Beyond Conflict
in the Horn

A
VERY HAPPY
and
BUSY
BIRTHDAY.
ON THIS
5Hth
JUMP!

Continue to "HASTEN
THE DAY" as you seek
out more languages, and
shorten the list of
THE WORLD BY 2000

Beyond Conflict
in the Horn

Prospects for
Peace, Recovery and Development
in Ethiopia, Somalia and the Sudan

Edited by
Martin Doornbos, Lionel Cliffe
Abdel Ghaffar M. Ahmed
and John Markakis

The Institute of Social Studies
The Hague
in association with
JAMES CURREY
London

James Currey Ltd
54b Thornhill Square, Islington
London N1 1BE

© Institute of Social Studies, The Hague 1992
First published 1992

British Library Cataloguing in Publication Data

Beyond conflict in the Horn : prospects for peace, recovery
    and development in Ethiopia, Somalia & the Sudan.
    I. Doornbos, Martin
    963.07

ISBN 0-85255-361-7
ISBN 0-85255-360-9 Pbk

Based on the proceedings of the International Workshop on the Prospects for Peace,
Recovery and Development in the Horn of Africa, Institute of Social Studies, The
Hague, The Netherlands, 19-23 February 1991.

Typeset in 10/10 Bembo by Opus 43, Cumbria
Printed in the United States of America

Contents

III Recovery and Long-Term Development

Rural Production Systems: Crisis and Sustainability

The Political Economy: 'Structural Adjustment', the State and Civil Society

Acknowledgements

This volume and the workshop on which it is based have been made possible thanks to the efforts and collaboration of various individuals and institutions. Special appreciation is due to Bea Stolte, pioneer and key member of the organizing committee, for her crucial role in mobilizing institutional support and transforming the initiative for the workshop into the actual event. The Institute of Social Studies, a long-time meeting place for scholars and students from the Horn as well as from other regions, accepted to host the workshop and to make available logistic support for its preparation by the organizing committee. The assistance received in this connection by the ISS Research and Project Office, more specifically by Berhane Ghebretnsaie and Liesbeth van Nispen, greatly contributed to the workshop's smooth functioning and success. We would also like to record our debt to Gary Debus, Publications Office head at the ISS, for his role in turning the workshop's actual proceedings into the present volume, to Anne Webb for doing a truly excellent job in editing the manuscript and preparing it for publication, and to Joy Misa for her tireless assistance in the production of the text.

Contacts were established at an early stage with the Centre for Development Studies at the University of Bergen, Norway, which in 1989 had held a workshop with the related objective of reviewing the prospects for reconciliation between north and south Sudan, with leading participants from both regions. The ISS workshop was organized to further extend this initiative thematically and across the region as a whole, and has benefitted greatly from the collaboration with the CDS, Bergen, and its Director, Gunnar Sørbø.

We are sincerely grateful for the support and interest which first NOVIB, then various other international NGOs have contributed to make the workshop possible: CEBEMO, the Commisson on Interchurch Aid of the Netherlands Reformed Church, the European Human Rights Foundation, ICCO, MISEREOR, and OXFAM Canada. As the scope and objectives of the workshop grew, it was thanks to a generous grant from the Netherlands Ministry of Foreign Affairs that we were able to realize these broadened aims and subsequently to prepare this volume for publication. Special appreciation in this connection is due to the constructive support and collaboration received from the NGO, Education and Research Programmes Section of the Ministry.

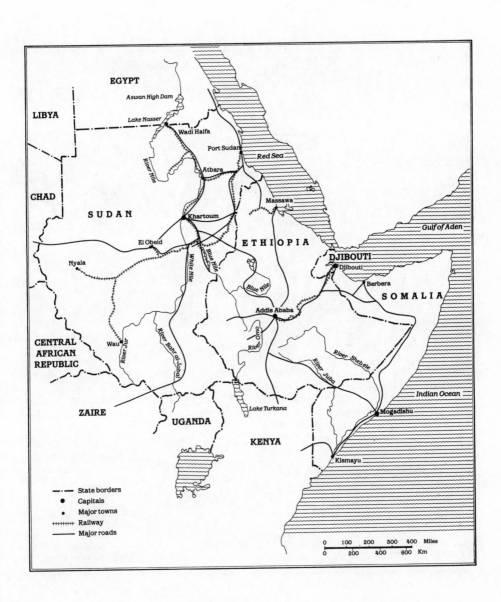

Map 1   The Horn of Africa

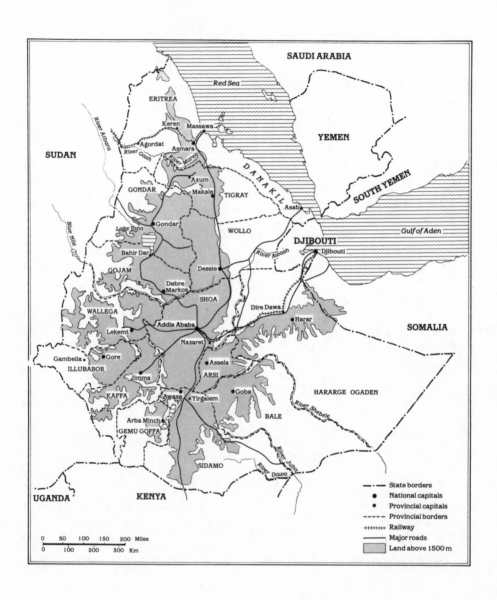

Map 2   Ethiopia

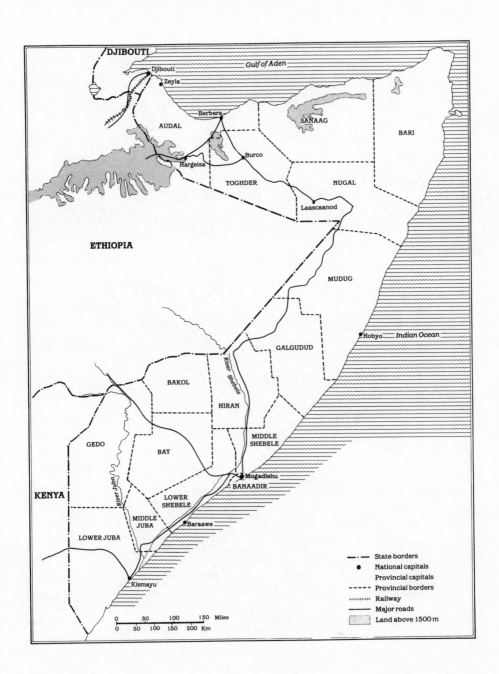

Map 3   Somalia

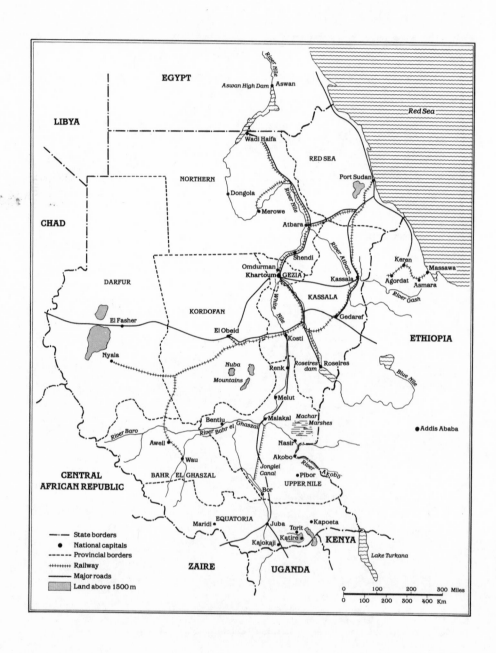

Map 4   Sudan

Introduction

This volume addresses the requirements and possibilities of a situation which until recently many regarded as entirely illusionary: a post-conflict situation in the Horn of Africa. In such a situation not the grievances of the past but the urgencies of the future would get primary attention; not the externally fed and ideologically clothed disputes, but the most pressing internal social needs and policy issues would be highest on the agendas of those responsible for making basic decisions. Rather than narrow fixations on maintaining central control, hegemonic power and tight state boundaries, visions of alternative and diversified state and non-state political involvements, processes and structures might guide the search for meaningful political action.

These were the ideas and aspirations which motivated many concerned leading intellectuals and political activists from all the countries and regions of the Horn to come and participate in a workshop held at the Institute of Social Studies, The Hague, in February 1991. The present volume constitutes a record of their views and exchanges on the prospects for peace, recovery and development in Ethiopia, Somalia and the Sudan. Their contributions reflect their realistic assessments of the primary requirements and needs as well as of possible openings and new approaches to the creation of a more humane environment and the conditions for lasting peace.

The idea to hold this workshop was conceived at a time when events in the Horn of Africa itself and also internationally appeared to signal the approaching end of the manifold and prolonged conflict in that region. Having exhausted the material and political resources at their disposal, the beleaguered regimes in the region were facing defeat, and that prospect was forcing them to seek negotiations with the opposition. The end of the Cold War drew to a close the long-standing superpower rivalry in the Horn which had exacerbated and prolonged the conflict. Concern for resolving regional conflicts meant that instead of providing the weaponry for war, the superpowers were beginning to press for peace in that corner of Africa. After nearly three decades of violence, the military option seemed about to be discarded.

The time had come, then, to consider the many problems that would have to be faced when peace finally prevailed, problems which the parties to the conflict may not have been able to consider in the midst of the war. It was an awareness of the need to look ahead beyond the conflict that brought together the people who initially formed the workshop's organizing committee (Lionel Cliffe, Bea Stolte, Martin Doornbos and John Markakis) in the spring of 1989. The idea had first emerged in contacts between some of the members of the organizing committee and several concerned NGOs who found themselves working on both sides of some of the battle lines in the Horn. Faced with what seemed to be an insolvable stalemate, it was felt an NGO initiative might possibly create an opening. This was at a time when there were mounting expectations internationally as to the role that NGOs might be able to play in a number of fields, and the NGOs themselves began to test the elasticity of the political parameters of their actions.

The organizing committee's initial task was to determine the theme of the workshop. Undoubtedly, the most serious problems in the region to be faced immediately would be political, and would have to do with the redistribution of power and rearrangement of the political system in each of the three countries. Being requisite to the resolution of the conflict, such issues had dominated discussion in the Horn and abroad up to this time. The results had been meager, mainly because this discussion had no effect on the agenda determined by the parties to the conflict. Consequently, it was considered prudent to reverse the usual order in which the various conflict situations in the Horn were commonly approached in efforts to develop a perspective on possible reconciliation. Instead of first trying to find the key to political solutions and, thereby, presumably create conditions for subsequent reconstruction and development in the social and economic spheres, the workshop focused on problems that peace itself would create once conflicts were resolved, and issues of long-term development in the region – something thought to be an indispensable requisite for lasting peace. One imagined that this approach might also stimulate thoughts about political solutions.

It was not expected, however, that solutions to the problems that will emerge after the introduction of peace would be worked out in the workshop, or that detailed plans for action would be drafted. It was expected that some of the issues would be identified and highlighted so that they could be taken up in other forums in the future by those best qualified to handle them. Furthermore, it was hoped that by focusing attention on the common post-conflict concerns all warring parties will face, an awareness of the enormity of the task that lay ahead would be promoted, and this might lead to forward-looking planning. It was also hoped that this focus might encourage some of the antagonists to lift their sights above the immediate military and political objectives that have dominated all discussion thus far. Finally, the workshop adopted a regional frame of reference, and an attempt was made to view all issues in that wider context. This is because the nature of many of the key issues transcends the geopolitical boundaries controlled or claimed by the antagonists.

The workshop programme and the invited papers largely reflected these basic objectives. In inviting papers, special efforts were made to ensure a reasonably balanced representation from each of the countries concerned, and as much as possible to have discussants from other countries or regions comment on the various contributions. By and large, these efforts were successful, except on two fronts. Firstly, as the workshop coincided with the intensification of armed conflict in Somalia, it became impossible for invited speakers from Somalia to leave the country. Also, several Somalis abroad were engaged in urgent political talks on the country's future and were unable to come to The Hague. An invited contribution from Abdi Samatar, who could not come to the workshop, in addition to the paper by Hussein Adam, greatly helped to compensate for this gap. Secondly, despite persistent efforts on the part of the organizers to minimize a gender imbalance among the workshop contributors, a coincidence of last minute cancellations by invited women resulted in a notable dearth of women contributors. Fortunately, a concerted action by six women participants served to keep gender issues among the workshop's concerns.

All in all, over one hundred workshop participants represented all states, most regions, and many of the embattled political movements in the Horn, as well as European non-governmental organizations operating in that region, and academic and research institutions in the Horn, Europe and elsewhere. The proceedings served the workshop's modest purposes well, and it was thought useful to publish them to give them wider circulation. In doing so, we have also included several contributions focused on the concerns of particular movements or groups which cover material not easily available elsewhere, if at all.

In addition to the main presentations and discussants' comments which are included in this volume, extensive discussion took place in plenary and group sessions, parts of which are included in condensed form. The various recommendations made in relation to each of the main themes, given in 'Prospects for the Future', reflect these discussions and may form a basis for future policy as well as research attention and action. The discussions, like the presentations, were for the most part very well informed and thoughtful because they engaged persons with long and intimate experience of the issues. In the course of them, one of the workshop's premises was proven correct. While focusing on the situation that lay beyond the conflict, people of opposing political views often found themselves in agreement on fundamentals, or at least became involved in a dialogue. Conversely, people of the same political persuasion sometimes disagreed. For instance, the question of how to deal with the foreign debt burden was debated without reference to current political divisions.

Although an objection was raised by one participant, who quoted the maxim 'man does not live by bread alone', the sense of the discussion supported another guiding premise of the workshop, that resource scarcity and maldistribution, and the loss of material security lay at the root of many of the region's conflicts. Therefore, it was generally possible to address this issue in many of its forms, undistracted by political and ideological preconceptions.

The undermining of subsistence was identified as the most crucial effect of resource scarcity, while the failure of rural production systems was considered a major cause. State directed efforts in agricultural development were recognized as dismal failures throughout the region, but when it came to considering alternative approaches there was a distinct lack of certainty deriving from avowed political persuasions. Neither the free market nor communalism were regarded as the remedy for the problem of food insufficiency.

The workshop's regional perspective was accepted as valid, and not only for such issues as the sharing of the Nile waters, over which there was a good deal of discussion. One opinion had it that before entering regional arrangements, one first ought to put one's own house in order. However, the tenor of the discussion implied that no one's house can be put in order in isolation. Discussion of ports, trade, transport, the environment, pastoralism, labour, minerals and so forth revealed the extent of regional interdependence.

The Inter-Governmental Authority on Drought and Development (IGADD) emerged as the institutional focal point of hopes for intra-regional co-operation and integration. Nearly all relevant projects that were suggested in the workshop were deemed appropriate for IGADD to administer, if only because this young and untested institution is the sole regional body in existence. The representative of IGADD itself pointed out the narrow mandate and limited resources of this organization that circumscribe its potential. Opinion in the Horn certainly favours strengthening this institution, and also creating others for specific regional purposes.

The felt need for a regional approach is commensurate with the perceived failure of the unitary, centralized and authoritarian post-colonial states in the Horn of Africa to peacefully resolve the contradictions inherent in ethnic, regional and class divisions within their borders. Ramifications of such divisions and the many regional linkages were cited as proof of the need for a regional approach to conflict resolution. The use of violence by the state to contain such contradictions has destroyed, among many other things, the prospect of building a civil society as the foundation of human freedom and dignity. The necessity to decentralize and diffuse political authority was taken for granted.

That is the way events *seemed* to be moving in the Horn during the months that preceded and followed the workshop. The long and bloody stalemate began to dissolve as the workshop was about to convene, making its timing particularly auspicious. The regimes in Somalia and Ethiopia collapsed under the onslaught of many armed opposition movements, leaving both countries in ruin. In the Sudan, the military regime continued to wage a desperate struggle to ward off a similar fate, with scarcely any hope of success. During 1991, all three countries were in the grip of severe famine, which the regimes did nothing to prevent. In the Sudan, the regime did not wish to recognize the existence of famine, resorting to the euphemism 'food gap' instead, and it obstructed rather than facilitated international efforts to provide famine relief.

The end of the regimes in Somalia and Ethiopia came with unanticipated swiftness and finality. None of the grandiose political schemes and institutions hatched by the fallen regimes survived, and in view of the fragmentation of the opposition, the resulting vacuum itself posed a problem. The Somali opposition forces were organized on a clan basis, and power at the centre was claimed by the force that captured Mogadishu in January 1991, the United Somali Congress, whose constituency is the Hawiye clan in the vicinity of the capital. The Somali National Movement, which represents the Ishaq clan in northern Somalia, gained control of the north, while numerous other clan organizations emerged and fought for local control. All rejected the legitimacy of the United Somali Congress government in Mogadishu, and scattered fighting among them continued in many parts of the country.

In Ethiopia the campaign that finally caused the collapse of the regime was mounted mainly by a regional movement, the Tigray People's Liberation Front (TPLF), whose forces entered Addis Ababa in May 1991. The TPLF operated within a coalition called the Ethiopian People's Revolutionary Democratic Front (EPRDF), which it had formed with several smaller groups. Opposition movements in other regions of Ethiopia, whose relationship with the TPLF in the past had not been friendly, accused the latter of intending to dominate the state, and refused to accept the authority of the EPRDF government in Addis Ababa. As in Somalia, they seemed intent on retaining power in the areas under their control, and clashes with the new government seemed likely.

Whatever the future may bring, an era has come to an end in the Horn of Africa. It is not just regimes that have come to grief in this region, but also the state system they defended. These are states with a brief history – having come into existence during the colonial period – and resting on shallow foundations, for they were formed by force and lumped together diverse ethnic groups and disparate regions whose people never had a say in the matter. Of course, there is nothing unique in this as far as the continent of Africa is concerned. Unlike most other states in Africa, however, the states in the Horn have been dominated by the elite of certain ethnic groups which used state power to secure what in that poverty stricken region is inordinate privilege. To defend this privilege, the ruling classes turned the state into a highly centralized and authoritarian system of oppression.

The states in the Horn have a record of spectacular failure in many fields, including economic development. This meant that the inherited disparity in material and social resources between regions, ethnic groups, and social classes attained further grotesque proportions. More than any other factor, this disparity was responsible for the wave of dissidence and rebellion that mounted steadily since the 1960s. The state played a dominant role in the production and distribution of resources in this region, especially under the pseudo–Marxist military regimes that held power during the past two decades. Access to state power became imperative for human welfare, and such access was not equally available to all groups in the Horn of Africa; to some it was not available at all. As a result, the state became the object of conflict, as well as the means with which the conflict was waged. In the end, the centre in Somalia and Ethiopia collapsed, and the state structure it upheld collapsed with it. It is a fair guess that the Sudan will follow suit eventually.

The collapse of the centre in Somalia and Ethiopia cleared the way for the restructuring of the state, and for the decentralization of power along the lines commonly advocated by the victorious opposition movements. Two major alterations have already taken place. One is the declaration of independence by the northern region of Somalia under the Somali National Movement, and the other is the *de facto* separation of Eritrea from Ethiopia under the control of the Eritrean People's Liberation Front. Furthermore, the declared policy of the TPLF in Ethiopia, as well as of most other opposition movements in that country, is for a pluralist, decentralized state system with regional autonomy. Regional autonomy is also the declared policy of the Sudanese People's Liberation Movement, which is likely to play a major role in shaping the future of the Sudanese state. The political situation in the Sudan makes it unlikely that any other system will prevail in that country.

Therefore, it appears that one key issue identified by the workshop, that is the character of the state, is now on the agenda of the political forces in the Horn. If this issue is successfully resolved, peace will follow, and then other issues will have to be faced. Since the centres of decision making will multiply with the proliferation of self-governing units, while the resources at their command will be relatively small, a regional approach will prove essential, as foreseen by many participants in the workshop. One such issue came to the fore immediately in Ethiopia where one of the new government's first acts secured Asab as a free port for the use of Ethiopia following an agreement with the Eritreans.

Since ethnicity had become the main basis for political mobilization against the fallen regimes, it emerged also as the preferred basis of political solidarity afterwards. Clans became the pillars of political regrouping in Somalia, while the first efforts to organize political representation in Ethiopia were addressed primarily to ethnic groups. This was one development not anticipated nor discussed in the workshop. Ethnicity was always a crucial political factor in the Horn of Africa, and ethnic domination was the most obvious cause of the conflict. Those who dominated the post-colonial state sought to establish class as the basis of political solidarity, and adopted Marxism in the 1960s. Their efforts failed and most of their opponents, while also espousing Marxism in theory, appealed to ethnicity for political support.

The new governments in Ethiopia and Somalia were immediately confronted with numerous problems of security and welfare, many of which had been identified in the workshop. There were many unanticipated complications. The collapse of the centre in these countries was such that the main pillar of the state, the military establishment, disintegrated completely. Consequently, the question of demobilization concerned not only the guerrilla armies, but the soldiery in their hundreds of thousands who had dispersed with their arms and no means of livelihood. Refugee repatriation and resettlement presented other complications. People returning to Ethiopia from Somalia and the Sudan in utter destitution found themselves stripped of refugee status and, therefore, ineligible for assistance. Those returning to Eritrea, a region under guerrilla control but not yet a recognized state, were likewise in limbo. A new wave of refugees appeared in the making as people not considered native to Eritrea started to leave that region. The worst fate was reserved for the southern Sudanese who were forced to flee refugee camps in south-western Ethiopia by the changed political situation in that country. Upon entering the Sudan they came under air attack by the Sudanese army which considered them rebel supporters.

As the dust begins to settle in parts of the Horn, regret over loss of life and opportunities on an untold scale may promote an awareness of the possibility of an alternative scenario: a scenario in which political authorities demonstrate basic respect for civil rights of men, women and children; in which constituent groups within civil society are in a position to keep their leaders accountable; and in which efforts to create welfare and equity of opportunity constitute basic political pursuits. The search to give fresh meaning to the concepts of social justice and human rights, for ways of empowering suppressed groups and individuals, and for a thorough rethinking of the relationships between state and civil society, constitutes a fundamental challenge not only to the people and intellectuals of the Horn, but to people throughout Africa. These issues and needs are indeed of continental proportions; however, people in the Horn countries have carried more than their share in the struggle against injustice and the search for an equitable social order. If they succeed in shaping meaningful political frameworks and relationships, the significance of this will undoubtedly extend throughout the continent.

The Editors

1 Prospects for Peace, Recovery and Development in the Horn of Africa

BONA MALWAL

It would be foolhardy, and nigh on impossible, to formulate plans and ideas for a future 'new order' in the Horn of Africa without first suggesting the appropriate means by which the present conflicts in the region can be peacefully settled. It would be futile to talk about reconstruction and development, the repatriation of refugees, the provision of post-war famine relief, the re-establishment of links between the countries of the region, the demilitarization of the war zones and the demobilization of the armies, guerilla or otherwise, without first considering the prospects for peace. Therefore, it is necessary to consider how many of the conflicts could possibly be settled by either the regional forces at play or the intervention of international politics and diplomacy.

Regional linkages

In one of the many recent articles on Africa's depressing decline, Richard J. Barnet observed that 'no one has yet come up with a formula for assuring sustainable growth, a decent standard of living for all, and the promise of a more equitable distribution of wealth'. He notes 'the paths to development are different for different countries, depending upon their histories, cultures, and politics, but that for the poorest countries the paths are well hidden' (1990). Nowhere in Africa are the paths to development more obscure than in the Horn of Africa.

International discussion of the Horn of Africa is a relatively recent phenomenon which presupposes some kind of uniformity in the conflicts in the various countries. Whereas there is a certain degree of similarity between the problems faced by the three major countries of the region – Somalia, Ethiopia and the Sudan – it would be a mistake to assume that such similarities are sufficient to warrant generalizable solutions to these problems. The conflicts in each of these countries have arisen out of their own particular circumstances and histories. It is important to keep the differences between the countries firmly in perspective when making any linkages, and to retain a degree of flexibility in the solutions being proffered.

It is true, for example, to say that Somalia, Ethiopia and the Sudan all have had internal military conflicts which can be described as civil wars. The conflicts in Ethiopia and the Sudan shared such a characteristic with Somalia, but involved much more than the desire to overthrow a repressive regime. The conflicts in these two countries brought into question the very existence of these states in their present forms. In addition, in Ethiopia it is impossible to talk about one civil war because there have been many wars fought, in Eritrea, Tigray, and other areas of the country. The objectives of the groups which fought these wars were by no means the same. Therefore, in order to prescribe possible solutions for the region's conflicts, it is necessary to address each one in turn.

6

Somalia

Somalia is probably the one country in Africa where the people can justifiably claim to be of the same origin. The various clan groupings notwithstanding, there is a remarkable degree of homogeneity in the origins of the Somali people. Theoretically, therefore, one might presuppose it should be reasonably simple to devise workable solutions that could cater for the aspirations of all the various groupings in Somalia. A democratic political system that could ensure equal participation of all groupings would be a step in the right direction. However, finding that system proves to be a major and almost insurmountable challenge facing Somalia today.

Whilst the search for a pluralist form of democratic constitution is the key challenge in the case of Somalia, in the cases of Ethiopia and the Sudan an even more complex series of issues will have to be addressed alongside those of democracy and establishing an equitable political system because of the conflicting nationalities and cultures within these two countries.

Ethiopia

As with Somalia and the Sudan, Ethiopia has been afflicted with a repressive and totalitarian government. The Mengistu regime in Addis Ababa long utilized all the tools of overt repression against the different nationalities within the country. This led to rebel movements in all parts of the country which were dedicated to securing either the overthrow of the Dergue in Addis Ababa or the separation of their region from the rest of the country. The vastly differing objectives of these movements complicate talk about the attainment of liberal democracy and multiparty politics as appropriate solutions to the country's problems.

Perhaps the biggest challenge to the continued existence of Ethiopia as a nation-state is the movement for the liberation of Eritrea and the other nationalist movements. The war in Eritrea has been Africa's longest running war and so it would be foolhardy to present simple solutions to a conflict nearly 30 years old. The Eritrean rebellion was initially intent upon restoring autonomy to the area within a federated Ethiopia, but that has since been modified to the complete separation of Eritrea from Ethiopia and the formation of an independent state. With some justification, the Eritreans have laid wide open the whole question of a people's right to self-determination. However, by accepting autonomy within Ethiopia between 1952 and 1962, the Eritrean people accepted the principle of a federated unity with the Ethiopian state. Of course, Ethiopia needs to be censured for Haile Selassie's abrogation of that autonomy and for inflicting a painful war upon the region, but at the same time, Eritrea's future is surely somehow linked with that of Ethiopia.

If a solution can be found which includes a form of affiliation of Eritrea in a federated Ethiopia, then surely such a solution will be the answer to the other regional disputes within that country. With greater autonomy in the regions, there ought to be room for the peaceful resolution of most of today's grievances. Once the issues of power and resource sharing and of the future political system are established, the introduction of a pluralistic democratic system of government should be within reach.

Sudan

There is a great deal to be said for suggesting that the Sudanese conflict is even more complex than those of Ethiopia or Somalia. The Sudanese situation is characterized by racism and cultural and religious bigotry. The people of the Sudan have fought two civil wars within 35 years. During this period, the intentions of the government of the day have been very clear from the outset; that is, the total destruction of their opponents.

The numerical composition of the Sudanese population, with regards to race and religion, makes simple solutions to the conflict tenuous at best. The major regions in the country were thrust together through historical accident, and it was through another historical accident that political power was handed over to the minority Arab population upon independence in 1956. This minority used race to great effect as it sought to establish dominance over all the other racial groupings in the country. However, now that this minority has found itself inexorably entangled in its own web of racial politics, it has attempted to cloud matters through the introduction of the religious issue. While it is true that the Moslem population of the Sudan outnumbers all other religious groupings put together, it is also true that non-Arabs form a larger majority in the country. It is unclear whether the rights to power ought to remain with the racial or religious majority. However, it is clear to all that those who are today advocating that power should remain in the hands of the religious majority are the same Arab minority which not so long ago were playing the racial card.

In the 1950s, at the outbreak of the first civil war, such had been the lack of contact between the people of southern and northern Sudan that the southern opposition movement displayed separatist tendencies. This policy was based on the inaccurate assumption that northern Sudan was entirely Islamic and inhabited by Arabs and, therefore, was perceived as a region with which the non-Islamic and African south could not possibly co-exist. Over the subsequent decades, communications improved between the north and south, and as a result the struggle in the south against the Arab and Islamic fundamentalist domination of power in Khartoum opened the eyes of non-Arab communities in northern Sudan to the real nature of the conflict. This educational process, however, is not about to resolve the conflict. The ruling Arab minority is entrenching itself in power through the rabid application of religion. The introduction of Islamic fundamentalism as a political system and the repression which goes with it has set back attempts to liberalize the political system.

The Sudan of the 1980s and 1990s is not a country of separatist movements, but that does not mean it is any closer to resolving its conflict. The Sudan People's Liberation Army (SPLA), which is leading the military struggle against the government in Khartoum, has continually stated that it is not a separatist movement. Its stated objectives are the creation of a Sudan in which no one race, especially a minority race, nor one religious grouping, especially the Islamic fundamentalists, are able to dominate political and economic power. This is the point at which a whole new set of problems enters the equation. Both the powers that be in Khartoum and the SPLA know that such a new Sudan would mean ending the Arab minority's monopoly on political and economic power which it has held since 1956. The ruling elite is therefore staunchly resisting such a change.

The SPLA is the only guerilla movement in the whole of Africa, perhaps in the whole world, which advocates the introduction of a multiparty democratic political system based upon a universal electoral franchise. Furthermore, the SPLA advocates the removal of religion from politics on the grounds that there is no room for religion in the politics of a multicultural, multi-ethnic and multireligious state. The ruling minority is resisting these progressive policies and, therefore, is prolonging the war by holding onto a narrowly based political system that excludes the majority of the people of the Sudan. The Islamic fundamentalists have advocated separatism rather than reduce their own power. This is the first example in Africa of controllers of the state system proposing to carve up the state rather than calling for stronger national unity; they have essentially handed over the objective of defending the unity of the country to the opposition movement.

The way to peace in the Horn

There have been several efforts by the superpowers and others in the international community to bring the various feuding factions in the Horn together to initiate a peace process. It would appear that not much success is possible in a situation in which the international community primarily sees its role as one of facilitating the process of bringing the contending parties together around a negotiating table and then withdrawing, much like a referee, to allow the contenders to talk it out. Little progress has been made in these kinds of negotiations. The inherent problem with this situation has been the international community's insistence upon peace for its own sake, without concerning itself with the issues which have caused the conflicts in the first place. All the groups involved in the conflicts claim to want peace, but each and every one of them is interested in securing peace only on their own terms. Until the international community pronounces its stand on the various issues which must be addressed there will be little incentive for certain groups in these conflicts to give ground on their negotiating positions. The international community can be a catalyst for change in these conflicts. War will not end, of course, merely by coming down in favour of one side or another, or by placing an embargo on the weapons of war. Those weapons have become many and complex, including the use of famine which so devastated the Horn of Africa during the 1980s. But clear pronouncements would inform undemocratic and repressive regimes that the international community will censure and not vindicate them. That would be the first step toward isolating these groupings from the international community and forcing them to change their ways. It would also provide additional moral backing to those groupings whose causes are recognized as just by the international community.

It is very unlikely that Siyad Barre would have remained in power so long in Somalia if he had not received the tacit support of the international community. If there had been international condemnation of his totalitarian regime and recognition that he was a major obstacle to the attainment of democracy and to the unity of Somalia, then there would have been much greater pressure placed upon him to change. By engaging in business as usual with such regimes, the international community has been sending the wrong signals to the despots of the world, making the successful conclusion of the peace process far more difficult. Equally, if the international community had made it clear earlier to both the Ethiopian government and the EPLF what it expected of them in the formation of a new Ethiopian Federation which could repair the damage of the abrogated Eritrean autonomy, then a more timely breakthrough in that conflict might have been possible. Similarly, in the Sudanese situation, an international condemnation of religion and racism in politics would likely still produce dramatic results on the path to peace.

Africa's experience and possible solutions

War has been most costly not only in the material destruction of state structures, but also in the most vulnerable sectors of the society. In all of the countries of the Horn the clock has been rolled back in all fields of social development. To cite only a few:

1. child mortality in the countries of the Horn, as elsewhere in Africa where there is civil strife (Angola and Mozambique, for example) is three to four times higher than the continent's average. Children in these war states die of preventable or easily treatable or curable diseases such as diarrhoea and malaria;
2. diseases which have almost been eliminated in much of Africa – such as smallpox – still claim children's lives in the war states;
3. whole generations of school-aged children have been denied education because of the war. At least three generations have received no education at all in large areas of the three Horn countries due to the civil wars and the states' incapacity to provide these services;
4. life expectancy in the countries of the Horn of Africa has gone down by 10 to 20 years in the last three decades;
5. per capita income of the region has decreased in the last 30 years by at least 50 per cent;
6. famine has become endemic in the region, claiming massively larger numbers of lives than the wars themselves. Famine is, of course, a direct product of the wars.

If and when the international community decides to take Africa's conflicts seriously and moves to resolve them in earnest, it should bear in mind Africa's most recent experiences in the field. It would be wrong to assume that African states will be starting from square one with regard to resolving conflicts. After all, Africa's most populous state, Nigeria, has successfully rebuilt its national unity out of the ruins of a civil war. The net result has been the strengthening rather than the weakening of the federal system of government.

Nigeria may not be the most positive example to use considering that the civil war only ended after the military victory of one side over the other. It is also not a very good example on matters pertaining to democracy as it has suffered more military interventions in its post-independence history than most African countries. However, Nigeria is perhaps the most outstanding example of an African state respecting and adhering to a system of regional pluralism. Nigeria has continually striven to strengthen the powers of the regions under its federal system in the very important areas of economic policy and revenue sharing, law and order, and political representation at the national level. Ethiopia and the Sudan, as multi-ethnic societies, could learn a great deal from the Nigerian experience in this regard.

Generally speaking, Africa's political experience over the past 30 years can be quite instructive. The initial political evolution – which happened in many post-independence African countries – from strict nationalism opposed to any kind of regional dissension on patriotic grounds, which resulted in heavily centralized systems of control and administration in the hands of the educated few, was found to be entirely wanting. So have been the centralized systems under the control of the military authorities when they have opted to intervene following the political failures of the nationalists.

For the countries of the Horn, perhaps war has become a convenient excuse to which the powers that be resort in order to excuse their failure to run these states. Africa's disappointing economic, social and political performance and development is a general indictment of the centralized state. The search for an alternative to a centralized system can no longer be avoided. Self-governance – a policy where the people are able to seek and develop partnerships with one another in the development process; where they can fulfill their potential for self-organization at multiple levels; and where they hold the rights and diverse resources to engage in collective action – must be explored and must evolve in all the countries of the Horn, indeed in the whole of Africa. Professors James Wunsch and Dele Olowu argue in a most powerful way in a recent book that the centralized state 'is the cause of underdevelopment in Africa' (1990).

Separation based upon ethnic homogeneity has not proven to be a better alternative for marginalized peoples. Internal ethnic rivalries are as potently divisive and dangerous as the external ones. Therefore, on a continent-wide basis, Africa urgently requires a more equitable and balanced system of state management. There is no reason why the new mood for democracy which is sweeping the rest of the world should exclude Africa.

Any search for a system suited to Africa's peculiarities will need to take into account Africa's traditional and indigenous experiences and blend them with the best of successful democratic systems elsewhere in the world. Whatever systems evolve in the countries of the continent, it is apparent that central to the search for solutions must be the principle of multiparty democracy based among other things on the multi-ethnicity of the countries involved. It is certainly possible to envisage solutions to the continent's conflicts, including those of the Horn of Africa, although each solution will be specific to a particular country.

Interstate mistrust

Interstate rivalries and suspicions have definitely helped fuel the civil wars within the Horn of Africa. For example, the Ethiopian and Somali states, in spite of repeated agreements, remain highly suspicious of each other. These mutual suspicions have resulted in phoney and direct wars between the belligerents. Ethiopia's relationship with the Sudan is in an even worse condition than that with Somalia. The Sudan's commitment to regional co-operation in the Horn remains questionable. Through its own internal politics, which have tilted towards pan-Arabism, or in more recent years towards Islamic fundamentalism, the Sudan has failed to strike an external balance between its commitment to Africa and to the Arab world. The country's facilitation of the flow of Arab support to the Eritrean movement provoked the charge that the Sudan wanted the Red Sea to become entirely Arab-controlled. The suspicion that this was the motivating force for the Sudan's interest in Eritrea was, to no small extent, a reason why the SPLA enjoyed so much support from the Ethiopian government. Balancing these interstate regional suspicions is as important as finding solutions to the internal conflicts that are currently engulfing the Horn of Africa.

The transition from war to peace

Assuming that all these balancing and counter balancing acts are possible, the process of moving these countries through the transition from a state of war, division, famine and death to one of rehabilitation, reconstruction, development and social tranquillity can be engaged, however difficult it may prove to be. In relation to development, the Sudan and Ethiopia possess vast areas of fertile agricultural land and more than adequate water resources if utilized to their fullest potential. With the right inputs, there is no reason why this area should not become the bread basket of Africa and the Middle East. The two countries also possess vast untapped mineral deposits waiting to be exploited for the benefit of the area's people. Furthermore, the two states and Somalia are regular stopping points on important trading routes between the Mediterranean and the Indian Ocean. The Sudan is an important political, commercial and cultural link between Africa and the Middle East, between Africa and the Arab world, and between Northern and sub-Saharan Africa.

During the transition from war to peace in the Horn of Africa, both the role and the assistance of the international community will be crucial. This is not only a region devastated by war, famine and drought, but it is one that has become increasingly dependent upon handouts from the world at large as a result of the mismanagement and ineptitude of the governments which have run the individual states. Such a dependence on international assistance is likely to increase rather than diminish during the transitional period.

The process of rehabilitation will demand vast resources that are currently unavailable to the states of the Horn. Short-term programmes should include the demobilization of the warring parties, the demilitarization of the war zones, the provision of food and other relief for the displaced, and the repatriation and resettlement of those who fled the war, famine and drought. Much of the experience gained in 1972 with the repatriation and resettlement of refugees in southern Sudan following the peaceful settlement of the Sudan's first civil war will be useful in the future for the Sudan. However, the Sudan's domestic resource base is much weaker today and would be unable on its own to sustain such a vast operation. The region would depend upon the international community bearing the brunt of the short-term material needs, as well as of the medium- and long-term needs. Planning ahead on a regional basis might prove more practical than planning on a country by country basis, and would also have the added benefit of limiting the effects of donor fatigue which has become more noticeable in recent years. It would, of course, be futile to set up a regional institution for the development of the Horn of Africa without first being certain that the move towards peace in the region is an irreversible one.

The medium-term phase would consist of social welfare issues such as the reconstruction of state facilities destroyed or damaged during the conflict, the rehabilitation of social services, and the provision of the necessary tools and seeds for people being resettled in their areas of origin. This phase should also include the re-establishment of all regional interstate links which were destroyed by the conflicts.

The long-term phase would involve the restoration of a peacetime economy and a civil society. It will only be possible to achieve this once the first two phases have been well and truly implemented and set in motion. As with the first two, this third phase will require outside investment and technical assistance of enormous proportions. At least in this phase the resources to be developed or supported will become clear. It will be a process of investment by both the donor institutions and the individual states involved for their mutual benefit. Clearly this will be a more capital intensive phase than the first two and, therefore, it is difficult to imagine the states of the Horn of Africa being capable of sustaining a peace process without the steady input of international development assistance.

General observations and conclusions

In recent years the Sudan has experienced the almost total breakdown of its material and physical infrastructure, as well as of its public service system. Things are not likely to be any better in either Somalia or Ethiopia which, along with the Sudan, are among the poorest countries in the world. A certain culture of destruction, indiscipline, inefficiency, corruption, and disregard for public property and the rule of law has permeated the fabric of Sudanese society. It is now the rule, rather than the exception, for public funds and property to be misappropriated. In the past, the Sudan has experienced the failure of large investment projects not only because of bad planning and inappropriate allocation of resources, but also because of misappropriation, theft and mismanagement. The Sudan is currently heavily debt-ridden with very little to show for it. Serious attention will need to be paid to this area of state affairs if the country is to move away from the war culture of destruction and embezzlement. Furthermore, no substantial development will be possible in the Sudan, nor in Ethiopia and Somalia, even if peace is attained unless the public services are properly reconstructed, with regulations designed to prevent blatant political abuse, and services given the necessary authority to operate as independent state institutions.

In the Sudan public services have been dominated by one ethnic grouping to the detriment of all others. The civil service has been as responsible as any partisan politician for the denial of services and development projects to those regions considered by the ruling elite to be rebellious. It is precisely for this reason that requests have recently been made for any foreign assistance intended for the displaced or war-affected people of the Sudan to be delivered directly to the people in need under the supervision of the international relief agencies. The conversion of international aid into economic and political power for the ruling elite is something that the international community should consider when determining how to reconstruct the war-ravaged Horn of Africa. There is plenty of evidence that, due to the defectiveness of the system of aid so far, too much aid intended for the poor in our countries has gone into the private pockets of many of our public servants and aid officials (Hancock, 1990). The administration of aid requires a coalition of the aid donors, the local people and the local authorities, not the central administration.

Generally speaking, it is difficult to imagine solutions to the problems in the Horn of Africa which will leave intact the present state structures. Only a complete dismantling of these structures and their replacement by new representative institutions which reflect their constituencies will restore public confidence in state bodies. Close international supervision and monitoring will be needed for such a process to be successful. International and regional organizations, friendly governments and international institutions will have a role to play.

The civil wars, rebellion and instability in the Horn indicate the failure of the systems of government in these states, and the refusal of the governed to accept being betrayed by these systems. The people are tired, but not defeated. A commitment by the international community to the cause of the people, rather than to the continuous strengthening of the regimes that oppress them, could make a world of difference.

References

Barnet, R.J. 1990, May. 'But what about Africa? On the global economy's lost continent' *Harpers Magazine*.
Hancock, G. 1990. *Lords of Poverty: The Power, Prestige and Corruption of the International Aid Business*, New York, The Atlantic Monthly Press.
Nickel, H. 1990, January 31. 'Democracy or disaster for Africa' *The Wall Street Journal*.
Wunsch, J.S. and Olowu, D. (eds.) 1990. *The Failure of the Centralized State: Institutions and Self-Governance in Africa*, Boulder, Westview Press.

Comment   ABEL ALIER

During the last two years political and economic liberalization has taken place in Eastern Europe, Latin America and some parts of Africa. In addition, events of a slightly different nature have been taking place in the Gulf region, which are strategic for Arab oil, world trade and various other interests which make Somalia, Djibouti, Ethiopia and the Sudan lands and people no longer compartmentalized and sealed off from the rest of the Red Sea littoral. These events are likely to inject political realignments and reforms which will have an impact on the conflicts in the Horn. All these trends suggest that more changes are likely in Africa, including the Horn.

Bona Malwal's paper offers perceptive insights into the various aspects of the subject under discussion. The topic on which he has written is key to the other themes of the workshop. The question, what are the prospects for peace in the Horn of Africa, is a loaded one on which everything else revolves. The problem of Eritrea and Ethiopia was resolved after World War Two when a federal system which assigned wide powers to Eritrea was provided, but the arrangement did not last more than a decade. The settlement concluded in the Sudan in 1972 lasted for only 11 years. Both Ethiopia and the Sudan have since been gripped by civil wars and have suffered all the painful things that wars inflict on human lives, human progress, property and civilizations. We now know that once these types of wars are started they are difficult to bring to a conclusive end, whether by decisive military victory or by diplomatic and political resolution. The Nigerian war ended in a military victory; and that of the Sudan through internal diplomatic and political resolution. But these, as we view the world of similar conflicts in Palestine, Iraq (the Kurds), Angola, South Africa and now, again, Ethiopia and the Sudan, are noted for their longevity and killing power. Millions have died in the Sudan and Ethiopia during these civil conflicts.

The primary concern of people of ideas should be how to resolve the issues of contention which brought about and fuel the civil wars. Bona Malwal boldly suggests that problems which justified the wars in the Horn are not likely to be resolved unless the international community intervenes and supplements efforts made toward that end by regional forces. The suggestion is worthy of examination and should be floated for further debate. Who should be the internal participants in the resolution of the issues of contention? Which part of the international community should be involved and in what ways? Furthermore, it may be worthwhile to ask what factors contributed to the settlement in Eritrea/Ethiopia in 1952 and in the Sudan in 1972. In short, what do you feed into the computer to get a political settlement?

The related question of why the settlements of the political conflicts in Ethiopia/Eritrea and the Sudan were abrogated by the central governments of Ethiopia and the Sudan should be explored and answered, if only to guarantee that similar reverses are prevented in the future when fresh agreements on similar problems are reached. Two things seem clear: there are no chances of settlements surviving if they (a) do not provide for responsible pluralist democratic systems of government at all levels, and (b) are not backed by economic reforms, a restructuring of the economy and massive economic aid. Solutions that provide democracy at local and regional levels of government and maintain dictatorships, feudalism and other forms of authoritarianism at the central government level have no chance of long-term survival. This is so whether the solution agreed upon is federalism or another form of decentralization. Those were the primary causes for the abrogation of Eritrea's and southern Sudan's autonomy. Dictators and feudal rulers in the Sudan and Ethiopia were frightened by the presence of democratic practices in the regions as these could possibly be expanded even to the centre where the rulers wielded monolithic powers.

It is important to provide, as part of the settlement, details of what a pluralist democratic system of government requires. Such a system should liberalize the economy by subordinating the role of the state to that of the private sector and the market forces;

permit freedom of association to allow social, trade and professional associations to organize and engage activities and training which will strengthen their vocations; allow freedom of the press; reform the system of representation; and provide ground rules for the observation and exercise of democratic practice within the machinery of political parties.

Post-war states in the Horn

It is indeed crucial that post-war problems be identified and addressed even before political settlements are secured. The relief and resettlement of displaced people costs a lot of money. And there are other social and security considerations which make management of this immediate post-war activity not only difficult in itself, but also crucial to the success of the whole settlement. It is, therefore, important to have accurate figures of displaced persons, to know how many are outside and inside the borders of their country, and to know their identity as peasants, pastoralists, school-aged children, skilled workers, combatants and so forth. It is necessary to know numbers and identities for relief purposes, for health and education programmes and for reconstruction.

Political settlements will likely generate goodwill among members of the international community toward Horn countries and that goodwill can be translated into substantial material support for post-war projects of relief, reconstruction and development. On the basis of identified post-war problems and on the basis of commitment to broad economic reforms and restructuring, it is proposed that international debt be forgiven and written off, probably in its entirety. The Sudan's debt alone stands at 14 billion US dollars, Ethiopia has 3 billion US dollars outstanding and Somalia is probably more indebted than Ethiopia. Future loans for, or purchases of, arms should be outlawed as part of the growing trend toward arms reduction world-wide. Priority should be given to economic restructuring, reconstruction and development. But, until a political settlement is reached in Somalia and the Sudan, it is essential to continue relief operations for displaced people caught in the midst of the civil wars.

Regional co-operation

The Horn of Africa countries need to explore suitable and profitable fields for co-operation. Time and resources should be channelled toward regional relations rather than conflicts. To begin with, existing areas of co-operation should be reviewed and strengthened to the mutual benefit of the people and states in the Horn. The Inter-Governmental Authority on Drought and Development (IGADD) can be a starting point for such co-operation, along with the OAU's Economic Commission for Africa. The IGADD charter singles out three tasks it has to address, namely (a) to provide for food security for the member states, (b) to use the water of the Nile for irrigation and (c) development of infrastructure, that is, highways linking the borders and improvement of ports. Significantly, however, Ethiopia, the Sudan, Kenya and Uganda, as members of IGADD, have so far not established workable relations which allow for practical co-operation in the use of the Nile waters. For Ethiopia and the Sudan the Nile Valley still raises problems rather than grounds for co-operation.

References

Davidson, B. and Cliffe, L. 1988. *The Long Struggle of Eritrea for Independence and Constructive Peace*, Nottingham, Spokesman.
EPLF. 1978, April 28. EPLF Position Statement. (This document was issued in reply to the distortion by *Pravda*, the Soviet Union's official organ, of the basic facts of the Eritrean struggle).
Trevaskis, G.R.N. 1966. *Eritrea: A Colony in Transition, 1941-1950*, London, Oxford University Press.

I

IMMEDIATE NEEDS AND PROBLEMS THAT WILL BE POSED BY PEACE ITSELF

Victims of War

2

Children and War in the Horn of Africa

SAMIA EL HADI EL NAGAR

According to available reports and studies, most of those who have been displaced or are refugees as a result of civil conflicts and natural disasters are women and children. As a result of war, millions of children in the Horn of Africa have experienced violence, sickness, torture, exploitation, separation from parents and hunger. Many have died. These conditions have had profound effects on the general quality of life, health and education of these children.

Considerations of how to bring about peace and the expected problems and prospects facing such attempts must consider the impact of war on children. Children constitute the future generations which will have to maintain that peace and ultimately undertake the development of their countries. Therefore there is a real need to know the conditions of displaced and refugee children as well as of those who remain in the war-affected zones, to ask what needs they have, see to what extent these needs are fulfilled, and consider their psychological well-being.

There is a serious dearth of information on the condition of children in conflict situations. This is due to the fact that children have not constituted a significant area of inquiry in the countries in question, particularly children in situations of crisis. Thus exact estimates of the number of displaced children, of children remaining in war affected areas, and of refugee children are not available. Similarly, detailed studies on the socio-economic conditions in the Horn of Africa are lacking. Sample surveys and reports are currently the best available sources of information.

Displaced children

To escape death, many people in war-affected areas flee to safe zones within the same country. In most cases men stay behind and send women and children away from the dangerous area, but sometimes parents send children away alone. The result is a large influx of people in towns and villages distant from the war areas. Data from the Sudan show that about 1.7 million southern children are currently displaced in urban centres within the country. These children suffer from poor health and lack of adequate educational facilities. Many of them have been forced to work to support themselves and their families. The displaced usually leave without any assets and, due to poverty, many parents cannot support their children once they are away from the family's homelands. The net result is the numerous abandoned children found on the streets of urban areas in the countries of the Horn.

Health facilities in most urban areas in the Sudan are hardly adequate for the settled population, let alone for the displaced. In most settlements for the displaced health facilities are non-existent except where NGOs are working, but even these tend to be inadequate and uncoordinated. The implications of this are that diarrhoea, vaccine preventable diseases, acute respiratory infections and malnutrition are common among displaced children. According to a survey conducted by the Sudan Council of Churches (SCC) in 1987, 23 per cent of the southern displaced children below three years of age were malnourished. The report also estimated that 36.8 per cent suffered from two-week diarrhoea, and 4.6 per 1000 experienced night blindness. Among the causes of child mortality, diarrhoea ranked highest followed by measles and respiratory diseases, 28, 26 and 14 per cent respectively.[1]

A nutrition survey carried out by the SCC in eight settlements for the displaced around Khartoum in August and September 1989 found that malnutrition was prevalent among 16.2 per cent of children under two years, and among 14.6 per cent of children over two years. The survey attributed malnutrition mainly to the poor quality diet especially of young children (SCC, 1989). A survey carried out in some Eritrean villages showed a very high incidence of moderate and severe malnutrition. In one village 75 per cent of displaced children were found to be clinically anaemic, and a high incidence of active trachoma was noted (March & Tool, 1984).

War has also profoundly hampered southern Sudanese children's education. Of the 60,730 displaced students, only about one-sixth have found educational opportunities in the regions to which they moved (Republic of the Sudan, 1989). Many southern children are not allowed to enter the government schools unless they produce birth certificates and documents showing previous levels of education. This is a great limitation for people driven from their home areas by the war. Another limitation is that many of the displaced live in unplanned areas where no educational facilities are even available.

Some schools have been established in the displaced settlements and are run by NGOs, but attendance at these schools is very poor. A SCC survey of 600 households in eight settlements in Khartoum in 1989 showed that only 33 per cent of displaced children are in primary schools and 12.5 per cent in kindergartens. Fourteen per cent did not attend school because of the high costs, 30 per cent because of the non-accessibility of schools, and 15 per cent were kept home by parents to help with domestic work. About 4 per cent were suffering from sickness or malnutrition (Awet, 1989). Given these figures, it is not surprising that a large number of displaced children are illiterate. Of a sample surveyed, 54.7 per cent of the boys and more than 60 per cent of the girls were illiterate (SCC, 1989).

Because of poverty and high rates of unemployment in Sudanese towns, displaced families rely on their children to contribute to the family income. According to SCC data, 25.4 per cent of southern displaced children in Khartoum are in the labour force. Given that the majority of children are under five years of age, 40 per cent of those above five years are in the labour force washing cars, vending in the markets and hawking cigarettes. Many southern children between 9 and 16 years work as domestic helpers (SCC, 1989).

However, a considerable number of the displaced children become vagrant. According to some social welfare institutions working with street children, southern children constitute two-thirds of the 25,000 estimated street children in Khartoum. These are mostly boys over ten years of age. Although some of them may take on casual activities, most of them support themselves by begging, theft and support from NGOs. It is common to see street children eating or collecting articles from garbage bins.

Many diseases are prevalent among these children. A recent sample survey shows that anaemia, bilharzia and venereal diseases are found among street children from the southern regions. Their health is further endangered by the bad habits and practices – such as smoking, benzine and glue sniffing, drinking alcohol and smoking hashish (Cannabis Saliva) – which are spreading among them (Dodge, 1989; Atti, 1989). No accurate statistics are available on the magnitude and severity of these addictions.

Children in war affected areas

The lives of children in the war areas in the countries of the Horn are directly endangered by raids, bombings and shooting. They also suffer from the disruption and destruction of the infrastructure, production activities and other food supply channels. Many children have lost their lives in the course of raids by the fighting groups in villages, but death among civilians is largely caused by hunger and disease. In 1987 about 250,000 people in southern Sudan died of hunger and diseases (UNICEF, 1990). As a result of the war, limited food supplies and limited health services were available in the region, and thus thousands of children who suffered from infectious diseases and malnutrition died. The prevalence of illnesses like malaria, measles, diarrhoea, dysentery, and pneumonia was aggravated by poor sanitation, the inaccessibility of services and low food production.

In SPLA controlled areas, although malnutrition and cases of kwashiorkor have been reported for children under 12 years, surveys show that children have better nutritional status than expected (Swiderski, 1989). However, with the continuation of the hideous war, the displacement of rural food producing populations, and the generally deteriorating conditions, nutrition levels are likely to decline. Furthermore, the cessation of immunization programmes in many areas of conflict, and the limited coverage of other areas, encourages the spread of diseases such as measles, pertussis, diphtheria and tetanus. This has been the case in many areas in southern Sudan lately (Abu Zeid et al., 1988).

In recent years, millions of civilians in war-affected areas in Eritrea were in dire straits. Harvests have been non-existent and grain stores empty. In addition there has been a shortage of water in some areas and consequently poor hygiene. The result of these conditions has been a high infant mortality rate of 52 per cent in some areas. Cases of extreme and moderate undernourishment are reported among children, as are several diseases which are considered side effects of undernourishment. Of the children examined, 43 per cent suffered from protein deficiency, 67 per cent had clinical signs of anaemia, and 23 per cent were in the last stages of undernourishment. They were often infected by diseases and were clearly at a low level of physical and mental activity (March & Tool, 1984). Although such a survey may not have been representative of the situation in general, it indicates a serious condition which needs to be considered.

Only a small number of schools and educational institutions are currently functioning in war-affected areas and, consequently, many children do not have access to education. Because of the disruption of the social and economic life of the people in the war zones, attendance is far below capacity. In addition, the functioning schools are likely to be inefficient due to poor buildings, equipment and educational materials, and a shortage of teachers. In the Sudan, recent data from the Educational Consultant of the southern region shows that over 95 per cent of the schools in the three southern regions are closed. Only a very negligible number of schools (eight primary schools, four secondary schools and no high schools) have been functioning in the Upper Nile since 1983, the area being the major scene of the war activities (Republic of the Sudan, 1989).

Refugee children

The refugee population in the four countries that constitute the Horn has been estimated to be two million. According to the most recent figures, there are 838,458 Ethiopians in the Sudan; many have been in exile for years. The number of Sudanese in Ethiopia recently jumped to 375,000, and the estimated 400,000 Somalis who fled across the borders to Ethiopia and Djibouti is continuously increasing due to the ongoing war in Somalia (UNHCR, 1990).

Although the host countries welcomed the refugees, the situation of refugees, particularly children, is rather unsatisfactory. Most of the host countries have been suffering from internal wars (with the exception of Djibouti) and a deteriorating economic situation aggravated by famine, drought and floods. Djibouti, having poor resources, is also experiencing difficult economic conditions.

About 47.7 per cent of Ethiopian refugees who live in camps in the Sudan are children less than 15 years of age according to estimates quoted by El Bashir (1990). However, the number of children in some refugee camps exceeds 50 per cent as shown by Economic and Social Research Council (ESRC) surveys in 1982 and 1989. Although restrictions are not imposed on the Ethiopian refugees' use of public health services, as indicated earlier government health institutions are already underequipped and understaffed. Medicines are in short supply and sometimes not available. Thus high incidences of diseases are prevalent among refugees, particularly children. Even in the organized settlements in the Sudan where the government health services are supported by NGO activities, refugee children suffer from malaria, diarrhoea, respiratory diseases and eye infections. Kuhlman (1990) reported that in Kassala (an urban area with large numbers of Ethiopian refugees) children suffer from malnutrition; out of 31 children admitted to a Mother Child Health (MCH) clinic in one month, 22 suffered from afflictions related to malnutrition. Data from the ESRC (1989) shows a prevalence of chickenpox, measles and anaemia among children in Southern Tokar refugee settlements.

Ethiopian refugees in the Sudan have had access to education in government schools. In addition, there are some schools established by NGOs in organized refugee settlements, and several schools are run by the liberation fronts. A number of refugee children are also in private schools in the urban areas. Despite such opportunities, the education of refugee children raises serious problems. The proportion of refugee children in schools is generally much lower than their proportion among the general population; 55 per cent of school-aged refugee children never attend school (Kuhlman, 1990; Mohamed-Salih et al., 1990). In addition to the constraints of accessibility, inadequacy, and the requirement of birth certificates, many refugee parents exhibit considerable resistance to Sudanese curricula and the Arabic language. Furthermore, many Ethiopian refugees in urban areas cannot afford the transportation, uniforms, and stationery needed for children in schools.

Due to the language problem and the general socio-economic conditions, many children have few prospects of being promoted from primary to secondary schools. At the post-primary level the number of places in English speaking institutions is extremely limited. In addition, there are no vocational training centres for non-Arabic speaking refugees. The few available avenues which were available to Ethiopian refugees in some higher education institutions were being closed with the adoption of Arabic as the language of instruction at these institutions.

With the presence of Ethiopian refugee children in government schools, private schools and liberation front schools, using the Arabic, English and Ethiopian languages and different curricula, the same generation of children is exposed to completely different systems of education. More significantly, the relevance of the Sudanese system of education to the needs of Ethiopian society is highly questionable. The result of such problems is a high illiteracy rate among Ethiopian refugee children in the Sudan.

The situation of Somali refugees is somewhat different from that of other refugees in the Horn of Africa. Since 1988, the war in northern Somalia has caused thousands of refugees to move to Ethiopia and Djibouti. The majority are in Djibouti where many Somali refugees find members of their clan groups. It is relatively easy for Somalis to integrate into these communities and share their dwellings and food, but this has created a critical situation for both the refugees and inhabitants of Djibouti. The host country has limited natural resources, is in a difficult economic situation, and has poor social services and a high rate of unemployment. Such an arrangement also creates difficulties for the NGOs working in the country; because there are no camps, it is difficult to identify displaced Somalis (UNHCR, 1990). NGOs are providing food and medical care to Somali refugees. Somali children living in congested places and mostly in poor areas are vulnerable to high incidences of diseases. The children are likely to suffer poor health as medical services in the host country are poor and overburdened. Somali children have no access to education in Djibouti as the schools are also overcrowded. Moreover, Djiboutian education is in French whereas Somalis tend to use English and Arabic.

Some Somali refugee groups in Ethiopia also live in very difficult circumstances. They live in camps in areas where water is scarce and, as a result, some had to move out of the camps, while others were forced to exchange their food rations for water. Other supplies are also limited, as are health services. Children suffer poor health although they are given priority in the medical centres available. Conditions are generally becoming worse with the increasing influx of refugees (UNHCR, 1990).

Other effects of war on children

War has significantly increased the number of mutilated and disabled children in the Horn; the number of disabled children is far higher than the estimated 10 per cent considered as a base in the world by WHO. In one camp of a few thousand displaced southern Sudanese in Khartoum, there are about 1000 children suffering from blindness (Mohamed-Salih, 1990). A survey in Eritrean villages reported a high incidence of reduced levels of physical and mental activity in some areas. The presence of many blind children was also acknowledged. Considering the need for further health and education services in the country in general, it is not surprising that provision of special health care and educational facilities is rather difficult.

In addition to physical disabilities, children will likely experience psychological disturbances as a result of the war. Such an effect cannot be presented statistically as psychological disturbances are mostly treated in traditional ways and may not be reported. In addition, psychological illnesses may go unnoticed among children, particularly among orphaned, unaccompanied and abandoned children.

The experiences children are subject to during war and the conditions under which they live in war-affected areas, as displaced people or as refugees, may cause and reinforce psychological problems. One significant result of war for many children is the loss of their home. This means the loss of cultural symbols, identity, status, familiar patterns of behaviour, in addition to the loss of many human relationships built up over a lifetime (Kuhlman, 1990). Even those remaining in the war-affected areas experience disturbances of their cultural symbols. Another consequence of war is that children experience or witness killing, torture, death of close relatives and starvation. Such experiences are likely to remain in the children's minds and cause them disturbances (Kuhlman, 1990). The magnitude and severity of such problems depends fundamentally on factors linked to family and community conditions and responses. For the thousands of unaccompanied children the psychological impact of war is dreadful. Separation from the family is traumatic, and this is compounded by their insecure conditions (Ressler, et al., 1988).

Life in the camps for refugees and the displaced may contribute to children's psychological problems. In the camps the essential ingredients for the socialization process may not be accessible because of economic pressures faced by parents and children. In addition, many camps are crowded with different ethnic groups and this likely blurs cultural patterns. Such a situation may threaten the self-identity of the individual and thus is likely to result in psychological problems for children and adults. Symptoms of distrust of oneself and others, distress, fearful aspirations and depression should be expected (Ressler et al., 1988).

The psychological disturbances experienced by children during the war may range from minor anxiety symptoms to changed behaviour and extremely aggressive behaviour. The gravity of such problems depends on the ability of parents to cope with the emotional difficulties of their children. Such ability is reduced by pressures which parents themselves experience. In addition, children may not have access to other help as the governments and NGOs concentrate mainly on material needs (Mohamed-Salih, 1990; Burr, 1990). A serious problem that has to be recognized by any peace agenda is identity diffusion and its related psychological problems. Identity diffusion is a result of different factors such as cultural differences among groups, long periods of exile from home-areas, and difficulties related to the integration of displaced and refugee people into the society.

The role of the government and NGOs

The governments in the Horn countries are attempting to reduce the stressful situations of war, but such efforts have been greatly constrained by the continuity of the wars and political aims. Government assistance to victims of war is largely dependent on NGO support. Many NGOs are distributing food and clothes, and providing health services in displaced camps and refugee settlements. Some NGOs provide educational services and many projects have been established, particularly in the Sudan and Ethiopia, with the aim of achieving self-reliance among refugees. UN organizations have succeeded in delivering thousands of tons of food and medical assistance in war zones; Operation Life Line in southern Sudan is a case in point. However, it must be emphasized that the efforts of NGOs have been greatly curtailed and constrained by conflicting parties in the Horn countries.

Considering the policies generally, there seems to be a great concentration on provision of immediate material needs, mainly food and clothing. Thus some settlements, particularly of displaced people, suffer problems of water shortages, poor sanitation, and the spread of contagious diseases. Thousands of people in war zones suffer starvation and lack basic needs. Children share such suffering as no particular efforts are directed to consider children's needs, with the exception of the limited health and educational services provided in some displaced and refugee camps.

To sum up, it can be said that war in the countries of the Horn of Africa has had differential effects on children. They suffer from illiteracy, poor health and an insecure future. However, the gravity of such problems differs with the situation of children. Any future thinking must consider the problems of vagrancy, poor health, illiteracy, irrelevant education and training, lack of awareness of and indifference to national problems, identity diffusion, and the numerous physical and psychological problems among children.

Recommendations

1. Any prospects for peace must give special priority to data collection on children.

2. Government policies must be directed to recognize that children have separate needs which must be addressed strategically and comprehensively if the numerous and serious problems are to be minimized when conflicts are resolved.

3. There must be co-ordination between the activities of the different NGOs engaged in activities related to displaced and refugee children.

4. Generally the government and NGOs should be encouraged to make a serious effort to improve the health of children by combating diseases and malnutrition, and by providing basic food needs.

5. Specific efforts need to be made to improve the literacy of children generally in the Horn of Africa, with particular consideration given to those affected by war. Here emphasis should be on the relevance of the education of refugee children to their home country. Skills needed for the post-war period should be considered in training programmes.

6. There is a need for immediate action to improve the environment in refugee and displaced settlement camps. The provision of social services is essential.

7. Regeneration of the family and of community life is needed to reduce psychological problems and provide the social milieu needed for the socialization of children.

8. Measures must be taken to protect children and their families in the war zones and to ensure their continuing access to food, medical care and basic services. Efforts must be made to avoid children's exposure to violence and hostility in the war zones.

9. Special attention should be paid to those refugee children who are psychologically disturbed and displaced.

10. The problem of vagrancy should be seriously considered.

Note

1   Use has been made of the report titled *Impact of War on the Sudan* by Mohamed-Salih, M.A., et al., presented to UNICEF, Nairobi, September 1990. Most of the figures and facts used in this paper are from this report. For a detailed reference on some of these points, the reader is advised to refer to this report.

References

Abu Zeid, A., et al. 1988. *War Wounds: Development Costs of Conflict in Southern Sudan. Sudanese People Report on their War*, London, The Panos Institute.

Atti, A.H. 1989 (unpublished). *Children and Vagrancy in Sudan*.

Awet, I.O. 1989. *Primary Education for the Displaced in and Around the National Capital*, Khartoum, SCC.

Burr, M. 1990. *Displaced Persons: A Decade of Despair*, Washington, Committee for Refugees.

Dodge, C.P. 1989. 'Among survivors: Street kids in Khartoum' in Myres, W. (ed.) *Protecting Working Children*, Khartoum, UNICEF.

El Bashir, Z.S. 1990. 'Socio-economic effects on refugees in Sudan', paper presented at the conference on *Problems of Internal Migration and Displacement in Sudan*, held by the Population Centre, Sudan, University of Gezira.

ESRC. 1982. 'Socio-economic survey of spontaneously settled refugees in Port Sudan', *ESRC Research Report No. 13*, Khartoum, Economic and Social Research Council.

ESRC. 1989. 'Socio-economic survey of South Tokar District, Eastern Region', *ESRC Research Report No. 30*, Khartoum, Economic and Social Research Council.

Greuzen, A. 1988. *The Displaced People of Khartoum*, report of an exploratory mission, Holland, Sudan, Médecins Sans Frontières.

Khier, A.M. 1989. 'Status of displaced children in Sudan', paper presented at the seminar on *Children's Rights in Sudan* held by Scova, Wad Medani, Sudan.

Kuhlman, T. 1990. *Burden or Boon? A Study of Eritrean Refugees in the Sudan*. Amsterdam, VU University Press.

March, H. and N. Tool. 1984. *Eritrea Nutritional Survey*, Sudan, Eritrean Relief Association and German International Relations Office.

Mohamed-Salih, M.A., et al. 1990. *Impact of War on the Sudan*, unpublished report presented to UNICEF, Nairobi.

Nobel, P. (ed.) 1987. *Refugees and Development in Africa*, Uppsala, Scandinavian Institute of Africa.

Republic of the Sudan. 1989. *Final Report and Recommendations*, Khartoum, The Steering Committee for the National Dialogue on Peace Settlement and Initiatives.

Ressler, E.M., et al. 1988. *Unaccompanied Children, Care and Protection in Wars, Natural Disasters and Refugee Movements*, New York, Oxford University Press.

Rogge, J.R. 1985. *Too Many, Too Long. Sudan's Twenty Year Refugee Dilemma*, Totowa, New Jersey, Rowman and Allanheld.

SABAH. 1989. *Semi Annual Report on Activities of SABAH Voluntary Association for Street Children*, SABAH.

Save the Children Fund. 1988. *Progress Report on the Programme of Assistance to Displaced Southerners in South Darfur*, Save the Children Fund.

SCC. 1989. *Survey of Displaced People in Khartoum*, Khartoum, SCC.

Swiderski, A. 1989 (unpublished). *Nutritional Surveillance Program in SPLA Controlled Areas in the Southern Sudan*.

UNHCR. 1990, February. *Refugees*, no. 72.

UNICEF. 1990, April. *Intercom*, vol. 2.

Comment   L. JAN SLIKKERVEER

The shift in focus of Samia El Hadi El Nagar's paper away from the groups traditionally in the 'limelight' of political discussions in similar settings, and toward a particularly vulnerable and difficult to reach group which has remained for too long outside the general arena of scientific investigation, is pioneering. Such an overview of the situation in Somalia, Djibouti, Ethiopia and the Sudan is useful for regional comparisons and conclusions; it opens further avenues for future investigation into such processes as migration, border-crossing, regrouping and repatriation. Moreover, the urban–rural distribution of war-affected children could provide for important comparisons within particular war stricken areas.

An area which would be particularly useful to address in the future is the susceptibility of children to influences that will permanently affect their health. If we were to consider this particular vulnerability, the wider context of the child would become more explicit in terms of the equally vulnerable mother. This approach would evoke the atypical risk factors of war, such as displacement, stress, alienation, malnutrition, intercurrent illness and disease, as well as the general hazards of pregnancy and birth. In this context, particular vulnerability to disease is the result of the generally known factors – biological, genetic, environmental, socio-psychological – thwarted by war conditions.

Such a widening of the research focus will enable future studies to also analyse background characteristics such as household–composition, age, sex, marital status of the mother, social economic status, education and so forth to be collected from household surveys. Moreover, in relation to recommendations for planning and the improvement of conditions, remedies such as the newly developed strategy of the 'risk approach in health care', with special reference to maternal and child health (WHO Public Health Paper No. 76, 1984), could be brought in from an applied point of view. The introduction of the close social context of the child in terms of the mother and the young family, often enhanced by the 'illness management group', would enable future research to include perceptions, attitudes, values and belief systems in the analysis. Only through the study of these perceptions and behaviours will we be able to develop an adequate body of knowledge and, subsequently, practical guidelines for possible solutions to the problem.

3

Eritrean Refugees in the Sudan: A Preliminary Analysis of Voluntary Repatriation

ELIAS HABTE-SELASSIE

Introduction

Conventionally the voluntary repatriation of refugees is conceived of in a formal and organized manner involving the UNHCR, the host government and the government of the refugees' country of origin. These three actors often conclude a tripartite agreement before the process commences. This presumes that refugees are returning to territories under the control of the home government. The UNHCR's role in such an operation is to provide the returning refugees with transportation facilities, material assistance for relief and rehabilitation, and legal protection (UNHCR, 1980).

Eritrean refugees did not fall within this pattern or modality of repatriation. This was chiefly because the *de facto* authority in the liberated parts of Eritrea was a liberation front which lacked official international recognition (for a comparable dilemma in the Tigrayan case of repatriation of 1985–7, see REST, 1987; Hendrie, 1990a). Therefore, a trilateral agreement between the UNHCR, the Sudan government and the EPLF was not yet feasible. Owing to mandatory limitations, the UNHCR claimed it could not officially organize repatriation programmes into EPLF controlled and administered territories, let alone finance rehabilitation programmes for returnees inside Eritrea. Moreover, NGOs lack institutional memory and advance preparedness to immediately respond to such emergencies.

However, these legal and institutional constraints notwithstanding, voluntary but spontaneous repatriation of Eritrean refugees has been taking place for quite some time now. Until quite recently, Eritrean refugees who wished to return home did so without much trouble to anyone concerned. They were neither accorded legal protection nor material assistance, but simply trekked back home using whatever minimal resources they had. Though presumably fully aware of these spontaneous and unassisted refugee movements, neither the UNHCR nor the Sudanese Commissioner's Office for Refugees (COR) gave this problem adequate attention. Decisions to repatriate were based on each individual household's comparison of the situation in the home country and in the Sudan. Refugees usually rely on their own network of information obtained from accounts made by new arrivals, temporary visitors, and persons who occasionally visit Eritrea. This was the most common pattern of spontaneous and voluntary repatriation preceding the historic liberation of the port of Massawa in February 1990. But under all circumstances refugees have their own strategy for returning home. In the Tigrayan case, Hendrie stressed that the strategy adopted involved sending the heads of households and productive adults before the rest of the family members (Hendrie, 1990a, 1990b).

The liberation of Massawa was quite eventful not only in the military sphere, but also in political and diplomatic terms. Diplomatically it became the 'golden key' which was to open hitherto closed doors. Politically, above everything else it heightened the Eritrean people's long cherished hope for independence. Concurrent with such enhanced hopes came the desire to return home. Hence, the accelerated liberation of major towns during 1990 became a strong 'pull' factor motivating refugees to return home. Complementing this was the 'push' factor of the deteriorating economic and political situation in the Sudan. The generalized food shortage situation coupled with this year's widespread drought has made life in the settlements and urban areas absolutely unbearable. Both these 'pull' and 'push' factors simultaneously caused a change in the patterns and modalities of repatriation of Eritrean refugees. In general, governments and international agencies began to give the EPLF semi-official recognition and status. As a consequence both the UNHCR and COR also started, timidly, to treat the Commission for Eritrean Refugee Affairs (CERA) as a covert 'partner'. As is discussed later in this paper, the semi-official and organized repatriation operations of CERA during June and July 1990 exemplified such a change of attitude.

The principal aims of this paper are, therefore, to (1) discuss the patterns and modalities of the evolving trend in voluntary repatriation of Eritrean refugees and present a preliminary analysis of the causes and effects of the process; and (2), to identify needs and potential project areas for the integration of returnees in their respective areas of resettlement. Such an analysis, however sketchy, will hopefully inform local authorities and international public opinion about potential large-scale homeward movements of Eritrean refugees and the financial and material assistance requirements involved in operationalizing such large-scale repatriation and rehabilitation programmes. By extension, the Eritrean repatriation experience could become a lesson for future repatriation programmes with other refugee categories in the Horn of Africa.

Official policy versus practice

The right to return to one's homeland is a basic human right under international law (see the Universal Declaration of Human Rights, Art.13, Parg.2; International Covenant on Civil and Political Rights, Art.12, Parg.4; African Charter of Human and Peoples Rights, 1981, Art. 12, Parg.3). In so far as declarations of statements of intent are concerned, voluntary repatriation is universally seen as the most desirable of durable solutions. The UNHCR and member governments put this as a priority option, if and when possible. However, in practice two patterns have emerged in the sphere of voluntary repatriation: official, organized and assisted, and spontaneous and unassisted. Experiences to date establish that the large majority of refugees repatriate through the spontaneous and unassisted channel. It is even officially acknowledged that the number of refugees using the unofficial spontaneous repatriation channel may be up to ten times higher than for those passing through the framework of official repatriation (Coles, 1985).

The Sudan's refugee policy is widely believed to be one of the most generous and coherent on the continent (Nobel, 1982). This should not, however, be construed to mean that there is concurrence between policy and practice. The Sudan's refugee policy is based on the assumption that refugees are 'temporary guests' who are expected to depart once the causes for their flight cease to exit. Thus the Sudan's policy does not encourage the permanent settlement and integration of refugees (see Regulation of Asylum Act, No.45, 1974, Sudan Gazette No.1162, Legislative Supplement 183, 1974). Some refugees have stayed for close to 30 years and continue to be treated as temporary residents. Some Eritrean refugees born in settlements such as in Qala en Nahal, have become heads of families but continue to be regarded as refugees since even being born in the Sudan does not entitle them citizenship rights.

Extended residence in a deteriorating socio-economic and political climate does inevitably lead to 'compassion and hospitality fatigue' on the part of the host society and government. This may be one of the factors which led to the stricter policy recommendation made by a high level refugee policy task force in 1989. In connection with voluntary repatriation, this task force suggested that:

Since the feasibility of voluntary [formal and organized] repatriation has not yet been exclusively
proved owing to the lack of political agreement in the refugee exporting countries, it is hence
imperative to explore and deduce new methods to encourage refugees to choose the [route of] voluntary return.
(COR, 1989, emphasis added)

A question that could readily arise here is: what new methods are there to explore? If
voluntary repatriation through the official tripartite agreement is considered unfeasible
for the majority of refugees in the Sudan, only two alternatives appear to avail themselves.
The first is to force repatriation through the use of direct force or indirect pressures; the
second option is to overcome existing legal and diplomatic limitations, and work in
collaboration with legally unrecognized liberation movements in repatriating refugees to
areas outside the control of recognized governments.

The first option was tried in Djibouti in 1982 and in subsequent years when the
UNHCR, the Djibouti government, and the Dergue in Ethiopia concluded a tripartite
agreement against the expressed wishes of the majority of the refugees (according to the
author's interview with escapees met in Somalia in March, 1983). Many refugees
repatriated to Ethiopia under duress, and some who attempted to escape lost their lives.
The same model is being applied to refugees in Somalia. In this latter case, the international
community is pressuring the Somali government to grant citizenship rights to those who
do not wish to return home. The international community's threat of terminating 'food
aid' to refugees in camps, has left refugees hard-pressed to 'choose' one of two equally
questionable options: 'voluntary' repatriation, or permanent resettlement as Somali citizens
(UNHCR, 1990a, 1990b). Such a move sets a highly dangerous precedent and is a flagrant
violation of people's fundamental right to self-determination (UN Charter, Art. I;
UNHCR 1951 Refugee Convention, Art. 33; OAU Convention of 1969, Art. V). Using
relief as a weapon with which to compel refugees to return to the country from which
they fled is an outright violation of a fundamental principle of international law.

The second option is more relevant to Eritrean refugees in the Sudan. As will be fully
discussed in subsequent sections, a semi-official and rather timid repatriation of Eritrean
refugees, involving the UNHCR, COR and CERA, was undertaken in June and July
of 1990. However, this somewhat experimental repatriation of 801 Eritrean refugees (235
families) was of a limited nature and scale. Assistance measures were restricted to the
provision of transport to the border, some kitchen utensils, and a limited supply of food
relief. The important rehabilitation component was totally left out.

High level officials in COR admit that refugees, when and if they so wish, have a right
to return home and to seek assistance during the entire repatriation process. The only precondition set by Sudanese COR officials is that the decision to repatriate is made freely
and without any force or pressure whatsoever. This, of course, is in conformity with
UNHCR standards (UNHCR, 1983, Part 2). However, if one probes beyond the surface
of such expressions one becomes suspicious. It is widely believed that the government of
the Sudan uses refugees to obtain international assistance (Habte-Selassie, 1988; USCR,
1988). The UNHCR, on the other hand, is looking for a way out of its costly refugee
assistance programme in the Sudan. It has been pouring a substantial amount of funds into
the refugee sector for over two decades and yet refugees are far from being self-sufficient.
At present, due to a 25 per cent reduction in the UNHCR's programme of assistance to
the Sudan, it would be in the High Commission's best interest to encourage repatriation
of refugees, whatever the modality, in order to 'honourably' withdraw from the impasse
in which it finds itself. A variant of the Somali scenario is a possibility that could evolve.

Owing to these divergent views and conflicts of interest, COR and the UNHCR are
'off the record' exchanging accusations and counter-accusations. Given the complex set
of realities, one wonders what the Sudan's policy task force meant by proposing to *'explore
and deduce new methods to encourage refugees to choose the [route of] voluntary return'*. What
procedures and measures would encouraging refugees to repatriate involve, *persuasion or
compulsion?* How can one persuade refugees to return home unless and until they
themselves perceive that the situation at home is conducive to their return? And if
compulsion is used at all, would this entail direct force, or indirect pressures such as the
termination of relief or other assistance?

CERA's first experience in organized repatriation

During the Second and Unity Congress of the EPLF and the Eritrean Liberation Front (ELF) Central Leadership, held inside Eritrea in March 1987, the Commission for Eritrean Refugee Affairs was constituted and charged with the responsibility of dealing with all matters (legal, social, economic and cultural) concerning Eritrean refugees everywhere. However, CERA only became fully operational in 1989, and even then it was operating with very limited human and financial resources. Furthermore, while CERA was in the process of institution building, it was confronted with the issue of repatriation; CERA had neither direct experience with this issue nor adequate familiarity with the repatriation experiences of other countries. It was under such unusual circumstances that CERA had to undertake its first organized, semi-official repatriation operation in June and July 1990, and it is this pioneering but limited experience to which much of this section is devoted.

Factors influencing decisions to repatriate

Organization and logistics

Reports of several refugee households wishing to return home from various settlements in eastern Sudan came to CERA's headquarters in Khartoum as early as September 1989. This first group of applicants was chiefly influenced by the subversive activities of various Eritrean organizations which operated from inside the Sudan. The Eritrean Jihad Front, an Islamic fundamentalist organization, figured prominently among these groups. However, both the nature of the reasons for returning and the number of applicants changed after the liberation of the port of Massawa in February 1990. While the earlier applicants were concentrated in a few settlements, such as in Khashim el Girba and Shagarab, after the liberation of the port applicants for repatriation came from nearly all settlements. This became a matter of great concern to CERA, other EPLF departments and the Eritrean Relief Association (ERA).

In early June, CERA began contacting the embassies of major donor countries, the UNHCR and COR to highlight the evolving trend of repatriation to EPLF administered territories, and to discuss repatriation procedures and possible assistance measures. Given the reduction of the 1990 UNHCR programme of assistance, and the UN system's mandate dilemma regarding assistance measures inside Eritrea, the US embassy was approached for assistance. However, because US policy on assistance to refugees requires that such assistance is channelled through the UNHCR and/or NGOs, the UNHCR, the US Embassy Refugee Co-ordinator's Office, and CERA held a meeting on 10 June 1990 to discuss the modalities of repatriating 400 Eritrean refugee households, assess assistance requirements, and work out the logistics of the operation. All parties agreed that those who freely chose to return to Eritrea should be assisted, but it was proposed that complete information on these applicants ought to be made available to the UNHCR and host governments. It was also agreed that COR should be duly informed about the matter by the UNHCR representative. And, once all the official formalities and procedures were met, the process of repatriation would resume. The US Embassy representative affirmed that a request for the required funds would be submitted to Washington; upon approval, funds would accordingly be released to the UNHCR which would, in turn, fund COR operations.

Prior to this, CERA held a meeting with the Sudanese Commissioner for Refugees to discuss the growing number of Eritreans who wish to return home and the assistance measures required for their repatriation and rehabilitation. The Commissioner expressed COR's readiness to fully co-operate with CERA provided that the voluntariness of the Eritrean refugees' wishes to repatriate is unequivocally ascertained in advance. He further affirmed that it is the right of every refugee to voluntarily return home and to be assisted in both the repatriation and rehabilitation phases.

Following this meeting, CERA staff proceeded to Showak in the east to discuss the details of the first group of repatriants with COR and UNHCR regional offices. It was at this point that CERA came to learn that UNHCR/COR assistance measures consisted of only transport trucks from settlements to the border, one month's food ration of only dura and cooking oil, and a limited supply of kitchen utensils. Despite CERA's appeal for more assistance it was not possible to alter the decision. Before a day was fixed for the actual movement of returnees, security clearance had to be arranged by COR with the Kassala government, and a transfer point – where refugees would be handed over – had to be chosen by CERA. Once the repatriation dates were fixed, CERA, in collaboration with the EPLF Commission of Transport and Supplies and the EPLF department of Public Administration, arranged the resources and logistics required for the inland post-hand over operation. In spite of the rather modest number of people involved (801 people; 235 families) in this repatriation operation, given CERA's limited resources and the rather limited level of co-ordination existing at the time between the other EPLF Departments concerned, the task proved to be quite a feat. The task will even be more difficult when larger numbers of returnees are involved in the near future. However, the exercise provided CERA with invaluable experience on the basis of which future repatriation programmes can be planned and carried out.

The situation of returnees in their home country

Unlike in other repatriation cases in which a tripartite agreement guarantees the home country authorities emergency relief and rehabilitation assistance (UNHCR, 1980), in the Eritrean case the entire burden of care, maintenance and resettlement of returnees has become the responsibility of the EPLF and its affiliates. The UNHCR ceased being responsible for providing legal protection and material assistance (both for emergencies and rehabilitation) once the refugees crossed the Sudan–Eritrea border.

Due to their proximity to the border, the town of Tessenei and the surrounding villages received and resettled approximately 3,000 returnees between April 1989 and December 1990. Upon the closure of Tessenei, chiefly owing to over-crowding and an inadequacy of suitable housing and public services, new returnees were relocated to nearby estate towns such as Ali Gider, Telat'asher and Arba'atasher. At present Tessenei and its vicinity are only used as transit centres for returnees who wish to proceed further inland.

Although most returnees prefer to resettle in towns, the economies of many towns could not sustain a larger population. For example, 90 per cent of Tessenei's residents are returnees and nearly 95 per cent of the town's economic activities are centred around the service sector. Productive activities, if the climate permits, are confined to the agricultural sector. Many of the returnee families in the areas of Tessenei and Ali Gider have been allotted 1 to 4 hectare plots of land; however, poor rains have frustrated hopes for immediate food self-sufficiency and, owing to the absence of other sources of income, many returnees have to rely on the ERA until the next harvesting season.

Many urban centres have suffered deliberate bombing attacks by the Ethiopian Air Force. In these towns the infrastructure, services and utilities are in very poor shape and would require considerable amounts of funds to rebuild and re-establish. As a result there are critical housing and water shortages in most of these towns and reconstruction activities are urgently needed. Similarly, in a highly devastated physical environment the traditional sources of energy (firewood and charcoal) are difficult to come by; alternative sources of energy need to be developed and renewable energy sources established. Alternative construction materials will also be needed if the housing needs of large numbers of returnees are to be met without inflicting further damage on the rather limited and scarce forest resources remaining in Eritrea. In the meantime tents and other temporary housing materials are urgently needed to meet the needs of returnees.

While the above picture characterizes most urban centres in Eritrea, there are some rural villages, such as Tekombia, Shambeko, Mogollo, Mogoriab, and so forth, which have a relatively greater absorptive capacity and better prospects for early economic recovery. Most of these villages lie within the Gash Basin and offer diverse economic activities such as crop production, livestock rearing, and petty commodity trade. Generally speaking, however, if these rural areas were to absorb more returnees they would require the provision of basic services (health, education, transport, and so forth), utilities (water, flour mills, electricity), and markets for non-farm consumer commodities. Priority should be given to the provision of health and education services which refugees have been intimately acquainted with in the Sudanese refugee settlements.

All of these components are of paramount importance in the design and implementation of rehabilitation programmes for returnees, but require the commitment of considerable amounts of financial and material resources which are at present beyond the means of the authorities in Eritrea. When the number of repatriations and associated logistical requirements increase with time, the sums involved will increase exponentially. This fact reveals the constructive role the international donor community *can* and *should* play in assisting rehabilitation and development programmes for returnees over and above that of emergency relief. Without this external input the situation could easily retrogress and result in an emergency, in which case recovery will prove to be much more difficult and costly.

Some demographic and socio-economic features of returnees

The Commission for Eritrean Refugee Affairs' Register of Returnees indicates that 1,576 households (approximately 8,000 individuals) returned to Eritrea from eastern Sudan between April 1989 and December 1990. This figure does not, however, include those who spontaneously and elusively returned to join their kin as tracking down these returnees would be an onerous task. Furthermore, the above figure does not includes the 300 households which returned from Tigray in northern Ethiopia during the course of 1990.

The returnee population represents diverse ethnic origins, age and gender structures, and socio-economic backgrounds. To illustrate this, a sample of 380 households which returned in the third quarter of 1990 was analysed. About 68 per cent of the returnees came from organized settlements and reception centres, while some 32 per cent came from spontaneous settlements in rural towns and villages and major towns (CERA, 1990a).

The sample constituted about 30 per cent of the total population of the 1,256 households which were repatriated from the Sudan between 1 January and 30 September 1990. Of the 380 households, 273 (71.84 per cent) were male-headed, and 107 (28.16 per cent) were female-headed. However, of the 1,361 returnees, 693 (50.9 per cent) were females and 668 (49.1 per cent) were males. The fairly balanced sex distribution in this sample tends to refute the commonly held assumption that the refugee population in the Sudan is predominantly female. The number of youths of marriageable age was small relative to the total population of returnees. One plausible explanation for their low numbers is that many may have decided to remain behind for fear of being conscripted into the Eritrean People's Liberation Army (EPLA).

Socio-economic status of returnees

Returnees have come from various types of settlements in the Sudan (land-based agricultural, wage-earning, and spontaneous settlements, both rural and urban), but the majority are from organized land-based and wage-earning settlements in the rural areas. A considerable number among them were also spontaneously settled in the Sudanese urban centres. The bulk of the returnees (over 70 per cent) wished to resettle in towns in Barka and Gash regions. This rather high percentage of returnees wanting to resettle in urban areas may be due to the proximity of the towns to the Sudanese border and hence easier access to the Sudan if and when the need to return arises; to some returnees residing in these towns before flight; and to the degree of urbanization and social change that has been occurring during the returnees' extended stay in large settlements in eastern Sudan (with a refugee population of 20,000–30,000), and the craving for the amenities of urban life enhanced by these changes.

The last factor is particularly true with regard to women and children. For most refugee women who belong to patriarchal and 'feudal' socio-political systems, life in the refugee settlements has been to a limited degree a liberating experience. Piped-water delivery systems in the settlements have relieved women of the arduous task of collecting and carrying water on their backs, and flour mills in the settlements are a deliverance for women who traditionally perform back-breaking grain grinding activities. Likewise, the existence of markets and transportation facilities have markedly reduced the time absorbed by those activities. The availability of health services has generally improved the health situation of the settlements' populations, particularly of women and children, and the provision of primary education in the settlements has given children access to education which was not available to most in their pre-flight situations.

A review of the returnees' pre-flight economic history indicates that about 85 per cent were primarily engaged in rural economic activities, while 15 per cent were engaged in the urban (formal and informal sector) economies. This ratio changed considerably as a result of extended residence in the Sudan. According to a review of the post-flight economic history of returnees, 35 per cent of the total number of household heads were engaged in non-agricultural economic activities. All of these changes are important parameters to recognize in the design and execution of resettlement and integration programmes for returnees.

Factors that encourage or hinder organized and spontaneous voluntary repatriation

Repatriation as a special phenomenon of population movement is influenced by a host of socio-economic, politico-military, institutional and operational factors. It is not possible to be exhaustive in such a limited though indicative case study, but the study will touch upon the major factors in both the host and home countries that may enhance or hinder voluntary repatriation, be it organized and assisted or spontaneous and outside the traditional framework of tripartite arrangements and formal programmes of assistance.

In the case of Eritrean refugees in the Sudan, voluntary repatriation is a function of situations prevailing in both the host and home countries, as well as of the international political climate which has a bearing on the quantity and quality of assistance obtainable at any given time. The inherent political and institutional/legal constraints facing the UNHCR have manifestly determined its role in the repatriation of Eritrean refugees. This 'mandate dilemma', coupled with the bureaucratic delays of UNHCR organized repatriation programmes, discourages many refugees from relying on the official channel. Thus refugees often rely on their own networks and means even in situations where there is no mandate dilemma or political impasse.

Other factors which motivate refugees to voluntarily repatriate relate to a host country's social, political, and economic realities. At present the situation in the Sudan, aptly characterized as a 'total crisis', is a major 'push' factor accelerating the repatriation of refugees. Excessive political control through neighbourhood *lijnas* (associations), a variant of the *kebeles* in Ethiopia, has made refugee life generally unsafe; generalized food and commodity shortages have caused a rapid deterioration of living conditions as well as sparked harsh attitudes towards refugees and stigmatized them in the eyes of the national population. Recent statements by Sudanese government authorities (see *Sudanow*, October 1990) blaming refugees and NGOs working in the refugee sector for food shortages are, to say the least, provocative and unwarranted. Furthermore, the deliberate inflation of refugee population figures in the country to three million (the official estimate at the end of 1990 being 749,000), has created widespread anxiety and a feeling of extreme insecurity among refugee communities. All of these factors have enhanced the desire of refugees in the Sudan to return home.

Reinforcing the above noted factors on the host country's side are military and political developments in the refugees' home country. Owing to the rapid change in the military balance of the Ethio-Eritrean war, many Eritrean refugees' perceptions and attitudes have markedly changed in recent months. Refugees, who have been frustrated by life in exile, are voluntarily deciding to return home. However, variations in people's attitudes and perceptions with regard to the timing of repatriation still exist.

As a recent Euro-Action ACORD survey illustrates, refugees' decisions as to when and how to return home are influenced by both endogenous and exogenous factors.

Endogenous factors include the perceptions and personal experiences of individual refugees; the economic status and level of income in the host country; the political views and allegiances to political fronts/organizations, and perceived treatment by the home authority; and family ties and situations, and so forth. Exogenous factors include the means by which the conflict is terminated; drought and famine situations in the host and/or home country; the enemy's possible military actions against economic targets and civilian populations, such as air raids or the confiscation of farmers' and pastoralists' produce to feed the occupying army; socio-economic realities of the host country; the international community's provision of assistance and the actual accessibility of such assistance both in the refugee settlements and across the border in the home country for returnees and drought victims; and opportunities for resettlement in countries such as the USA, Canada and Australia.

As stated in ACORD's survey report, the various Eritrean political movements have, though in varying degrees, influence among the refugee communities. Of a total of 149 interviewees, 61 were members of the EPLF and 88 possible sympathizers. In terms of types of responses, the ACORD survey noted that 81.5 per cent of those who stated they would return immediately were EPLF members, while 84.3 per cent of those whose return depended on the circumstances were not EPLF members. This suggests that the decision to repatriate and particularly the timing of repatriation is very much a function of a refugee's political allegiance. It is also worth noting that 71 per cent of those who expressed a wish to return to EPLF sponsored and administered settlements consisted of EPLF members, but only 29 per cent of the non-members made the same choice. This significant discrepancy between the two groups may be attributable to the traditional divisions within the Eritrean struggle which continue to exist.

Religion is another determinant factor among certain sectors of the refugee communities in the Sudan. This element ought to be seen in relation to the propaganda campaigns waged by some Islamic fundamentalist groups within the refugee communities. Although now on the decline, largely due to the EPLF's recent diplomatic successes and military prowess, Islamic fundamentalists have always tried to characterize the EPLF as too radical, pro-Christian and anti-Muslim (see EPLF, 1990).

A last factor which should be introduced in this analysis concerns the policies, attitudes and actions of the home authority, the EPLF. Here it is not what the EPLF feels and does which is determinant, but the refugees' perceptions of the organization and its policies and practices. Given the long drawn-out war and the painful history of a series of civil wars in Eritrea, the EPLF needs wisdom, patience and tolerance in dealing with the issues of refugee repatriation. The matter is not solely the domain of politics, but should primarily be seen from a juridical, humanitarian and human rights protection perspective.

It is instructive to stress that whatever the objective conditions at any given time and place, ultimately the subjective element, that is the refugees' own perception of the situations in both the home and host countries, is the determinant factor. Therefore, the most ideal condition which could motivate refugees to return home is the cessation of the very factors and forces which in the first instance caused their flight: 'no greater incentive to return home [can] be offered refugees than the elimination of the conditions which caused their flight' (Gordenker, 1987:130). Pursuing this viewpoint a bit further by bringing in the element of the inviability and failures of attempted local integration programmes, Kibreab argues, that 'as long as the root and immediate causes to the problem remain unresolved, almost all African countries will continue to treat refugees within their territories as refugees and are not willing to accord them equal rights with their citizens'(1990b:30).

Experience in Africa invariably illustrates, however, that most refugees are unwilling to relinquish their national identity even when citizenship rights are offered by host governments, as in the cases of Tanzania, Somalia, and to a limited extent Botswana (see Christenssen, 1983; Kibreab, 1990a). The attitudes of refugees and host governments are therefore concurrent in that both are opposed to the idea of permanent settlement in the countries of first asylum. The Eritrean refugee experience (Tesfai, 1990; CERA, 1990; Kibreab, 1990a), and that of the Tigrayan refugees in 1985-7 (Hendrie, 1990a) also substantiate this viewpoint.

The economics of repatriation and reintegration of returnees

The scale of the problem

Mass distress migration clearly entails tremendous costs for the population involved and the state in the country of origin. Refugee movements imply enormous losses in human resources, particularly of skilled and professional workers who often are in short supply. Repatriation programmes also demand considerable material and financial resources in all phases, including the movement of repatriates, rehabilitation and reintegration of returnees, and reconstruction and development programmes in the returnee hosting areas.

There are close to 100,000 Eritrean refugee households (500,000 individuals) in central and eastern Sudan. The majority of these refugees came from rural Eritrea and are now located in rural Sudan; from CERA's 1990 registry of returnees, of a total of 1,256 households repatriated to Eritrea in 1990, 74.3 per cent came from rural areas in the Sudan, and 25.7 per cent from urban centres. Children under 16 years of age constituted 57 per cent of the total population of returnees. Such a predominance of youth and children will have a considerable bearing on rehabilitation and development programmes.

Domestic capacities and resources

Due to a lack of official aid, the authorities in Eritrea have been operating with limited resources and under extreme difficulties. Conducting an all-out conventional war for national liberation and managing a modern administrative structure with all the institutions and service-rendering infrastructures, and at the same time being confronted with one of the worst droughts in years, has not been an enviable challenge. This combination of commitments and constraints has meant that a large portion of the EPLF's resources has been allocated to furthering the war and mitigating the effects of the drought. The EPLF's resources are by and large drawn from its own sources; however, the limited emergency relief and economic recovery and reconstruction programmes engaged could not have been successful without the work of the Eritrean Relief Association (ERA). The ERA is an indigenous NGO which, since its establishment in 1975, has developed partnership relations with a host of foreign voluntary agencies which are the principal sources of funding for its emergency relief and rehabilitation programmes. Inside Eritrea, the ERA has found implementing partners among various EPLF technical/sectoral departments. In collaborative efforts, the ERA acts as a conduit for funds mobilized abroad, while the sectoral departments execute projects.

In spite of the frequent appeals the ERA launches for emergency relief assistance, and the funds and other essential inputs it raises for a broad range of rehabilitation and development projects, the needs of the Eritrean people are far from being satisfied. External assistance in a situation where domestic resources are exceedingly limited is still needed. Eritrea, after all, deserves substantial rehabilitation and development assistance from the international community to reconstruct the war damaged economy and environment. And, since the Eritrean people are themselves the country's principal resource, their return home is of highest priority. The significance of CERA's voluntary repatriation programme ought to be seen in this light.

References

CERA. 1990a (unpublished). *Annual Report*.
CERA. 1990b. Quarterly reports on situation of Eritrean refugees (mimeo in Tigrigna language), Khartoum, CERA.
Christenssen, H. 1983. *Survival Strategies for and by Camp Refugees*, Geneva, UNRISD.
Coles, G.J.L. 1985, July. *Voluntary Repatriation: A Background Study*, Geneva, UNHCR.
COR. 1989. Refugee Policy Document, Government of Sudan.
Crisp, J. 1985. 'Voluntary repatriation programme for African refugees: A critical examination' *Refugee Issues*, vol. 1, no. 2.
De Beer, G. 1989. 'The United Nations and Namibia: Betrayed confidence?' *Netherlands Quarterly of Human Rights*, vol. 7, no. 2.

EPLF. 1990. 'Questions and answers of the Secretary General' *Sagam*, vol. 2, no. 10.

Gordenker, L. 1987. *Refugees in International Politics*, New York, Columbia University Press.

Gorman, R.F. 1984. 'Refugee repatriation in Africa', paper prepared for the *Symposium on Refugees in Africa: Alternative Viewpoints*, organized by the Refugee Studies Programme, QEH, Oxford University.

Habte-Selassie, E. 1988. *The Political Economy of Refugees in Northeast Africa: Case Studies from Somalia and the Sudan*, M.A. thesis, The Hague, Institute of Social Studies.

Hendrie, B. 1990a. *The Tigrean Refugee Repatriation: Sudan to Ethiopia, 1985–1987*, a study prepared for Intertec Institute, Dallas, Texas.

Hendrie, B. 1990b. *Power and Rationality: A Critique of International Disaster Relief*, M.Sc. thesis, London, University College.

Horn, N. 1984. 'The role of government organizations in the repatriation of refugees in Africa with special emphasis on refugees from Zimbabwe', an expanded version of a paper presented at the 1983 *African Studies Association Conference*, Boston, MA.

van Hovell tot Westerflier, W.J.E.M. 1989. 'Africa and refugees: The OAU Refugee Convention in theory and practice' *Netherlands Quarterly of Human Rights*, vol. 7, no. 2.

Kibreab, G. 1990a. *Refugees in Somalia: A Burden, An Opportunity, and A Challenge*, Ottawa, International Development Research Council.

Kibreab, G. 1990b. 'Host governments and refugee perspectives on settlement and repatriation in Africa', paper prepared for a policy seminar on *Development Strategies on Forced Migration in the Third World*, The Hague, Institute of Social Studies.

Kuhlman, T. 1990. *Burden or Boon? A Study of Eritrean Refugees in the Sudan*, Amsterdam, VU University Press.

Nobel, P. 1982. 'Refugee law in the Sudan' *Research Report No. 64*, Uppsala, Scandinavian Institute of African Studies.

OAU. 1969. *OAU Convention Governing the Specific Aspects of Refugee Problems in Africa*, Addis Ababa, OAU.

Refugee Studies Programme. 1990. 'Refugee voices from Indo-China' *Refugee Participation Network*, no. 7.

REST. 1987. 'Refugees return home in optimistic mood: Special features on health services in Tigray' *Rest Newsletter*, London, UK Support Committee.

Smyer, W.R. 1985, Fall. 'Refugees: A never ending story' *Foreign Affairs*.

Tekie, M. 1990. 'The Eritrean refugee problems in the Sudan: Issues and challenges', paper prepared for AFSAAP, Geelong, Australia, Deakin University.

Tesfai, M. 1990. 'Eritrean refugees' attitudes towards returning home', report prepared for Euro-Action Accord, London.

Tieleman, H.J. and T. Kuhlman (eds.) 1990. 'Enduring crisis: Refugee problems in eastern Sudan' *Research Report No. 41*, Leiden, African Studies Centre.

Toole, M.J. and R.J. Waldman. 1990. 'Prevention of excess mortality in refugee and displaced populations in developing countries' *The Journal of American Medical Association*, vol. 263, no. 24, pp. 3296-3302.

UNHCR. 1980 (sic). *Conclusions on the International Protection of Refugees*, adopted by the Executive Committee of the UNHCR Programme; Excomm. Conclusion No. XXXI of 1980, No. XXXVI of 1985 (regarding voluntary repatriation).

UNHCR. 1983. *Handbook for Emergencies*, Parts 1 and 2, Geneva, UNHCR.

UNHCR. 1990a. *Fact Sheet on Djibouti, Ethiopia, Somalia and the Sudan*, vol.4, no. 1. Geneva, UNHCR.

UNHCR. 1990b. 'The Horn of Africa: An Uncertain Future' *Refugees*, no. 72.

USCR. 1988. *Beyond the Headlines: Refugees in the Horn of Africa*, Washington DC, United States Committee for Refugees.

Comment   MEKURIA BULCHA

Experience from the past 30 years of independence shows that repatriation is the ideal solution to the refugee problem in Africa. There is no doubt that it is also the best solution to the refugee problem in the Horn. However, the question is under what conditions are refugees willing to return to their countries of origin? Is the cessation of armed conflict enough for governments and international organizations to repatriate refugees? What is peace or who defines peace?

Elias Habte-Selassie's contribution provides some clear answers to these questions, but his discussion is limited to Eritrean refugees in the Sudan. Since the points he raised regarding repatriation and post-repatriation problems are also relevant to other refugee situations in the Horn, the following comments elaborate on some of his points and put them in the wider perspective of the refugee problem in the Horn.

Repatriation, while being the ideal solution to refugee problems in the Horn, is not in itself free from problems. As one writer has aptly commented, it has a Janus-faced quality, that is it can be the best solution when voluntary and a very bad one when involuntary (Gorman, 1984). This observation touches upon the issue of who decides if and when refugees should repatriate. International conventions provide clear guidelines on this point. All regional and UN legal documents stipulate that repatriation must be voluntary and that voluntary repatriation is possible only when refugees themselves pursue it as a genuine option to end their exile.

This leads us to ask, are refugees generally willing to go home if the authorities leave that decision to them? How can we be sure that they will not choose to stay in the host countries in order to benefit from the assistance they get from the international community? Every survey and research report on existing refugee situations shows that the dream of most African refugees is to go back to their countries of origin and live among their relatives in dignity. This includes many of those who sought asylum in Europe and North America and are relatively economically secure. Research shows that more than 95 per cent of the Ethiopian refugees in the Sudan, including those who have been in exile for decades, are eagerly awaiting the chance to go home (see Bulcha, 1988). The spontaneous repatriation of 400 Eritrean refugees described by Elias clearly indicates the eagerness with which refugees respond to changes that make repatriation to their countries possible.

In most cases refugees voluntarily repatriate once clear cut and fundamental changes have taken place which eliminate the root causes of their flight. But the way refugees respond to changes can depend upon factors other than the end of a civil war, a change of government or the attainment of independence. Eritrean, Oromo, Tigrayan and Amhara refugees responded differently to the question: 'Under what circumstances would you be prepared to return to your home country?' For Eritrean refugees the precondition for voluntary repatriation was the military and political victory of their liberation movement and the attainment of national independence (Bulcha, 1988). As Elias pointed out, for some Eritreans not only should independence be in place before they return home, but hostilities between the different political factions inside Eritrea must cease and peace must reign.

The response of Oromo refugees was somewhat similar to that of the Eritreans. Most saw Oromo–Ethiopian relations as colonial and the Amhara dominated government as alien. Therefore, they genuinely considered the decolonization of Oromoland and the establishment of a democratic Oromo state as a necessary precondition for their voluntary repatriation. The majority of the refugees from Tigray said that they expect a change of government and the restoration of peace and order in Ethiopia before returning home. The concern of the Amhara refugees was very ambiguous and shifting. Until about the middle of the 1980s, most Amhara refugees were for an overthrow of the Mengistu regime. Today, the obstacle to a voluntary return to their home country seems to be the lack of security and the deep economic crisis in Ethiopia.

Generally speaking, what each category of refugees is waiting for is the restoration of peace. However, they differ considerably when it comes to the definition of peace. For example, it does not make much difference to some of them, particularly the Amhara group, if peace and order are established through military victory over the various liberation fronts or through a negotiated settlement. For others the defeat of the liberation fronts does not necessarily lead to a just peace. Peace devoid of justice is, of course, nonsense.

One may ask, is the Horn of Africa on the threshold of a post-conflict period? The fall of Siyad Barre seemed for some time to be the beginning of the return of peace to Somalia. As the guerrilla forces entered Mogadishu, Somali refugees around the world hoped for a safe return to their country. However, the demise of the Barre regime did not result in the end of conflict. Hostilities have continued between the United Somali Congress (USC) which controls Mogadishu and the other clan-based fronts that control different regions of Somalia. These conflicts are now producing new waves of refugees.

The situation in the Sudan is a stalemate. The war between the Sudan People's Liberation Army (SPLA) and government forces is raging on and thousands of refugees from the south are pouring into south-western Ethiopia and northern Sudan. The situation in Ethiopia has undergone dramatic changes. However, at this point it is difficult to predict what the outcome will be with respect to the regions of Ethiopia, specifically in Eritrea, Tigray and Oromoland, now that the Dergue has been expelled. The Oromo question has been played down by most of the Ethiopian organizations that aspire to replace the Dergue. The exclusion of the Oromo Liberation Front (OLF) from peace negotiations and continued armed conflict in Oromoland certainly have affected peace, and will have a significant impact on the repatriation of refugees and economic recovery in the region. A large proportion of refugees in the Horn, particularly in Somalia, are Oromo and most of the fertile agricultural land and known mineral deposits in the region are found only in Oromoland.

In short, a comprehensive peace that involves all conflicting parties must be achieved in all three countries of the Horn in order to have a successful programme of refugee repatriation, and to embark on socio-economic reconstruction and development. As indicated by Elias Habte-Selassie, the process of refugee repatriation if and when peace is restored in the Horn will involve three main problems: identification, transportation or movement and integration into the societies of origin. Identification of those who have decided to return home, the first stage in the process, entails a number of problems and questions regarding how repatriation should be organized and conducted. Elias has described the approach used by the Commission for Eritrean Refugee Affairs (CERA) whereby applications are received from those who wish to return home and then processed. Such an approach cannot be applied to all refugee groups or on a large scale in the Horn. I do not think that it is even applicable to most Eritreans in the Sudan.

What is needed once peace is restored is a survey of every refugee household to ascertain the wishes of its members. Such a survey involves certain difficulties such as locating spontaneously settled refugees scattered in urban and rural settings. Furthermore, since the operation would involve tens of thousands of households, it would require considerable resources even when conducted in organized refugee settlements and camps. These problems, without a doubt, can be surmounted with proper planning and provided there is co-operation between the host government, the UNHCR, NGOs, and refugee representatives and their organizations.

In addition to identifying prospective returnees, a survey needs to get a clear picture of their demographic profile: age, sex, household structure, economic status and destination in the country of origin. This provides valuable information needed to plan the technical aspects of repatriation, such as assembling and providing returnees with proper transportation and other facilities (food, water, medicines, and so forth) on route. Moving tens of thousands of families over long distances involves not only seeing them over the border, but also helping them return to their places of origin where they might still have relatives or a claim to property. It is an operation that takes much time, requires a lot of money and calls for proper pre-planning and organization.

Some of the Horn countries have sufficient experience in receiving and settling returnees after long years in exile. A good example is the Sudan which, following the cessation of the civil war in the south in 1972, received and settled some 280,000 returnees from the neighbouring countries. However, given the economic crisis which the countries in the Horn are now experiencing, repatriation on a large scale cannot be conducted without international co-operation. Once peace is restored, resources will be needed for the reintegration of returnees and the rehabilitation of internally displaced people whose numbers run into the millions in each country.

Elias Habte-Selassie's paper provides a good introduction to the problems that can arise with the absorption of returnees. One can imagine how difficult it will be to settle and integrate 400,000 to 500,000 returnees in an environment that has been destroyed and has degenerated and a society which has largely disintegrated due to an extended war. For most rural refugees who have been in exile for a long time and whose villages have been ravaged by war and the inhabitants killed or scattered, there is no living community to return to. In Ethiopia this includes those areas where the rural communities were uprooted and displaced by the much criticized resettlement programme of the military regime. In these areas returnees must build new communities and new social networks from scratch.

One of the changes that flight has brought about or has accelerated is the rate of rural to urban migration. Many refugees of rural origins have drifted to towns and major urban centres in the countries of asylum in search of subsistence. According to the Sudanese government, by October 1990 there were over 85,800 Ethiopian refugees in Khartoum (in *Horn of Africa Bulletin*, 2(7), 1990:21). Other cities such as Gedaref, Kassala and Port Sudan also accommodate tens of thousands of refugees from Ethiopia. As Elias has pointed out, a very large proportion of the rural refugees, not only in the Sudan but also in the other countries of the Horn, live in large settlements of 20,000 to 30,000 people. These settlements are very different from the hamlets in which most of the refugees lived before their flight; they have urban characteristics with modern facilities and services such as clinics, schools, running water, flour mills and so forth. The point is, many of the refugees who have lived in urban areas and large settlements for a long period will want to settle in similar environments after repatriation. This will, however, be almost impossible as during the last two decades of economic crisis there has been little or no development of urban facilities in the Horn. Furthermore, the urban population in the region has increased many-fold because of the huge displacement of people from the rural areas due to war and famine. The existing urban facilities, therefore, do not have the capacity to accommodate and absorb returnees. These are some of the many problems that need to be tackled in order to absorb and reintegrate returnees in the post-conflict period in the Horn.

Repatriation, even when voluntary, could be unsettling for many refugees, particularly for those who were born and brought up in exile. There are many refugees in that category in the Horn. The rehabilitation of these and others who have lived for many years in exile requires understanding and in some cases the need will arise to (re)educate them in some aspects of life in their or their parents' country of origin. Some will prefer to stay in the host countries and these people should be given the chance to do so and be treated as citizens in those countries.

Returnees come back home not only with problems but also with resources and skills. Skilled and educated refugees can play important roles in the recovery and development of their societies' conditions once they return. Perhaps it is necessary to conduct a survey of refugee skills at the start of the repatriation programme so that their rehabilitation is planned properly and their skills put to use.

References

Bulcha, M. 1988. *Flight and Integration: The Causes of Mass Exodus from Ethiopia and the Problems of Integration in the Sudan,* Uppsala, Scandinavian Institute of African Studies.

Gorman, R.F. 1984. 'Refugee repatriation in Africa', paper prepared for the *Symposium on Refugees in Africa: Alternative Viewpoints,* Oxford.

Comment   ABDEL RAHMAN A. AL-BASHIR

Voluntary repatriation is generally perceived as the most desirable solution to refugee problems, although it is by no means easy to achieve. Elias Habte-Selassie has presented the unique and fascinating repatriation experience of a group of refugees chosen from different settlements. The significance of this experience is that it was organized by an indigenous refugee organization, and that the desire to return never waned during the long years of asylum.

The flight of Eritrean refugees to the Sudan began in March 1967 when 30,000 refugees crossed the border from the lowlands of Eritrea to the Sudan near the town of Kassala. Successive waves of refugees followed throughout the years, and by 1990 there were more than 560,000 refugees of Eritrean origin in the Sudan.

Since their arrival, the refugees have been received with a tradition of hospitality and openness. Due to the existence of ethnic affinities and the political sympathy of the local Sudanese hosts, their reception and settlement went on without notable difficulties. Large areas were set aside to accommodate the refugees in settlements, while the rest, who were greater in number, settled themselves in the local communities.

Notwithstanding occasional indications of friction or 'utterances' by some members of the government, the refugees enjoyed an integrated and peaceful stay with the local people. The fact that not a single case of refused entry was registered during the past 26 years reflects the commitment of the Sudanese people to their Eritrean guests. Refugees are allowed to stay until it becomes possible for them to return. For this reason it is necessary to maintain a reasonable degree of integration to enable the refugees to pursue their lives as normally as possible. The policy of integration does not lead to naturalizing the refugees; it is not in the interest of the Sudan to depopulate a neighbouring nation. It is worth noting that the refugees who arrived in 1967 were similarly against any policy that would, in their view, lead to their naturalization. For this reason, there was some objection to the settlement and the distribution of agricultural plots to households on the grounds that it was a step toward granting them citizenship.

The paper refers to some allegations that the refugees had been used to obtain international assistance. Such allegations are, to say the least, unfair. Whatever assistance has been 'poured in', it has never been enough to meet the requirements of the refugees. It does not take into account the loss of resources and the pressure on services and the infrastructure. The acceptance of refugees should not be viewed in terms of material losses and gains.

The experience of repatriating this group of refugeees, unique as it is, is a highly organized one; therefore, it could not be described as spontaneous. The constant flow of refugees, by its very nature, is contradictory to any spontaneous return. It is known, however, that occasionally refugees risked 'sneaking in' in order to meet with relatives who were left behind and to follow the news on their property, animals and agricultural fields. Such clandestine movements were generally unobstructed.

Elias refers to the factors that lead to this voluntary repatriation. The 'push' factor of the deteriorating conditions in the Sudan, and the liberation of Massawa and other major urban towns and rural tracts were events which enhanced the recognition of the EPLF and gave Eritreans confidence that their long-awaited aspirations would be realized. In my view, the successes scored by the EPLF, rather than the other factors, are behind the increase in repatriations.

The civilian institutions, the Eritrean Relief Association (ERA) and the Commission for Eritrean Refugee Affairs (CERA), were established to cater for the administration and the welfare of the civilian population inside and outside Eritrea. Through the extension of services and the implementation of some developmental projects among the refugees, these two indigenous institutions have acquired a high level of efficiency and organizational skill. This has enabled them to successfully implement the repatriation and resettlement of their own people.

This experience in which civilian life in large zones in conflict areas is run by would-be governments demonstrates the possibility of achieving aims outside the traditional norms. The experiment has revealed the importance of careful planning and the provision of the necessary logistics to ensure the smooth transfer of the returnees to their abodes inside Eritrea.

To avoid any frustrations that could lead to serious setbacks, the returnees should continue to be provided with detailed information on what to expect once they cross the border. They should be provided with services as close as possible to those which they enjoyed during their asylum. It is expected that the politically enlightened refugees would understand that under such circumstances, a lower standard of basic services is rather inevitable. For the rank and file refugees, the provision of services in their new home prior to their transfer is necessary.

It is conceivable that in view of the facilities that were available, repatriation had to be limited to a small number. The question posed by Elias is most valid: What should be lone to persuade the international community to respond effectively to these new situations? The international system of the UN, entrenched in its rigidity, has not developed itself to meet the new challenges. For this reason, matters of war and peace in many parts of the world remain unsettled.

In its endeavour to resolve the deadlock, the Eritrean leadership may decide to:

1. achieve national unity amongst all liberation fronts in accordance with a political programme accepted by all parties. The importance of this achievement is that all refugees will decide to be repatriated once their leaders agree on the programme;
2. make a commitment to democracy and power sharing;
3. distribute the programme for repatriation, resettlement and rehabilitation widely to donors;
4. address potential donors directly (given the limitations of the UNHCR's mandate) to finance and to join through their national NGOs in implementing the programmes in conjunction with the indigenous refugee institutions; and
5. assert the voluntary nature of repatriation.

4

Demobilization and Employment of Combatants: Two Perspectives

I MELAKOU TEGEGN

Once peace is achieved, a pertinent question in the process of reconstruction is the demobilization of armed fronts and state armies that have been involved in the Ethiopian or Eritrean conflicts. The demobilization of combatants from the Ethiopia–Eritrea conflict first depends on the modalities under which the Eritrean conflict is finally resolved. If, as seems likely, Eritrea becomes independent after the military victory by the Eritrean People's Liberation Front (EPLF), then the guerrilla army will become a national army. One problem, however, is what will become of the armies and members of the other fronts. Political democracy becomes the basis for the solution of such a problem. The EPLF should then enter into an agreement with the other fronts as to how to form an Eritrean national army. The agreement must be basically political for the problem is not military. If democracy in general and universal suffrage and a multiparty system in particular is agreed upon, the danger of a civil war can be averted by agreeing on the formation of a national army.

If the Eritrean conflict were to finally be resolved by the proposed referendum opting for some kind of extended regional autonomy through a federal or confederal relationship with Ethiopia, the nature of the disposition of the various Eritrean armies will then be subject to a different kind of agreement. In such a situation, converting the combatants of various organizations to an Eritrean regional army under the direct command of the local Eritrean government will be one solution.

The actual demobilization of the combatants themselves, on an individual basis, poses particular problems in a country ravaged by a protracted war. The processes of demobilization and the prospects for employment are tied up with what the combatants themselves want to do, and what they want to do depends on their previous position in the society. This leads us to glance at the class composition of the various guerrilla armies.

Almost all the combatants in the guerrilla organizations have peasant origins. The picture within the EPLF is slightly different where the leadership above the platoon level is mostly composed of ex-high school students and the various departments are run by ex-college students or even graduates. In the Tigrayan People's Liberation Front (TPLF) the top leadership is composed of ex-university students, and the political, medical and financial departments are composed of either ex-university or ex-high school students. The Ethiopian People's Revolutionary Party (EPRP) which, during its heyday, had from six to ten university graduates in a single platoon, now has the same composition as the TPLF, although the EPRP leadership is predominantly made up of college graduates.

Given their peasant background, the collective life they have led in the guerrilla army, and the deep mutual attachment and camaraderie that they have developed, ex-combatants may still opt to stay in the army. Some may prefer to return to their previous occupations while others may prefer to start a new life. Briefly probing into these possibilities reveals the practical problems the demobilization process may entail.

1. The army option

The option to stay in the army goes hand in hand with the nature of the resolution of the conflict and the political settlement reached. If regional autonomy is agreed upon for various regions, and if the various guerrilla organizations become regional sections of one national army (as was set out in the Addis Ababa agreement that ended the civil war in the Sudan), the possibility of keeping the combatants in the army will be high and may also be significant if there is a separate national army for Eritrea. Under such circumstances, many combatants may opt to stay in the army if only to avoid unemployment. But either way, keeping a large standing army costs money. One further issue is whether this option will be available to women fighters: in Namibia and Zimbabwe they were excluded from the professional army after fighting as guerrillas.

2. The farming option

As most combatants are of peasant origin, some of them may opt to return to farming. Under such circumstances, they will need assistance to re-start this way of life. With the knowledge, experience and culture they acquired in the army, they will definitely want changes in the ways of rural life. Modern education, health care and the introduction of technical know-how will be immediately required. In such a case, material as well as advisory assistance is needed. In Zimbabwe ex-combatants organized in co-operatives to help settle themselves, but material assistance is still crucial and its provision may require foreign assistance: Zimbabwe was fortunate enough to have resources to pay all ex-fighters for two years.

3. Options for youth

Others, particularly the young combatants, may seek a new way of life. Children as young as ten have been active in the various guerrilla organizations. Although all peasant combatants acquire a great deal of knowledge and new experience while in the guerrilla army, children's perceptions are very different. For children it is not a mere acquisition of knowledge; they are brought up with the army. Most young fighters may thus opt to start a new life. They may want to go to school or undergo various training programmes. In such cases, they will be the most needy ones. Due to the large-scale social dislocation created as a result of the government's resettlement and villagization programmes, many young combatants may not find their parents even if they want to return to their villages. In their quest to start a new life, the urban areas will be their most likely residence. Problems of shelter and food will follow. A great deal of assistance is also required in this area.

4. The banditry option

A fourth and very real possibility for ex-combatants is banditry. Ethiopia (and Eritrea) has a history of all sorts of banditry, and those who fled south from Addis Ababa may resort to this unless there is a credible offer of amnesty. All cases of banditry are not viewed as entirely negative. Rebelling against a given political order, ruler, policy or even a certain decree is quite common. In the tradition of the Ethiopian peasantry, dissent or opposition often finds expression through banditry. Furthermore, this form of expression is likely to follow any political settlement which is not acceptable to all fighters. A political and social mechanism must be worked out to prevent ex-combatants from following this route.

The demobilization process in the case of the guerrilla organizations in Ethiopia proper involves similar problems to those discussed in relation to Eritrea. Political democracy is also the basis to work from. But Ethiopian democracy will have one unique advantage; it should deter other secessionist trends. The introduction of political democracy and the emergence of civil society will deter the nationalist undercurrent which is caused by feudal autocracy and military dictatorship.

Within the demobilization process the involvement of the Ethiopian diaspora is crucial to the country's reconstruction. A large section of the country's intelligentsia is abroad in forced or self-imposed exile, and the consequences of this 'brain drain' are obvious. The rebuilding of the country cannot do without the participation of the intelligentsia abroad. For two decades now the flow of Ethiopian intellectuals abroad has continued unabated. In the demobilization process, therefore, a climate of political democracy is an essential precondition if the participation of the country's intelligentsia in the reconstruction process is desired. The same holds true for gender equality and the participation of women in this process. A possible conflict between generations is another problem which faces post-independence Eritrea and post-liberation Ethiopia. The young generation which was born and brought up in the West will have difficulties coping with Ethiopian society which is patriarchal, hierarchical, paternalistic and avowedly religious. Here, again, political democracy serves as the basis on which the possible generation difference can be bridged.

Peace by itself will not automatically solve all the problems and heal all the wounds. According to one Amharic saying, the offender may forget but not the offended. Mistrust, prejudices and certain problems that are reflections of these phenomena may linger on. They can only be dissolved over time and, above all, by maintaining the democratic process and the political agreements reached. The case of the settlement of the southern Sudan conflict can be a good example in this case. The present civil war there basically emanated from the violation of the Addis Ababa agreement which had ended the civil war in southern Sudan in 1972.

Particular attention and effort should also be directed to enabling women ex-combatants to participate fully and equally in social, economic and political life. Special training and economic opportunities must be provided. The problem of women ex-combatants re-integrating into society, where they may not find opportunities to realize the 'equality' they experienced in the guerrilla army, must be recognized. Special efforts must be made to enable women to retain legal and political gains they have made, to remain independent and equal, and to retain positions of leadership.

Furthermore, special attention and facilities must be given to the rehabilitation and full re-integration into socio-economic life of disabled combatants. The uninterrupted war that was fought for the last 30 years gave rise to a huge population of disabled combatants in Ethiopia and Eritrea. One major task in the process of reconstruction is the rehabilitation of these combatants.

II   HIZKIAS ASSEFA

The theme of this conference challenges us to consider how we could possibly influence the peaceful resolution of the current conflicts in the Horn by focusing on what might happen beyond the conflict. If we view our task that way, then the discussion ceases to be hypothetical or merely an intellectual exercise. Indeed, there is a school of thought in conflict resolution theory which postulates that a creative look at 'beyond the conflict' can be a useful tool for peacefully resolving conflicts between adversaries.

One factor which can hinder peace agreements is the way in which combatants view their absorption into society at the end of a conflict. If termination of a conflict is to mean combatants will face severe unemployment, or grave difficulties in resuming normal life after a peace agreement, the enthusiasm among combatants for pursuing peace could be greatly reduced. Alternatively, if it can be shown that aside from addressing the grievances that started the conflict, there could also be demonstrable benefits, peace becomes a more attractive option.

The current situation in the Horn does not seem to offer a very promising future for combatants, even if peace were to prevail tomorrow. Creating the number of jobs that would be needed in the region to absorb them would itself be an enormous task. Employing and rehabilitating war veterans into normal social life was a major problem for an economically advanced country like the United States after the Vietnam war. Invariably, for many combatants in the Horn, the end of the conflicts might mean having to start from scratch. The challenge of looking 'beyond the conflict' is to establish how it might be possible to reduce the pain of demobilization, repatriation, and rehabilitation processes.

Another possible method could be to undertake the resettlement and rehabilitation processes in a way that cuts across past conflict lines. During the resettlement process, a safe and supportive environment could be created in which people from formerly conflicting sides could interact and collaborate with each other, so past stereotypes and negative attitudes could perhaps be broken down and a new atmosphere of tolerance and co-operation between former enemies fostered.

In relation to the Nairobi Peace Initiative, we have had a lot of discussions with various agencies on the subject of how development projects could be used to enhance peace. One approach could be to design programmes or projects in such a way that former perceived or real adversaries work together. An interesting example of this approach comes from a small sewing co-operative project in northern Sudan. At first this project involved women who had come from the south and who were non-Muslim. As their work and needs expanded, they included northern Muslim women who would sew shirts which were then decorated by southern embroiderers. As these women worked side by side, their work relationship expanded to include other positive social relationships such as coffee groups, and they took part in small mutual aid activities. When the factory became more productive and began to generate a good income for the employees, the funders called all the employees together and told them that from then on the employees were to run the co-operative, and that the success or failure of the enterprise depended on them. The women got together, discussed the future of the enterprise and, with the help of the funders, wrote the by-laws of the co-operative. They demonstrated their determination to continue their co-operation in order to make the enterprise successful, but also identified some of the issues that could subvert their co-operation. Since religion was one of them, they wrote in their by-laws that religion would not be discussed in their gatherings. Such rules isolated the issues that divided them, and enabled them to build on their common interests and needs. This is a simple example but its implications are interesting. The demobilization and resettlement of combatants, refugees, and exiles could be handled in such an imaginative way and could be an instrument for either creating an incentive for peace or for reinforcing peace.

Realistically it must be doubted how one major source of employment, absorption into the national and regional armies, could create enough employment. Although this may appear to be one solution, its full implications for peace, democracy, and economic prosperity for the area have not been fully explored: what would the absorption of all these combatants do to the size and the strength of the military forces in these areas? Can these societies afford to support such huge armies, especially if the major preoccupation of the societies after the war becomes economic rehabilitation and reconstruction? What would the effect of such militarization be on civil society? If there are so many battle-hardened veterans in the various armies, how could fledgling democracies flourish under the shadow of such forces? How easy would it be to settle social disputes peacefully and democratically and not by resorting to violence if one has so many people in arms?

Return to Normalcy

<table>
<tr><td rowspan="2" style="font-size:3em">5</td><td>Relief, Rehabilitation and Reconstruction in the SPLM/SPLA Administered Areas During the Transitional Phase and Beyond
JOHN LUK</td></tr>
</table>

The Sudan People's Liberation Movement and Sudan People's Liberation Army are responsible for the welfare of approximately five million people in the areas under its administration. This responsibility requires immediate attention while the struggle for the realization of a more peaceful Sudan continues. The immediate needs of the civilian population in the liberated areas are, therefore, a primary preoccupation of the SPLA/SPLM.

The main objective of the civil war as far as the SPLM/SPLA is concerned is the creation of a new Sudan of peace, prosperity and happiness for the Sudanese people. This requires a clear plan for the future development of the country which will use its abundant natural and human resources to alleviate the present abject state of poverty and underdevelopment.

The issues which this paper addresses can be broadly divided into: (1) food needs of people in SPLA areas arising from the present famine situation, and possible measures to boost food production in the liberated areas; and (2) the rehabilitation of social services and basic infrastructures. The paper finishes with the SPLM/SPLA's proposals for long term local development.

SPLM/SPLA administration:
The effect of war on people and services

The SPLM/SPLA now controls the whole of southern Sudan except for a few towns. It is entrenched in southern Blue Nile and Southern Kordofan, and the south's international borders with Ethiopia, Kenya, Zaire, Uganda and the Central African Republic are under SPLM/SPLA control.

Of the approximately eight million southerners, about 1.6 million have migrated to northern Sudan in search of food. The majority have situated themselves in and around Khartoum, Southern Kordofan, Darfur and the central region. Nearly half a million have sought refuge in the neighbouring states of Ethiopia, Kenya, Zaire and the Central African Republic, while the same number are entrapped in government held towns in the south.

Since the outbreak of war in May 1983, southern Sudan and the adjacent northern areas of Southern Kordofan, Southern Darfur and southern Blue Nile (Angessana area) have suffered massive destruction in terms of human lives, properties and basic socio-economic development infrastructures. The south experienced the highest level and most tragic of this destruction. So far nearly half a million people have perished from war, famine and other preventable causes. About five million cattle, two million sheep and 1.5 million goats have died due to the war, disease and floods, thereby depriving a large

42

proportion of pastoralists of an important source of livelihood. These numbers continue to grow due to lack of vaccines against common animal diseases.

Basic infrastructures and public utilities in the SPLM/SPLA administered areas have also suffered considerable damage. Towns have been levelled to the ground, roofs of buildings removed and used in the construction of shelters by government forces, most bridges have been blown up, and several roads and tracks could not be maintained and are consequently overgrown with trees and bushes to the point of being unsuitable for motor transport. Education and health services have also been seriously disrupted by the civil war. Most schools, hospitals and other public and private buildings in SPLM/SPLA controlled towns have suffered physical damage from mortar and aerial bombardments. In most places the roofs, windows and doors have been removed leaving nothing but roofless walls.

Drought and food needs

Of the eight million people at risk from starvation in the Sudan, 1.5 to 2 million are in SPLM/SPLA administered areas. The present famine resulted from the failure of the rains in most parts of the country. In some places rain came too late to save the stunted crops, or it resulted in floods. The situation in the south has been aggravated by the civil war which has resulted in a massive displacement of the civilian population. Consistent bombing of villages by the government air force also has prevented farmers from regularly working on their farms as villages were abandoned to avoid bombs.

A large number of people are currently moving to the south from Khartoum, Southern Kordofan and other adjacent areas. These returnees or displaced persons are coming to northern Bahr el Ghazal and Upper Nile where food shortages are even greater. Within the south itself the population is on the move. People are moving into neighbouring Ethiopia from as far as Bahr el Ghazal and from all areas of Upper Nile. In Bahr el Ghazal, over 150,000 displaced persons recently returned from Khartoum on the government's assurances that food would be made available to them as soon they arrived. However, the same government failed to respect the assurances it had given and refused to allow relief trains of the United Nations Operation Lifeline Sudan to move food to Bahr el Ghazal. These displaced people are now moving to SPLA held towns such as Yirol, Kapoeta and Bor. Some will even try to make the two month journey to Ethiopia.

As can be seen from these examples, the general food situation in the Sudan is tragic. The whole country is on the brink of a disaster much worse than the famine of 1984–5. Forced by the grave concern expressed by the international community about the looming human disaster, the regime of General al Beshir only recently acknowledged the existence of a critical food gap of 1.2 million tons. It has, however, not changed its obstructionist policies toward international efforts to deliver food to the needy civilian population in SPLA administered areas. Western and eastern Sudan face the same fate as the south.

The Khartoum regime has hampered food deliveries by the International Commission of the Red Cross (ICRC) and the United Nations sponsored Operation Lifeline Sudan (UNOLS) as of November 1990. Trains and steamers scheduled to move food to the south under the direction of UNOLS have remained loaded and docked for the last one and a half years. The journey has been prohibited by the government even though the SPLA has given its assurances that it will not interfere with relief operations. Needless to say, the government's attitude has angered and frustrated the international donor community which is making efforts to provide assistance.

Given the intransigence and indifferent attitude of the Sudanese government towards the welfare of the southern Sudanese in SPLA administered areas, and the Sudanese people in general, the SPLA has called upon the international donor community to intervene promptly by giving support to organizations that are ready and willing to deliver humanitarian assistance to the people in SPLA areas. (For possible delivery routes suggested by the SRRA, see Appendix 1.) Only in this way can we avoid a recurrence of the 1988 tragedy in which more than 250,000 southerners died from starvation, unnoticed by the world.

The production of food security

The effects of the civil war, as indicated in the preceding sections, are tragic and far reaching for both the inhabitants of the war zone and the basic economic infrastructures. Both the production and service sectors of southern Sudan's economy have suffered greatly from the nearly eight years of civil strife. Agriculture and animal husbandry, the backbone of the economy of the south, have been severely undermined by the war and the unfavourable environmental conditions. Other important economic activities such as fishing, blacksmithery, carpentry and so forth have also not fared well due to the instability of the population and the lack of raw materials and equipment which previously could be procured from bush shops that have since disappeared.

However, since 1989, when the whole area east of the Nile – from Nimule on the Ugandan border to the mouth of the Sobat just a few miles south of Malakal (an area larger than Ghana) – fell to the effective control of the SPLA, the civilian population in this area began to enjoy a reasonable degree of peace and security. The SPLA is, however, more than aware that real security for the people under its administration can only be guaranteed if there is enough food for everyone to eat, that is, if there is food security. Accordingly, one of the top priority tasks of the SPLM/SPLA during this transitional period is to raise the people's productive capacities in the field of food production in order to minimize dependence on food assistance from abroad.

In this regard the SPLM/SPLA is now focusing its attention on the following:

1. the need to provide farmers in the SPLA administered areas with adequate agricultural hand tools such as hoes, axes, mallodas, pangas and sickles so that they may be self-reliant in food production;
2. the need to provide more seeds of various types to farming households in SPLA areas, particularly maize, sorghum, cowpeas, groundnuts and so forth. Over the last two years farmers in rural southern Sudan have made maximum use of seeds and hand tools which have been provided by international relief agencies. Table 1 shows the impact of the seeds and agricultural hand tools programmes on food production in some selected areas of the SPLA administered region in 1990. It should be noted that the areas of Ayod, Nasir, Kapoeta and Chukudum were severely affected by drought and that the quantities of seeds and tools supplied were not sufficient for the farming families in the programme areas.

Table 1   Impact of Seeds and Tools Programmes on Food Production in Selected Areas

Areas	Seed rate/ feddan	Yield kg/ feddan	Seed input MT	Prod- uction MTS	Seed cost US$	Equivalent food cost US$	Percentage of total food production
Torit	15kg	450	820	24,600	1,066,000	12,300,000	34%
Bor	16kg	450	184	5,520	239,000	2,760,000	23%
Kajo Keji	12kg	900	207	15,911	269,100	7,955,500	14%
Ayod+	12kg	180	14	252	18,200	126,000	2%
Nasir+	11kg	90	70	594	91,000	297,000	4%
Kapoeta+	9kg	180	45	942	58,500	471,000	8%
Chukudum+	13kg	180	60	850	78,000	1,105,000	10%
Pibor	10kg	180	14	252	18,200	126,000	26%
Total	20	300	1,414	48,921	1,837,900	25,140,500	14%
(Ratio)						1 : 14	

3. The SPLM/SPLA is also focusing on enabling the Sudan Relief and Rehabilitation Association (SRRA) agricultural officers to help farmers with essential extension services by providing more training for SRRA officers;
4. preparing for the opportunities for large-scale mechanized agricultural production which will open up as security and stability become more consolidated in SPLA held areas. Procurement of development aid directly through NGOs will be of paramount importance in this next phase; and
5. supplying the fishing communities in SPLA administered areas with fishing equipment. The rivers, streams and swamps of southern Sudan are an invaluable source of fish. Before the civil war surplus dry fish used to be exported to Zaire. If supplied with sufficient fishing equipment such as hooks, lines, nets and so forth, fishing communities in the SPLA administered areas could easily meet an essential part of their food needs with fish and thus reduce their dependence on food aid from abroad.

In the long run the question of food security will have to be tackled in a more comprehensive way. Investment in agriculture will have to be given top priority. Development policies will have to be geared toward the promotion of agricultural production and recovery, with emphasis on the improvement of food production techniques and giving assistance to the Sudanese people in rural Sudan. It will be important to build a strong agro-industrial base and a diversified economy. The major pre-condition, of course, for the success of any policies in the Sudan, however sound they may be, is the existence of political stability and a genuinely pluralist political system in which all Sudanese both have a stake and feel obliged to preserve and defend.

Rehabilitation of social services and infrastructures

Rehabilitation work in SPLA administered areas is assigned to the Sudan Relief and Rehabilitation Association (SRRA) which has its headquarters in Kapoeta, in the southern Sudan, and branches in Kenya, Ethiopia, Europe and North America. Since the beginning of 1989 the SRRA, with the help of relief agencies, has made concerted efforts to rehabilitate essential social services which suffered heavy damage due to the civil war. The priority areas for rehabilitation and reconstruction in which the SPLM/SPLA and SRRA are engaged are education, health services, roads and transport, clean water and sanitation, and the vaccination of livestock.

Education

Education in the south came to a standstill shortly after the outbreak of the war due to the lack of security. Southern children have spent the last seven years without schooling. The three main southern towns of Juba, Malakal and Wau kept a limited number of schools open with a very insignificant number of pupils attending. Government figures indicate that out of the 1,417 schools existing in the south before the war, 1,171 of them had closed down (figures from the National Dialogue Conference on Peace held in Khartoum in 1989). From 1983 onwards the SPLA's military campaign against government forces in the different areas of the south was its primary preoccupation. Other matters, including education, became secondary. Some limited opportunities were available to southern children who moved north in 1984 and afterwards, but the conditions were harsh as a result of the poor living conditions of displaced people in Khartoum and other towns of the north.

The situation changed dramatically in 1989 with the SPLA's successive military victories which resulted in their effective control of a vast territory as described in the preceding section. With the recent SPLA capture of Western Equatoria, the government's presence in the south is now limited to the three main towns of Juba, Malakal, and Wau, plus half a dozen beleaguered garrisons. The greatest challenge now for the SPLA, as the effective authority in most of the south, is the reorganization of local administration in these areas and the rehabilitation and provision of such essential social services as education and medical care.

Before the hundreds of thousands of school-aged children can start attending classes, basic school materials, trained teachers and, of course, reconstructed or new school buildings have to be provided. So far the SPLM/SPLA has opened 300 primary schools in the liberated areas with the help of several voluntary relief agencies which provided limited school materials. However, the demand for education remains high. The question is how to provide the resources required to meet this overwhelming need.

Health services

The importance of health care for a displaced, malnourished and exhausted population like the one in the SPLA administered areas is second only to the importance of food. For seven years people in the rural south were left without medical care as the existing hospitals in the region closed down because of insecurity. With the restoration of security and stability in most parts of the SPLA administered areas (except for occasional bombings by the government air force), the SPLA is now striving to rehabilitate the region's health services.

In addition to suffering physical damage, hospitals in SPLM/SPLA administered towns lack all that hospitals should normally have in terms of medicines, equipment and qualified personnel. There are currently nine hospitals in the SPLM/SPLA administered areas catering for a population of nearly five million. Each hospital has only one doctor and very few qualified paramedical staff. Some of these hospitals even lack essential drugs for the treatment of diseases such as kala-azar, bilharzia, tuberculosis and malaria which are endemic in most of the liberated areas. Some voluntary organizations have donated medicines and equipment to some of these hospitals. The majority of these hospitals are, however, in a bad state of repair and need to be maintained and replenished with supplies, equipment, trained personnel and repaired structures.

Further facilities and programmes required to restore the provision of health services to a normal level include the implementation of child immunization programmes, the provision of mobile dispensaries which can take health care to the majority of the rural population, and the establishment of an orthopaedic workshop which can provide artificial limbs for those who lost limbs as a result of the war.

Roads and transport

Most roads in the south became impassable either because land mines made them too dangerous for any traffic or because essential bridges linking them were destroyed by either of the parties to the conflict. However, since the appearance of international relief agencies in the south in 1986, maintenance work has been carried out on some major roads by the SPLA to facilitate the movement of food convoys into famine stricken areas. The SPLA administered areas enjoy road links with Uganda, Kenya, Ethiopia and Zaire. Within the areas there are also feeder roads for internal distribution.

The majority of these feeder roads can only be used by motor vehicles during the dry season (December to May). Since the success of relief work will depend on the state of the roads in the region, assistance is required to strengthen the SRRA's road maintenance capacity and to establish a transport system in the form of vehicles for internal distribution. A mechanical workshop for the maintenance of vehicles and provision of spare parts and lubricants will be an essential component of this system.

Clean water and sanitation

Access to clean drinking water is a major problem facing the population in SPLA administered areas. The SRRA, with the help of the Medic Water Programme, has managed to dig a number of boreholes and install hand pumps to provide clean drinking water in some areas. The need, however, is so overwhelming that more resources are needed to enable the SRRA to provide a clean water supply to areas that are accessible to it. Some areas of Eastern Equatoria and Jonglei have desperate water needs.

Vaccination of livestock

Animal husbandry is an important economic activity for a large proportion of the southern population. The number of cattle, sheep and goats in the south has in recent years constantly declined as a result of diseases, natural disasters and war. The remaining animal wealth needs to be protected from such endemic diseases as rinderpest, foot and mouth disease, contagious bovine pleuro pneumonia and so forth. So far limited vaccination of cattle has been done by the SRRA in Kapoeta, Bor and Yirol. The demand for more vaccines is on the rise as more areas become accessible to the SRRA and relief agencies.

Economic enterprises for local development

With the aim of providing essential goods and services to the population under SPLM/SPLA administration, in accordance with its humanitarian mandate, the SRRA plans to introduce 12 types of enterprises in the liberated areas. These economic enterprises, although tied to the educational needs of the population, are designed and intended to cater for the long-term needs of the whole population in these areas. The enterprises are tailoring, leather training and shoemaking, soap production, carpentry and woodwork, agricultural farming, poultry farming, ginning and textile, dairy and beef production, school materials production, flour milling, fish production, oil seed pressing.

There are four economic projects already existing in the SPLA administered areas which need rehabilitation. These are the Katire saw mill, the Talanga tea factory, the Anzara textile mill and the Yirol oil mill. These projects were under the regional government of the south before its demise in 1983. They were then taken over by the regional government of Equatoria, and are now under the control of the SPLA. The raw materials for these projects can be obtained locally, however the technical expertise, fuel and spare parts needed for their rehabilitation may not be locally available.

Conclusion

In the absence of peace, the SPLM/SPLA will continue its efforts to normalize life in the areas under its administration and to seek the international donor community's support for these efforts in the form of humanitarian assistance. The primary task of the SPLA at present is to make it possible for the civilian population under its administration to lead a tolerable life even before an overall solution to the conflict is found.

In a post-war period in which, hopefully, all the root causes of the Sudan's chronic political instability will have been totally removed, some of the immediate concerns will be the following:

1. meeting the basic needs of the people to improve their living standards through reviving the economy and strengthening their productive capacity;
2. voluntary repatriation and resettlement of refugees and internally displaced persons;
3. rehabilitation of basic socio-economic infrastructures, with top priority given to areas devastated by war;
4. food security;
5. eradication of epidemic diseases;
6. normalization of relations with neighbours and promotion of regional co-operation, especially in the areas of trade and management of common resources;
7. development of natural resources, particularly oil and other important minerals whose exploitation was impeded by the civil war;
8. reorganization of the civil service and training of personnel; and
9. construction of roads and improvement of river transport.

Finally, the Sudan will need a leadership which has a vision and commitment to the country's development and the people's welfare. The current call by the SPLM/SPLA for a new Sudan in which all the various Sudanese nationalities can interact and integrate with the spirit of give and take deserves to be taken seriously. The Sudanese must rid themselves of sectarianism and other divisive factors if the dream of a united, peaceful, prosperous and stable Sudan is to be realized.

Appendix 1   Routes Through Which Food Can be Delivered to Southern Sudan

The SRRA in its food appeal for 1991 indicated six possible routes through which food could be delivered to southern Sudan.

1. The first route is from Loki in Kenya, through Kapoeta, Torit, Bor to Ayod, Waat and Akobo. Alternatively, one can pass through Kapoeta to Boma, Pachalla and Pibor. It is to be noted that the Kapoeta–Boma–Pachalla road becomes difficult with the first rains.
2. The second route is from Uganda, through Nimule, Torit, Bor, to Ayod, Waat and Akobo, and from Bor to Pachalla. It is to be pointed out that food intended for the lake provinces, Akon, Mayen Abun and Leer areas, has to be delivered to Bor and then be moved by barges to Shambe and Adok.
3. The third route is from Uganda, through Kaya to the interior.
4. The fourth is from Uganda to Kajokaji and beyond.
5. The fifth is likely to be from Zaire to Yambio, Tambura and Maridi.
6. The sixth route is from Ethiopia (Gambella) by both land and river through Itang and Jokou to Nasir, Ulang and Abuong. The land route is inaccessible during the rainy season. The river route is possible, however. The final routes are by train from Muglad to Aweil and Borges and from Kosti to Malakal.

6

Famine, Conflict and the Internationalization of Public Welfare

MARK DUFFIELD

In approaching the question of recovery and reconstruction in the Horn of Africa, and the role that non-governmental organizations (NGOs) have in this process, one is presented with a situation which has been defined by two interconnected developments. Firstly, there is a growing understanding that 'African famine' is a complex and deep-seated problem. Secondly, in response to this situation a world historic internationalization of public welfare has occurred. During the 1990s policy debate will centre on the adequacy or appropriateness of the latter in relation to the former. This paper is an attempt to sketch the relation that exists between the two and to argue that the system of public welfare that has emerged is in need of urgent reform. The paper divides into four main sections. The first examines the social background; the second analyses the nature of internal conflict; the third describes the growth of food insecurity; and the fourth discusses the contradictions and limitations of the donor/NGO safety net.

The social and economic background

The specificity of African famine

It is increasingly recognized that contemporary famine in the Horn, as well as in other parts of Africa, is a symptom of wider and long-term economic and political difficulties (Duffield, 1990). In particular, enviro-economic and conflict factors have increasingly combined to produce the appearance of countries plagued by economic decline, political fragmentation and growing food insecurity. Until recently, the contribution of conflict to this scenario has either been ignored or its effects minimized (Green, 1987). Given its concern with public welfare, this paper seeks to redress this imbalance. In order to develop a better understanding of what could be called the specificity of African famine, a useful starting point is a consideration of de Waal's (1990) recent work.

Briefly, de Waal has argued that African definitions of famine allow for a far wider range of meanings than the term usually denotes in English usage. These meanings can range from poverty, to dearth, to increased mortality and frank starvation. African peoples normally deal with famine with coping strategies which include such practices as labour migration or the collection of wild foodstuffs, and the management of assets such as livestock or craft skills. Coping strategies are the single most important means by which African peoples deal with famine and in recent famines, for example in northern Sudan in the mid 1980s, they were much more effective than food aid in keeping people alive. Because coping strategies involve a variety of decisions, including the decision to go hungry in order to preserve assets, the epidemiology of enviro-economic famines is complex; they usually take the form of disease crises rather than of starvation. In Africa, however, there is a close connection between famine and conflict. Violence disrupts people's coping strategies or prevents them from operating at all. In these circumstances, especially when such actions are deliberate, frank starvation is often the result.

This paper seeks to add to de Waal's model of African famine by arguing that the importance of coping strategies is underscored by the growing instability of semi-subsistence as a way of life. Furthermore, by analysing the logic of internal conflict in Africa, which makes semi-subsistence and coping systems necessary targets, it attempts to make an organic connection between instability, conflict and food insecurity. This complex set of relations and outcomes provides the context in which the internationalization of public welfare has occurred.

The intensification of production

Although there has been a widespread decline in economic performance in Africa since the 1970s, this should not hide the crucially important fact that, in attempting to achieve growth, there have been significant attempts to intensify the production of primary products, including food. Although these efforts have fallen short of their goal, from the point of view of this paper their importance lies in their connection with the environment, vulnerability and conflict.

In market economies intensification has usually taken the form of an increased capitalization of agriculture. In the Sudan, for example, there has been a large-scale mechanization of agricultural production. Such developments usually involve various forms of state subsidies. In planned economies, such as in Ethiopia, there has been less emphasis on technical developments and more placed on the provision of basic tools and seeds. There have been major attempts to socially reorganize the society through resettlement, the formation of communal villages and the promotion of village based co-operatives.

Few systematic studies of the social effect of these 'core' developments upon the groups living at the 'periphery' of the countries concerned have been attempted (see Iliffe, 1987). From the fragmented evidence an argument can be made that core developments have indeed had a considerable impact. The specificity of the African situation is that these developments have occurred in areas characterized by groups living by various, and often complex, forms of semi-subsistence. Moreover, they have often been directed by politicians or planners who were unaware or uninterested in this condition. In some countries, such as in Chad and the Sudan, inherited regional differences have been accentuated and new ones have been established. The result has been the widespread marginalization of peripheral groups and the transformation of social and family relations.

Patterns of social transformation

The transformation of subsistence economies is a complex issue. The diversity of such economies, together with differences in local conditions, means that no single model of the process can be given. It is clear, however, that change has indeed taken place. The high rate of urbanization is indicative. Albeit starting from a low level, Africa currently has the fastest rate of urbanization in the world. Its 35 major cities are growing at an annual rate of 8.5 per cent which means they are roughly doubling in size every nine years. According to current trends, by 2020 more than half of Africa's entire population will be living in towns (Harris, 1989). The pattern is for subsistence economies to weaken and collapse under the combined effects of market forces, political intervention, environmental change and the direct and brutal consequences of conflict. Here only a few pointers can be given.

The recent intensification of primary production in Africa's market economies witnessed the decline of transnational labour migration. The expansion of labour opportunities in West Africa, for example, has reduced the need for migration to the Sudan. Within the Sudan, labour for its mechanized schemes now comes from internal sources, with southern Sudan playing an increasingly important supply role. In short, the period has been synonymous with the development of national labour markets. This is a most significant event and suggests that patterns of semi-subsistence, that is, partial reliance on wage labour or relations of market exchange, rather than being limited to specific groups or distinct seasons of the year, have become generalized and an essential addition to family or group directed activities of subsistence.

Evidence from the period of growth during the 1960s suggests that semi-subsistence economies existing within market societies were not necessarily unstable. Under the present conditions, however, the mix is not conducive to stability. Impoverished agriculturalists, for example, have to compete with commercial farmers while at the same time making do with reduced family labour due to migration. They have responded by intensifying their methods of production. Time and labour saving techniques, such as reducing inter-cropping, crop rotation, strict sowing and weeding regimes, extensive terracing, and so on, have become prevalent across the Sahel (see de Waal, 1987). In many respects this intensification has taken place at the expense of traditional methods of resisting drought, thus adding to the erratic nature of food production. A form of intensification has also occurred amongst pastoralists. The reduction of available rangelands and accessible water due to the expansion of mechanized agriculture has stimulated a change in herd composition and herding techniques. One trend has been for large stock (camels, cattle) to be replaced by small stock (goats) which require less in terms of rangelands, browse requirements and supervisory labour (see Abu Sin, 1982).

Changes such as these at the economic level not only underscore the poor performance of domestic food production in the face of continued population growth, but also engender a change of family and gender relations. Labour migration and the penetration of market forces has had the effect of transforming relations between generations in favour of the youth. In many groups, political power has shifted away from traditional lines of authority. At the same time, given that farming is work done by women in many regions of the Horn, the development of national labour markets, together with the growing necessity of labour migration (usually a male activity), has frequently increased the burden of agricultural and domestic work that women bear and, as group support tends to weaken, to leave them more exposed to external uncertainties.

The tensions and contradictions intrinsic to the process of social change at a local level constitute an unstable complex of relations. This complex is an essential ingredient in the dynamic of internal conflict in Africa. Its configuration suggests that, over the long term and under the present conditions, it is questionable whether semi-subsistence is a viable socio-economic system. The trend toward urbanization would tend to support this supposition. In recent years drought and conflict have fuelled its rapid growth. However, insofar as increasing food insecurity is connected to the decline of local subsistence economies, and that this decline, moreover, is related to conflict, then drought and conflict themselves further compound the instability of semi-subsistence.

Effects on the environment

The local level changes sketched above have major environmental implications. Some of the identified causes of environmental degradation are already familiar: the overgrazing of restricted rangelands, deforestation due to population growth, the geographical confinement of rural settlements, unplanned urbanization, and so forth. Of crucial importance, however, is that the intensification of peripheral agriculture and pastoralism denotes an important shift in the relationship between the environment and subsistence and semi-subsistence modes of existence. The former mode was dependent upon the finite and renewable properties of nature and was careful to manage these properties. Indeed, cultural life revolved around this necessity. Semi-subsistence, however, as a result of having to adjust to market forces, has adopted an attitude toward the environment similar to that found in core commercial activities; nature has become an infinite resource that can be exploited at will for short-term gain. This shift in attitude is another factor that marks the instability of semi-subsistence under the current conditions.

The intensification of core and peripheral production methods since the 1970s has not only seen declines in yield per hectare as a result of the short-term practices involved, but has also contributed to accelerating the shrinking of Africa's resource base. The pasture, soil, livestock, water and forest which are being consumed under prevailing conditions of high population growth, coupled with ineffective and short-term resource management, is essentially non-renewable. In the absence of other value-creating activities, such as widespread industrialization, this creates a situation prone to local, national and regional competition and conflict.

Coping with change

The question of how peripheral groups cope during times of hardship, especially during enviro-economic stress, has attracted increasing attention over the past two or three years (de Waal, 1987, 1990; Swift, 1989). The body of work which deals with this question is important since, not only does the operation of coping strategies partly define the specificity of African famine, but it also provides a valuable comment on the nature of semi-subsistence.

Coping strategies are more complex than relations of market exchange. They denote a range of family or group directed activities which exploit a stock of assets, some of which are of a subsistence nature, at times when food is scarce or expensive. Swift (1989) has divided assets into investments (including education and productive instruments), stores (including food and valuables) and claims (including debt and patronage). Some strategies involve the sale of assets such as livestock or jewellery. Others exploit movement through labour migration to centres of employment, the temporary relocation of families to centres of food availability, the collection of wild foodstuffs, the collection of grass and wood for sale, and so forth. The prevalence and operation of coping strategies means that under enviro-economic famine conditions (that is, in the absence of conflict), the social trajectory that a famine can take would be unclear to outsiders without an appreciation of the coping decisions involved.

There are a couple of aspects of coping strategies which need to be emphasized to increase one's understanding of the impact of conflict. In the first place, coping strategies are not only normal, they are also the most effective response that African populations can adopt at times of scarcity or expense. It has been estimated (de Waal, 1987) that during the mid 1980s famine in western Sudan, farmers were able to grow only 35 per cent of their food requirements, while food aid provided only an additional 10 per cent. Apart from going hungry, the balance was met by the resourceful operation of coping strategies. In other words, coping strategies met around half the food requirement and, although the last 10 per cent was of vital importance for many people, the strategies were five times more effective than food aid in dealing with the effects of famine. There is no reason to believe that these orders of magnitude are not reflected in other enviro-economic famines.

The other important consideration is the crucial importance of market centres for the effective operation of coping strategies. Without local markets (a frequent target in conflict situations) most of the exchange-based strategies, such as the sale of assets, petty trade, and casual labour, cannot work. In addition, a lack of markets suggests an absence of transport, and this both reduces the effectiveness of labour migration and means that food available within the region cannot be traded. Little or no communication with other areas reduces the availability of information upon which coping decisions can be based. In the absence of markets, coping strategies could well be reduced to living off stored food and the collection of wild foodstuffs, providing of course these options exist. In other words, the effectiveness of coping strategies is greatly reduced.

Whilst the study of coping strategies is important, it should not obscure the fact the activities involved are either modifications or extensions of what are, essentially, the normal conditions of semi-subsistence. In other words, coping strategies, effective as they can be, are not immune from the instability that characterizes semi-subsistence. They are based upon assets and during times of famine assets are consumed. For example, with regard to the current famine in northern Sudan, there is a concern that peripheral rural groups have not recovered their losses in livestock, movable wealth, and so on, incurred during the last famine of the mid 1980s. In addition, due to intermittent drought, the availability of wild foodstuffs is also restricted. In other words, the trend is for assets to diminish. This process should be seen as part of the wider shrinking of Africa's resource base. Indeed, although there are no figures available, the loss of peripheral group assets as a result of enviro-economic and conflict factors must be the major, if not the largest, component of the current reduction of resources.

The nature of internal conflict

Understanding conflict

Under (pre-colonial) subsistence conditions, conflict between groups was common – it was an important means through which groups could adjust to underlying economic and environmental changes. It could play this role, however, only insofar as it was part of a balanced system of reciprocity (Alvarsson, 1989). Moreover, although resource questions may underlie conflict (see Ulrich, 1989), at a more immediate level violence was a means through which groups expressed their political identity and aspirations. It should be stressed that under subsistence conditions, there is no distinction between physical and political survival. The only way that individuals, families and groups could conceive of staying alive was through the survival of their way of life (Turton, 1989). This is an important connection to make since it helps explain some of the notable characteristics of internal warfare.

Colonial powers, with varying degrees of success, attempted to police local conflicts by way of their superiority and monopoly of arms. The decay of governance in many parts of Africa since the 1970s, together with the spread of modern automatic weapons amongst peripheral groups, are important ingredients in the process of transformation, as is the increasing instability of semi-subsistence. This instability is part and parcel of a general decline in reciprocity. Many peripheral groups, for example, have become increasingly dependent upon agriculture at a time when, due to adverse climatic and market conditions, it has become a marginal activity. Under such circumstances, exchange relations between groups, including agriculturalists and pastoralists, begin to break down (Almond, 1989). A shrinking resource base, reinforced by core economic and social programmes, further undermines reciprocity. Under conditions of stress, ethnic identities can tend to harden and, with the transformation of family relations, especially between generations, traditional lines of authority are also weakened. It is as if, under the present conditions, the threat to the way of life of peripheral groups has never been greater; yet, at the same time, both the external (governance) and internal (reciprocity) means of resolving the inevitable violence are at their lowest ebb.

Internal war

It is common in Africa to find that internal war uses local conflict as its vehicle. So far, the question of imbalance among groups and the decline of reciprocity has only been mentioned in relation to enviro-economic factors. By far the greatest source of imbalance, however, is the political integration of local conflicts into wider internal wars. One aspect of this type of imbalance concerns access to modern automatic weapons. Internal conflicts have led African governments to spend staggering amounts of precious hard currency on armaments. In the case of the Sudan, which is by no means atypical, 40 per cent of government expenditure is currently spent on arms. This order of expenditure in otherwise poor countries has meant that many governments and opposing groups have entered into concessionary relations with superpowers and neighbouring states in order to secure arms supplies. Local conflicts have become linked to internal wars which, in turn, are the chess pieces of international rivalries.

With the exception of Eritrea and Tigray, within the context of internal war it is not uncommon to find that combatants frequently view non-combatant populations in a mercenary light. They are seen as a means to subsistence and/or a source of conscripts which has to be controlled or, if they happen to be in areas contested by opposing combatants, they have to be prevented from providing opponents with similar services. Although some parties to conflict in Africa frequently use the rhetoric of national liberation, their practice on the ground often challenges the conventional wisdom that in order to operate, a guerilla movement needs the support of local people. An extreme case is represented by RENAMO in Mozambique where, it would appear, all that is offered to non-combatants under RENAMO control is a precarious possibility of remaining alive (Gursony, April 1988).

The prevalence of the more mercenary attitude must be linked with the connection between physical and political survival within a semi-subsistence ethos. If the survival of people as political beings depends upon the survival of their way of life, it then follows, quite logically but tragically, that if you wish to intimidate them politically, you must destroy or incapacitate their way of life. This logic is further reinforced if, due to declining resources, such dominance is necessary for the survival of the opposing ethnic group. The various and complex patterns of semi-subsistence and of coping strategies are both the front line targets and defensive strongholds of conflicting internal forces in Africa.

Since the emergence and development of politico-military groups and movements – and in some cases their amalgamation – is fought out on a terrain of semi-subsistence economies, one cannot underestimate or emphasize enough the enormous price in dislocation and human suffering that this implies. Groups and movements do not simply require conscripts to fight; they need porters to carry weapons, supplies and booty; sappers to clear mines; informants to disclose enemy positions; and, importantly, a ready access to food. How such goods and services are secured in the field is not something only quartermasters need worry about, but rather it is the central dynamic of internal warfare. The idea of food as a weapon in internal conflict has become popular in recent years. What is less frequently recognized, however, is that obtaining food is also a necessary goal of conflicting forces. The civil war in the Sudan is a good example.

The political economy of the Baggara in western Sudan

Before the drought of the mid 1980s, the various Baggara Arab pastoralist groups living on the western borders between northern and southern Sudan had already felt the effects of marginalization. The loss of stock during the drought compounded these difficulties. The Baggara are the northern neighbours of Dinka pastoralist groups living in southern Sudan. Due to their geographical position, Dinka cattle were relatively protected from the effects of the drought. Periodic raiding had characterized relations between Baggara and Dinka for generations, but this conflict had been kept within limits by a wider system of reciprocity which linked the two groups (Howell, 1951). The present civil war began in 1983 with the formation of the SPLA in southern Sudan. The leadership of the SPLA is based upon the Dinka, the largest ethno-linguistic grouping in the south. The combination of a local material imbalance amongst the Baggara and the government's need to prosecute the war has produced catastrophic results for the border Dinka.

In 1985, the northern government began to arm the Baggara pastoralists with modern weaponry and to encourage attacks upon the unarmed Dinka to the south. These attacks were led by a younger generation of political leaders who had emerged during the process of social transformation. From this period an orgy of violence spread south (Africa Watch, March 1990). Armed militia, sometimes several hundred strong, roamed the countryside looting, killing, raping and enslaving. Thousands of people were killed and maimed, tens of thousands of cattle stolen and, by 1988, hundreds of thousands of Dinka had been displaced leaving the region virtually depopulated. The break between conflict being a means of adaptation to it being an agent of destruction is starkly portrayed. The events of this period are out of all proportion in relation to local conflicts of the past. Terrible as this example is, similar events have all too frequently come to characterize internal conflict in Africa.

The political economy of the SPLA in southern Sudan

In southern Sudan the SPLA has consolidated its presence in areas not previously under its influence in what is essentially a three-stage process. The first stage involved the formation of tactical alliances with local groups and, where necessary, the military defeat of government sponsored militia. The fate of the Murle and Mundari militia is an example of the latter. The disturbed nature of the Sudan's Ethiopian, Kenyan, and Ugandan border areas has already been referred to. During the mid 1980s, in order to secure a safe base and access to food, the SPLA's strategy in south-west Ethiopia was to play on the differences and traditional hostility between the two linguistically related branches of the Nilo-Saharans: the Chai and Mursi on one side, and the Nyangatom, Toposa and Turkana on the other (Alvarsson, 1989). The selective arming of these groups by the SPLA not only helped the army build alliances, but the increased scale and ferocity of attacks upon their relatively unarmed rivals provided, in the form of looted grain and cattle, a vital means of subsistence. In 1987, for example, the SPLA's arming of the Nyangatom enabled the SPLA to mount a devastating attack upon the Mursi (Turton, 1989). In this attack between 500 and 1,000 Mursi (10 to 20 per cent of the entire population) were killed. As in the Baggara/Dinka example, killing on this scale destroys the traditional system of checks and balances which exists between groups.

As the SPLA has extended its influence in the areas which border Kenya and Uganda, a similar strategy of playing on group hostilities, selectively arming, and forming complex patterns of local alliance has been engaged. One consequence has been the widespread displacement of the defeated populations throughout the area. In 1986, for example, in order to establish a base and provisions in southern Sudan near the Ugandan border, the SPLA made use of the long-standing hostility between the Acholi and the Madi. The Madi had been associated with the Amin regime and, following its collapse, Madi refugees were settled in international camps across the border in Sudanese Acholi territory. These camps were attacked and looted by local Acholi and SPLA forces causing thousands of Madi to stream back into Uganda, and sparking off one more in a succession of population displacements.

Evolving from this process of alliance and defeat, the second stage of the SPLA's consolidation of its presence has involved attempts to cement its emerging structure through local conscription and the training of recruits in its Ethiopian base camps. Using this local cadre, the current and final stage of consolidation involves establishing a systematic structure of internal taxation.

The SPLA has significantly transformed the socio-political system over large areas of southern Sudan. By increasing the imbalances within that system through the selective strengthening of groups at the expense of others, it has caused some ethnic groups, in the sense of distinct socio-economic units, to cease to exist. The advent of the UN's Operation Lifeline Sudan, insofar as significant amounts of relief food and seed have been appropriated by the SPLA, can be argued to have reduced tension in some areas by relieving SPLA pressure on non-combatant populations. In other words, the misappropriation of relief supplies has, ironically, made it easier for these populations to cope.

The logic of food denial

Because groups and movements need to secure or protect sources of food in order to survive physically and politically, a counter-logic stipulates that those sources are themselves legitimate targets for the opposition. This is the classic territory of counter-insurgency operations. There are two main forms of food denial. One of these rests upon the relocation or corralling of groups to prevent them from providing sustenance to opposing bodies. Government forces in Ethiopia and Uganda, for example, have used these techniques. Such operations have not been noted for their sensitivity or observance of human rights. The other form of food denial involves actually withholding a given area's or group's food supplies. There are many examples of this in Africa. It is usually encountered in cases where an area or group deemed to belong to the enemy is already suffering the effects of war and/or enviro-economic stress. Examples of this are the attempts by the Sudanese and Ethiopian governments to prevent relief supplies from reaching southern Sudan or Eritrea and Tigray respectively. Movements, however, also attempt to interdict food supplies. The SPLA's attempts to blockade the government towns in southern Sudan is a case in point.

War and famine

With regard to the structural or underlying connection between war and famine, several observations can be made. In some respects internal wars in Africa are still partly cast in an earlier mould. That is, they are fought by groups whose existence is based upon different forms of semi-subsistence. Modern conflict, however, arises not as a process of regulation and adaptation, but from the instability and crises of semi-subsistence which have been increasing since the 1970s. Modern warfare, moreover, proceeds not by resolving tensions, but by massively increasing imbalances and disparities between groups. It does so because the political economy of internal war dictates that systems of semi-subsistence are both targets and points of defence. The polarization of ethnic groups and the destruction of assets reinforces the instability of semi-subsistence. Conflict in Africa should not, therefore, be seen as a secondary or separate issue; it is a long-term trend and a defining characteristic in the growth of food insecurity. Indeed conflict, impoverishment and drought appear to have become central players in a complex, antagonistic and mutually self-reinforcing syndrome which has pushed many countries toward widespread food insecurity and political fragmentation. In other words, enviro-economic factors are the sub-structure of African famine whilst conflict is its superstructure.

This paper has already examined the central importance of coping strategies in attempts to survive enviro-economic famines. In defining the specificity of African famine the prevalence of conflict has also been noted. The effect of conflict, both indirectly and as a deliberate strategy, has been to restrict or destroy people's means of subsistence and ability to cope. Under conflict conditions, people's vulnerability increases dramatically. If drought is also part of this situation it compounds the vulnerability equation. If one then adds military strategies which actively promote, or in some cases prevent, population movement, or which deny the availability of or access to relief food, rather than the health crises of enviro-economic famines, frank starvation is often the result. Some recent examples of starvation under conflict conditions would include Karamoja in northern Uganda (1980), the worst areas of northern Ethiopia (1984), Ethiopian resettlement camps (mid 1980s) and displaced Dinka in western Sudan (1988).

Limitations of existing international conventions

The way internal conflicts are fought systematically violates the international conventions on the conduct of war, particularly those dealing with the treatment of civilian popula-tions.[1] In terms of the international response to internal conflict in Africa, the International Commission of the Red Cross (ICRC) should, in many respects, be the ideal agency to intervene in order to protect civilian populations. The ICRC, however, has faced many difficulties in Africa. It is common for conflicting parties not to recognize one or all of the various conventions and furthermore, the conventions themselves were primarily designed to govern inter-state war between industrialized nations. Indeed, one can see them as a form of reciprocity which attempts to direct and limit the effects of such wars. Non-international or internal war is therefore something of an anomaly within inter-national law, and many aspects of the relevant Articles and Protocols have a customary rather than a definitive status.

One result of these difficulties has been that, at best, the ICRC has been ineffective in the Horn. The same could be said, however, in relation to the UN humanitarian mandates. Internally displaced peoples, together with the existence of extra-legal states, mean that the UN system only has a limited sphere of operation. The situation in the Horn has indicated in stark relief the growing mismatch between international regulatory institutions and the situations actually existing in third world countries. This mismatch also relates, especially in Africa, to increasingly divergent development trajectories within the world economy.

The growth of food insecurity

The global position of Africa

The information revolution that has embraced the advanced industrial countries has not been reflected in the development trajectory of Africa. Indeed, since the 1970s, the pattern has been for various developments to reinforce rather than change an earlier division of labour based upon the export of primary products. This occurred at a time when other developing countries, especially those in the Far East, were switching to the export of manufactured goods (Josling, 1987). Given the simultaneous technological changes taking place in manufacturing, especially the growing use of synthetic materials (Kaounides, 1990), the increased reliance upon traditional primary products is a major concern and deserves to be considered apart from the adverse market trends which also accompanied this development.

One factor which has reinforced the old division of labour has been the decline in foreign direct investment (FDI) in African industry. Although in relative terms FDI in much of Africa has never been great due to a lack of infrastructure, high production costs and the spread of internal conflict, it has declined since the 1970s (World Bank, 1989). If one takes the case of Britain as indicative, over the past decade British FDI in Africa has virtually collapsed. During this period around a third of the companies previously involved have disengaged, leaving Africa's share of British FDI at 0.4 per cent of the British world total (Bennell, June, 1990). A similar decline in direct investment has been observed in South Africa (Smith, 1990). Investors have found Europe and America better propositions.

Dependency theorists may see cause for quiet optimism in this trend. Since the early 1980s, however, African policy makers have become increasingly concerned. Based upon the experience of the Far East, an emerging view is that trade and investment between rich and poor countries can be beneficial, especially if it results in technology transfer. In the prevailing climate, however, the prospects for developing such links are not encouraging. The IMF/World Bank structural adjustment programmes, together with market reforms that some countries have independently initiated, can be seen as additional factors which have tended to entrench the old division of labour as they are predominantly aimed at boosting the production of primary products.

The emergence of food insecurity

The growth of food insecurity[2] in Africa is a complex phenomenon. Different countries have often arrived at a similar end despite travelling separate routes. In general terms, Africa has continued to sustain a high level of population growth at the same time as per capita food production has declined. This has resulted in a growing number of countries becoming food deficient. Reflecting an increasing urban demand, there has been a corresponding increase in the import of commercial foodstuffs. So far, this trajectory is not untypical of a normal development scenario. Many economically robust countries are food deficient and regularly import to make up the difference. In the case of Africa, however, the situation is different. In the absence of industrialization, Africa has continued to rely on the export of traditional primary products to furnish the hard currency needed to purchase commercial imports. This has occurred at a time when the price of primary products has dropped, effecting a corresponding increase in the cost of these imports. Deficit situations have therefore become increasingly difficult, and in some cases impossible, to bridge.

The highly erratic nature of African food production, due to climate or instability, has often compounded such deficit situations. Moreover, where local surpluses may exist, a lack of infrastructure often limits the scope for internal market solutions. A major consequence has been the increasing role for external food aid at the same time as it has declined in the rest of the world. In 1987–8, for example, the IGADD countries (Djibouti, Ethiopia, Kenya, Somalia, the Sudan and Uganda) alone received 13 per cent of the total world food aid (IGADD, 1990).

Food insecurity is now an established feature of the African condition. The statistics are staggering. Amongst IGADD members, for example, 45 million people, or 39 per cent of the total population, are regarded as food insecure. With the exception of Malawi and Zimbabwe, a similar situation exists amongst the members of the Southern African Development Co-ordination Conference (SADCC) – Angola, Botswana, Lesotho, Malawi, Mozambique, Swaziland, Tanzania, Zambia and Zimbabwe (Morgan, 1988). With respect to the food insecure themselves, the two largest groups (aside from the growing number of urban poor) are poor rural households and those affected by the spread of internal conflicts. In the IGADD countries about 35 per cent of the food insecure (nearly 16 million people) are classified as war affected.

Since the mid 1980s, food insecurity relating to internal conflict has grown dramatically in SADCC countries. It is now estimated that some 12 million people are involved (one third the population of Angola and half that of Mozambique). They include 6.1 million displaced within their own countries, 1.9 million refugees in neighbouring countries, and four million urban people affected by the resulting economic breakdown (Smith, 1990). When the situation in Southern Africa is taken into account, at least half of the total population of food insecure in Africa have been affected by war in some way.

The donor/NGO safety net

The internationalization of public welfare

Africa's economic decline and growing food insecurity since the 1970s have been matched by a growth in welfare aid directed to the continent. Multilateral aid to Africa has steadily grown at the same time as it has fallen off in other areas of the world. In 1987, sub-Saharan Africa received 36 per cent (12.6 billion US dollars) of the world's total multilateral aid, this being the largest single regional allocation. The case of British bilateral aid is instructive. At the same time as British foreign direct investment has collapsed in Africa, bilateral aid has increased. It grew from 28 per cent of the total in 1971 to 48 per cent in 1988 (ODA, 1989). Again, this has been at the expense of British aid flows to other areas of the world. This pattern is also reflected in the expenditure of NGOs. During 1989–90, for example, OXFAM spent 80 per cent of its £17 million emergencies budget in Africa's war affected countries (OXFAM, 1989–90). There is a symmetry between the decline in economic performance and foreign investment, and the increase in foreign aid. It would seem that Africa has been reintegrated into the new world order, not by decisive economic ties but by the internationalization of public welfare.

This internationalization is based upon the projection of a two-tiered welfare system that has emerged in connection with the neo-liberal restructuring of the welfare state in the West. Here, the economically active sectors of the population are increasingly expected to seek welfare services in the market place, whilst a safety net, partly constructed from contractual relations between local authorities and voluntary agencies, is being put into place for the remainder (Stoker, 1989). In the case of Africa, structural adjustment is attempting to stimulate market reform whilst a welfare safety net is increasingly being provided in the form of contractual or project agreements linking donors and NGOs. Current approaches to food security, for example, fall into this two-tiered mould (Maxwell et al., 1990; IGADD, 1990). One can discern the beginnings of a loose meshing of approaches and institutions. Although government bodies are frequently involved in existing safety net agreements, it is an essentially donor/NGO system since this is the main finance and implementation axis.[3] Whilst there are exceptions,[4] in most contracts government bodies play a 'sleeping partner' role. Given that donor/NGO systems have emerged due to the incapacity of government structures, it would be surprising to find otherwise.

The internationalization of public welfare, especially its donor/NGO safety net, has grown considerably during the 1980s. Its expansion can largely be attributed to the growing enviro-economic and increasingly war related emergencies of the period. Large bilateral/NGO operations have developed in the Sudan and Ethiopia since the mid 1980s, and have grown in Uganda and Mozambique. A new departure, beginning in 1989, was the emergence of a UN/NGO operation in southern Sudan. A similar structure is now being developed in Angola. Experience is growing within these bodies and wider national and international linkages are developing amongst and between them.

These developments are of world historic importance. If one takes a sober and objective view of the trends, several conclusions appear inevitable. Long-term political instability and internal conflict is compounding problems of economic decline, government decay and food insecurity. The internationalization of public welfare has been the inevitable outcome of this set of circumstances. Trends would suggest that these two processes are not only linked, but that they will continue to grow and develop during the 1990s.

This development has several important implications. In the first place, the relief/development debate,[5] which may have had relevance in the 1960s and 1970s, has now become meaningless. The effect of the crisis is such that agency activity has increasingly taken on the appearance of basic public welfare interventions either of a direct, relief type or an indirect, self-help variety. Two-tiered welfare is also the administrative expression of a socially polarized society, one part of which exists in a state of permanent crisis. In the 'global cities' of the leading industrial countries this takes the form of a growing underclass of ethnic minorities, casual workers and the unemployed (Sassen-Koob, 1989). In Africa, the long-term instability of semi-subsistence gives rise to conflict which further increases instability. The 'underclass' here comprises the war and enviro-economic casualties of this process. The existence of 'developmentalism' within NGOs, especially the view that relief work is somehow undesirable, tends to work against a proper appreciation of the full significance and historic weight of present developments. It therefore minimizes the urgent need to reform the welfare system that is now developing.

The case for reform

The main policy debate during the 1990s will be around the issue of whether or not a two-tiered welfare system of the type currently emerging is adequate or appropriate to deal with the specificity of African famine. NGOs have rightly prided themselves on developing a direct relationship with project partners and beneficiaries. During the 1990s, it is possible that due to the combined effects of enviro-economic and conflict factors, together with the decay and disintegration of governance, difficulties over access and the ability to help will increase. In such a situation growing attention must be given to the institutional framework of the donor/NGO system as a whole. The case for the reform of this system rests on two factors: (a) it is, and will remain for the foreseeable future, the only effective means of assisting people in dire distress (the case of northern Sudan is instructive here); and (b), it is fraught with problems, limitations and gross inadequacies.

The question of targeting

In a two-tiered welfare system, safety nets are defined in terms of their ability to target assistance. The conventional wisdom in Africa is that targeting is the only way to reduce the unsustainable cost of generalized nutritional subsidies. Moreover, the savings achieved by limiting such subsidies more than compensate for the relatively high administrative costs that a targeting system represents (World Bank, 1986). The neo-liberal logic within this position propels targeting systems toward minimalist levels of input. This stands in contrast to agency concerns for community-based needs and for the needs of women. In the Sudan and Uganda, for example, NGOs such as OXFAM have attempted to develop relief targeting systems that are reliant in some way upon communal forms of redistribution, or support the semi-subsistence economy involved. This is important work which has not yet been fully evaluated. Although interest in targeting systems is growing, it has not as yet reached a wider audience. OXFAM's experience in the Sudan's Red Sea Province, for example, is arguably one of the most systematic attempts at targeting attempted so far in Africa, yet it appears practically unknown outside the organization (Walker, 1987). In the case of enviro-economic stress, where coping strategies and transformations in family and gender relations create a complex situation, sensitive targeting is difficult. Indeed, it is regarded as still being in its infancy (Maxwell et al., 1990).

In relation to conflict, which is responsible for possibly half of the food insecure in Africa, the issue of targeting has received little or no attention. The logic of internal war means that no one in such a situation can be neutral and, consequently, actions are seen as either helping one side or the other. This raises many issues including that of compensatory aid in conflict situations. In western Sudan during 1988, in what is generally regarded as a successful emergency operation, it was only possible to relocate and support displaced Dinka, in what was a potentially hostile Arab region, by providing compensatory aid (water, health and educational inputs) to the indigenous population. This approach is also common, usually due to political pressure, when dealing with refugees. The political issue of equability quickly arises in cases of displacement or resource destruction. It may not be possible or even desirable to ignore pressure for compensatory aid.

For a variety of social as well as physical reasons, war affected populations may require far greater inputs than conventional targeting would allow for. War affected populations are also bereaved populations, and food aid can play an important role in providing the resources to allow groups to complete burial and mourning rites. The psychological and traumatic effect of war also has to be taken into consideration. If one cannot separate physical survival from the survival of the group, then many displaced people whose way of life has been destroyed will have lost everything, including their psychological and cultural foundations. This is an element of targeting which is rarely even thought about, let alone acted upon. In all of these instances, neo-liberal minimalist conceptions are open to challenge.

The logic of internal conflict, that is, the taxing of non-combatants, strategies of food denial, and so on, throws up even more issues. Mention has already been made of the case in which the appropriation of food aid by the SPLA in southern Sudan may have eased the tax burden on non-combatants, thereby increasing their ability to cope. Whilst no one could seriously argue (or could they?) that the best way to help non-combatants in an internal conflict is to feed combatants, it illustrates the complexity of these problems. It also indicates that, targeting aside, the main difficulty in a conflict situation is that of access.

The question of access

If one excludes the logistical and technical considerations, difficulties of access are composed by the compounding of two problems: (a) the political economy/logic of internal conflict; and (b), the unilateral nature of the donor/NGO system. With regard to the latter, whilst there can be a constructive dynamic between neo-liberalism and the neo-populism of NGOs, there are certain aspects of the relation which give cause for concern. The transfer of funds away from governments and toward NGOs is a defining feature of the donor/NGO system, but donors have never discussed this with any African government. Nor, for that matter, does it appear ever to have seriously been discussed with NGOs. Rather than through a process of all party agreement, it has emerged as a donor condition which all too often is founded on ill-defined and assumed roles.

The unilateral (yet ill-defined) donor/NGO system maintains contradictory and even antagonistic relations with African governments. Many are uneasy with the new found wealth of NGOs and their populist leanings. This is a serious weakness in the international system of public welfare and it undermines attempts to construct a welfare safety net in numerous ways ranging from disinterest to outright hostility and obstruction. In the case of the Sudan, beginning with government attempts in 1986 to deny food to the south, a steadily worsening relationship developed between the government and donor/NGOs. Until recently, a similar situation existed in Ethiopia. Whilst in Uganda and Mozambique relations can be said to have begun cordially, problems are now beginning to arise. If the trend continues, in two or three years' time these countries could well resemble the virtual paralysis that has existed in the Sudan. These problems are a structural feature of the donor/NGO system.

In attempting to play a humanitarian role, the donor/NGO system has to confront the logic of internal conflict. The difficulties and weakness inherent in this system are magnified in such circumstances. It is a logic, moreover, which means that national NGOs are either aligned or they cannot operate. With a system which is ill-defined and non-negotiated, positions can harden and polarization easily occurs. In these situations, all too often relief policy is made on the move and interventions occur when and where possible rather than according to need. In many instances of dire distress, no access at all is possible.

These difficulties can only be resolved through protracted negotiations between all parties at national and international levels. Such negotiations would have to at least (a) work towards defining more precisely the contractual relations between government, donors and NGOs, including questions of targeting; and (b) pursue the reform of the rules of non-international war to ensure they take into account the nature of internal conflict. Whilst initially these negotiations would have to take place in stages and at different levels, the final aim would be to work toward the amalgamation of the two levels. In other words, the intention would be to reform the contractual relations that define the donor/NGO safety net in such a way that they are comprehensive, binding on parties, including government, and based upon a modernization of the rules of war.

The question of sovereignty

This paper has sought to show the important position occupied by food in internal conflict. It is both a weapon and a goal. In this situation the donor/NGO system exercises a good deal of influence, some of which may be unintentional but, nevertheless, is unavoidable. The UN/NGO cross-border relief operation into southern Sudan, for example, is both an indirect recognition of the SPLA and, since it represents a means of preventing further population displacement, it means that the north can never (if it ever could) force a military conclusion. In other words, the donor/NGO safety net has been drawn into the partitioning of the Sudan.

In the case of Eritrea and Tigray, although donors and NGOs have always kept a low profile to avoid the recognition issue, it must, nevertheless, be the case that the huge amounts of food relief that have crossed the border from the Sudan since the mid 1980s have helped retain the population and thus to sustain the movements in these areas. Whilst there have been no designs other than of a humanitarian nature, these examples indicate that the donor/NGO system has little choice but to operate along the fault lines of African sovereignty. This is a further complication in the government and donor/NGO relationship. Events within the Russian Empire and, in particular, the real possibility of Eritrea's independence, with the agreement of the OAU, could well increase pressure for change in the essentially colonial pattern of African sovereignty. These considerations increase the need for the reform of the donor/NGO system.

Concluding remarks

It may well be that it is not possible to disengage the donor/NGO safety net from the nexus of national and international political relations in which it is currently embedded. At best, attempts at reform may achieve only a partial freeing up of elements and secure but a limited space for operation. Such an attempt is necessary, however, because not only do millions of people in Africa need assistance, but during the 1990s the welfare dependency of many African countries could deepen. Tackling the limitations of the emerging system should, therefore, be accorded due priority.

Notes

1   Notably, Common Article 3 of the Geneva Conventions (the rules of war governing non-international armed conflict), Protocol II of the Geneva Accords and the Land Mines Protocol.

2   The concept of food security reflects a change in thinking about hunger and malnutrition. It focuses upon the operation of food systems (production, distribution and consumption) in relation to the lives of the poor and vulnerable (see World Bank, 1986).

3   Since the 1970s, the amount of bilateral aid given to NGOs has increased at the same time as the implementing capacity of many African governments has declined. Between 1975 and 1988, for example, the British government increased its support for NGOs from £5 million to £42 million (ODA, 1989).

4   As with the nature of internal conflict, the major exceptions are Eritrea and Tigray. In both cases ERA and REST, being the humanitarian wings of the main military movements, operate in a self-directed manner and monopolize welfare activities in their areas of operation. International NGOs, at most, act as donors

with regard to these activities. This level of autonomy and the organizational capability that is represented is unique in Africa.

5   That is, that emergencies are essentially secondary/short-term phenomena dealt with by temporary remedial action which re-establishes a normal state of development.

References

Abu Sin, M.E. 1982. 'A change in strategy of animal herding among the nomads of the Butana, Eastern Sudan' in Heinritz, G. (ed.) *Problems of Agricultural Development in the Sudan*, Gottingen, Edition Herodot.

Africa Watch. 1990, March. *Denying 'The Honour of Living'. Sudan: A Human Rights Disaster*, New York, Washington, London.

Almagor, U. 1979. 'Raiders and elders: A confrontation of generations among the Dassanetch' in Fukui, K. and D. Turton (eds.) *Warfare Amongst East African Herders*, Osaka, Senri Ethnological Studies, no. 3, pp. 119–46.

Almond, M. 1989. *The Complexities of Pastoral Development as They Relate to OXFAM's Pastoral Programme in Sudan*, Oxford, OXFAM.

Alvarsson, J. 1989. *Starvation and Peace or Food and War? Aspects of Armed Conflict in the Lower Omo Valley, Ethiopia*, Uppsala, Uppsala Research Reports in Cultural Anthropology.

Bennell, P. 1990, June. 'British industrial investment in sub-Saharan Africa: Corporate response to economic crisis in the 1980s' *Development Policy Review*, vol. 8, no. 2, pp. 155–78.

de Waal, A. 1987. *Famine That Kills: Darfur 1984–85*, London, Save the Children Fund.

de Waal, A. 1990. 'A Re-assessment of entitlement theory in the light of the recent famines in Africa' *Development and Change*, vol. 21, pp. 469–90.

Duffield, M. 1990. 'Sudan at the crossroads: From emergency preparedness to social security' *Institute of Development Studies Discussion Paper, No 275*, Sussex, IDS.

Green, R.H. 1987. 'Killing the dream: The political and human economy of war in sub-Saharan Africa', *Institute of Development Studies Discussion Paper, No 238*, Sussex, IDS.

Gursony, R. 1988, April. *Summary of Mozambican Refugee Accounts of Principally Conflict Related Experience in Mozambique*, Bureau for Refugee Programme, Department of State.

Harris, N. 1989. 'Aid and urbanisation: An overview' *Urbanisation and British Aid: Papers and Proceedings of a Workshop*, London, Overseas Development Administration, pp. 174–85.

Howell, P.P. 1951. 'Notes on the Ngrok Dinka' *Sudan Notes and Records*, vol. 32, pt. 2, pp. 239–93.

IGADD. 1990. *Food Security Strategy Study*, Volume 1, prepared by IDS University of Sussex, DAG University of Birmingham, FSG University of Oxford.

Iliffe, J. 1987. *The African Poor: A History*, Cambridge, Cambridge University Press.

Josling, T. 1987. 'The changing role of developing countries in international trade' in Clay, E. and J. Shaw, (eds.) *Poverty, Development and Food*, London, Macmillan.

Kaounides, L. 1990. 'The materials revolution and economic development' *IDS Bulletin*, vol. 21, no. 1, pp. 16–27.

Maxwell, S., J. Swift and M. Buchanan-Smith. 1990. 'Is food security targeting possible in sub-Saharan Africa? Evidence from north Sudan' *IDS Bulletin*, vol. 21, no. 3, pp. 52–61.

Morgan, R. 1988, September. *Social Welfare Programmes and the Reduction of Household Vulnerability in the SADCC States of Southern Africa*, Mozambique, UNICEF.

Overseas Development Administration. 1989. *British Overseas Aid: Anniversary Review*, London, ODA.

OXFAM. 1989–90. *Emergencies Unit Annual Report*, Oxford, OXFAM.

Sassen-Koob, S. 1989. 'Growth and informalization at the core: A preliminary report on New York City' in Smith, M.P. and J.R. Feagin (eds.) *The Capitalist City*, Oxford, Basil Blackwell.

Smith, S. 1990. *Front Line Africa: The Right to a Future*, Oxford, OXFAM.

Stoker, G. 1989. 'Creating a local government for a post-Fordist society: The Thatcherite project?' in Stewart, J. and G. Stoker, *The Future of Local Government*, London, Macmillan.

Swift, J. 1989. 'Why are rural people vulnerable to famine?' *IDS Bulletin*, vol. 20, no. 2, pp. 8–15

Turton, D. 1989. 'Warfare, vulnerability and survival: A case from southern Ethiopia' *Cambridge Anthropology*, special issue, *Warfare in Africa: The Local Experience*, pp. 67–85.

Ulrich, R. 1989, April. *Environment and Security in the Horn of Africa*, report for United Nations Environment Programme.

Walker, P. 1987. *Food for Recovery: Food Monitoring and Targeting in Red Sea Province, Sudan, 1985–1987*, Oxford, OXFAM.

World Bank. 1986. *Poverty and Hunger: Issues and Options for Food Security in Developing Countries*, Washington DC, World Bank.

World Bank. 1989. *Sub-Saharan Africa: From Crisis to Sustainable Growth*, Washington DC, World Bank.

Comment   SOLOMON INQUAI

Mr Duffield's paper is interesting both for what it states and what it does not. The paper tends to reduce all conflicts in Africa to the scarcity of the means of subsistence, that is, of land. Land is unquestionably a finite and as such a scarce commodity. It is at the heart of economic well being, or lack of it, especially for the peasant and pastoralist societies in the Horn of Africa. Land scarcity breeds insecurity and could possibly lead to conflict by aggravating the people's deprivation, but it does not follow that all conflicts in Africa in general and the Horn in particular can be said to emanate 'from the growing instability and crisis of semi-subsistence'. The paper should address the root causes of the conflicts in Africa.

If one examines the various conflicts, one soon comes to realize that they are caused by differing circumstances. Present day conflicts in Africa seem to fall into two broad categories. Firstly, there are those that flare up because those in the seats of power deny the peoples in a country freedom and justice – generally this is known as a lack of democracy. Autocratic regimes, despots and dictators breed conflict. People take up arms in order to change the political structure of the society they live in. To suggest that struggles for justice and freedom, and for self-determination are nothing more than struggles for subsistence or semi-subsistence and for food security is to underestimate the higher ideals of Africans. Secondly, there are those conflicts that are instigated, financed, and funded by foreign powers. In these types of conflicts, the participants are nothing more than armed bandits implanted to destabilize a country whose political philosophy is not acceptable to some foreign powers. RENAMO in Mozambique is an example of this. There are other types of conflicts, but the concern here is that the paper does not discuss the political motives behind the many struggles in Africa.

To move on to famine and famine management and the role of the NGOs, contrary to de Waal's claims, there is nothing unique or peculiar about famine in Africa. The only thing different is that it is current among the famines of the world. It is occurring in a period of media explosion and as a result is widely publicized. Africa is in no way different from the countries of the world that were famine prone only recently. During the period in history when Africa was feeding itself, and Ethiopia was exporting cereals and other farm products, others were suffering from famine. The great famines of India, China, Russia, America and indeed Europe should not be forgotten. Who would have forecast 40 or 30 years ago that India and China would ever get out of that vicious cycle of ever recurring famine and become self-sufficient, let alone producers of surpluses, leaving the question of equity and distribution aside? The effect of famine on the peoples of India and China was just the same as it is on the peoples of Africa today and, as the famines in India and China have been reversed, African famine is also reversible given peace and stability.

Among the factors that have distorted African food production and the continent's capacity to feed itself are: (a) the archaic mode of production, (b) over-population, (c) lack of development input, (d) demand for foreign goods, (e) the ever-declining price for primary commodities, (f) conflicts and civil wars, and (g) the IMF's adjustment policies. The drawing of Africa into the market economy has also been a major contributor to the African food deficit. Primary commodities, as stated above, fetch less and less money every year. Africans, in order to service debt and to purchase the foreign goods on which they have become so dependent, are forced to devote more and more acreage to cash crops which leaves less for growing food. For instance, the Sahel devotes more hectares to the production of export crops such as groundnuts than it does to food production. In Kenya it is criminal, punishable by law, to uproot coffee bushes and plant maize. It is no wonder that these policies coupled with the vagaries of nature continue to result in a food deficit in Africa.

As the struggles for freedom and justice in the Horn of Africa succeed and usher in a period of peace, major exercises of reconstruction and development have to be undertaken. This has already begun in Tigray under the TPLF. The NGOs, especially those with proven track records for justice and fair play, will have a major role to play as partners. However, whatever is done will have to be initiated and led by the people as they are the ones solely responsible for setting the agenda with regard to the kind of work that is to be undertaken. The days when aid agencies look down upon the people of Africa and speak of them as 'children needing guidance and direction because they don't know what they need' are finished. Aid or 'international welfare' will only be accepted on the terms and conditions set by the people and their elected representatives; aid can only be supplementary to the efforts of the people themselves, as has always been the case.

People will use their resources and their energy to reverse the current trends as they work for permanent solutions. A democratic Ethiopia will, over a short period of time, be able to move from a food deficit country to a food surplus country; areas of deficiency will be countered by areas of surplus. Over the last few years the Relief Society of Tigray (REST) has seen people building terraces, building hundreds of kilometres of road, and building dams, water catchments, sink wells and so forth. Using whatever resources people have and the limited aid they get, the major reconstruction work has already begun.

Quoting the following statement seems an appropriate way to conclude: 'thirty years of international experience shows that technology and knowledge do not in and of themselves bring development. It is people's development of their own expertise that underlies genuine development.... No one develops any one. People and society develop themselves' (Anderson & Woodrow, 1989)

Reference

Anderson, Mary B. and Peter J. Woodrow. 1989. *Rising From the Ashes,* Boulder, Westview Press.

Comment   HASSAN A. ABDEL ATI

Mark Duffield's paper contributes to our conceptualization of famine and the safety net that could cater for it. The paper is also very definitive in illustrating the complexities of the issue of food production, and its sustainability and accessibility locally, nationally and internationally. The following comments respond to the major points and issues raised by the paper, and discuss what could be the role of NGOs in the post-war period in establishing a safety net for the conflict victims.

The paper outlines the nature of the world order that has emerged since the early 1970s and its implications for Africa. This order was stimulated by the reinforcement of the colonial division of labour, the deterioration of traditional production systems, internal conflict as a part of greater international conflicts, a decline in foreign investment, and the increasing importance of food and welfare aid mediated by the international community. Against this background, the paper raises a number of issues relevant to the present situation in the Horn of Africa, the most important of which have been summarized below.

1. The complexity of African famine both in form and causes is due to such factors as environmental calamities, conflicts and the consequent socio–economic transformations that have occurred.
2. The strong link between conflict and food shortages and famine emerges in the paper very clearly as food is identified as a cause and a goal of conflict, as well as a

weapon in the conflict (the withholding of food, for instance). As a result of the problems of environmental degradation, conflict, and the collapse of local markets and production systems there are large numbers of helpless victims in Africa. This has, due to the scale of the problems encountered, led to the emergence of a situation in which the welfare of the victims in Africa has been internationalized (both in assessing or deciding the needs and responding to them).

3. In Africa, although instability and local conflicts have disrupted traditional survival and coping strategies, they have largely been overlooked in analyses.
4. The paper predicts the concern of the 1990s policy debate to be the relevance, adequacy and appropriateness of the internationalization of welfare for the complex African situation.
5. The paper stresses the failure of attempts to increase production of primary products and links these failures to the environment, vulnerability and conflicts.
6. The difficulty of neutrality on the part of NGOs operating in the conflict zones is also discussed.

However, the paper in stressing the failure of the various attempts made to increase primary production, especially of food, seems to overlook two important factors. The first point overlooked is the emphasis on cash crop production by international and other donor agencies which have directly and indirectly contributed to the decline of subsistence farming and food production. Secondly, even when food is produced aspects such as prices, accessibility, distribution and sustainability are largely ignored.

The role of NGOs

Available information strongly indicates that the contributions of NGOs to the alleviation of the immense social problems in the Horn of Africa, both now and in the post-war period, are not only desirable but also critical and inevitable for a number of reasons. As shown in the paper, these include: the poor resources of recipient countries and their misuse and/or mismanagement, and the massive humanitarian as well as developmental requirements expected in the post-war era; the high costs of debt servicing; the decline in direct foreign investment as a result of high production costs and poor infrastructure; the contradictions and widening gap between the structural adjustment requirements (targeted toward governmental and state machinery) and the requirements of the social welfare safety net targeted to the needy social groups (mostly by NGOs); the increase in bilateral aid via NGOs which parallels the decrease in investment; and the antagonism and mistrust, whether real or imaginary, between donors and African governments which has resulted in the transfer of funds away from governments to NGOs.

These issues have to be seen in the context in which they will be influential. If one is to speculate about the working environment for NGOs during the post-war period, it is more likely to be characterized by a continuous gap between national governments in the recipient countries and the NGOs operating there, unless some clear policies and common objectives are decided for a common understanding between the two parties *vis-à-vis* the tasks undertaken. Furthermore, there is likely to be a reinforcement of what Mark Duffield calls 'developmentalism' and developmentalist attitudes within the NGOs which would make them less ready to accept other models, be it from the government or local NGOs.

In light of the presently emerging 'New World Order' in the 1990s, the Horn and Africa in general are likely to be competing for Western resources (both from governments and NGOs) certainly with Eastern Europe and possibly with a post-apartheid South Africa, to mention two examples. The requirement for Western resources will be compounded by the domination of the 'structural adjustment' requirements and 'values' in the region which will further degrade national governments' capacities to address social problems and welfare issues.

Finally the high degree of volatility and change resulting from the geographical and occupational mobility of the population both during the conflict and afterwards in the resettlement process may continue. Regional and local imbalances might be increased further during peace time. In fact, contrary to what the paper suggests, imbalances tend to emerge and grow during peace rather than conflict time, especially when market forces have free rein – ultimately this leads to conflicts.

Experience with NGOs in Africa

Although NGOs have records of some very clear positive accomplishments in Africa, the organizations have their drawbacks and if these are not addressed the net result in the post-war era might be disastrous. The dominance of and preoccupation with 'developmentalism' on the part of NGOs at the expense of basic social and humanitarian activities is one such drawback. The problem is not with NGO developmental activities *per se*, but these activities should not be implemented at the expense of immediate needs, or in isolation from governmental machinery or the activities of local NGOs if conflict is to be avoided now, and sustainability is to be ensured in the future.

The apparent rivalry or antagonism between NGOs and national governments precipitated an attitude among the needy of mistrust, scepticism and helplessness towards their national governments. This has been compounded by the tendency among some NGOs to embark on building a parallel system of administration rather than rebuilding or strengthening existing systems to improve their efficiency and credibility. The distribution of relief during the 1984–5 famine is a case in point. Another area of concern is that the tendency of NGOs to impose measures and methods of work on national governments through collective bargaining will shape the post-war situation as governments as well as beneficiaries would not have much choice. The unfortunate incidence of sending unqualified and mostly uncompromising staff (experts, consultants) from the headquarters to the field to determine not only the fate of the needy but also that of the future development of the country reinforces this concern.

The general unwillingness among NGOs to undertake infrastructural activities (this applies to UN agencies) is a considerable drawback given that infrastructural development is vital if the market place is to operate and reliance on welfare aid is to be reduced. A final constraint is the failure of NGOs to exploit or use the traditional survival mechanisms and/or social structures, or to develop them to strengthen their resilience and capabilities.

What is to be done?

In view of these problems and the desirability of NGOs in the post-war period, a clear plan of action must be prepared before embarking on any activities. This will require sufficient information collection – which should, if possible, start now – and a clear definition and division of roles. Local NGOs and local institutions must be involved from the outset of the planning stage and be equipped to become part of executing post-war tasks. Furthermore, a continuous dialogue between NGOs, donors, government institutions and local organizations should be initiated so that they can respond quickly to changing circumstances. Sufficient attention must be given to infrastructural projects (by donors and UN agencies) and to strengthening the administrative and management capacities of the concerned government institutions and local organizations. All this obviously requires sufficient information and goodwill on the part of all the actors if the reconstruction effort is to succeed.

7

The Changing Position of Eritrean Women: An Overview of Women's Participation in the EPLF

WUBNESH W. SELASSIE

Women's traditional position in Eritrea

Like any other traditional society, Eritrean society is patriarchal; the male is considered the preserver and transmitter of the family line and property, and the female is just a subordinate member of the family. This traditional attitude is exhibited as soon as a child is born. A mother who gives birth to a boy is happy and proud of having fulfilled the demand of the husband and the clan, while on the other hand, she who gives birth to a girl is humiliated and sad. Disappointment grows as the number of females born to the family increases. A mother's disappointment arises partly from the reaction of her family and community, and partly from her own negative experience as a woman in the society into which she has brought a daughter. This attitude towards females deeply entrenches a feeling of inferiority in them while it gives the upper hand to males, right from the beginning. As a result, the entire society practices traditional values that suppress women. In addition, religion mixed with traditions influenced by feudal norms has contributed substantially to the passivity of women. Both Christian and Islamic religious leaders have taught women to be passive, obedient and faithful servants of their husbands and kinsmen.

The 60 years of colonial rule in Eritrea, prior to the Eritrea–Ethiopia conflict, to some degree altered traditional gender roles in the country. The colonial state confiscated large areas of agricultural land, conscripted men into military service leaving female-headed families behind, and installed large- and small-scale factories in various towns in Eritrea. These changes necessitated the creation of a labour force which comprised both sexes. Still, the salaries paid to women were half those of men doing the same type of job. All technical and administrative positions were assumed by men, mostly the colonizers, while women worked in textiles, plantations, and factories that required less skilled labour.

The emergence of the Eritrean People's Liberation Front (EPLF), following the annexation of Eritrea to Ethiopia, can be regarded as a turning point after which many of the backward traditional values and practices that created a gap between the sexes and various social classes in Eritrean society were uprooted. The EPLF, aware of the protracted nature of the Eritrean struggle for social transformation, of the future prospects for development and stability, and of gender and nationality issues, introduced the concept of maximum participation of all nationals in the process of liberating the country. This policy was to run alongside the equitable production, distribution and consumption of commodities and services.

The process of raising awareness within the EPLF

The gradual process of altering traditional values, including the subordination of women, began within the EPLF with the fighters. Within this group it was possible to impose new laws that would bring about changes, and to undertake an intensive process of convincing fighters of the need for social transformation. The resulting changes could be used as guidelines for civilians. Education was regarded as the most appropriate tool for convincing the latter group. The task was tackled cautiously and in steps. Intensive awareness-raising activities preceded action. Priorities were set up and measures taken to integrate women and various nationalities within the country into action, but this was done without directly confronting male supremacy or traditional practices.

The EPLF's plan involved integrating all nationals, regardless of gender, age and ethnic origin, into action to satisfy the demands of the ongoing struggle and of the people themselves. Efforts were then made to make participation more comprehensive in order to fulfill the current political, social, cultural and economic needs and to set up the basis for tomorrow. As it is impossible to think of a satisfactorily positive outcome being achieved without a realistic approach to the gender issue, women were given special attention in order to make the social transformation more effective. Such attention included exploiting women's labour potential, recognizing and validating their role in the society, and integrating them into fields previously regarded as out of women's reach. Furthermore, measures were taken to increase women's confidence, to narrow the power gap between men and women, and to facilitate women's struggle for economic independence and for equality in power structures so that they can ensure that their interests are better served. Women's participation (which accounts for 40 per cent of the EPLF) in the lengthy armed struggle demonstrated their capacity to Eritrean society and developed among women the ways and means of defending their own rights.

Reducing the gender gap in EPLF administered areas

Education has been regarded as the basis for social transformation in EPLF administered Eritrea. Under colonialism the provision of education was limited in capacity and localized to the main towns. A few urban girls who had parents who could afford the costs went to school as an indication of status or to make them more attractive for marriage, but the vast majority of women in Eritrea were uneducated. Since rural Eritrea did not have access to modern education, the percentage of illiteracy was very high among women and men. Consequently, providing education has been one of the EPLF's major challenges. Women have been the greatest beneficiaries of this programme as, because they were completely isolated from the limited educational institutions in traditional Eritrea, there was 100 per cent illiteracy among women in Agraa in the Sahel province, Maria-Tselam in Senhit, and Shelalo in the western region. A massive literacy campaign was introduced in the early 1980s, and by 1989 illiteracy was reduced by 50 to 70 per cent. Through education, many women in EPLF administered areas developed their ability to analyse the real causes of their marginalization, and learnt skills that facilitated their involvement in traditionally segregated work areas. Many women in these areas came to realize that equality cannot be achieved as long as they are seen as marginal to men, society and development.

The EPLF has also introduced appropriate technology which has contributed to reducing the long hours of hard work burdening women both in urban and rural Eritrea, particularly in the latter. The application of appropriate technology led to the development of small-scale income generating projects which can contribute to women gaining economic independence, which they regard as a step toward their emancipation. Such projects are particularly attractive to women who shoulder family responsibilities as single mothers due to the political situation. For women who work in the fields, collect firewood, fetch water, return home to do household work, care for their children, take care of animals, and so forth, appropriate technology has simplified their burden.

Primary health care programmes in EPLF areas have given special consideration to women and children. As in all other fields, women have been trained to play an active role in the medical field. They make up about 60 per cent of the medical workers in the EPLF health institutions, and some are experts and senior administrators. In addition, between 1985 and 1989, 354 civilians were trained as traditional birth attendants in four districts. These attendants assist expectant mothers in remote areas as deliveries are normally complicated and hazardous both to mothers and the foetus due to traditional practices of circumcision.

Women have been assuming senior political decision-making positions, both within the EPLF hierarchy and in the civilian administrative system, to safeguard their interests. Similarly, traditionally male-dominated village assemblies have begun to include 15 to 30 per cent women. Legally, women in EPLF administered areas are treated as equals. Old traditional patriarchal marriage laws are being replaced with new democratic marriage laws that serve the interests and needs of both sexes, and women judges and implementers of the laws are already installed. New land tenure laws allow women to own plots of land, and labour laws which prescribe an equal labour market and equal wages for the same types of jobs are being adopted. There is no room for a gender-based division of labour within the EPLF departments. This approach is also being adopted by civilian institutions in the liberated areas. Skill training for women has been continuous, and efforts have been made to create job opportunities for women.

Women's involvement in EPLF structures

The following incomplete statistical figures from the Research and Information Department of the National Union of Eritrean Women (NUEW) show the percentage of women in EPLF units in 1989 and the range of their involvement.

Field of work	Participation by %
Front line combat fighters	23.0
Public administration	35.0
Industry	29.5
Transportation	25.9
Health	55.2
Construction	19.6
Agriculture	19.8
Electronics	25.0
National guidance	1.7
Finance	9.5
Communication	33.1

The above figures can be further broken down to show the extent and diversity of women's participation in every department (see page 70).

The shift in women's position from their traditionally restricted role to their extended involvement in the national struggle was not achieved without overcoming obstacles. Some of the first women fighters to join the EPLF were not welcomed in some of the commands they were assigned to until they proved that they were capable of doing what their male colleagues could do. Women's education or taking part in the armed struggle was in some areas regarded as contrary to religious norms. Some men of peasant background were reluctant to give up the small privileges they possessed, while some educated men felt insecure about their positions with the advancement of women. Some women were reluctant to enter new fields; others attempted to enter as quickly as possible, without considering the impact of rapid changes on their society. A case study carried out by NUEW shows that reforming marriage laws in Sheeb took up to eight years, while avoiding the circumcision of women in Rora Habab area took over four years. Similarly, land distribution to women and minorities who were not allowed to own land was preceded by many years of education on the right of every villager to own land and on the rights of women in general.

Women's Participation in EPLF Departments

Industry	%	Transportation	%
Metalwork	21.5	Mechanics	25.0
Electrical shop	23.9	Electricians	30.0
Woodwork	22.8	Drivers	1.3
Leather shop	29.6	Welders	18.0
Tailors	38.5		
Food factory	34.4	Construction	
Shoe factory	26.6	Auto mechanics	2.0
Sanitary napkin factory	42.5	Surveyors	7.0
		Carpenters	1.0
Health			
Doctors	8.3	Electronics	
Lab tech.	48.7	Researchers	20.0
Midwives	96.7	Data	20.0
Pharmacists	26.4	Comm. equip. repair	12.0
Dentists	88.8	Watch repair	30.0
Anaesthesia	77.7		
X-ray	20.0	Finance	
Barefoot doctors	43.0	Bookkeepers	12.4
OR tech.	87.5	Accountants	6.6
National guidance		Agriculture	
Journalists	0.5	Veterinary	30.0
Teachers	11.0	Agri. field workers	11.1
Publishing	1.5	Tractor drivers	5.8
Artists	1.7	Dairy	50.0
Handicraft	0.5	Agri. experts	2.3
Photography, video & film	1.5		
Broadcasting	0.3	Communication	
News writers	0.2	Communication workers	33.1
Documentation	0.2	Communication experts	9.8

With experience and time, women developed new skills and professions that helped broaden their thinking, and increase their self-discovery and awareness. The diversity and depth of women's participation in the Eritrean liberation movement is unique relative to other similar movements. Women in the EPLF are not just fighters, but also share their maternal duties and household work with their male compatriots. They are factory workers by day and armed base guards by night, or they are civil servants under relatively normal conditions and front-line combatants when war breaks out. Their action is significant with regard to educating and conscientizing the society, and they are prepared to provide assistance to the civilian population in case of need. Having opened their eyes to various activities, women have developed an eagerness to learn more and this strong will has facilitated their self-development and increased their self-confidence.

As the figures clearly show, however, women still represent a minority in many of the previously male-dominated jobs. Most of the fields are new to women. Fifteen years ago women never imagined they would work in these fields, nor were they permitted to do so. Currently women's participation in all fields is not controversial among the majority of the fighters or in many parts of the EPLF administered areas. Furthermore, many women never stop to think whether or not they are capable of doing a certain job when assigned to it; due to experience, women are confident and able to do every task given the right conditions. The responsibilities shouldered and gaps filled by women are well recognized by the Front and by the society as a whole, as is the necessity of engaging this force in the enormous task of reconstruction in the context of peace.

The role of the NUEW in empowering women

The National Union of Eritrean Women was founded in 1979 as a result of the efforts of the EPLF in its mass mobilization of the Eritrean population, and of experienced women fighters in the Front. The major aim of the Union is to organize and empower women through educational means in order to maximize their participation in the struggle. Social transformation is a pre-requisite for the democratization of the society and, consequently, for the transformation of women's status.

Without creating antagonistic attitudes between the sexes, NUEW runs programmes to promote grass-root women's self-discovery and awareness, and sponsors short- and long-term projects and education programmes that tackle women's immediate needs, change women's socio-economic, cultural and political positions, and develop their skills so that they can be more involved in developmental and administrative work. The Union also provides nutrition and health care education programmes, works on creating job opportunities for women, and is involved in the introduction of appropriate technology.

Finally, the achievements of Eritrean women in the EPLF are significant, but the final goal has not been reached. There is a continuous and determined effort by both women and the Front to keep the pace of women's progress going. The future will to a great extent depend on how wisely and determinedly women exploit the opportunities open to them, the extent to which they can preserve the achievements obtained so far, and the continuity of the democratic system of the EPLF. However, the process of women's emancipation has become deeply entrenched over the last three decades, and it cannot easily be reversed. Women, having gained awareness of themselves and having learnt the techniques for avoiding oppression as a result of their exposure to the struggle, will continue to safeguard their rights.

The position of women in the EPLF after independence

The rehabilitation of combatants, regardless of gender, will be a challenging issue for the government that takes power in Eritrea after independence. Eritrea, being impoverished by three decades of war and successive droughts, will be starting the process of reconstruction almost from scratch. Up to two million Eritreans are dependent on food aid as a result of the total failure of their harvests and the complete collapse of the job market. Furthermore, tens of thousands of displaced persons, the majority of whom are women, need to be rehabilitated. Given this reality, a country that aims to restore an effective economic structure and democratic political system cannot afford to discriminate against female combatants or women in general. The situation might even require an immigrant labour force from outside the country. Therefore, without even considering the fairness of the system which is to be restored, the situation in Eritrea is going to demand high personnel resources, including the full participation of women in various fields.

In the EPLF administrative system, which will greatly influence the new administration after independence, the tradition of allocating personnel according to their qualifications, with considerable gender sensitivity, has been practised for years. At present, the mayor of the Akeleguzay provincial capital, deputy mayors of two other provincial towns, head of the social affairs, co-head of the health institutions, head of the economic commission supply unit are some of the women who hold high-ranking administrative positions within the EPLF. Many others also work at various levels in the public administration, political and military institutions, and economic sectors. This tradition of engaging women according to their qualifications is very likely to continue in the administration of free Eritrea.

However, the position of women is not only the responsibility of the future administration. Women themselves, being aware of their roles and responsibilities, will exert pressure on the government and challenge social pressures, male dominance and all kinds of difficulties they might encounter in order to keep their present status. The new laws adopted, such as the land tenure laws, the marriage laws, the laws that give women equal opportunities in utilizing their potential in all fields, like any other citizen, will continue to exist in free and democratic Eritrea.

8

The Need for Gender Analysis:
A Comment on the Prospects for Peace, Recovery
and Development in the Horn of Africa[1]

AMINA MAMA

Those currently exploring the possibilities for post-conflict development in the Horn of Africa are paying very little attention to gender divisions in their societies, despite the fact that the oppression of women is as much a characteristic of all the cultures and the rapidly changing socio-political formations in the region as class and ethnic differentiations. If the sex of the scholars, researchers and policy makers currently planning the future development of this region is anything to go by, one could be forgiven for wondering how many women have survived the wars, droughts, famines and political strife that have characterized the recent history of the Horn. Since we know that a great many women have indeed survived and continue to do so, albeit under some of the harshest conditions on the African continent, then we must pose the questions beyond survival: what is the present situation and what is the nature of women's and men's potential participation in development efforts? Are these the same, or will they be gender differentiated? If they are to be gender differentiated, what are the bases on which this should be so, given the rapidly changing character of social and political life, and the acute needs of the region and its peoples?

The disturbing absence of women amongst the policy developers and analysts working in and running the countries of the Horn suggests that very few are in a position to participate in drawing up the plans for the future. This situation and the conditions under which it has emerged must be addressed. The experience of other African states is useful in this respect, and is, therefore, discussed here with reference to the economy (particularly agricultural development) and the participation of women in African state structures. It is hoped that even this brief intervention will draw attention to some of the likely costs and implications of conducting development work which does not fully acknowledge the changing gender dynamics of African societies. It is also intended to alert concerned researchers and policy makers to the existence of areas of research and policy that may be useful if they wish to avoid some of the errors that have resulted from gender blindness in African development planning, and the shortcomings of some of the strategies that have been deployed in the name of 'integrating women into development'.

Studies and research on African women:
Implications for planners and policy makers

Gender has been addressed in academia internationally under the heading of 'women's studies', and we have seen the development of gender consciousness in social research. Women's studies courses (and in some cases departments) have been set up in a number of African universities in recent years (in Uganda, the Sudan, Kenya, with plans being

72

discussed in Ethiopia, Ghana and Nigeria). The establishment of these is a result of the growth of women's studies internationally, and the increased availability of international funds since the UN Decade for Women (1975–1985). Women's Studies in universities provide an institutional base for redressing the historical neglect of women in academic work, and often have the additional spin-off effect of encouraging greater involvement of women in research and teaching by creating a space that is not as male-dominated as the rest of academia. If African centres of women's studies manage to resist being ghettoized and marginalized from the mainstream (as has tended to happen in the West), they offer an opportunity to stimulate greater gender awareness in the rest of academia, and so usefully contribute to the emergence of an intellectual culture suited to a more democratic post-colonial Africa.

At the present time only a minority of African social scientists exhibit gender awareness in their work, and most of these continue to be women. This is not a desirable situation because there are already so few women employed in African academic institutions that relying on them to redress the male bias is likely to compound their marginalization. Furthermore, if we accept that gender affects and structures the lives of men as well as women (albeit differently) in sexually differentiated societies, then revealing and analysing the production of male domination and its consequences for a society should not be the sole responsibility of women scholars.

The extent to which the knowledge and insights yielded by women's studies and gender analysis in academia can be made accessible and meaningful to African people and feed into national cultures remains to be seen. This will inevitably, as elsewhere in the world, be related to the political character of the societies and the role that educational institutions and intellectuals play in the rapidly changing circumstances of the region.

At present educational and cultural institutions in the countries of the Horn suffer from chronic underdevelopment and impoverishment, with gender inequality being manifested in different ways in different places at different times. As elsewhere in Africa, women continue to be denied equal access to education, and the higher one goes the more marked this inequality becomes. The education that they do get is constrained by ascribed notions of women's place in society which are counterproductive; it concentrates on the old colonial 'home economics model' of women's education, rather than on equipping women with the skills and scientific and technical expertise that is required for them to participate more equitably in the production and development of their societies. More specifically, women's access to education during the early years of independence in countries such as the Sudan increased, but this development has been subsumed by the Islamization policies of the present government. Separate women's universities (such as Ahfad University, which like the University of Khartoum offers specific courses in women's studies) provide one of the more acceptable avenues for the education of women under a repressive regime that has introduced complete segregation of the sexes and embarked on wholesale circumscription of women's access to public life. In contrast to this, in Somalia, where women are guaranteed equality by law, education has been desegregated for many years. The experience of Somalia indicates the way in which gender inequality can persist long after equality has been decreed by a dictatorship. It also raises deeper questions about the extent to which liberation can in fact be decreed by repressive regimes, and the motivations of the regimes making such decrees in the absence of democratization.

In the literature now being grouped under the heading of 'African women's studies'(Robertson, 1987) the countries of the Horn of Africa are underrepresented. Vast areas of great relevance to development planners working in this subregion are hardly touched upon. The few widely available (that is to say, Western published) books that do exist address the area of sexuality.[2] This is important, but when it is the main area of research and publication on women, there is a danger of reproducing societal constructions of women as primarily if not exclusively sexual, whose 'natural role' centres on procreation and child care. In the absence of reliable and systematically gathered information on women, gender assumptions and images of women are likely to be drawn from stereotypical media images which do no justice to the diversity and complexity of women's lives and gender relations. This dearth of information makes the task of development vulnerable to both fantasy and failure.

Furthermore, gender relations are undergoing rapid changes. Despite their oppression, even in the most highly segregated and patriarchal of our societies, women have been central to the survival and sustenance of the peoples of Africa over the centuries. Since policy cannot be drawn up and strategies cannot be developed in the absence of a sound information base, research and documentation are urgently needed if policy makers and strategists are to redress a situation in which women's oppression constitutes a major obstacle to democratization and development. This requires gender-sensitive methodologies and terms of reference in all research and information collection, as well as specific attention to women. Basic areas for such research include women's existing participation in socio-economic life, in agricultural and industrial production and in political processes. It must also include the role of gender differences – the ways in which women and men participate differently because of their different and varying positions in the societies under consideration. At this point we have little knowledge of women's lives, of their participation in the survival, production and reproduction processes in the Horn of Africa.[3]

The burgeoning research literature on African women has its own limitations, but these do not excuse the fact that existing research of great relevance is often ignored by policy makers and planners. For example, the omission of women from economic planning has long been identified as a major shortcoming of policies, plans and strategies. Moreover, gender blindness in economic development planning has been identified as adding to the subordination of women and worsening the exploitative terms under which women labour. We now know that from the micro-level of the household and small-scale production processes, through to the macro-level of national economic planning, gender divisions operate to texture and construct all aspects of labour and life, and so all aspects of people's participation in social life. If a concerted effort is not made to include this dimension, there is a danger that old errors will undermine existing and prospective development efforts in the Horn of Africa, as they have elsewhere in the region.

Women and state structures

Since the UN Decade for Women (1975–85) a number of African regional and national state structures have been set up in response to global resolutions. The 1974 Addis Ababa Plan of Action for the Integration of Women into Development was followed in 1980 by the World Plan of Action adopted in Copenhagen, and in 1985 the Women's Decade culminated in the Nairobi Declaration. The African Centre for Training and Research of Women (ACTRW) was established under the auspices of the United Nations Economic Commission for Africa (ECA) in 1975. Following this a number of governments have established women's desks, women's commissions or other structures. 'Integrating women into development' is now officially part of regional and national planning, and international funding has been available for women's projects (see Mama, forthcoming).

In the context of the political and economic crises that have continued to devastate much of the region, these structures have been unable to prevent a situation in which the quality of life for the majority of people in Africa has deteriorated rapidly through the 1980s. Within this situation, it is now commonly acknowledged that the situation of women, rendered vulnerable by their subordinate status, has worsened disproportionately. This is particularly evident in the countries of the Horn. Under these dire conditions, neither the structures for women nor the inclusion of a few individual women in decision-making and planning structures have effectively prevented the continued decline in the life chances of African women, or forestalled their continuing exploitation and marginalization.

Historical evidence suggests that, overall, African women have experienced increased subordination and marginalization, first with the establishment of colonial administrative structures, and subsequently in post-independence states. The almost complete exclusion of women from meaningful participation in independent states has been one of the defining characteristics of African state formation:

> Women have neither played a significant part in the creation of the modern state system on the continent, nor have they been able to establish regular channels of access to decision-makers. State policies towards women have, as a result, exhibited varying degrees of discrimination and coercion. (Chazan, 1989:187)

This spectacular exclusion has been variously attributed to the processes of class formation and capitalist penetration, the gendering of these processes, the complex and locally specific interplay of ideological, social, relational and administrative factors, and a range of other factors and dynamics.

It is clear that women's access to state structures and resources, and so to major areas of social, political and economic participation, has been heavily circumscribed, even where equality policies and women's structures exist. A great deal more in-depth research is needed on the processes (only some of which have been identified as yet) in each given context. However, there is nothing to suggest that the countries of the Horn of Africa will be better or worse than other African countries on this account. Each one faces a different situation. At the present time, women are experiencing steadily worsening repression in the Sudan, while in Somalia it is difficult to assess what the after effects of the ousted Barre regime's apparently progressive ('socialist') policies on women will be, given the wider context in which these were instituted. Whether the Eritrean People's Liberation Front and its militia will become central to the governance of Eritrea, and whether their active inclusion of women in power structures will be continued, or prove to have been merely instrumental means of coping with the demands arising from their specific situation, all remains to be seen. Gender inequality is not just perpetuated and reified at the level of the state, however, and it is worth looking at the terrain of social relations more generally in analysing gender processes.

Women and the economy

It is in consideration of the economy that gender research has made some of its most useful contributions. Studies of African gender relations during colonialism and throughout the post-colonial development era have generated insights so profound that they have influenced the whole field of women and development, both in research and in policies and planning. For example, the early work on women in agriculture drew attention to the fact that the division of labour was not a neutral process, but differentiated according to gender. The sexual division of labour, means that women and men often perform different tasks, just as the various class, ethnic and religious positionings of people have implications for their participation in and contribution to the economy. All these must be taken on in the documentation and analysis of prevailing situations if we are to engage in reality-based planning.

Gender blindness has often meant ignoring women's productive and reproductive work, both within the household and in the production processes outside the household (Boserup, 1970; Rogers, 1980). These 'discoveries' led to widespread criticism of the colonially imported 'home economics' model of development which failed to take account of the numerous tasks that African women perform in various spheres of economic life. It became common knowledge in development circles that this gender blindness and ignorance of women's contribution undermined their productive capacity.

Since most of the Horn is agrarian-based it is worth elaborating this point. Numerous studies and project appraisals have demonstrated that the failure to address which sex does what in African agriculture has often resulted in the failure of agricultural development projects which have assumed that 'the farmer' is male where the reality has been that women are farmers. Overlooking this fact has meant delivery of land, resources and technology to men, and an undermining of women's productive capacity by decreasing their access to land and their ability to command labour and resources. In many instances women farmers have been subordinated by this type of 'development'. Some have even been redeployed as wage labourers on the farms of their own husbands or other local men on more exploitative or completely unremunerated terms that have led to their marginalization and impoverishment. The EPLF's advanced land redistribution policy is unique in the degree to which it allows women to own and inherit land and improves their rights of access to land in the event of divorce, widowhood or not marrying (see Wilson, 1991).

Diane Elson's work on macroeconomics and the more recent structural adjustment programmes has highlighted the ways in which male bias in macroeconomics has not only undermined the possibility of sustainable development, but threatens the ability of many underdeveloped societies to reproduce themselves by so overtaxing women that even their invisible contributions to the maintenance and reproduction of the labour force may be eroded beyond repair.

> Male bias in macro-economics is not only bad for women, it is also bad for the prospects of setting in train a process of sustainable development.... There is a hidden set of assumptions underlying macro-economic thinking which is deeply imbued with male bias. This hidden set of assumptions concerns human ... reproduction and maintenance. It is assumed that human resources may be treated as if they were a non-produced factor of production, like natural resources and as if they were costlessly transferable between different activities. (Elson, 1991: 165, 166)

We now know that the penetration of capitalist production relations, wage economies and the accompanying emphasis on cash crop production and industrialization, has negatively affected the productive capacities of many African women and, by proliferating new class divisions or reifying old ones, has negatively affected less powerful groups – subsistence producers and small farmers (many of whom are women), widows and single women.

At a more general level, many African countries have experienced increased dependency and indebtedness, both locally and internationally. Women and men have contributed economically in many unacknowledged ways, in both the formal and informal sectors of the labour market, although men initially entered the formal waged sectors more than women. Furthermore, the predominantly male participation in the waged economy has itself depended upon women's contribution to their maintenance, upkeep and well-being through their domestic roles as housewives, daughters and mothers. In the context of falling real wage levels, this contribution has become proportionately larger, with women increasingly bearing the burden of subsistence production and income generating as well as reproductive and domestic labour.

The limited access that women did have to waged jobs is retracting in many countries. Women's access to waged work outside the household increased briefly after independence, but has subsequently been undermined. It cannot be coincidental that the calls for women to return to the home (often on religious grounds) have resurged during the economic crisis, when unemployment has risen. In any case, real wage levels have fallen so much that even if women are driven out of regular jobs in the formal sector, they are obliged to find other (often more exploitative) ways of earning incomes and continuing to contribute financially to the maintenance of their households. Very few African men are in a position to sustain one or more wives and their other dependents, even if this were to be a desirable situation.

In the Horn of Africa, the underdevelopment of the productive forces has had its own characteristics, but here too these have been gender differentiated. The various wars, for example, have meant gender differentiated mobilization of women and men, and this must have implications for demobilization. Where only men have been conscripted (as in the huge Ethiopian army) women have been affected in as yet unspecified ways by the voluntary and coerced absence of men from the household, from the community and the labour force. Where large numbers of women have been involved in military action, as in the case of Eritrea, the post-conflict situation will need to address persisting gender differences and the changes in gender relations in constructing possibilities for women, and for men. In short, the years of war will have changed gender relations in ways that are contingent on what their involvement over the past decades has been, and these will need to be thoroughly researched, analysed and taken into account in devising development strategies. Before we romanticize the Eritrean future, we would do well to remember the example of Algeria, which should caution us that even the much celebrated involvement of women in armed struggle does not necessarily translate into equality in a post-independence state. We now have enough experience to realize that the participation of women in nationalist movements does not necessarily or automatically carry over into more equitable participation of women in the independent states. More thorough analysis of the terms of their participation would perhaps have produced less of the shallow optimism, and then the disappointment, that the literature displays. What economic policies are to be developed to ensure the economic viability and therefore the survival of the large numbers of women (and their dependents) who do not have access to land, to education, to adequately remunerated work?

Conclusion

All major socio-economic questions require gender analysis if we are to be at all realistic. The strategies that women and men have been deploying to survive the ravages of the wars and conflicts racking the countries of the Horn will need to be assessed and documented to provide the information base on which more equitable development planning can rest.

Detailed case studies of women's changing participation and the changing gender relations in all the communities of the region in the post-independence period must be conducted if pessimistic simplifications or romantic optimism are to be avoided. The transformation of gender relations must be an integral part of the wider social transformation that must take place as a prerequisite for development in the interests of the people of the region.

Much will depend on the political changes and the economic circumstances of each country. In the Sudan and Ethiopia, which have existed as centrally governed but undemocratic states for a substantial period, the situation is, and will probably continue to be, very different from that in Eritrea, where social transformation has been initiated (intermittently, according to the progress and setbacks of the war) in the liberated areas. The considerations and prescriptions must also be different and based on thorough appraisals of the existing situations. Ultimately, gender questions, like class and nationality questions, are manifested in the distribution of power, resources and labour, and it is these that must be analysed in ways that take account of the objective realities of all of the people.

Notes

Special thanks to Amel Hamza, Zahra Siad and other participants of the ISS Women and Development Programme for discussions on women and education and women's studies in the Sudan, Somalia and other African countries, which have contributed to my thinking and to the writing of this commentary.

1   This comment follows up on the interventions made by six women (Mrya Geerling, Djamila Hamid, Samia El Hadi El Nagar, Wubnesh W. Selassie, Bunie Sexwale and myself) who attended the workshop and expressed concern about the low level of gender awareness characteristic of much of the thinking about post-conflict situations in the countries of the Horn of Africa.
2   See A. Cloudsley's 1983 *Women of Omdurman: Love and the Cult of Virginity*. In one year a single publisher brought out the only two books it has on women in the countries of the Horn and both were on the controlling practices of clitoridectomy and infibulation (El Dareer, 1982; Abdalla, 1982, both from Zed Books). Other books on African women brought out by the same publisher also concentrate on sexuality and culture (e.g. El Sadaawi, 1980; Amadiume, 1987), whereas other Zed publications on Africa tend to focus on political economy and to be completely gender blind.
3   At a recent conference of African social scientists, the neglect of gender considerations in social science research was identified as a major constraint on intellectual freedom and on the potential usefulness of African research to national and regional interests (Imam and Mama, forthcoming).

References

Abdalla, R.H.D. 1982. *Sisters in Affliction: Circumcision and Infibulation of Women in Africa*, London, Zed Books.

Amadiume, I. 1987. *Male Daughters, Female Husbands: Gender and Sex in an African Society*, London, Zed Books.

Boserup, E. 1970. *Women's Role in Economic Development*, UK, George Allen and Unwin.

Chazan, N. 1989. 'Gender perspectives on African states' in Parpart, J. and K. Staudt (eds.) *Women and the State in Africa*, Boulder, Lynne Rienner Publishers.

Cloudsley, A. 1983. *Women of Omdurman: Love and the Cult of Virginity*, London, Ethnographica.

El Dareer, A. 1982. *Woman, Why do You Weep? Circumcision and its Consequences*, London, Zed Books.

El Sadaawi, N. 1980. *The Hidden Face of Eve: Women in the Arab World*, London, Zed Books.

Elson, D. 1991. 'Male bias in macro-economics: The case of structural adjustment' in Elson D. (ed.) *Male Bias in the Development Process*, Manchester, Manchester University Press.

Fanon, F. 1965. *A Dying Colonialism*, London, Writers and Readers Publishing Co-op.

Imam, A. and A. Mama. (forthcoming) 'The role of intellectuals in limiting academic freedom' in CODESRIA *Academic Freedom and Social Responsibility of Intellectuals,* proceedings of Kampala symposium.

Kadr, S.A. 1987. *Egyptian Women in a Changing Society 1899–1987,* Boulder, Lynne Rienner Publishers.

Mama, A. (forthcoming) 'Gender and African development economics: Challenging the production and reproduction of women's subordination', Economic Commission for Africa.

Parpart, J. and K. Staudt (eds.) 1989. *Women and the State in Africa*, Boulder, Lynne Rienner Publishers.

Robertson, C. 1987. 'Developing economic awareness: Changing perspectives in studies of African women, 1976–1985' *Feminist Studies,* vol. 13, no. 1, pp. 97-135.

Rogers, B. 1980. *The Domestication of Women: Discrimination in Developing Societies*, London, Tavistock Publications.

Wilson, A. 1991. *The Challenge Road: Women and the Eritrean Revolution*, London, Earthscan.

AREAS OF POTENTIAL REGIONAL COLLABORATION AND JOINT MANAGEMENT OF RESOURCES

9   The Management of Water and Irrigation: The Blue Nile

TERJE TVEDT

Conflicts over the Horn of Africa's freshwater resources will certainly threaten future regional stability and co-operation. There has been a tendency for this issue to be neglected and overshadowed by perhaps more visible ethnic, religious and cultural conflicts. In order to identify potential areas of conflict and possible forms of co-operation, it seems useful to discuss some past experiences of control and allocation of Nile waters. The focus here is the relationship among the Blue Nile riparians: Egypt, the Sudan and Ethiopia.

Introduction

Nature has enthroned Ethiopia as the potential water power of the Horn of Africa. On the one hand the country commands all the big rivers; the Blue Nile (or Abbai), the Atbara and the Sobat, together with their tributaries, combined contribute more than 80 per cent of the waters of the main Nile. Furthermore, the Gash runs from Ethiopia into eastern Sudan, the Omo feeds Lake Turkana in Kenya, and the Dawa, the Shebele and the Juba water Somalia. On the other hand, Ethiopia is one of the poorest countries in the world – with a GNP per capita estimated at 115 US dollars – which suffers recurrent droughts and famines. Irrigated land accounts for about 1 per cent of cropland (World Resources, 1990:280). Installed hydro-electric capacity in 1987 was 230 megawatts, compared to a technical potential of 4,000 megawatts (World Resources, 1990:320).[1] Most likely intensified use of the water resources, including those of the Nile, will be put high on any national development agenda. With a population predicted to increase from an estimated 24.2 million (1960) to about 112 million in 2025 (World Resources, 1990:254), the government will face a growing demand to narrow the gap between the country's level of development, on the one hand, and its position as the region's water tower on the other.

The strongest political, economic and military power in the basin, Egypt, depends totally on its present share of Nile waters. The Egyptian government has for a long time considered development of hydraulic technology and water control a top priority. The introduction of perennial irrigation, symbolized by Mohamad Ali's decision to construct the Delta Barrage in the 1840s, revolutionized Egyptian agriculture, while the introduction of modern irrigation methods in the Sudan dates back to the development of the Zeidab concession in 1904. A British engineer in Cairo expressed an attitude predominant in the ruling circles of Cairo in the 1890s[2] when he hailed water planning as 'man's' effort to take the 'Nile in hand'. Human control over the Nile was boosted by British colonialism and was achieved through the construction of the Nasser Dam which transformed the river in Egypt into an irrigation ditch.[3] Egypt's total dependence on the Nile has resulted in a process of technological and agricultural change which, at the end of the twentieth century, has left Egypt with what in terms of international river jurisdiction is called 'established rights' to more than two-thirds of the entire flow of the river. This *downstream* state has, contrary to the norm in international river basins, been the strongest negotiator and by far the most favoured by past water sharing agreements. Among the upstream riparians, the Sudan has also been a beneficiary of past allocation agreements. The most profitable parts of Sudanese agriculture and the electrification of the country rely on utilization of the Blue Nile waters.[4]

To summarize the crux of the matter, more than 80 per cent of the flow of the Nile originates in Ethiopia, but that country utilizes less than 1 billion cubic metres (bm^3). Egypt contributes nothing, but is entitled to two-thirds of the waterflow. The Sudan is legally entitled to a little less than one-fourth of the waterflow, has large areas of irrigable land, but contributes only marginally to the riverflow. This imbalance between water contribution and water use will become increasingly contentious in the Blue Nile basin as a result of demographic, economic and developmental factors which are more or less independent of the will of the leaders of the countries concerned. Skilful and practical state management in all the riparian states is required if open hostilities and water wars are to be avoided, and negotiations and successful basin-wide agreements achieved.

These water problems in the Horn might become clearer if seen in a wider geopolitical and water-political context. Most observers agree that the world faces a water shortage. Peoples, nations and the world depend on a resource which is finite and very important from the viewpoint of power politics and conditions for peace: water is endlessly and continuously transcending international boundaries. Uneven development among riparians makes renegotiations of earlier agreements necessary and continuously legitimate, but reconciling different attitudes and perceptions has proven difficult. Rational management is threatened by real contradicting interests and by great perceptual differences between groups of actors.

Unfortunately there are no firm and well-established laws governing international river basins which could support co-operation and rational management of the Nile basin. This is not a minor issue as half the world's population lives in such international river basins. At this point only some broad guidelines exist and there have been some discernable changes in attitudes over time.

Until the middle of the nineteenth century the governing principle was the Harmon doctrine which permitted the riparian state a free hand in the exercise of its sovereignty over that portion of the international river which passed through its territory. Gradually the attitude that 'rights' should be accompanied by certain 'obligations' toward other riparian states received more prominence. The United Nations began preliminary studies on the issue in 1959 (Falkenmark, 1986), but the International Law Commission, an organ of the General Assembly of the UN, has had difficulties even in agreeing on the concept of an international river (Falkenmark, 1990). In Helsinki in 1966 the International Law Association, an NGO based in London, established a set of rules providing guidelines for the utilization and administration of international river basins. However, in 1973 when the UN General Assembly invited UNEP to develop guidelines, the draft principles forwarded to the General Assembly in 1978 were severely criticized by several upstream countries. The UN Conference on Water held in Mar del Plata, Argentina, in 1977 was also unable to reach an agreement on how to strike a balance between sovereignty and responsibility *vis-à-vis* neighbouring countries, differences in incentives between upstream and downstream countries, the problem of confidentiality of water data and so forth (Falkenmark, 1990). This lack of success reflects the differences between the perceptions held by upstream and downstream states, and the contradictory interests which are difficult to reconcile when such vital interests are at stake.

The many water wars since the Second World War testify to this difficulty. Pakistan came into conflict with India over Indus, Israel and Jordan/Lebanon clashed over the Jordan and Litani rivers, Iraq struggled against Iran over Shatt al-Arab, Sikhs stood up against New Delhi over the national water allocation policy, and so on. One recent example which might indicate some of the difficulties facing rational planning and co-operation in international river basins is the conflict over Eufrat and Tigris between Turkey, Syria and Iraq. Turkey, as the upstream state, has controlled the water as if it were national property. In January 1990, Turkey unilaterally withheld water from the rivers in order to fill the Atatürk Dam. The country justified the action on the basis of rational hydrological arguments, but other states considered the act as one of employing water as a weapon against Syrian support of the Kurds in Turkey. The Atatürk Dam will reduce the flow downstream and thus affect the economies of Syria and Iraq and, what is perhaps more important in the power politics of the region in the long run, it will symbolize who has the strategic upper hand in the basin.[5]

Hydrological characteristics and the potential for conflict

The potential for conflicts over the uses of the Blue Nile and its tributaries cannot be explained without presenting some basic hydrological data. The River Nile has a basin area of about 2.3 million km^2, extending from 4° south to 31° north. It includes the whole of Uganda, almost all the cultivated land of Egypt, one third of Ethiopia, a substantial portion of the Sudan, and parts of Rwanda, Burundi, Tanzania, Zaire, and Kenya. The river is the longest in the world, but its waters are relatively modest compared to other great river systems. When entering Egypt the main Nile, according to official measurements at Aswan, carries on average a little more than 80 bm^3 annually. This amount is not more than that of the Rhine, whose length is only one-fifth of the Nile's 6,825 km. The Amazon carries 3,000 bm^3 annually, or more than 35 times that of the Nile, while the Congo discharges 1,400 bm^3 annually. This contradiction between extreme length and modest discharge increases the potential for water stress and provides ample grounds for competition among autonomous interest-maximizing actors experiencing a growing water demand.

Table 1   The Nile in Comparison with Other Major River Systems

River	Length (km)	Drainage (km^2)	Annual discharge (bm^3)
1. Nile	6,825	3,100,000	84
2. Amazon	6,700	7,050,000	3,000
3. Congo	4,700	3,700,000	1,400
4. Mekong	4,200	795,000	400
5. Niger	100	1,890,000	180
6. Zambesi	2,700	15,300,000	500
7. Rhine	1,320	162,000	80

The problem is further aggravated by other hydrological characteristics such as varying annual and seasonal fluctuations in water discharge, long-term scenarios regarding total water flow, and the role of the main tributaries within the hydrological system. The mean annual discharge for the period 1871–1953 was 92.4 bm^3, but from 1871–1901 the mean was 107 bm^3. From 1899 to 1959 it was about 84 bm^3 according to the 1959 Nile Waters Agreement accepted by both the Egyptians and Sudanese. During the early 1970s the mean annual discharge was close to 90 bm^3 as a result of high years in the 1960s, but for the past decade (1977–87) it was recorded at 72 bm^3. From 1984 to 1987 the mean flow was about 30 per cent of the average annual flow during the decade. The standard deviation from the mean has been almost 20 bm^3. The maximum flow was measured in 1878–9 when the total discharge was 150 bm^3, and the minimum years, 1913–14 and 1984–5, yielded 42 bm^3. The dramatic fluctuations in river discharges have repeatedly demonstrated the riparians' degree of vulnerability, and have thereby underlined the need for water control.

The Blue Nile and Atbara contribute about 70 per cent of the total annual discharge of the River Nile, while the White Nile carries the rest. The Blue Nile collects its flow from Lake Tana (7 per cent) and from the Didessa, Dabus, Fincha, and Balas tributaries, among others, before reaching the Sudan where the river is fed by Dinder and Rahad, (both of which have headstreams on the Ethiopian plateau). It has its maximum flow in August when it can discharge as much as 60 times its low season discharge. The Atbara, with its main tributary the Setit, also carries a torrential discharge, but of about one-quarter the volume of the Blue Nile. Compared with these, the White Nile brings a steady waterflow northwards. It has its headwaters in the Equatorial lakes, the most distant source being the river Luvironza, a tributary to the Kagera River which is the main supplier of Lake Victoria.[6] The maximum discharge of the White Nile is generally no more than three times that of the low season. Most of this variation is caused by the Sobat which is fed by the Baro and Pibor tributaries. The Sobat is, therefore, another tributary with an Ethiopian catchment area.

The role of rivers as a potential source of conflict is, of course, related to their importance for the riparians. The importance of the different Nile tributaries for Egypt and northern Sudan has been reflected in changes in the countries' water technology and irrigation economies. After the introduction of year-round irrigation in the nineteenth century and during the period of British rule in Cairo, water planners regarded the White Nile as the river of importance for Egypt.[7] The aim was to even-out natural fluctuations by storing excess water from the period of surplus and releasing it during the period of shortage. Much of the water of the Blue Nile and Atbara was, for technical reasons, thought to be not storable. The silt that inspired the saying of Herodotus, 'Egypt is the gift of the Nile', and which made the Blue Nile the river of importance during the many thousands of years of basin irrigation, created insurmountable problems for engineers aiming at perennial irrigation.[8] Only the tail-end of each flood could be stored if the reservoirs were to be prevented from silting up. A big dam on the main Nile, like that later built by Nasser, was thus partly opposed by the British in Egypt. But, since an increased water supply was a central aim of the British, the existence of this silt influenced the direction of their Nile valley policy and the focus of their regional diplomacy, and it has consequently influenced the relationship between Egypt and Ethiopia to the present.[9]

By the early 1890s the British government in Cairo had already proposed to dam the Equatorial lakes.[10] It was claimed that by raising the water level of Lake Victoria (covering almost the same area as Scotland) by one meter, Egypt would be guaranteed a discharge of 'fully 30 times more than is wanted' (Ross, 1893:189). But, as was already known then, in the extensive swamps in southern Sudan the river flow is reduced considerably due to a complex interaction of topography, swamp ecology and flooding patterns.[11] The annual amount of water retained in the swamps is proportional to the discharge of the Bahr al-Jabal at Mongalla, on average about 13 bm³. In other words, the losses rise as the inflow into the swamps increases. By improving the White Nile river channel the amount of water in the White Nile downstream could be increased in the so-called 'timely season' (that is, in the summer season when water was most scarce, especially after the rapid expansion of cotton cultivation) both by reducing the losses in the swamp area itself and by bringing more water down from the Equatorial lakes.[12] Because of these prospects, Britain, and later Egypt and the Sudan, planned for about 90 years to change the course of the Nile in southern Sudan. The optimistic plans formulated in the 1970s and 1980s hoped to increase the flow of the river by close to 20 bm³ per year.[13] Such gigantic projects are in the present political and economic situation unrealistic, but the existence of the plans has kept Egypt's focus on the White Nile.

Some recent trends have increased the water stress. Reports suggest that unchecked growth of the water hyacinth in the Nile in the Sudan, discovered for the first time in the late 1950s, results in a yearly loss of up to 10 per cent of the river's water yield. The past fluctuations in the Nile's discharge will probably not be lessened in the future. On the contrary, research suggests that as a consequence of the greenhouse effect there may well be an increase in these fluctuations in the Nile basin, and the generation of quite a different seasonality in the contributions to the main Nile's discharge (Hulme, 1990:72).

Perhaps it will increase the precipitation over the inter-lacustrine region while reducing it over the Ethiopian plateau. The severe droughts in the 1970s and 1980s worsened the already critical food situation in the upper parts of the Nile basin. It is possible that long periods of low Nile floods, as experienced from 930 AD to 1070 AD and 1180 AD to 1350 AD, might be repeated.

Not surprisingly, the establishment of proper control and management of water for both horizontal and vertical expansion of agriculture has, by many, been put forward as the future solution. North of 15° north in the Sudan the rainfall is less than 200 mm, and the Cairo area receives about 18 mm annually. In these areas irrigation is the only means of sustaining agricultural activities. In central Sudan, between 200 mm and 800 mm isohyets, irrigation is very important owing to the unreliability of the rainfall. Winter crops, such as long staple cotton, legumes, wheat, fruit, and garden crops, can only be grown on irrigated land. The total area suitable for irrigation in the Sudan has been estimated at more than four million hectares and, in addition to this area, there is an extensive clay plain in southern Sudan. In the rest of the Nile basin rainfall has on average been more than 800 mm per year, but here irrigation is also considered very productive as relatively small inputs can reduce the unreliability of the rainy season. Irrigation has, however, not been extensively developed in the upstream countries (see Table 2).

The first preliminary surveys for possible water works in the Blue Nile and Sobat basins were conducted from 1958 to 1964 by the Ethiopian government, with the assistance of the US Bureau of Reclamation. The surveys indicated the possibility of developing about 434,000 hectares with an annual estimated water requirement of 6 bm³. The schemes were primarily located in the plateau valleys around Lake Tana, on the Sudanese-Ethiopian frontier, and on the Anger and Fincha tributaries (Bureau of Reclamation, 1964). The four major Ethiopian hydro-electric projects would have an initial active storage capacity of about 51 bm³ and an annual electricity generation of over 25 billion kwh, or about three times the actual production of the Aswan High Dam (Whittington, 1985:4). But, as the title of the report indicates, this study covered only *Land and Water Resources of the Blue Nile Basin: Ethiopia*. There are, however, a large number of smaller tributaries in the upper parts of the Blue Nile catchment where there are 'extremely convenient sites' which have not yet been surveyed (Jovanovic, 1985:82). For instance, the tributaries of the White Nile – Baro, Ghilo and Akobor – have not been studied, nor have the Atbara, Takazze and Mareb Gash tributaries of the main Nile in Ethiopia, except in a report issued by an Italian consulting company which was based on aerial reconnaissance. The government has made proposals for diverting the Setit river, a tributary of Atbara, to develop 70,000 feddans, requiring about 300 million m³ of water per year (Ibrahim, 1984:102). Consultants employed by the Ethiopian government have put forward proposals for irrigation that would deprive the Sudan and Egypt of '23 per cent of today's available water if Ethiopia irrigates land inside the Nile catchment only, and 39 per cent if irrigation is extended to land outside the Nile catchment' (Jovanovic, 1985:84–5).

The irrigable area in the Tanzanian Nile basin has been estimated at 120,000 feddans, and as requiring an annual water supply of 500 million m³. In 1978, the Kagera Basin Organisation (KBO) estimated the possible irrigated land areas in the Kagera tributary and in the Victoria basin outside the Kagera basin, that is in Burundi, Rwanda and Tanzania, to be about 1 million hectares (KBO, 1978:70). The irrigable area in Uganda has been estimated to be about 1 million acres, and as requiring about 1.5 bm³ of water annually. Kenya's potential remains uncertain. The above assessments are, of course, dependent on the choice of technology, whether intra-basin transfers are considered or not and, primarily, on considerations of internal economic capabilities and donor interests. Water technology is developing very rapidly. Kenya, a contributor of water to the Nile through the six rivers which flow into Lake Victoria, and as a country in which two-thirds of the land is classified as arid or semi-arid, has discussed plans for inter-basin water transfers. In Ethiopia there has been discussion of a proposal which suggests diverting the Blue Nile into the Awash catchment by drilling a very long tunnel (Jovanovic, 1985:84). That such projects are possible has been demonstrated by Libya's Great Man-Made River, which takes water from the Nubian sandstone aquifer in southern Libya and transports it to the coast through a 4,000 km system of underground pipelines. This technological accomplishment demonstrates how natural constraints can be overcome and the potential for water transfers. It also demonstrates, however, how this can increase the potential for conflict.

Table 2 Cropland and Irrigation, 1975–87

Land	Cropland total area (hectares) 1987	Cropland (hectares per capita) 1989	Irr. land as percentage of cropland 1975–7	Irr. land as percentage of cropland 1985–7
Burundi	1,332,000	0.25	4	5
Egypt	2,560,000	0.05	100	100
Ethiopia	13,930,000	0.30	1	1
Kenya	2,420,000	0.10	2	2
Rwanda	1,120,000	0.16	0	0
Sudan	12,478,000	0.51	14	15
Tanzania	5,230,000	0.20	1	3
Uganda	6,705,000	0.38	0	0
Zaire	6,690,000	0.19	0	0

Source: Adapted from *World Resources 1990–1991*: 280–1.

Secondly, the oil embargo of October 1974 and the rapidly escalating cost of oil signalled the end of the era of cheap energy. The Gulf war of 1991 demonstrated again that oil is an uncertain, conflict ridden and costly source of energy. Global concerns about the environmental effects of fossil fuels have directed the attention of both donors and governments to hydro-electric developments. This combination of factors will focus more attention on hydro-electric schemes in the Nile basin. Table 3 shows the discrepancies on a national level between installed capacity and technical potential for hydro-electric production in the Nile valley countries.[14]

The installed capacity of all the hydro-electric power projects in the Nile basin represents only about 18 per cent of the potential capacity. The hydro-electric potential, if fully developed, would be expected to generate about 80,000 GWH a year, which is almost equivalent to the rest of Africa's hydro-electric production (Ibrahim, 1984:104). Currently the average consumption of energy is thought to equal about 115 kg of petroleum per capita. (That of the industrialized countries is more than 3,500.) Hydro-electric power stations do not withdraw much water from the river system used and the Nile is, of course, not the only possible source of hydro-electric energy. In the Blue Nile basin it is central from a technical point of view that such projects should not cause concern downstream. However, as the prolonged negotiations between Egypt and British Uganda over the Owen Falls dam showed in the 1940s, downstream states want to have guarantees as to the management of hydro-electric power stations.[15]

Thirdly, the sharp rise in population increases demand on available water resources, not only in the agricultural and industrial sectors, but also in terms of domestic water use. The rates of population growth in the countries concerned are above 3 per cent per year. If a population doubles, the maximum per capita availability of water decreases to 50 per cent of its present level. The figures for population increases in the basin countries (see Table 4) are, of course, uncertain and partly 'guestimates', but still they demonstrate the magnitude of the problem. The total population of the basin countries is thought to have increased from about 105 million in 1965 to approximately 245 million in 1990, and it is expected to grow to 614 million in 2025. In Egypt the per capita crop area decreased from 0.73 feddan in 1821, to 0.29 feddan in 1975. Over the same period the cropped area more than trebled. In this country the population increases by one million every ninth month, and the country already imports more than 50 per cent of its food. Time will also change the demographic profile within the basin as projected population increases show that in 2025 Ethiopia will be by far the most populous country.

Table 3 Hydroelectric Resources

Land	Technical potential (megawatts)	Installed capacity 1987 (megawatts)
Burundi	289	12
Egypt	3,210	2,700
Ethiopia	4,000	230
Kenya	814	354
Rwanda	600	56
Sudan	380	225
Tanzania	4,000	259
Uganda	1,200	156
Zaire	120,000	2,486

Source: Adapted from *World Resources 1990–1991*: 320–1.

Table 4 Size and Growth of Population

Land	Population (millions)		
	1960	1990	2025
Burundi	2.9	5.5	13.1
Egypt	25.9	54.1	94.0
Ethiopia	24.2	46.7	112.3
Kenya	6.3	25.1	77.6
Rwanda	2.7	7.2	18.1
Sudan	11.2	25.2	59.6
Tanzania	10.0	27.3	84.8
Uganda	6.6	18.4	55.2
Zaire	15.9	36.0	99.5

Source: Adapted from *World Resources 1990–1991*: 254–5.

The present water demand is close to the maximum level sustainable but, while Egypt is utilizing more than it is entitled to, the Sudan is using less than 70 per cent of its 18.5 bm^3 share. Ethiopia, like the other upstream states, is using almost no Nile water. This is water to which, moreover, this country has no legal rights.

It is easy to be alarmist in assessing the future of Nile water use. Water planners have been crying 'wolf' at least since the 1890s. As early as 1893 the former British Inspector General of the Egyptian Irrigation Service wrote that the 'available natural supply has been completely exhausted' (Ross, 1893:188). The greatest authority on the Nile this century, H.E. Hurst, warned in 1946 that 'it is obvious that preparation for what is sometimes called "the far future" must be begun now.... In fact we may say that the "far future" is already upon us' (Hurst, Black & Simaika, 1946:9). John Waterbury projected that a water shortage of great but varying severity was likely to occur during the 1980s and beyond (Waterbury, 1979).

As developments have shown, this pessimism in the 1890s and 1940s was, on the whole, unwarranted mainly due to the introduction of new and improved dam building technology, such as was used in the construction of the first Aswan Dam in 1902, and the Nasser Dam which opened in 1971, and which had the capacity to store the entire Nile discharge for two successive years. In the 1970s and 1980s water demand did not reach predicted levels mainly due to economic and political crises in the countries concerned. Projects which would have increased the Sudan's water demand by close to 10 bm^3 could not be implemented because of both political and financial reasons and, therefore, attention was given to the rehabilitation of existing projects. The other riparians have also been burdened by political instability, debt and a lack of money for investment in costly irrigation and hydro-electric projects.

The Nile is a finite resource and the potential for relieving pressure on the water through controlling its flow is limited (except for the Sudd-projects).[16] The potential for a new technological revolution in Nile control (similar to those of 1902 and 1971) as the answer to predicted increases in levels of demand is illusory. The internal conflicts in the Sudan, Uganda and Ethiopia have, from this point of view, helped to postpone possible inter-state conflicts over the Nile waters.

It has been argued that Egypt has realized its future resource situation, and will try to meet its growing food requirements from imports rather than from utilization of Nile waters (Allan, 1990:184). The government has announced its resolution to give priority to the modernization of its old, inefficient irrigation system, and thus to focus on increasing the efficiency of its water use. But Egypt has, in the same period, put forth the idea of irrigating the Sinai with Nile waters, arguing that north of Cairo the Nile has a drainage basin which extends eastward to the Sinai mountains. These mixed signals might indicate Egyptian uncertainty about how to adapt to the present and future water situation. At a conference in Cairo in June 1989 it was, however, reported that additional water resources have been discovered. The study revealed that there is perhaps twice the previous estimate of the quantity of underground water in the driest part of the Egyptian desert (*Time International*, 1990:40).[17] In the long run this new resource might liberate Egypt from its total dependency on Nile waters and may reduce the water scarcity in the basin. The Nile will, however, because of economic and technological circumstances, remain the region's main resource and Egypt's life-blood.

Regional considerations and agreements

How will the Nile basin countries and their political leaders react to a situation where the gap between water demand and supply most likely will increase, and where difficulties might be aggravated because there are no clear international rules to guide and curtail their actions? Certainly their reactions will not be based on hydrological factors alone, but will be influenced by past experiences, levels of mutual understanding, psychology, geopolitical considerations, and so forth. The political importance and role of 'hard' hydrological data is, of course, related to the circumstances in which such data become important. For instance, where hydrological conditions would benefit from co-operation, conflicts can still prevail due to 'soft' factors such as distrust, or a lack of understanding. Some of the most important Ethiopian plans for the Blue Nile, for example, would, on balance, not have detrimental effects on the waterflow downstream. On the contrary, it has been argued that a reservoir at Lake Tana would be a more rational site for water storage than the High Aswan Dam (Whittington, 1985). Evaporation would be reduced considerably; currently more than 10 bm^3 of water evaporates from Lake Nasser in Egypt and Lake Nubia in the Sudan every year. Egypt's opposition to such a reservoir upstream as a replacement for the High Aswan Dam is, however, based on the country's fear of losing national control of its most important resource, a fear continuously nurtured by Egypt's vulnerable geopolitical situation.

Although our focus is the Blue Nile basin and the Horn, the nature of the river system makes a discussion confined to this geographical area insufficient. The relationship between Ethiopia, Egypt and the Sudan will be affected by developments in water withdrawals, hydraulic technology and political relations in and among the White Nile states. Water sharing and water planning problems are, therefore, regional in the broadest sense of the term: what takes place in the Kagera basin directly affects Ethiopia's options and *vice versa*. And, if the Jonglei Project Phase I and Phase II and the other projects for draining the Marchar marshes and improving the Bahr al-Arab should succeed in increasing the supply of water by about 20 bm³, an amount which the Sudan and Egypt could share on an equal basis between themselves, then the pressure on the Blue Nile waters would be relieved.[18] An Ethiopian decision to withdraw water from the Blue Nile or the Setit would, in such a situation, be less harmful. If, on the other hand, big water works were constructed in, for example, the remote inter-lacustrine region in Tanzania or Kenya for the use of these upstream states, then Egypt's dependency on a secure and steady Nile supply from Ethiopia would grow. Any plans Ethiopia had for utilizing water from the Blue Nile, Sobat or Atbara would be threatening to both Egypt and the Sudan. Also, if Ethiopia started to implement some of the plans drawn up for withdrawing Nile waters, the total amount to be shared among the other eight riparians would be equally reduced. Possibilities for stability and peace in the Horn of Africa are, therefore, intimately connected to developments in the 'Heart of Africa'. In this way there exists a fundamental interdependence among the Nile basin countries. The river is a potential source of both co-operation and conflict.

The question of control of the Nile waters has, for centuries, affected political relationships among upstream and downstream states in the basin.[19] Well known are the alleged threats made by the Ethiopian Emperor, Tekle Haimanot (1706–8), *vis-à-vis* Egypt: 'if we are inclined to revenge, the Nile could be sufficient to punish you since God has put into our hands this fountain' (in Budge, 1970:433). The Egyptians, in turn, could refuse to appoint new leaders of the Koptic church when they thought the water was diverted deliberately. Partly with the aim of liberating Egypt from its vulnerable geopolitical position, Khedive Ismail employed a military strategy which aimed to make the entire Nile an Egyptian river.

The Nile waters played a crucial role in the imperial strategy of Britain and Cromer, their 'puppet master in Egypt'. The British perceptions of the Nile and its tributaries strongly influenced how the continent was partitioned among the European powers (see Tvedt, 1987). Not only Tekle Haimanot, but also the British explorer and imperialist Samuel Baker argued in favour of a policy of exerting control over Egypt by threatening the country from an upstream position. Already in 1884 he urged the British to conquer the Nile upstream, after they had occupied Egypt in 1882, because: 'The Arabs have drunk at these wells [the Nile] for thousands of years. Erect a fort so as to command the wells, and the Arabs are at your mercy. No water, no Arabs' (Baker, 1884).

Since the occupation of Uganda in 1894, and of the Sudan in 1898, and up until the Suez crisis in 1956, London was well aware of Britain's upstream position and the possibilities which that provided for exerting pressure on Egypt. At the same time, and especially when faced with European competitors, Britain (and later Egypt, to counteract British plans) tried to establish the principle that no upper basin state had the right to interfere with the flow of the Nile. This paper cannot go into these historical questions in detail, but will refer briefly to some of the most important treaties and agreements.[20]

In March 1891, Italy and Britain signed a protocol for the demarcation of their spheres of influence in eastern Africa. A provision in Article III stipulated that 'the Government of Italy undertakes not to construct on the Atbara any irrigation or other works which might sensibly modify its flow into the Nile' (British Foreign Office, 1920:93–4). On 15 May, 1902, King Menelek of Ethiopia signed an agreement with Britain regarding the frontiers between Anglo-Egyptian Sudan, Ethiopia and Eritrea. Article III provided:

His Majesty the Emperor Menelek II, King of Ethiopia, engages himself towards the Government of His Britannic Majesty not to construct or allow to be constructed, any work across the Blue Nile, Lake Tana or the Sobat, which would arrest the flow of their waters into the Nile except in agreement with his Britannic Majesty's Government and the Government of the Sudan. (Gleichen, 1905:295)

In 1925 Italy recognized, in an exchange of letters with Britain, 'the prior hydraulic rights of Egypt and the Sudan', and agreed that it would not construct on the head-waters of the Blue Nile, its tributaries or affluents 'any work which might sensibly modify their flow into the river' (in Okidi, 1982:170). Ethiopia, both under Haile Selassie and Mengistu, obviously has questioned the validity of the agreements and opposed the notion that they are binding (see Tilahun, 1979); the arguments, among others, being that none of these treaties mentioned anything about Ethiopia's 'natural rights' to a certain share of the water and that Britain, by recognizing the annexation of the Ethiopian empire by Italy, invalidated all previous agreements between the two countries.[21]

The 1929 Nile Waters Agreement between Egypt and Britain did not deal explicitly with the Blue Nile head-waters. The Sudan was given 4 bm^3, and the complete flow of the 'timely' water from January 20 to July 15 each year was the preserve of Egypt. Within this context, Egypt raised the Aswan Dam in 1933 and constructed the Jebel Aulia Dam on the White Nile, and the Sudan developed the Gezira scheme. Most important in relation to these water works are the arguments put forth by the President of the Egyptian Council of Ministers in paragraph 4(b) of his note to Lord Lloyd, the British High Commissioner in Cairo, and accepted by the latter:

> Save with the previous agreement of the Egyptian Government no irrigation or power works or measures are to be constructed or taken on the River Nile and its branches, or on the lakes from which it flows, so far as these are in the Sudan or in countries under British administration, which would, in such a manner as to entail any prejudice to the interests of Egypt either reduce the quantity of water arriving in Egypt, or modify the date of its arrival, or lower its level.

The status of the 1929 Agreement, as well as the agreements between Britain, King Menelek and Italy, have stimulated discussion. Some of the upstream states support the Nyerere Doctrine on state succession treaties, a doctrine formulated in 1962 which opposes the view which implies that the independent sovereign Tanzania should inherit the Nile agreement applied to territories under British colonial administration. On 21 November 1963, Egypt replied in a Note that, pending further agreement, the 1929 Agreement 'remained valid and applicable' (in Okidi, 1990:202). Egypt and the Sudan have argued in line with their interpretation of Articles 11 and 12 of the Vienna Convention of 1978 about State Succession and Treaties. They claim that treaties dealing with the delineation of international boundaries or with territorial status remain valid and that the obligations are to be carried by successor states.[22]

The most recent and important agreement was the Agreement for the Full Utilization of the Nile Waters signed by Egypt and the Sudan in 1959. Despite the name of the agreement, representatives of seven out of nine countries were not sitting at the negotiating table. Seen from the perspective of the absent riparians, the main feature of this agreement was that they were excluded. Nevertheless it has endured the stresses and strains of political upheaval since 1959, and thus has proven to be an accomplishment. It provided for the annual allocation of the whole flow after evaporation was deducted. Of the total annual flow of 74 bm^3, Egypt was allotted 55 bm^3 and the Sudan 18.5 bm^3; any increase in the natural flow of the river should be shared equally. In addition, the costs of upper Nile projects were to be shared on an equal basis, compensation was to be paid to the Sudan for the movement of the Nubians from the site of the Nasser Dam, and a Permanent Joint Technical Commission was to be established. In the Sudan the Khasm el-Girba on the Atbara and the Roseires Dam on the Blue Nile, both completed in 1966, were a consequence of the agreement.

The 1959 Agreement has been considered 'one step in a long road' toward a multilateral agreement by the Sudan and Egypt (Khalid, 1984:11). Some upstream states, however, have not wanted any new agreements on Nile allocation because they regard themselves as weak in terms of negotiating strength; they are not yet as economically developed as the Sudan and Egypt, and do not have equivalent international political status. Some of the countries have not even formulated national water management plans. This resistance to a new basin-wide agreement should not simply be interpreted as a sign of bad will, but should be seen as arising from emphasis on interest-maximizing policies which prioritize national development.

Some of the riparians have moved toward what has been called an 'integrated approach'. In August 1967, Egypt and the Sudan agreed jointly with the governments of Rwanda, Burundi, Kenya, Tanzania, and Uganda to undertake joint hydro-metereological surveys of the catchments of the central African lakes. The declared aim of the surveys was to carry out studies and collect data which could assist the participating countries in planning water conservation and development. The governments of the Sudan and Egypt have particularly underlined the preambular part of the plan of operations which stipulates that the project also 'provides the groundwork for *intergovernmental cooperation in the storage and regulation and use of the Nile*' (Khalid, 1984:20). This statement has been interpreted as one which 'indicates clearly the future trend in Nile water management' (Khalid, 1984:20). In 1977 the Sudan and Egypt proposed to establish a Nile Basin Commission comprising all nine states of the Nile valley. Some steps have been taken in this direction, partly through the Endugu grouping[23] which Egypt especially has held out as an example of how co-operation can be organized.

Conclusion

Different proposals for a comprehensive Nile waters treaty have been put forth. Such a treaty could perhaps have been negotiated and signed in the first decades of British rule, when London controlled most of the valley from the central African lakes to the Mediterranean, but since the 1930s there have been few opportunities for achieving agreement on such a treaty. This holds also for the foreseeable future as the different riparians disagree on too many basic issues, including the need for negotiations or renegotiations. Some say that what is needed is a renegotiation of previous agreements, while others claim that there are no such previous agreements to renegotiate. Whether previous agreements are binding has itself been a conflictual issue. Some of the upstream states have favoured the postponement, rather than rejection, of new agreements so as to prevent the present allocation pattern from being perpetuated indefinitely. No single institution has either been delegated the overall responsibility of developing a comprehensive overview, or has acquired sufficient competence to act.

Given the uneven development of the states in the Nile basin, the historical relations and experiences, and the level of mutual distrust between some of the riparians, it is not likely that one such institution can be established in the near future. Consequently, others argue that the most efficient way of promoting co-operation and avoiding conflicts is to have a more modest, but perhaps more realistic aim: the riparians should try to create an atmosphere of co-operation step by step, and institutionalize this co-operation in a wide range of areas. One aim could be to establish forums for discussions and a code of conduct relevant to the formulation of national development plans and policies. What is needed is progress in other areas such as communication, regional trade, cultural interaction, and in the solution of the remaining boundary problems.[24]

It is also important that donor agencies internalize the understanding that the Nile waters are finite resources. Waterbury (1979) has illustrated the unfounded optimism of aid agencies regarding water supplies in Egypt. This lack of realism regarding the developments which the river Nile can stimulate and sustain has also been widespread among agencies working upstream. The Kagera Basin Organisation, Hafslund Engineering, Norconsult, the World Bank and other consultancy firms and aid organizations have drawn up plans partly disregarding both the international character of the river and its finite resources.[25] Future Nile development cannot be expected to proceed along the lines previously planned, neither upstream nor downstream in the Blue Nile basin.

Notes

1 The exactness of the figures in *World Resources* is highly questionable. For a discussion on the problems of such aggregated data collections see Hill, 1986. Data on electrification and irrigable land tend, however, to be more exact than data on living standards and so forth. For the broad comparative purposes of this article they can safely be used.

2 Quotations from Colin Scott-Moncrieff (1895), the Under-Secretary of State for Public Works in the first decade of Lord Cromer's rule.

3 For a discussion on developments of Egyptian irrigation during the first decades of British colonialism, see Tvedt, 1990:108–22.

4 The products of irrigated agriculture based on Nile waters (mostly Blue Nile waters) accounted in the beginning of the 1980s for 40 per cent of GDP, 40 to 50 per cent of government revenue, and about 90 per cent of export earnings. Hydro-electric installations generated about 70 per cent of the total power supply.

5 In the industrialized world there is, due to climatic and developmental conditions, a tendency to focus on water quality rather than quantity. In the World Commission on Environment and Development report, *Our Common Future* (1987), the problem of international rivers and conflicts over water as a scarce resource is not mentioned at all. The general message is that water is an ubiquitous substance like air, the foremost problem being its quality.

6 As the International Law Commission could not agree on the boundaries of a river basin, Egypt and the other White Nile riparians have disagreed on whether Luvironza belongs to the Nile basin, and consequently whether Tanzania has a pertinent claim on Nile waters. This issue shows that the Sudan and Egypt also can disagree regarding conditions upstream. In October 1960, the Sudan invited representatives from Kenya, Tanganyika and Uganda to Khartoum, and acknowledged the claim of the British authorities in Tanganyika that parts of the country lie within the river basin (Khalid, 1984:12).

7 See for example Willcocks, 1984, Appendix III: 11.

8 Willcocks (1894) thought year-long water storage impossible due to his calculations of sediments in the Blue Nile. Sediment build up was estimated at 55,000 m³ annually.

9 The secondary importance of the Blue Nile in schemes for Nile control in this century is illustrated by the fact that as late as 1925 the British consul in north-west Ethiopia, Colonel R.E. Cheesman, could write that 'the latest maps showed the course of the Blue Nile as a series of dotted lines' (Cheesman, 1968), whereas the White Nile was carefully surveyed immediately after the Fashoda incident in 1898 (see the reports by Garstin). The British proposed to regulate Lake Tana as part of their integrated plan for the whole basin (Dupuis, 1904), and in 1927 Tafari, in Addis, sent a close confidant to New York to arrange for the construction of the Lake Tana dam by the American J.G. White Engineering Company (McCann, 1981:686) but, owing to a number of political, hydrological and economic reasons, the plan was never implemented. The first recorded journey down the entire course of the Ethiopian Blue Nile was undertaken during the late 1920s by Cheesman. The first known attempt to navigate the tributary was initiated by a wealthy American big game hunter, W.N. Macmillan, who hired B.H. Jessen, a Norwegian or Swede, in 1902 and 1905 to undertake the job. He did not succeed. According to the literature, the first person who managed to travel from the Blue Nile Bridge to Roseires in the Sudan was a Swedish canoeist, Arne Rubin, in 1965 (Blashford-Snell, 1970:43).

10 See Willcocks (1894), Garstin (1889, 1901, 1904) and Hurst, Black and Simaika (1946).

11 The literature on this aspect of Nile control and Nile hydrology is voluminous. For an overview, see Tvedt, forthcoming.

12 Garstin proposed to excavate a completely new canal from Bor to the Sobat junction, 'leaving the great Swamp Region altogether to one side' (1904:165). MacDonald's plan proposed to 'absorb all the water wasted' in the marsh and 'abolish it permanently' (1920:134–5).

13 The proposed projects and their estimated annual yields are, in addition to Jonglei Phase I, Machar Marshes, 3.6 bm³; Bahr al-Ghazal, 6.3 bm³; and Jonglei Phase II, 3.8 bm³

14 A number of pre-feasibility studies have been undertaken such as, for example, in southern Sudan regarding the Fola rapids (Hafslund, 1984) and in the Kagera river (Norconsult & Electrowatt, 1976; KBO, 1982).

15. The agreement for the construction of a dam at the outlet of Lake Victoria was concluded between Egypt and Uganda in 1949. The dam, completed in 1954, provides the capacity for long-term storage for the benefit of Egypt, and hydro-electric power (150,000 kw) for the benefit of Uganda. An element in the agreement is that the Egyptian government has the right to post a permanent representative at the dam site to monitor management of the dam.

16 The Sudd (in Arabic *sadd* or block) is a generic name applied to the huge marshes through which the Bahr al-Jabal, Bahr al-Ghazal and Bahr al-Zaraf and the lower portion of their tributaries wind their way and lose billions of cubic metres of water.

17 Reported in *Time International*, 5 November 1990:40. The paper reported on the first of a series of Global Water Summit Initiatives organized by the Washington-based Global Strategy Council. It was Farouk el-Baz of Boston University who announced an analysis of data collected by the US space shuttle and remote sensing instruments.

18 For a description of the Egyptian Ministry's plans see, for example, Samaha (1979) and Ali (1977). It should be noted that the Sudan's main interest has been in exploiting Blue Nile waters. More waters in the White Nile will, however, make it possible for the Sudan to withdraw more water from the Blue Nile since more of Egypt's requirements will be met from the increased flow of the White Nile.

19 See Langer (1968:103–4) and Hecht (1987) for descriptions of Ethiopian/Egyptian relations pertaining to the Blue Nile before 1800 AD.

20 For a review of some of the treaties from different viewpoints see Tilahun (1979) and Okidi (1982, 1990).
21 Other agreements of importance are those signed by Britain and the Independent State of Congo in London on 9 May 1906, and the tripartite Agreement and Declatation signed by Britain, Italy and France on 13 December 1906.
22 See, for example, the article written in 1984 by the then Foreign Minister, Mansour Khalid, regarding the official Sudanese viewpoint, and by Ahmed (1990) for the Egyptian opinion.
23 *Endugu* is a Swahili word meaning brotherhood. The governments of Egypt, the Sudan, Uganda, The Central African Republic, Zaire and, later, Rwanda and Burundi have taken part in ministerial-level meetings. The group was established to discuss and co-ordinate policies on many issues, among them and most important, the Nile waters. Kenya, Tanzania and Ethiopia have not, however, joined the group.
24 For a discussion of such matters see, Omer (1986).
25 See, for example, the World Bank study on the Sudan from 1979 in which it is estimated that the Sudan's water requirements in year 2000 will be more than 25 bm^3 annually.

References

Ahmed, S. 1990. 'Context and precedents with respect to the development, division and management of Nile waters' in Howell, P.P. and J.A. Allan, (eds.) *The Nile: Resource Evaluation, Resource Management, Hydropolitics and Legal Issues*, London, SOAS-RGS, pp. 225–38.

Ali, M.K. 1977. 'The projects for the increase of the Nile yield with special reference to the Jonglei Project' *UN Water Conference, Mar del Plata*, vol. iv, pp. 1799–1831.

Allan, J.A. 1990. 'Review of evolving water demands and national development options' in Howell, P.P. and J.A. Allan (eds.) *The Nile: Resource Evaluation, Resource Management, Hydropolitics and Legal Issues*, London, SOAS-RGS, pp. 181–93.

Baker. 1884. 'An interview with Samuel Baker' *Pall Mall Gazette*, 'Extra', 8, p. 12.

Beshir, M.O. (ed.) 1984. *The Nile Valley Countries: Continuity and Change*, Khartoum, Institute of African and Asian Studies, University of Khartoum.

Blashford-Snell, J.N. 1970. 'Conquest of the Blue Nile' *The Geographical Journal*, 36, pp. 42–55.

British Foreign Office. 1920. *Peace Handbooks No. 129: Ethiopia*, London, H.M. Stationery Office.

Budge, E.A. Wallis. 1970. *A History of Ethiopia, Nubia and Abyssinia*, Oosterhout, Anthropological Publications.

Bureau of Reclamation, US Department of Interior. 1964. *Land and Water Resources of the Blue Nile Basin: Ethiopia*, Main Report and Appendices I–V, Washington DC, Bureau of Reclamation.

Cheesman, R.E. 1968. *Lake Tana and the Blue Nile: An Abyssinian Quest*, London, Frank Cass & Co.

Dupuis, C. 1904. 'Report upon Lake Tana and the rivers of Eastern Soudan' in Garstin, W. *Report Upon the Basin of the Upper Nile with Proposals for the Improvement of that River*, Cairo, Ministry of Public Works.

Falkenmark, M. 1986. 'Fresh water as a factor in strategic policy and action' in Westing, A.H. (ed.) *Global Resources and International Conflict*, Oxford, Oxford University Press.

Falkenmark, M. 1990. 'Global water issues confronting humanity' *Journal of Peace Research*, vol. 27, no. 2, pp. 177–91.

Garstin, W. 1889. *Note on the Soudan*, Cairo, Ministry of Public Works.

Garstin W. 1901. 'Report as to irrigation projects on the Upper Nile' in *Foreign Office Blue Book No. 2*, in Despatch from His Majesty's Agent and Consul-General, Cairo.

Garstin W. 1904. *Report Upon the Basin of the Upper Nile with Proposals for the Improvement of that River*, Cairo, Ministry of Public Works.

Gleichen, C. (ed.) 1905. *The Anglo-Egyptian Sudan*, a compendium prepared by Officers of the Sudan Government, Volume I, London, Wyman & Sons.

Hafslund Consulting Division. 1984 (unpublished). *Fula Rapids Power Station: Feasibility Study*, submitted to the Democratic Republic of the Sudan.

Hecht, E.D. 1987, March (unpublished). 'Ethiopia threatens to block the Nile', paper presented at the *International Symposium on the Nile Basin*, Cairo, University of Cairo.

Hill, P. 1986. *Development Economics on Trial: The Anthropological Case for a Prosecution*, London, Cambridge University Press.

Howell, P.P. and J.A. Allan (eds.) 1990. *The Nile: Resource Evaluation, Resource Management, Hydropolitics and Legal Issues*, London, SOAS-RGS.

Hulme, M. 1990. 'Global climate change and the Nile Basin' in Howell, P.P. and J.A. Allan (eds.) *The Nile: Resource Evaluation, Resource Management, Hydropolitics and Legal Issues*, London, SOAS-RGS.

Hurst, H.E., R.P. Black and Y.M. Simaika. 1946. *The Nile Basin, Volume III: Future Conservation of the Nile*, Cairo, Ministry of Public Works.

Ibrahim, A.M. 1984. 'Development of the Nile River system' in Beshir, M.O. (ed.) *The Nile Valley Countries: Continuity and Change*, Khartoum, Institute of African and Asian Studies, University of Khartoum.

Jovanovic, D. 1985. 'Ethiopian interests in the division of the Nile River Waters' *Water International*, 10, pp. 82–85.

KBO (Kagera Basin Organisation Secretariat and Beyrard Mission). 1978. *Examination Report of the Technical Report 'Development of the Kagera Basin'*, Phase II, volume III, New York, United Nations Development Programme.

KBO (Kagera Basin Organisation Executive Secretariat and UNDP). 1982. *Energy, volume III, Development Programme of the Kagera Basin: Final Report*, New York, United Nations Development Programme.

Khalid, M. 1984. 'The Nile waters: The case for an integrated approach' in Beshir, M.O. (ed.) *The Nile Valley Countries: Continuity and Change*, Khartoum, Institute of African and Asian Studies, University of Khartoum.

Langer, W. 1968, second edition. *The Diplomacy of Imperialism: 1890–1902*, New York, Alfred A. Knopf.

MacDonald, M. 1920. *Nile Control. A Statement of the Necessity for Further Control of the Nile to Complete the Development of Egypt and Develop a Certain Area in the Sudan, with Particulars of the Physical Conditions to be Considered and a Programme of the Engineering Works Involved*, vol. 2, Cairo, Government Press.

McCann, J. 1981. 'Ethiopia, Britain, and negotiations for the Lake Tana dam, 1922–1935' *The International Journal of African Historical Studies*, vol. 11, no. 1, pp. 1–32.

Moorehead, A. 1962. *The Blue Nile*, London, Hamish Hamilton.

Norconsult, A.S. and Electrowatt. 1976. *Kagera River Hydropower Developments: Rusumo Falls Hydropower Project, Kishanda Valley Hydropower Project, Kakono Dam Hydropower project*.

Okidi, C.O. 1982. 'Review of treaties on consumptive utilization of waters of Lake Victoria and Nile drainage system' *Natural Resources Journal*, vol. 22, no. 1, pp. 161–99.

Okidi, C.O. 1990. 'History of the Nile and Lake Victoria Basins through treaties' in Howell, P.P. and J.A. Allan (eds.) *The Nile: Resource Evaluation, Resource Management, Hydropolitics and Legal Issues*, London, SOAS-RGS, pp. 193–225.

Omer, Mohamed Ali Mohamed. 1986. *Proposal for a Nile Waters Treaty*, monograph series no. 26, Khartoum, Development Studies and Research Centre, Faculty of Economic and Social Studies, University of Khartoum.

Permanent Joint Technical Commission for Nile Waters. 1981. 'The permanent joint technical commission for Nile Waters: Egypt-Sudan' in *Experiences in the Development and Management of International River and Lake Basins*, Natural Resources/Water Series No. 10, proceedings of the United Nations Interregional Meeting of International River Organizations, Dakar, Senegal, New York, United Nations.

Ross, J.C.P. 1893. 'Irrigation and agriculture in Egypt' *Scottish Geographical Magazine*, IX, pp. 161–93.

Samaha, M.A.H. 1979. 'The Egyptian master water plan' *Water Supply Management*, vol. 3, no. 4, pp. 251–66.

Scott-Moncrieff, C. 1895, January. 'The Nile' in *Royal Institution of Great Britain, Proceedings*, 14.

Tilahun, W. 1979. *Egypt's Imperial Aspirations over Lake Tana and the Blue Nile*, Addis Ababa, United Printers.

Tvedt, T. 1987, March (unpublished). ' "Water imperialism" – on the British occupation of the Upper Nile', paper presented at the *International Symposium on the Nile Basin*, University of Cairo.

Tvedt, T. 1990. *Images of 'the Others'*, Oslo, Universitetsforlaget.

Tvedt, T. (forthcoming). *Bibliography on the Nile in Sudan*, Bergen, Centre for Development Studies.

Waterbury, J. 1979. *The Hydropolitics of the Nile Valley*, Syracuse, Syracuse University Press.

Whittington, D. 1985. *Implications of Ethiopian Water Development for Egypt and Sudan*, Khartoum: DSRC Seminar No. 60.

Willcocks, W. 1894. *Report on Perennial Irrigation and Flood Protection for Egypt*, Cairo, Government Printing Press.

World Bank. 1979. *Sudan: A Country Report*, Washington DC, World Bank.

World Commission on Environment and Development. 1987. *Our Common Future*, Oxford, Oxford University Press.

World Resources Institute, UNEP and UNDP. 1990. *World Resources 1990–1991*, Oxford, Oxford University Press.

Comment   SIDGI AWAD KABALLO

The paper's opening statement, that 'conflicts over the Horn of Africa's freshwater resources will certainly threaten future regional stability and co-operation', presents a pessimistic view which I do not share. Due to changes in the environment, the size of the population and development agendas, a need might arise for some upstream states (including the Sudan) to plan a new irrigation scheme or put more lands under permanent irrigation. This would require negotiations between and among the states of the Nile basin; it would not necessarily 'threaten future regional stability and co-operation', or bring about pressures which are defined in the introduction as 'independent of the will of the leaders of the countries concerned'. In short, I do not share the view that these states are on the edge of 'open hostilities and water wars'.

Let us first examine why such a need for new projects might arise. Of course one of the reasons is not 'to narrow the gap between [Ethiopia's] level of development, on the one hand, and its position as the region's water tower on the other,' because even if Ethiopia were rich it would need to utilize its water resources to feed its population and to generate cheap hydroelectric power. The need for new irrigation projects might arise because of environmental changes in the area; a sharp increase in population; development policies in the area of electrification and use of hydroelectric power, industrialization which requires both water and electricity, and expansion in agriculture (food and raw materials). In this context, the demand for water might rise when these countries deal with problems of uneven development within them rather than uneven development between them. For example, in the Sudan there will be a need for more water if agricultural development is to take place in southern and western Sudan (instead of being focused in central Sudan, the Gezira, and northern Sudan).

If we are convinced there is a need for new projects, what is the size of the problem? The paper provides the following figures:

1.	*Ethiopia*	
	Irrigation of 434,000 hectares requires	6.0 bm^3
	Irrigation of 70,000 feddans requires	0.3 bm^3
2.	*Tanzania*	
	Irrigation of 120,000 feddans requires	0.5 bm^3
3.	*Uganda*	
	Irrigation of 1 million acres requires	1.5 bm^3
4.	*Kenya*	
	Not determined	?
	Total	8.3 bm^3

The total water needed is 8.3 bm^3 which is about 9.9 per cent of the total water measured at Aswan!

Let us remind ourselves that the 1959 Nile Waters Agreement between the Sudan and Egypt provided for the two countries to prepare a united view when negotiating with other countries about the Nile waters, and that the water they agreed should be allotted to a third country should be deducted equally from the shares of the two countries. What is the problem then?

How can the Sudan and Egypt save 8.3 bm^3? Is it by forgoing their development projects? The answer is, of course, no! It is by more efficient water utilization, spraying instead of flooding, better preparation of the soil, seed improvement and so forth. It is also by increasing the water available through new projects like Jonglei, and by improving storage facilities in the upstream states to avoid evaporation losses. As Tvedt suggested, the use of underground water is another solution. There is a problem, but one which might peacefully be solved. Why the pessimism?

10 The Refurbishing and Expansion of Trade Networks in the Horn of Africa

MARUYE AYALEW

Introduction

Trade expansion among African countries has remained low in spite of the many attempts made to promote its development, particularly through the establishment of subregional and regional groupings. Over the last ten years a number of institutions have been set up in the different regions of Africa in order to promote trade and economic co-operation. In 1982, for instance, the Preferential Trade Area for Eastern and Southern African States (PTA) was established. The PTA became operational in 1984 with the main objective of promoting co-operation and development in all fields of economic activity, including trade, customs, industry, transport, communications, agriculture, natural resources and monetary affairs. All countries of the Horn belong to this regional grouping. In 1986 the Inter-Governmental Authority on Drought and Development (IGADD) was set up with the objective of co-ordinating the efforts made by countries in the Horn to establish food security and combat desertification through environmental protection. The six members of IGADD are Djibouti, Ethiopia, Somalia, Kenya, the Sudan and Uganda.

In spite of these efforts, the level of intra-African trade in general and of regional trade in the Horn in particular has not improved significantly. Trade within Africa has actually declined since the 1960s and early 1970s when it accounted for around 6 per cent of Africa's total trade. Table 1 gives a general picture of intra-African and intra-PTA trade since 1980.

Table 1 African Trade Directions (in millions of US dollars)

Year	African exports to the world	Intra-African total exports	% share of total	PTA exports	Intra-PTA exports	% share of PTA exports
1980	95,082.1	2,804.1	2.9	10,732.3	481	4.5
1985	66,827.5	2,346.5	3.5	9,124.6	361	3.9
1986	52,304.2	2,365.0	4.5	7,798.3	432	5.5
1987	55,850.9	2,863.0	5.1	7,731.6	392	5.1

Source: ECA Statistical Data Base.

The share of intra-African trade seems to increase during the 1980–7 period. However, the level is still very low (5 per cent) compared with the total exports and reflects the extent of Africa's dependence on external markets. At the intra-African level there is a tendency toward the concentration of trade between members of a subregion. For instance, trade within the eastern and southern regions ranged between 481 and 392 million US dollars during the 1980–7 period, accounting for more than 60 per cent of the region's total intra-African trade. This trade is facilitated by the existence of subregional economic groupings, transport, and relatively short distances. It can be argued that trade between East African countries could have been more extensive had there been peace and political stability in the region.

This paper sets out to analyse current trade activities among neighbouring countries in the Horn, identify major constraints to intra-regional trade, highlight potentials and prospects for co-operation and, finally, propose some policy recommendations. Djibouti, Ethiopia, Somalia and the Sudan are the focus of this study, although occasional references are made to Kenya and Uganda. Current trading activities within the region are identified as official (recorded) or unofficial (unrecorded). It is difficult to accurately quantify the magnitude of unrecorded trade, but some qualitative information is presented to show its significance and implications.

Main features of intra-African trade

Trade among African countries is dominated by three major groups of commodities. Mineral fuels and related materials made up 29 per cent of the total intra-African trade in 1987; food, beverages and tobacco accounted for 26 per cent; and manufactured goods contributed 20 per cent. As shown in Table 2, the importance of manufactured goods in intra-African trade has declined from approximately 45 per cent in 1970 to 20 per cent in 1987, while trade in mineral fuels increased form 11 per cent to 29 per cent. The share of food, beverages and tobacco has remained constant throughout the reference time.

Table 2 Structure of Intra-African Trade (in millions of US dollars)

Commodity	1970	% share	1980	% share	1987	% share
Food, beverages, tobacco	188	27.9	727	24.5	779	25.7
Crude materials excluding fuel	68	10.1	270	9.1	324	10.7
Mineral fuels and related materials	75	11.2	1,219	41.0	889	29.3
Chemicals	16	2.4	131	4.4	239	7.9
Machinery and transport equipment	26	3.9	87	2.9	190	6.3
Other manufactured goods	229	44.5	536	18.1	614	20.2
Total	672	100	2,970	100	3,035	100

Source: Computed from UN monthly *Bulletin of Statistics,* 1988–9.

Obviously, the structure of intra-African trade has not undergone any qualitative change toward the export of manufactured commodities. The declining share of intra-African trade in this product group is a sign of an increasing dependence on external sources for non-primary imports.

Regional trade in the Horn of Africa

Recorded trade

Most of the East African countries are fairly trade oriented. Exports from the region account for around 20 per cent of the area's GDP, and imports account for about 25 per cent. Their exports in absolute terms have shown significant increases since the beginning of the 1970s.

Table 3 Exports (in millions of US dollars)

Country	1970	1980	1984	1985	1986
Djibouti	11	13	13	14	28
Ethiopia	122	425	417	338	477
Somalia	31	133	45	91	107
Sudan	294	594	629	367	447
Kenya	305	1,389	1,082	989	1,217

Source: ECA, *African Statistical Year Book,* parts 1 and 3, 1986.

Trade *among* these countries is insignificant as at the beginning of the 1980s it stood at around 3 per cent of their total exports. This figure is, however, based on official statistics which do not include the substantial unrecorded trade in the region.[1] The following sections outline the extent of trade relations between countries of the region.

Djibouti and Ethiopia

The recorded and unrecorded exchange of goods between Djibouti and Ethiopia is the most extensive exchange among countries in the Horn. Historical relations and infrastructural links connect these two countries between which the rail link, established more than 80 years ago, has been the main factor in the expansion of trade. Officially Djibouti imports around 30 million US dollars worth of goods from Ethiopia annually. This does not include cereals, livestock, coffee, and other food items which enter the market illegally. In 1987, 9.3 per cent of Ethiopia's exports and 2.5 per cent of its imports were traded with African countries; about 90 per cent of this was exported to and 36 per cent was imported from Djibouti. Fruits, vegetables, sugar and chat are the major exports to Djibouti.

Djibouti and Somalia

Trade relations between Somalia and Djibouti date back to the colonial era. About 68 per cent of Somalia's total imports from the region and 6.4 per cent of the country's total imports come from Djibouti. However, most of the commodities imported originate in third countries outside of Africa. Of Somalia's exports to the subregion (1.2 per cent of its total export earnings), 61 per cent goes to Djibouti. Somalia's official regional trade is relatively low. Its exports to the region have rarely exceeded 10 per cent of its total exports.

Ethiopia and Somalia

Somalia's trade with Ethiopia is negligible. There was no recorded trade during the 1978–87 period due to the war of 1978 and the subsequent border conflicts. In the beginning of the 1970s, small quantities of cereals, vegetables, and other food products were exported to Somalia.

Somalia and Sudan

Somalia's trade with the Sudan is also minimal as these countries do not have a common frontier and are relatively far apart.

Ethiopia and Sudan

Ethiopia exchanges various types of commodities with eastern Sudan. Most of the border trade is, however, unrecorded or illegal. According to Ethiopian Government statistics, coffee was a major export to the Sudan until the beginning of 1980. By the end of the 1980s the major exports to the Sudan comprised only alcoholic beverages, petroleum products and spices. Ethiopia used to import small quantities of textile yarn, cotton and other consumer items from the Sudan, but Sudan's exports to Ethiopia significantly declined from 1.2 million birr to only 66,000 birr during the 1971–89 period. Reasons for the decline of official border trade include the prevalence of security problems in both countries and currency overvaluations.

Unrecorded trade

Unofficial or unrecorded trade in the region is a major activity involving many people not only from the border areas but also from the centres of these countries. In some areas there are very strong traditional links and ethnic and cultural relations among inhabitants across borders. Major commodities like cereals, sugar, oils, other consumer goods, livestock and coffee are traded widely. The direction of the trade flow between Somalia and Ethiopia depends on relative prices between the two countries and on the season. Usually consumer goods and cereal exports from Somalia originate in third countries. According to some estimates, about 40 per cent of unrecorded Ethiopian imports from Somalia in 1988–9 comprised cereals and sugar (IGADD, 1990:160). Unofficial Somalia imports are relatively minimal due to the country's small market and supply shortages on the Ethiopian side. However, some studies still indicate a considerable degree of smuggling of live animals and various cash crops (such as coffee) to Somalia.

Between Djibouti and Somalia livestock and cereals are the major commodities traded illegally. The major operators of this trade are Somalis residing in both countries. The major commodities traded unofficially between Djibouti and Ethiopia are cereal, rice, edible oil, flour and other consumer items (IGADD, 1990:19). In addition, live animals, fruits, vegetables, coffee and other products are traded informally.

Informal trade in cereals, pulses, food and other consumer goods exists between Ethiopia and its four neighbours: Djibouti, Kenya, Somalia and the Sudan. Ethiopia is the largest market in the region and the only country which shares borders with all members (except Uganda) of IGADD. The people in the border areas belong to the same ethnic groups as those on the Ethiopian side and consequently there is movement across the political boundaries by people with similar cultural, religious and consumptual habits. In these areas, official national marketing channels for livestock, cereals and pulses are not well developed, and the populations are poorly supplied with goods from the central regions where most agricultural and some industrial production marketing takes place. This is one of the main reasons for the prevalence of unrecorded border trade.

Commodities for trade are mostly carried by animals or people, and in some cases are transported by vehicles or the railway. The seller, in most cases, is the buyer of another item; this two-way trade implies a monopolistic or oligopolistic situation in the underground economy. Border trade, where recorded or not, follows the principle of surplus and deficit areas reflecting comparative advantages. It is interesting to note that similar agricultural commodities are exchanged in both formal and informal ways in the region.

Constraints on regional trade in the horn

As presented in the preceding section, official trade between neighbouring countries in the Horn of Africa has been stagnating and even declining over the years. In addition, the composition of this trade has remained basically unchanged. Constraints on the expansion of trade in the region can be seen as political, economic, institutional and also physical. Political differences between countries and political instability within countries in the Horn are largely responsible for the low level of official transborder trade in the region. Hostilities and border clashes between Ethiopia and Somalia since 1960 are the main reasons for the weak trade relations between them. Similarly, poor diplomatic and trade relations between the Sudan and Ethiopia are mainly a result of political differences. The long frontier between these two countries cannot be used for expanding official transborder trade mainly due to security reasons.

The relatively good political and diplomatic relations between Ethiopia and Djibouti, Djibouti and Somalia, and Ethiopia and Kenya have helped to improve trade relations among these countries. Ethiopia's trade relations with Djibouti are mainly due to existing favourable political conditions and infrastructural proximity. It is worth noting that, while the Djibouti port is the second main outlet for Ethiopia's exports, Somalia's similar ability to play such a role is totally hindered by political constraints. The infrastructure between Ethiopia and Somalia's ports is not as adequate as that to Djibouti, but this could have been improved during the last 30 years had good political relations existed between these countries. According to some studies, transport costs could be reduced significantly if Ethiopia used Somali ports for some of its exports. This would also mean the development and expansion of the service industry in Somalia.

Economic constraints on the expansion of intra-regional trade are attributable to the existing structure of production and distribution: there is a clear divergence between supply and demand patterns among neighbouring countries. All the countries in the region are mainly primary producers, while their demands are for manufactured goods and capital. Their limited demand for raw materials, which is a reflection of their low level of development, results in production being geared largely toward export to developed countries outside of Africa.

The Horn countries are producing more or less the same products due to their shared low technological threshold. The problem is that the difference in the quality of the goods produced is not enough to promote trade given high transport costs and other trade related constraints such as poor credit systems. Furthermore, most of the manufactured goods cannot compete with similar better and cheaper items imported from beyond the region. The limited national markets in the region restrict the range of products which can be made available as producers are not able to benefit from economies of scale. Internal markets in Djibouti and Somalia are small, as reflected by the size of their populations, while in Ethiopia and the Sudan, where the domestic markets are relatively large, factors such as inadequate transport and communications, and the low income of the rural people (the majority of whom have limited purchasing power) diminish the size of the rural markets in the region (see Appendix 1).

The pricing and exchange rate policies followed by each country and the persistent use of convertible currencies for trade transactions also hinder trade expansion in the region. In spite of the establishment of regional payment and clearing systems, many countries still prefer to trade in hard currencies. In addition, most countries have overvalued currencies which make their exports uncompetitive. This is one of the major reasons for the development and expansion of parallel markets in almost all border areas in the region.

Institutional constraints on regional trade in the Horn, such as a lack of information on regional demands and of marketing institutions, have contributed to the low level of trade in the region. Food production has remained at the level needed to meet demands at the country level when other parts of the region were suffering from shortages. Consequently, demand for food and other consumer items is generally met by imports from the developed countries while the capacity for increased production exists in the region (UN/ECA, 1989). Poor marketing channels, complicated export and import procedures, an absence of quality standards, and a lack of incentives and government support are also thought to be serious obstacles to trade expansion. Additionally, tariff and non-tariff barriers constitute a major obstacle to regional trade. Although provisions are made within the regional grouping of PTA for the reduction of tariffs and the removal of non-tariff barriers, they have not been easy to implement as tariffs are a major source of revenue for all countries in the region.

Macro-economic regulations of individual countries may also conflict with regional co-operation. For example, if the countries in the region follow inward-looking trade policies and try to promote their exports and reduce their imports, they will be pursuing policies which directly conflict with the principles of regional co-operation and trade expansion.

The fourth major constraint on the expansion of regional trade in the Horn is the inadequacy of transportation and communication (see Appendix 1) and maintenance systems in the region. Interstate road links in the Horn are not up to the required standard for all-season international traffic. Interstate roads do exist between Ethiopia and Kenya, Ethiopia and Djibouti, Ethiopia and the Sudan, Djibouti and Somalia, but they are not fully utilized for trade activities because of poor road conditions, security problems, and policy induced constraints.

The only existing interstate railway line runs between Djibouti and Ethiopia. It is 781 km long and the oldest railway line in Africa, but currently it cannot be utilized to its maximum capacity due to old age and a lack of adequate equipment. Maritime transport is also not well exploited. There is little or no coastal shipping between the Sudan, Ethiopia, Djibouti and Somalia in spite of the existing port infrastructures and vessel capacity. There are direct telecommunication links between Djibouti, Ethiopia and Kenya. Telex and telephone services to Somalia, however, are connected via Rome, and services to the Sudan and Uganda go through Paris. This is a serious obstacle to trade as it hinders fast communication and is costly. Air transport is one way in which all the countries of the Horn, except Ethiopia and Somalia, are directly connected, but this form of transport is the most costly. Clearly, transportation and communication infrastructures need to be constructed and rehabilitated in order to facilitate regional trade.

Prospects and potentials for trade co-operation in the Horn

All the problems and constraints analysed in the preceding section should not in any way reduce the potential for expanding and developing interstate trade in the region. However, this potential can only be realized if all countries involved can solve or at least minimize the above mentioned constraints.

Available trade statistics indicate that there is a growing market in the Horn for processed meat and meat products, cereals, fruits and vegetables, and manufactured goods (see Appendix 2). In addition, since some commodity groups – particularly food, beverages and tobacco, chemicals, machinery and transport equipment – are the main contributors to the large trade deficits in most countries of the region, it would be useful to restructure African production in order to increase the interstate trade of these commodities so that trade deficits could be reduced significantly. If all countries in the Horn were to open up their borders in a co-ordinated manner so that existing price differentials between import and export parity prices could be reduced, the scope to adjust the production and consumption patterns among neighbouring countries in accordance with comparative advantages would be created.

It is argued that regional trade co-operation could contribute to the implementation of risk-reducing strategies. Food security, for instance, could be handled in a better and cheaper way if countries in the region co-operated. Various studies indicate that cereal production fluctuations are much smaller at the regional level than at the national level; regional trade could be used to even out these fluctuations. According to one study, cereal production in East Africa (Kenya, Tanzania and Uganda) fluctuated by 6.4 per cent during the 1960–80 period, while it fluctuated by 9 to 10.8 per cent for the individual countries. It is important, therefore, to plan food production policies in co-ordination with all neighbouring countries with the ultimate objective of regional self-sufficiency.

It is often thought that adjacent nations like those in the Horn of Africa have similar production patterns arising from similar factor endowments, and hence have similar

Table 4 Export Similarity Indices

Country	Ethiopia	Kenya	Somalia	Sudan
Ethiopia	100.00			
Kenya	50.50	100.00		
Somalia	2.10	4.78	100.00	
Sudan	12.49	11.12	15.92	100.00
Uganda	72.76	41.66	0.00	2.59

Source: IGADD, March 1990.

export structures. This kind of assumption leads one to conclude that there is little potential for the development of regional trade. However, existing climatic and geographical diversity in the Horn does not support the above argument; there are more differences than similarities in the export structures of the Horn countries (see Table 4).

The prospects for trade expansion between Ethiopia and Somalia, Ethiopia and the Sudan, Somalia and Kenya, Kenya and the Sudan, and Somali, the Sudan and Uganda are considerable. The high similarity index for Ethiopia and Uganda is mainly due to their dependency on coffee exports. If we exclude the few agricultural export commodities which these countries depend on and for which the markets are already established outside the region, the potential for regional trade in other commodities (food and other consumer items) might even be higher (see Appendix 2).

Recommendations

In sum, at the national level it is necessary to reorganize production structures toward developing and expanding the production of food and consumer goods for domestic and neighbouring markets. Appropriate pricing and exchange rate policies should be adopted in general, and for agricultural products in particular, to provide adequate incomes to the rural population and also to create demand for manufactured goods. All countries in the Horn should remove tariff and non-tariff barriers in line with the principles of the PTA, and liberalize their trade regimes to facilitate transborder exchange in the region.

It is also important to provide incentives which will encourage indigenous entrepreneurs and businesspeople to promote trade in the region. This can be done through the provision of adequate credit facilities from regional trade and development banks. All countries should encourage their traders to use regional financial institutions such as the PTA clearing house in order to minimize the use of convertible currencies among themselves.

Key requisites to transborder trade are peace and the free movement of goods and people. These can only be achieved if there is political stability within each country and good political and diplomatic relations between neighbouring countries. It is hoped that membership of the Horn countries in subregional and regional groupings, such as IGADD and PTA, will strengthen these relations. The harmonization of economic policies among neighbouring countries, with the aim of expanding regional trade and development activities, could then be pursued. All Horn countries could first liberalize their domestic trading systems so that goods and services could move freely in the region. The aim should be to have similar rules and regulations for various economic and trade activities, including the establishment of common external tariffs.

An effective trade information network also needs to be developed so as to ensure up-to-date information on the region's market situation. In this respect the recently established Trade Information Network (TINET) within PTA has to be strengthened and supported by all member countries.

As noted earlier, roads also need to be improved. The PTA and IGADD have prioritized regional projects which set out to refurbish and improve highways which will facilitate the interstate movement of goods and services in the Horn region. It is also important to maintain national road systems which are currently in poor condition. As the major problem is the lack of adequate financial resources, it is necessary to mobilize additional local and external funds in order to provide adequate budgets for maintenance. In addition, the railway between Ethiopia and Djibouti needs to be rehabilitated and modernized in order to increase its existing cargo capacity. Finally, telecommunications would be improved if microwave links were installed in the missing areas so that all countries in the region could be directly connected.

Increased trading activities among neighbouring countries will contribute to the improvement of social welfare in the area, and this will help to bring about political stability in the region as common interests come to dominate existing differences. Existing regional groupings like PTA and IGADD can play a key role in co-ordinating various development programmes and in strengthening regional information centres. However, this can only be realized when these institutions are supported by the good will of all participating countries.

All these infrastructural programmes cannot be financed by the Horn region itself. The region can contribute considerable financial and labour inputs if, following peace, current non-productive expenditures are reduced and redirected toward development activities. In addition, financial and technical assistance from the international community can complement the region's development programmes as long as all countries in the Horn genuinely show initiative and fully participate.

Note
1 Some studies estimate that unrecorded intra-regional trade could be as high as 40 per cent of the total trade among the countries in the region.

References
Bird, R. 1972. 'The need for regional policy in a common market' in Robson, P. (ed.) *International Economic Integration: Selected Readings*, London, Penguin Books.
Customs and Excise Tax Administration. 1988. *Annual External Trade Statistics*, Ethiopia.
EUROPA. 1989. *The Europa World Yearbook*, vol. 1, London, Europa Publications.
ECA. 1986. *African Statistical Yearbook*, parts 1 and 3, Addis Ababa.
IGADD. 1989, December. *News*, Djibouti, IGADD.
IGADD. 1989. *Status Report for 1989 and Work Programme and Activities for 1989–1990*, Djibouti, IGADD.
IGADD. 1990, March. *Study of the Potential for Intra-Regional Trade in Cereals in the IGADD Region*, vol. 2, Oxford.
Kendie, D. 1975. *Prospects for Co-operation in North-East Africa between Ethiopia, Somalia and the French Territory of the Afars and Issas (Djibouti)*, The Hague, Institute of Social Studies.
UN/ECA. 1987, August. *The Development and Expansion of Intra-African Trade: A Policy Paper*, E/ECA/TRADE/85, Addis Ababa.
UN/ECA. 1989. *Intra-African Trade: Situation, Problems and Prospects, A General Analysis*, E/ECA/TRADE/89/15, Addis Ababa.

Appendix 1   Vital Statistics for the Northern PTA Region (1986)

	Djibouti	Ethiopia	Somalia	Sudan
Population (in millions)	0.372	44.6	6.1	22.3
Urban percentage	78.3	11.6	34.9	20.9
Railways				
Total length (km)	100	681	–	4,756
Locomotives	–	26	–	335
Wagons	–	640	–	6,580
Roads				
Total length (km)	3,515	37,600	21,470	9,700
Paved roads (km)	286	12,643	6,120	3,220
Sea-borne shipping				
Goods loaded (1,000s of tons)	329	577	290	1,287
Goods unloaded (1,000s of tons)	753	2,885	1,200	3,320
*Foreign trade (total)**				
Imports C.I.F. (in millions)	19,015	2,299	7,271.9	2,197.5
Exports F.O.B. (in millions)	4,976	988	7,703.9	117.5
Balance (in millions)	–14,039	–1,312	432.0	–1,080.0
*Intra-African trade***				
Imports (in millions)	4,300	47.8	428.2	34.7
Exports (in millions)	163	42.1	7.2	19.2

*   in local currencies of individual countries
o   data for Djibouti, Somalia and the Sudan refer to the years 1983,1982,1981 respectively.
Source: ECA, 1986.

Appendix 2   Potential Intra-Regional Trade as a Percentage of Foreign Trade (for IGADD
                Region)

Commodity	1971–5	1976–80	1981–4
Fresh meat	3.23	9.80	23.54
Dried meat	4.99	10.48	25.32
Prepared meat	3.56	26.29	41.27
Maize	54.89	53.60	11.90
Other cereals	23.94	7.65	12.92
Prepared cereals	2.05	11.51	11.39
Fresh vegetables	5.95	25.71	31.75
Prepared vegetables & roots	30.35	72.52	27.32
Fresh fruit	15.67	8.44	9.77
Dried fruit	27.20	25.70	32.20
Prepared fruit	21.64	14.76	19.21
Sugar and honey	2.10	27.68	54.83
Tea	20.39	15.24	27.00
Spices	46.09	70.39	71.83
Animal feed	8.75	14.05	48.59

Source: Taken from IGADD, March 1990.

Comment PAUL DOORNBOS

Mr Ayalew's excellent paper will hopefully one day become the blueprint for a comprehensive trade agreement between the countries of the Horn. He has analysed the economic, institutional, political and infrastructural constraints in a balanced manner, and has suggested ways and means to overcome them.

Regarding the orientation or focus of the paper, however, the figures the author uses are by definition figures pertaining to 'administered trade', derived from trade ministries and customs departments. This is the type of trade which requires letters of credit, import and export licences, and payment of export taxes and import duties. Seaports and airports in the countries of the Horn receive and dispatch almost all trade goods that appear in official statistics; in the Sudan, for example, almost all customs duties are generated in Port Sudan and Khartoum airport.

As Mr Ayalew has rightly mentioned, the flow of 'administered trade' is toward the North and/or the oil states, not toward neighbouring countries in the Horn of Africa. However, as he also pointed out, there is a very large volume of trade across land borders which by-passes the few customs posts and does not enter official trade statistics. Although non-payment of customs duties can be termed a public welfare loss, the sheer availability or the reduced prices of 'smuggled' goods constitutes a private, and often also a public, welfare gain. Large parts of the countries of the Horn continue to be supplied with essentials as well as luxuries not thanks to the inefficient and sometimes corrupt trade bureaucracy, but *despite* state intervention in trade. This raises a fundamental issue: given the sorry performance of the state in many areas, such as domestic and foreign trade, is further elaboration of a given state activity called for, or is a retreat called for?

Mr Ayalew's first recommendation is by far the most important precondition for expanding trade: trade is not fatally constrained because of political, institutional or infrastructural reasons, but because the volume of surplus production is so small and fluctuating, and because people have no purchasing power. As for the other recommendations, they seem designed to streamline 'administered trade' which never has had and will not in the foreseeable future have a bearing on cross-border trade. Overland traders will not be affected by the standardization or removal of tariffs. Traders work on a strictly cash basis or have credit arrangements among themselves which the introduction of formal credit and the improvement of regional financial institutions will not easily supplant. As for clearing houses, traders are experts at negotiating and adjusting exchange rates – on an hourly basis if necessary. Traders rely on large personal networks for information about supply, demand and prices, and ought to be the source rather than users of a proposed trade information system. Additionally, warfare and trade embargoes are notorious for not impeding trade as are widely differing economic and trade development policies which, given the many differences in subsidies, prices, and commodities, provide ample scope for brisk trade. Finally, in theory road building will have cost-saving effects, notably on fuel and tyres, but surfaced roads near borders inevitably give rise to customs posts, roadblocks, tolls and other costs.

The states in the Horn should retreat from many spheres of public life and concentrate on core issues. It is highly improbable that all the talent and initiative of a given country is vested in the state. On the contrary, many state laws and regulations (pertaining, for example, to trade) appear to be designed to enable government personnel to control, stifle and batten on what remains of the private sector. Ironically, the state's record in direct taxation (personal income and business profit taxation), which is a very legitimate role of the state, is dismal, with evasion of taxes and underreporting of profits and income the rule rather than the exception.

Therefore, the assumption that further elaboration of the state superstructure in the field of trade will be effective is questionable as long as the state's productive basis remains as weak and neglected as it has become over the past decades. There is ample evidence to suggest that this basis is rapidly eroding further, calling to mind images of pyramids teetering upside-down, propped up by foreign aid. However, this question leads us into the much larger discussion on the role of the state.

11 Adding Fuel to the Conflict: Oil, War and Peace in the Sudan

PETER NYOT KOK

To all those who have, more shall be given, and they will have abundance. From those who have nothing, even what they have will be taken away.
St Matthew ch. 25; v. 29.

We fought for 17 years without knowing oil existed underneath our soil. Now that we know, we shall fight longer if Nimeiri cheats us.
A southern Sudanese reaction to Nimeiri's decision to site the oil refinery in Kosti instead of Bentiu.

The above quotations roughly capture the basic attitudes of the main protagonists to oil and oil politics in the Sudan. The two attitudes are recipes for conflict, especially if both are backed up with military force as is actually the case in the Sudan. But the conflict in the Sudan, unlike the conflicts in Ethiopia and Somalia, encompasses a fight over strategic resources – oil and water. However, this paper shall deal with oil, specifically the configurations of political power in the Sudan since the early 1970s and their impact on the oil issue at the time.[1] The conflict itself is historically a conflict over the control, access to and the use of state power in the Sudan.[2] But since oil, like all other strategic resources, is a source of power, it logically becomes an important element in the conflict. Consequently, the present conflict cannot be fairly resolved without a generally acceptable resolution of the oil issue.

The discovery of oil in a relatively and transitorily poor country like the Sudan (with deep-seated problems of inequitable sharing of political power, wealth and so forth along ethnic, cultural and regional lines) can be a blessing or a curse, an opportunity to reconstruct a just national order or a danger to national unity. Whether it is the former or the latter depends, to a large degree, on the policies of those who wield power in the state and (more decisively perhaps in developing countries) the role of the relevant oil company or companies. In the Sudan the discovery and the commercial exploitation of oil occurred in a period (1977–83) when configurations of political power within the country were on a collision course, and when the oil company in question thought its interests would be best served if it allied itself with the stronger party. It failed to use its weight and its corporate diplomacy to press the government to act with justice and due consideration to southern legitimate demands and expectations with respect to oil.

The discovery of oil

Chevron Oil (a subsidiary of Standard Oil of California, SOCAL) obtained an exploratory licence in November 1974. Within a few years its concession was 516,000 sq km, lying mostly in the provinces of Southern Darfur, Kordofan, Upper Nile and Blue Nile.[3] The fields in the south, near Bentiu (revealingly named unity fields, and the wells named unity wells), were the most productive (*Sudanow*, March 1983:11). In 1980 these fields were estimated to contain about 300 million barrels of oil, of which 80 million barrels were deemed easily recoverable using the water injection method (*Sudanow*, March 1983:11). However, by 1983, following the surprise discovery of relatively huge quantities of oil (3,300 barrels a day) in the field called Unity 14, Chevron put the estimated oil reserves in the Unity fields at 900 to 970 million barrels, of which 240 million barrels could easily be recovered. They optimistically predicted that, 'based on experience in similar locations, additional discoveries of similar sized fields can be expected' (*Sudanow*, March 1983:9). Chevron's main effort was thus in the Bentiu area and in the Machar Marshes in the Melut-Malakal-Nasir triangle – all in southern Sudan.

For the Sudan, Chevron's findings were a historic breakthrough. Not since oil exploration began in the Red Sea littoral in 1959 had such news been received. Ominously, however, the ruling groups in the north, who were the first Sudanese to learn about the oil discoveries in the south, were gripped by fear of southern separatism inspired by oil.[4] Up until 1974 they had resisted giving exploration licences to oil companies wishing to work in the south. This was ostensibly for security reasons even though peace prevailed in the south at that time and no evidence of southern separatism could be adduced. However, fear of southern separatism does not adequately explain why the northern ruling circles handled the oil issue with paranoid possessiveness and studied exclusion of the southern regional government from petroleum affairs. The explanation, it is submitted, lies in the nature and attitudes of the political forces that were in power in Khartoum from 1978 to 1984, that is from the time of the announcement of the oil finds by Chevron to the time oil operations were shut down in the south.

The power structure in Khartoum (1978–84)[5]

The National Reconciliation of 1977 between Nimeiri on one hand and the National Front parties[6] on the other, brought into the government (the party – Sudanese Socialist Union – and the People's Assembly or Parliament) forces that traditionally espoused Arab-Islamic hegemony over the Sudan. They were the forces of sectarian and fundamentalist Islam which used religion to consolidate and extend a position of political and economic privilege which they had inherited from the colonial era. They felt that their position was challenged by the emergence of any other distinct political entity, especially in the south or in other regions of the Sudan.

Since independence, the National Front parties resisted granting federal status to the south. In the mid 1960s, when they were challenged by a rebellious south and a sophisti-cated socialist movement in the urban north, they countered with severe repression and with an Islamic constitution which provided superficial regional autonomy. From 1972 until they reconciled with Nimeiri, they opposed southern autonomy, seeing in it an obstacle to their hegemony over the Sudan and to their design of Islamizing the south as a prelude to Islamization of East and Central Africa.

The National Front was represented in the central government by two figures: El Sharif El Tuhami, from the Umma party, became the Minister of Energy and Mining from 1978 to 1985; and Hassan El Turabi, the leader of the Moslem Brotherhood, became the Attorney General. The former worked to marginalize the southern regional government from oil affairs, and the latter strove to undermine the legal and political basis of southern regional autonomy through crafty amendments of the Basic Law,[7] and by sponsoring the southern divisionists.[8] Both men succeeded in their designs, but at an incalculable cost for the Sudan and the Sudanese people as their policies contributed to the outbreak of the war. Nimeiri himself was not an innocent bystander. He effected the National Reconciliation to protect his presidency being fully aware that it was at the expense of the non-sectarian supporters of the May regime and of southern autonomy. Besides, he fully approved the policies of his two ministers.

The commercial bourgeoisie in the north followed the oil developments in the south with a keen appetite.[9] Benefits had, in fact, accrued to this class (even before the oil flowed) in the form of real-estate rents and support services for Chevron and its numerous sub-contractors. There was already a proliferation of petroleum services companies registered in anticipation of the oil finds. This class was, therefore, interested in ensuring stability in the north by unifying the northern front as it were. It was not by accident that representatives of this class mediated the National Reconciliation.

To all these forces – the forces of sectarian and fundamentalist Islam newly reconciled with Nimeiri, and the bureaucratic and commercial classes that formed the base of the May regime – oil was to be controlled and used to consolidate their hegemony; the aim was not to distribute it fairly throughout the Sudan. This, I submit, was the dominant perspective in north-central Sudan, and in the central government at the time.

Fears of southern separatism, which some of them (at least those in the ubiquitous intelligence apparatus) knew to be baseless at the time,[10] became a useful rationalization for a visceral attitude of dominance and exploitation. Control over oil would not only give them power over the Sudan, but would also give them badly needed respectability and stature in the Arab world, especially in the oil states where Sudanese rulers were regarded as welfare collectors, although dignified ones for that matter.

The situation in the south

In the south a different alignment of forces with a different perspective prevailed. Popular anger and disappointment over the hollowness (in socio-economic terms) of the regional self-rule was widespread by 1977, and this contributed to the change of regional government in the 1977–8 elections.[11] The new regional government, the 'wind of change', promised to adopt a hard-line approach *vis-à-vis* the central government so as to secure southern entitlements. However, it soon became evident that a hard-line approach without military hardware is a dangerous bluff that could be called. The central government exploited intra-southern quarrels and rivalries and, by 1980, a new government was elected in Juba under Abel Alier.

The new government, even though it operated from the start in an unhealthy environment of ethnic politics which was manipulated and orchestrated by the central government, was determined to seek a fair share of the national cake (Mawut, 1986: 24–40). The socio-economic deterioration of the south made a mockery of the civil peace that had prevailed from 1972 to early 1980. 'One does not eat peace' was a common slogan among southerners.

Ironically, peace had had unexpected results. In the north the proliferation of development and service projects was in evidence, while in the south central government projects stagnated due to lack of funds and managerial will. In addition, the central government starved the south of badly needed funds from 1972 to 1977. The region received, on average, only 23.2 per cent of the allocated sums annually from the central government from a special development budget.

Table 1 Special Development Budget for the South

Year	Budget allocation (thousand LS)	Actual expenditure (thousand LS)	Actual expenditure (percentage of allocation)
1972–3	1,400	560	40.0%
1973–4	7,300	730	10.0%
1974–5	7,100	1,150	16.2%
1975–6	7,200	1,630	22.7%
1976–7	15,000	3,610	23.6%

Source: The Southern Regional Ministry of Finance. Fadalla, 1986:23.

From 1977 to 1983 the development needs of the south were supposed to be met under the Six Year Plan (1977–8 to 1982–3). Out of the 225 million US dollars earmarked for the south under the Plan, only 45 million was actually paid to the south by 1982 (Prunier, 1989:415), that is only 19.6 per cent of the minimum investment recommended by the ILO in 1976 (ILO/UNDP, 1975:202). Apart from a few foreign financed agricultural projects in Equatoria, the south was, in development terms, 'where it was at the time of the conclusion of peace' (*The Economist*, 29 May 1982:31).

This lack of investment and development was reflected in a widespread shortage of services and high unemployment. Education was badly hit. Schools deteriorated. There was a lack of books, desks, chalk, teachers, food and so forth. Discipline broke down and standards dropped. The outlook for most students in junior and senior secondary schools was bleak. They were to form about 60 per cent of the SPLA forces in due course.

There was thus a conflict-laden situation prevailing in both Khartoum and Juba from 1978 to 1983. The government in Khartoum viewed the southern regional government with self-serving suspicion. In Juba there was a popularly elected government acutely aware of the popular disappointment and anger which had arisen over the socio-economic backwardness of the south despite eight years of peace. The southern masses felt that the central government should be more forthcoming in its financial and developmental obligations to the south than it had hitherto been. The oil was to be a test case of the central government's intentions. Whereas the southern regional government in mid 1981 was for a fair and equitable deal over the oil, the central government was for exclusive control. A collision was thus inevitable.

Patterns of exclusion and southern Responses

The central government was determined to exclude the southern regional government from oil policy making even before the formal announcement of oil finds in December 1978. The policies of exclusion were the inverse of the policies aimed at tightening the central government's grip (and that of Chevron) over the oil, and followed the pattern outlined below.

1. In 1974, following the Akobo incident, the government prompted Chevron to move its base camp from Malakal in the south, to Muglad in southern Kordofan (Alier, 1990:216).[12] This move deprived the town of Malakal and the adjacent villages of employment opportunities and other benefits associated with having an active oil base camp.
2. In an effort to dissociate oil from the south in the minds of northern Sudanese, the central government studiedly and constantly referred to the oil fields as 'located 450 miles south-west of Khartoum'.
3. Geographically neutral and politically 'reassuring' names – such as 'unity' – were conferred on oil fields and wells found in the south, whereas those in the north were given local names such as Barakat and Abu Gabra in Southern Kordofan. The government even went to the extent of translating a Dinka name, 'Thou', into an arabic one, 'Heglig' (a well known tree in the area), to name an oil field in the Bentiu area (Alier, 1990:219).
4. Southerners were excluded from the training programmes in oil technology sponsored by the Ministry of Energy and Mining and financed by a 150,000 US dollar grant from Chevron. The Minister was determined to exclude southern Sudanese from the 'oil secrets and management in the Sudan' (Alier, 1990:222).
5. Trips to the oil fields by the President, the Minister of Energy and Mining, and Chevron officials were never made known to the southern government or the commissioner of the province concerned.
6. Officials of oil companies operating in the south were instructed to avoid discussing their work with southern government officials – a directive which Total subsequently had to ignore after it was ordered to leave the south by the southern Minister of Energy and Mining.
7. Attempts were made to redraw provincial boundaries to incorporate the oil-

bearing areas in the south into the north (Badal, 1986:144–7).

8. Military units commanded by southerners were transferred from Bentiu area and replaced with larger units from the north commanded by northerners.

9. Southerners were excluded from the White Nile Petroleum Company (WNPC) which was formed in August 1981, to establish and run the refinery in Kosti and subsequently the pipeline.[13]

10. The central government decided to locate the oil refinery in Kosti, as opposed to Bentiu, and the latter opted for an export-oriented pipeline from the Bentiu fields to Mersah Nimeiri near Port Sudan. All these decisions were made with pointed disregard for southern preferences.

The southern reaction to all these measures of exclusion and control was by no means separatist or possessive. Angered by the surprise announcement made in San Francisco in late 1978 by Chevron and the Sudan government that oil had been found in commercial quantities in the Sudan and would be exported by pipeline via Port Sudan, southern students demonstrated and called for the construction of a pipeline to Mombasa. This demand, which was by no means the official policy of the regional government at the time, reflected, nevertheless, a widely held belief among southerners that the most deserving markets for Sudanese oil were the poor oil-starved countries of East and Central Africa.

Successive regional governments did not have a publicly known oil policy (if they had one at all) from 1978 to 1980. However, the southern people and government were forced to quickly take a stand when the President formally announced in April 1980 that the refinery would be built in Kosti because of its strategic location. The southerners were enraged and demanded an explanation. El Tuhami, Minister of Energy and Mining, added insult to injury by adding that Kosti had been selected for scientific, technical and economic factors in preference to Bentiu, 'which is in the middle of nowhere' (*Sudanow*, June 1981:18). The regional government, under considerable pressure from the southern public, insisted on having the refinery located in Bentiu. Once there, the provisions of the Southern Provinces Self-Government Act of 1972 would enable the regional government to collect taxes and other revenues which the central government would collect if the refinery was in the north. In addition, other revenues, employment, services and so forth would accrue to the south, at least to the Bentiu Area Council. At no stage did the regional government claim exclusive title to the oil.

Nimeiri ordered El Tuhami and Chevron's Managing Director to go to Juba to meet with the regional government. The meeting was heated but frank and ended with the parties agreeing to have a technical committee in which the region would be fully represented, to undertake a further technical study of the refinery location, and to take up other issues. A trilateral approach to oil affairs was, it seemed, finally beginning to take shape as it should have in 1974.

Unfortunately, El Tuhami misrepresented the Juba meeting to the President as indicative of a southern separatist attitude towards oil (Alier, 1990:220). The President then reaffirmed the decision to locate the refinery in Kosti, but made some minor concessions to the south.[14] The regional government accepted these sweeteners and agreed to 'cool off' to the bitter disappointment of the southern public who, as the then President of the High Executive Council (HEC), Abel Alier, put it, 'condemned me for not fighting, physically if need be' (Alier, 1990:221). At that point the regional government was not in a position to fight and did not want to bluff. Some southerners saw much wisdom in the HEC's decision not to stumble into a confrontation they were not prepared for. There was, however, no compelling reasons for the HEC to positively endorse the President's decision as it did. The south still had the right to reopen the issues of revenue sharing and participation in the oil industry no matter where the refinery was located.

The conflict over the location was also a conflict over philosophies of development. The central government wanted the refinery to be situated close to areas of industrial and agricultural production in central Sudan. The regional government, on the other hand, held the view that 'the principle of taking business to areas where infrastructure is developed would condemn the underdeveloped areas of the country to perpetual under development' (Alier, 1990:220) – an argument that was unacceptable to the hegemonists in Khartoum.[15]

Latent conflicts

There were also latent conflicts between Chevron and enlightened opinion in the Sudan. Chevron's concession was based on a production-sharing agreement with the Sudan government which was established in 1974 and underwent a number of revisions (Kok, 1980:473–85). However, the gist of it was that Chevron was entitled to recoup its costs from up to 30 per cent per annum of the value of oil recovered. From the balance, the government was to get 70 per cent and Chevron 30 per cent as long as production was under 250,000 barrels per day (b.p.d.). If production reached 250,000 to 500,000 b.p.d. the government's share would go up to 75 per cent, and to 80 per cent when productivity exceeded 500,000 b.p.d. (Kok, 1980:475). The government thus had an interest in higher production, which was then also in the interest of Chevron. It was thought that these shares unfairly favoured Chevron[16] and that the sharing formula encouraged the government to embark on a recklessly accelerated production programme which would lead to depletion of the oil before a well-conceived national policy was agreed on for the utilization of the resource.

A second point of conflict existed between the government and some intellectuals and concerned the role of oil in development and the restriction of oil policy formulation to a small group comprising the President, a few palace aides, the Minister of Energy and Mining, Chevron and a few expatriate mediators. Some wanted the oil to be used first to meet domestic needs before the surplus (if any) was exported (Kok, 1980:16–24). The government and Chevron were seen as exported-oriented, and hence not acting in the best interests of the Sudan.

In 1980 the Sudan was spending about 279 million US dollars on petrol and petroleum products, a sum which represented about 60 per cent of its foreign currency earnings.[17] This jumped to 437 million US dollars when the decision to build the 1,455 km pipeline to Mersah Nimeiri was taken. Government opponents argued that this sum would be saved if oil was used for domestic needs. However, close observers think that the Palace preferred to export oil because it promised handsome kickbacks and commissions from bidders and so forth (see Khalid, 1990:332).

The secrecy over oil policy-making thus had more to do with special deals than with operational requirements for confidentiality. Under the law, oil contracts are supposed to be entered into by the Petroleum Affairs Council and ratified by parliament. An amendment to the law conferred all powers to grant licences and enter into production-sharing arrangements on the Minister and the President. This arrangement suited both the Palace and the contractors as it ensured secrecy. But these conflicts over oil were overshadowed by the conflict between the central government and the southern government and people.

Preconditions for revenue sharing

The decision to construct a pipeline from the oil fields to the Red Sea was defended on the grounds that globally there was a surplus in oil refining capacity, especially in Saudi Arabia, and hence it was cheaper to construct a pipeline, export the crude and import it back refined than to construct an oil refinery of 25,000 to 50,000 b.p.d. capacity.[18] This argument did not convince most Sudanese for the reasons already mentioned. For the southerners, this decision confirmed the north's original plan of 1978 which aimed to transfer the oil out of the reach of the south.

In June 1983, Nimeiri divided the south into three regions and thereby weakened its political power. Hostilities broke out and in February 1984, three months after its camps were attacked in the south, Chevron shut down its operations in the Sudan. That was the only way of stopping the oil from being used by the northern ruling groups to consolidate their hegemony over the Sudan. Some northerners now admit that oil policies and the division of the south contributed to the outbreak of the war.[19] Since then, there has been talk among the ruling groups in Khartoum of equitably sharing resources. But this talk still betrays deep-seated hegemonic tendencies. It assumes that mineral resources, including oil, should be vested in the central government with producing region(s) being entitled to a *fixed* percentage. This formula, first advanced by Saddiq Al-Mahdi, was repeated in March 1991 by the present military government, which recommended the Nigerian model of revenue sharing (*Final Report,* 1989: 27–8). The newly announced federal structure in the Sudan, however, eloquently confirms the tight control by the centre over such a resource, despite the talk of revenue sharing.[20]

There can be no fair oil revenue sharing formula in the Sudan without a prior power-sharing scheme among the relevant groups/regions in the country. Oil is power, and neither it nor any other sources of wealth and power can be fairly shared in the Sudan without first putting in place a fair system of power sharing. The absence of these pre-conditions makes the sharing formulae from other countries, such as Nigeria, not very useful at this stage. In Nigeria, control of oil has implications for the strategic balance of political forces in the state and that probably explains why the Nigerian revenue sharing schemes have proved disturbingly unstable since the 1960s. Even the carefully worked out scheme by the Okigbo Commission (1980) proved highly controversial.

Importantly, despite the broad similarities between the problems facing Nigeria and the Sudan, there is a fundamental difference. In Nigeria, there is an inverse relationship between political hegemony on one hand, and socio-economic development on the other. The north (or the Fulani Hausa group of states) had and continues to have a commanding presence at the federal level despite its relative underdevelopment and its fear of southern domination in other fields. It has used state power not only to better its power position, but to check southern 'domination'. Even under military regimes, the north has never been a political underdog.

In the Sudan, on the other hand, state, financial, commercial and economic power are in the hands of the elites of north-central Sudan. They have used this power, under military and civilian regimes, to maintain and aggrandize their position, and to prevent other regions from breaking out of backwardness. This monopoly of state power on ethnic/regional lines first has to give way to a more equitable sharing of power before it can be complemented by a revenue sharing arrangement. Under such an arrangement, mineral resources should be the property of the people. The right to make administrative and technical arrangements for the exploitation of such resources on behalf of and for the benefit of the people can be vested jointly in the state and federal governments. For non-fuel minerals, such a right can be exercised by the state in which the minerals are found. The individual states and the federal government should be partners in all negotiations and agreements with the operating oil companies. This scheme should also include arrangements whereby rich states and the federal government are obligated to pay fixed percentages of their earnings to relatively poor states. Compensatory payments should also be made to those regions that have historically been deprived, neglected or exploited, to enable them to catch up, particularly in terms of infrastructure and services. Such are the post-conflict revenue sharing arrangements which one would like to see in the Sudan.[21] It presupposes an effective and just sharing of state power in the Sudan, which is not yet the case.

Notes

1 The conflict over water in the Sudan, especially over the digging of the Jonglei Canal, is not discussed in this paper. The reader may refer to Waterbury, 1979:60–80; and Alier, 1990:193–214.

2 There is a rich literature on the nature of the conflict in the Sudan, but the most recent works with fresh insights into the issues involved include: Malwal, 1983; Niblock, 1987; Alier, 1990; Khalid, 1990; Woodward, 1990; and Garang, 1987.

3 See Kok, 1981. A highly condensed summary appeared in *Sudanow,* December 1981:39. The figures and the locations cited here were authoritatively given by Mr. Pete Bellinger, the then Managing Director of Chevron (Sudan) who participated in the conference.

4 Southern separatism, to the extent that it has ever been definitively formulated, has been more a reaction

to the injustice, repression and intransigence of the northern ruling circles than a primordial categorical demand of the southerners. This view is adequately analysed in Wai, 1981 and Albino, 1970. Northerners (some scholars and politicians) tend to regard southern separatism as foreign inspired, and that the mainstream southern opinion is for unity of the Sudan. See Al-Rahim, 1968; Beshir, 1968; and Mahgoub, 1974. However, even if there was no foreign influence for separating the south from the north, and despite the fact that Western and Eastern powers and the neighbouring African countries were not for separation, the danger of southern separatism has been used by the northern ruling groups as a handy tool for mobilizing northern public support and the support of the 'sister' Arab countries for draconian measures against the south.

5   A useful exposé of the structure of political power in the Sudan after the National Reconciliation is to be found in Khalid, 1985; and Malwal, 1983.

6   These were: The Umma Party, led by Saddiq Al-Mahdi who was also the overall President of the National Front; the DUP, led by Sharif Al-Hindi, who was the Deputy Leader of the National Front; and the Moslem Brothers whose leader, Hassan El Turabi, never left the Sudan until the Reconciliation. For an account of the reconciliation process, see Hamid, 1984.

7   The Regional High Executive Council and the Regional Assembly Act, 1980 gave powers to the President of the Republic to dissolve these two institutions in the south. The President used this Act to dissolve these institutions in 1980, 1981 and 1983. The Act is unconstitutional as it purports to amend the Southern Provinces Self-Government Act 1972 in a manner contrary to section 34 thereof which prescribes that any amendment of the Act must be approved by three-quarters of the members of the National People's Assembly and two-thirds of the southern Sudanese in a region-wide referendum. Art. 6 Sudan Permanent Constitution, 1973, reaffirmed this provision.

8   The southern divisionists were those who espoused the division of the south into three or more regions. They were very closely sponsored and advised by a number of political personalities in the central government including the Attorney General.

9   Fatima B. Mahmoud (1984:73–148) gives a valuable account of this class and its role in contemporary Sudanese politics. Also see Niblock, 1987.

10 A State Security Report in November 1984 and made public after the fall of Nimeiri in April 1985 took the view that the subdivision of the south in June 1983 and the adoption of the Shariah laws in 1983–4 were the main reasons for the outbreak of the war.

11 Lazarus Mawut (1986) gives a valuable account of the mood in the southern region prior to the outbreak of the conflict in 1983.

12 Malakal airstrip, argued the government, was needed by the government for its air operations against the mutineers in Akobo. But when the Akobo incident was over, Chevron was not permitted to go back to Malakal.

13 There was not a single southerner on the board of directors of the company which was made up of the three shareholders: the central government, Chevron and the International Finance Corporation.

14 These were: the improvement by Chevron of Kosti-Malakal road to make it an all-weather road; health and educational services for the Bentiu Area Council in addition to a grant of one million Sudanese pounds in development funds; topping plant to produce refined products for adjacent oil fields; and special barges to ferry refined oil and oil products from Kosti to Juba and the intermediate towns. These tasks were to be undertaken by Chevron who, 'it became evident in the course of time, did not intend to fulfil its undertakings' (Alier, 1990:221).

15 In a perceptive article, D. Roden discusses the implications of these two schools of thought on Sudanese development. He observed that 'once a certain region has been able, through some initial advantage, to move ahead of other regions, the "backwash" or "polarization" *effect that arises as productive forces like labour, capital and commodities are drawn into the growth area will greatly restrict opportunities for development in the rest of the country*' (1974:502, emphasis added).

16 A view shared by all the Sudanese participants in the conference organized by the author in the University of Khartoum, in December 1981. See Kok, 1981:14–32.

17 A statement by the Minister of Mining and Energy, in *Sudanow*, July 1980:30.

18 Interview with Yusuf Suleiman, Minister of State for Energy and Mining, *Sudanow*, March 1983:14.

19 See, for example, the statements by Professor Muddathir Abd Al-Rahim in *Asharq-Al-Awsat*, no. 3980, 1989:3, and Dr El Turabi, in an interview with Helena Da Costa, *Radio France Internationale*, reproduced in *Politique Internationale* (Paris), November 1986:147. However, both speakers made these admissions in an attempt to show that Shariah laws were not the cause of the conflict, a view which even Nimeiri's security apparatus did not share as we have shown in note 10.

20 See the Constitutional Decree No. 4 promulgating a federal system for the Sudan. S. 33 (l)(a) for the limited sources of funds for the States, in contrast to the vast powers reserved for the central government under 33 (i)(j). See *El Sudan El Hadith*, 5 February 1991:2.

21 A federal-confederal constitution and a revenue sharing scheme were the subject of a study by the author in Kok, 1989.

References

Al-Rahim, M. Abd. 1968. *The Development of British Policy in the Southern Sudan 1899–1947*, Khartoum, Khartoum University Press.

Albino, O. 1970. *The Sudan: A Southern Viewpoint*, London, Oxford University Press.

Alier, A. 1990. *Southern Sudan: Too Many Agreements Dishonoured*, Exeter, Ithaca Press.

Badal, R. 1986. 'Oil and regional sentiment in the south' in Al-Rahim, M.A., R. Badal, A. Hardallo and P. Woodward (eds.) *Sudan Since Independence*, London, Gower.

Beshir, M.O. 1968. *The Southern Sudan, Background to the Conflict*, New York, Praegear.

Fadalla, B.O.M. 1986. *Unbalanced Development and Regional Disparity in the Sudan*, Khartoum, Department of Economics, University of Khartoum.

Final Report and Recommendations on Dialogue and Peace Issues. 1989, October. Khartoum, Government of the Sudan, pp. 27–8.

Garang, J. 1987. *John Garang Speaks*, Khalid, M. (ed.) London, Kegan and Paul International.

Hamid, M.B. 1984. 'The politics of national reconciliation in the Sudan: The Numayri regime and the National Front opposition', *Occasional Papers Series*, Washington DC, Center for Contemporary Arab Studies, Georgetown University.

ILO/UNDP. 1975. *Growth, Employment and Equity: A Comprehensive Strategy for the Sudan*, Geneva, ILO Office.

Khalid, M. 1985. *Nimeiri and the Revolution of Dis-May*, London, Kegan and Paul International.

Khalid, M. 1990. *The Government They Deserve*, London, Kegan and Paul International.

Kok, P.N. 1980. *The Role of Nation-States and Supra-National Entities in the Promotion and Regulation of Private Foreign Investment: The Case of the Sudan*, a J.S.D. thesis, Yale Law School.

Kok, P.N. 1981. 'Petroleum in the Sudan: Law, policy and practice', proceedings of a conference *Petroleum in the Sudan: Law, Policy and Practice*, Khartoum, Faculty of Law Library, University of Khartoum.

Kok, P.N. 1989. *A New Constitution for the Sudan*, Khartoum, The Sudan Council of Churches.

Mahgoub, M.A. 1974. *Democracy on Trial*, London, André Deutsch.

Mahmound, F.B. 1984. *The Sudanese Bourgeoisie: Vanguard to Development?*, Khartoum, Khartoum University Press.

Malwal, B. 1983. *People and Power in the Sudan: The Struggle for National Stability*, London, Ithaca Press.

Mawut, L. 1986. *The Southern Sudan: Why Back to Arms*, Khartoum, St. George Press.

Niblock, T. 1987. *Power and Class in the Sudan: The Dynamics of Sudanese Politics 1898–1985*, London, Macmillan.

Prunier, G. 1989. 'Le sud-Soudan depuis l'independance (1956–1989)' in Lavergne, M. (ed.) *Le Soudan Contemporain*, Paris, Karthala-Cermoc.

Roden, D. 1974. 'Regional inequality and rebellion in the Sudan' *Geographical Review*, vol. 64, no. 4.

Wai, D. 1981. *The African-Arab Conflict of the Sudan*, New York, African Publishing.

Waterbury, J. 1979. *The Hydropolitics of the Nile Valley*, Syracuse, Syracuse University Press.

Woodward, P. 1990. *Sudan 1898–1989: The Unstable State*, Boulder, LRP and London, LCAP.

Comment   JORDAN GEBRE-MEDHIN

Since the days of independence, irrespective of the oil finds, the basic and fundamental problem in the Sudan has been that political power in the country is under the hegemonic control of northern elites. From the start, the war between the north and south assumed a civil character. When the first armed confrontation was resolved in 1972 (after 17 years of fighting) the negotiated resolution of the conflict implied a fair degree of autonomy for the south in the federalist republic of Sudan. This, however, never materialized. The systematic imposition of ignorance concerning oil reserves in the south, and the direct and indirect diversion of oil revenue from its source, aggravated the contradiction further, leading to the second armed struggle by the south against northern hegemony. Peter Nyot Kok has made this very clear.

Kok is correct when he locates political power as the source of conflict in the country. However, historically the conflict between Ethiopia and Somalia was not so unlike the struggle in the Sudan as 'strategic resources' played a determinant role in the conflict. In the early 1940s, when Britain defeated Italy in the Horn of Africa, London assumed control of former Italian colonies – Eritrea, Somalia, Ethiopia and the Ogaden region. In 1944 Ethiopia was decolonized. Britain, frustrated by the nationalist movements for independence in its colonies, was by the late 1940s ready to abandon Eritrea, Somalia and the Ogaden. The USA was nervous as the Sinclair Oil Company of New York was already in the Ogaden, and Washington had established a foothold on the Red Sea with its Kagnew Base establishment in Eritrea. It is here that the USA made its first strategic error when it favoured the 'stable' Ethiopian empire state to replace Britain in the Horn. To this end, the USA helped the Ethiopian Crown gain control of the Ogaden and Eritrea.

The conflict between Ethiopia and Somalia was a contradiction between two repressive states with reactionary policies. The Ogaden became an excuse for the destructive wars between Somalia and Ethiopia, first in 1964 and again in 1977–8. The basic issue of self-determination for the people of Ogaden was of no concern to Somalia and Ethiopia. Further, Somali state nationalism was not informed by matching power. The fragile Greater Somali unity was further fractured when the Ethiopian empire state provided a fraction of the Somali opposition with arms and political support, destabilizing in the most accelerated form the entire political economy of Somalia. The perception that there were oil fields in the Ogaden was elementary to the war policies of Ethiopia and Somalia over the Ogaden. In this complex and difficult situation the liberation fronts in the Ogaden were never able to maintain a fair degree of independence. The case of Eritrea was different.

Emperor Haile Selassie and the dictatorial regime of Mengistu also took 'strategic resources' as one factor in their determined policy to hold on to Eritrea. When Ethiopia began sending armed bands to weaken Eritrean resolve for independence, Eritrean peasants reacted by forming militias to fight this violence induced by Ethiopia. This was in 1948. In the 1950s, when the Ethiopian monarch acted contrary to the UN based federal status of Eritrea, opposition against Ethiopia became vocal and active. The discovery of strategic resources in Eritrea, in part exploited by the Nippon Mining Company of Japan, did not change the historically rooted politics of the national movement in Eritrea. At a given conjuncture the Eritreans were to realize that a compromise solution with the Ethiopian empire state was impossible. The strategy of uniting with the democratic forces within the empire, to isolate and destroy the Amhara-dominated state and its apparatus, became central and key to the success of the Eritrean revolution, as well as to the success of popular forces within the country. Whether this example is of any importance in the case of the Sudan, the people of the Sudan will decide. It remains a fact, however, that the state policies of Somalia and Ethiopia with regard to the Ogaden, and the Ethiopian state's policy on Eritrea were informed by 'strategic resources' considerations.

12 An Introduction to IGADD

ALI AHMED SALEEM

The Inter-Governmental Authority on Drought and Development (IGADD) has six member states in the Horn: Djibouti, Ethiopia, Somalia, Kenya, the Sudan and Uganda. This institution is still young. It was born in 1986 as a result of a lot of discussion among the ministers of foreign affairs and the IGADD countries' UN representatives in the General Assembly. The severe drought of 1984-6 brought them together and they agreed among themselves to establish an institution with the sole purpose of working together to solve a common problem. They also wanted to pool their resources because one state cannot face the problem of drought alone. Not only does drought have no boundaries, but by pooling their resources they hoped to achieve some results. The organization received considerable assistance from the UNDP, and was also helped by the World Bank.

The organization has a supreme organ that consists of the heads of states and governments, a council of ministers, and an executive secretariat. The executive secretary, the head of the secretariat, is appointed by the council of ministers for a once renewable term of four years, and is entrusted with the implementation of the resolutions and programmes of action emanating from the council of ministers. All the programmes come from and are approved by the council of ministers. In particular, the executive secretary co-ordinates the environmental policies of the countries of the subregion and assists in the formulation of proposals in order to establish an ecological balance. Furthermore, the executive secretariat assists the member states in procuring technical assistance for the preparation of project documents for the rehabilitation of drought-stricken areas, and assists the member states in the assessment of emergency needs for famine relief. Finally, it seeks, mobilizes, and co-ordinates the resources needed for drought control projects and makes an effort to reinforce national organs and facilities necessary for the implementation of sub-regional development policies.

IGADD developed a plan of action after its establishment which defined three different areas for the authority's activities. It undertakes emergency drought relief measures which are beyond the scope of one member country; engages medium-term programmes for drought recovery and for laying the foundations for a fresh start; and takes on long-term programmes which are meant to guide socio-economic development of the subregion in an environmentally balanced way. In this plan of action there are certain priority areas which emphasize food security, environmental protection, water resources and desertification control, in that order. To pursue these areas, the executive secretary has started commissioning studies and formulating regional projects. In this connection, the key point is that IGADD is working on a regional rather than national basis. The organization helps the member countries develop by providing expertise and finance, but it does not handle national projects. Besides the priority areas, IGADD is working with the livestock sector, communication and transportation infrastructure, and human resource development, but on a smaller scale. For each project IGADD has a technological component. In the matter of grain marketing, for example, a grain technologist is incorporated in the project.

IGADD developed a food security strategy for the region, which was endorsed and accepted by all the member states in Kampala in October 1990; there was a political commitment by the ministers who attended the conference to pursue all that was recommended in the strategy. As a result a regional early warning food system project was established in Djibouti which now serves all the six member states. A sensing component of this early warning project is in Nairobi. The whole objective of this project is to develop a data bank which covers the entire food security spectrum. Currently the collection of information is a weak point for IGADD. The organization takes its information from the governments of the region and is not able to verify it. We are hoping to have complete data on the region soon; we started this project two years ago.

IGADD programmes started out being *ad hoc*, but the donors refused to finance unrelated projects. We had to develop a strategy. Now we have financing for most of the projects in the strategies, and we are pursuing the mobilization of funds from other potential donors. In relation to water resources, IGADD will concentrate its efforts on improving the level of water resources knowledge in the member states so as to be able to provide planners and decision-makers with reliable inputs; encouraging co-operation among the member states in planning and managing service and groundwater use; and enhancing the efficiency of water use by means of applied research. In addition, IGADD will set the foundation for the gradual introduction of multinational river management, and will concentrate on supporting training and research as well as subregional planning for irrigation.

On the environmental issue, IGADD also developed a strategy which was endorsed and accepted by all the member states at the meeting in October 1990. The pollution issue is taken care of in the environmental protection strategy. It is one of the key programmes. Oil pollution, for example, is taken up in this strategy.

Co-ordination is very important in IGADD's work. Not only is it essential to co-operate with other organizations, but we must know what they are doing. Consequently, the organization keeps in very close touch with the other organizations. The Preferential Trade Area (PTA) has produced a very good study on co-ordination and harmonization of intergovernmental authorities in East Africa and West Africa, and Southern Africa. In that report they recommended the categorization of organizations which have the same or similar objectives. Thus, IGADD was categorized with the Economic Community of West African States (ECOWAS) and the Southern African Development Co-ordination Conference (SADCC).

Comment   HUSSEIN M. ADAM

During its formation, IGADD learnt from other intergovernmental organizations, such as the Comité Permanent Interétats de la Lutte contre la Sécheresse dans le Sahel (CILLS) which stretches from Senegal to Chad. It was agreed that the organizational structure of IGADD would be very small but would grow in size, unlike CILLS which seemed to have started with a very large and cumbersome secretariat. It was also agreed that the member countries would pay for the secretariat, which was again different from CILLS. The procedure for adopting documents was as follows: UN experts would first draft the documents, then the country experts would critique and re-adopt the documents, then a ministers' conference would officially approve them, and finally the summit approved the whole thing.

At the time of the IGADD meetings, Egypt was very interested in being given observer's status. This is not surprising given Egypt's interests in the sources of the Nile and IGADD's clear expression that regional water development is one of its objectives.

Tanzania had also shown interest. Countries from outside the region were also very interested in IGADD, including the EEC. France naturally because of the base being Djibouti. But Italy seemed to be the heavy player. In fact, the Italian minister at the 1986 summit pointed out that this is a region where they have historic ties, that is in Eritrea, Ethiopia and Somalia, and in essence said to the heads of state at the summit that if they can agree to work with this structure, Italy will contribute as much money as it puts anywhere outside of Italy. This was an example of an outside donor interested in providing funding which goes beyond one country.

My view is that a structure like IGADD is ultimately the correct one for co-operation in the region. It is possible down the line that when these countries are ready to co-operate seriously, they may find that they need to modify IGADD structures, but it will be useful to analyse whatever mistakes IGADD makes. One of the things that IGADD did play a role in was the political sphere. At the first IGADD meeting in January 1986 Mengistu and Siyad Barre met for the first time and initiated a dialogue. And I think it was at the donors' conference or the summit that they met to ratify some other agreement for Ethiopian-Somali co-operation. So there were political results. Some people feel that it was a little too political, and in a way, that was true. In the appointment of the executive secretary, for instance, there was tremendous politicization of the fight. Other appointments were to be purely on merit; the jobs would appear in the six countries in the newspapers, and experts who fit the criteria would apply. But these positions were also very politicized; almost every country came with one candidate in its pocket. I think this comes back to the point that until the houses are cleaned inside, IGADD will reflect what the member states are. And if there is patronage in appointments in Somalia and in Ethiopia, and people are given jobs as a kind of hand-out, that just projects itself at the inter-regional level. That is one problem and, hopefully, that will change.

Comment: ABDULRAHMAN MOHAMED BABU

With respect to the economic formation of IGADD, I just want to emphasize one aspect of the East African Community which may be useful for future communities. East Africa had the longest lasting economic community, existing up to 1974. In fact, when in 1968 we went to Brussels to join the EEC as associate members, the EEC members commended East Africa by saying they had a lot to learn from us. We had to laugh at them because at that time East Africa already had a parliament and commissions of various kinds, thanks to the Phillips Commission. But why is it that this wonderful organization collapsed? The reality of the matter is that we do not have the material basis for co-operation. I remember when I was Minister of Trade, we set up a committee, a Council for East African Trade. Ministers of Kenya, Tanzania and Uganda came together to discuss what could be exchanged among themselves. Uganda said, 'we have coffee, we have maize, we have tea'. Kenya said, 'we have maize, we have coffee, we have tea'. Tanzania said, 'we have maize, 'we have tea, we have coffee'. Now what do we exchange among ourselves? We realized that we do not have the material basis for exchange. In fact, rather than co-operate, we compete. If there is drought in Kenya, we celebrate it in Tanzania because their coffee will go down, our coffee will go up.

This is the basis of all our problems in Africa. Our economies are not complementary. They are competing economies because these are colonial economies. They are not serving our interests – they are serving export interests. Therefore, with this new thinking in the region, especially in the Horn where there are wonderful opportunities, particularly in terms of labour-power, we should be thinking seriously about what are the bases, the material, economic bases which will bring these countries in the Horn and also in East Africa together.

13

Patterns of Internal Wage Labour Migration in the Horn of Africa: The Case of the Sudan

SALAH EL-DIN EL-SHAZALI IBRAHIM

Introduction

The wars that have ravaged the countries of the Horn of Africa have set into motion processes of population destabilization of considerable magnitude. Even before the escalation of war, the destabilization of rural communities, manifested in accelerated rural to urban migration (and more recently emigration to the oil-rich Arab countries), was a cause for concern. With the escalation of armed conflicts, destabilization of the countries involved has been further accentuated. The mass displacement of Sudanese, Ethiopian and Somali citizens, both within and outside their respective countries, produced around two million refugees who have been hosted by the countries of the Horn of Africa, and who constituted 40 per cent of Africa's refugees and 12 per cent of the total world refugee population in 1989 (*The Courier*, May–June 1990:72–3). Of these, 'more than a million Ethiopian (and Eritrean) refugees have sought asylum in Somalia and the Sudan, almost 350,000 Somalis have gone to Ethiopia and there are almost 450,000 Sudanese in Ethiopia and Uganda' (*The Courier*, May–June 1990:67). These statistics obviously do not include those refugees produced by these countries, but who found asylum in other parts of the world. Nor do they include those who were internally displaced, whose numbers are known to be much greater. In the specific case of the Sudan, the estimated number of people displaced by the war is just under three million.

The overwhelming majority of refugees and displaced people within the countries of the Horn are impoverished and illiterate agropastoralists who can only perform unskilled manual labour. In view of the general economic crises besetting the countries of the Horn, employment opportunities for both refugees and displaced people are quite limited, particularly in the large urban areas where both categories seem to concentrate. In regions outside the combat zones the economic crises have also accelerated patterns of (voluntary) labour migration from rural to urban areas and from both of these areas to the oil-rich Arab countries. The current conditions of war and economic crises, however, mean that very little is being done to deal with the problem of population mobility (forced and voluntary alike). The only exception takes the form of interventions which aim to evict migrants, refugees and displaced people from the large urban areas and rehabilitate them within traditional economic pursuits in the countryside.

Upon the restoration of peace conditions in the Horn a major task facing governments will be the stabilization of the population in productive pursuits. This requires the formulation of comprehensive and synchronized population and land-use policies and programmes. In view of the need to achieve far-reaching changes in socio-economic structures and processes throughout the Horn, however, formulation of the required policies and programmes amounts to a formidable task. If policies and programmes are geared to stabilize and rehabilitate the population through interventions which aim to restore former patterns and forms of production, particularly in the so-called 'traditional sector' within which the majority of the population lives, they may prove irrelevant and futile. As will be corroborated later in this paper, the 'traditional sector' is experiencing an intensive process of decomposition, and its viability has been consistently eroded over the years. The challenge, thus, is to be both innovative and realistic when formulating population and land-use policies.

The purpose of this paper is to illuminate aspects of the phenomenon of labour migration and how, in recent years, it has taken the form of population displacement. The central contention of the paper is that, although those who are displaced seem to follow relatively old established routes of labour migration, the dynamic of displacement indicates a thorough break from the logic of earlier patterns of labour migration. In order not to be too general, and in the process vague as well, the paper focuses on the specific case of the Sudan, and seeks to highlight some of the requirements that need to be satisfied to bring about population redistribution and stabilization in the context of a peace economy. Since the formulation of comprehensive population and land-use policies relating to refugees as well as to integrated resource management in the Sudan entails a fair degree of co-ordination with neighbouring countries, with Ethiopia (and perhaps an independent Eritrea) in particular, the paper also contributes to the identification of spheres for regional co-operation among the countries of the Horn of Africa.

The paper consists of six sections, the first being this introduction. The second section provides a general background to labour migration and the emergence of labour markets in colonial Sudan. The third section describes the processes that led to the acceleration of wage labour migration in post-colonial Sudan, while the fourth exposes salient features in the operation of agricultural labour markets in the country. The fifth section provides an account of the emergence of mass displacement as the dominant form of labour mobility. The final section recapitulates the main conclusions drawn in preceding sections and provides some suggestions for the formulation of policies which would adequately address the problem of population stabilization in the context of a peace economy.

Migration and the 'urban problem' in the Sudan

Since its independence in 1956, the Sudan has witnessed a process of rapid urban growth. As in other underdeveloped countries, urbanization in the Sudan is unevenly distributed between regions, a few major cities are dominant, and the population is concentrated in the capital. The population of Greater Khartoum increased from 245,735 in 1955–6 to 784,294 in 1973, and to 1,343,651 in 1983. Although this urban growth is partly a consequence of the relatively high fertility rates which are assumed to prevail in cities (Khalifa, 1979), the prime factor is said to be increased rural–urban migration. Urban growth has been intensified further since 1983 by influxes of refugees, drought victims and people displaced by the war. This has exacerbated concern over the 'urban problem' which is generally attributed to the 'massive drift' of rural people into the few large cities.

In response to its concern over the urban problem, the Sudanese authorities attempted, as have many other governments, to curb the migration of unskilled labourers into Greater Khartoum. Throughout the 1980s, regular raids (*kasha*) were launched to arrest unemployed migrants and unregistered refugees, although no effective measures were undertaken to evict them. Currently the Commission for the Displaced is sparing no effort to encourage the war displaced to return to their homes or to settlements in 'transition zones' which border the combat zone.

Elsewhere, it has been discussed (Ibrahim, 1986) how the assumptions informing official responses to the urban problem clearly overlook the causes of rural–urban labour migration. These responses also seem to grossly misunderstand the role of unskilled rural migrants in the acceleration of rapid urban growth in post-colonial Sudan, a mis-understanding shared by the dominant 'paradigms' in Sudan's urban studies. Official responses have not only failed to yield systematic explanations of the nature and origin of the proletarianization process underlying rural–urban migration of unskilled workers, but have also mystified the dynamics of urban growth in the Sudan in which migration by unskilled workers is only one of several, at least equally important, factors.

The point is simply that rural–urban unskilled labour migration does not constitute the sole, or even the predominant, form of labour migration in the Sudan. Leaving aside the seasonal movements of nomadic pastoralists, intra-rural wage labour migration is indeed more significant, not only because it concerns the overwhelming majority of rural migrants in the country (upwards of two million by one estimate), but also because without it the large-scale irrigated and rain-fed agricultural schemes, on which the Sudanese economy is heavily dependent, could hardly function. Taken together, the two forms of labour migration constitute aspects of one and the same process: labour migration in search of wage employment and/or 'income-generating opportunities'. Studies which hope to ascertain the causes of rural–urban labour migration should, therefore, simultaneously attempt to understand and explain the nature and origins of labour migration in general.

The formation of a Sudanese labour force and the emergence of labour markets are both recent developments in the Sudan. Before the turn of this century, labour markets were virtually non-existent (O'Brien, 1980, 1983a; Ibrahim, 1985, 1988a). Thus, following the establishment of the British colonial state in 1899, the colonial administration encountered real difficulties in its attempts to secure the supply of skilled and unskilled wage labourers needed for construction and other tasks. The majority of the economically active population consisted of domestic producers, small farmers and pastoralists who, to a large extent, were self-sufficient. Various forms of local level trade (including barter) served to consolidate the viability of subsistence production. The colonial state consequently had to introduce various policies in order to stimulate the 'natives' to seek wage employment, and it had to import labour from beyond the boundaries of the country in order to obtain the required labour force. Rather than create a fully proletarianized wage labour force, however, the colonial design was to set into motion a process of semi-proletarianization which would stimulate a small section of the domestic producers in rural Sudan to engage in forms of seasonal wage labour migration (Ibrahim, 1985; 1988a).

Throughout the British colonial period a basic government policy was to maintain conditions conducive to the continuation of domestic agricultural and pastoral production. The design was to promote cash cropping and the sale of animals among these petty commodity producers. This policy was reinforced by a number of measures that the colonial regime adopted to avoid setting into motion proletarianization processes. Among sedentary cultivators these measures included the reluctance of the government to expropriate land under crop, the strict control and monitoring of interactions between traders and small producers, and the avoidance of the emergence of a sizeable class of landless Sudanese through various stabilization measures, such as through bringing landless northern Sudanese back to agriculture as tenants on irrigated schemes. Among pastoralists stabilization was achieved through the demarcation of grazing lines, the allocation of exclusive grazing areas for each of the main pastoral groups, and a fair degree of influence upon the timing and direction of pastoral movement through synchronized comprehensive water, range and animal health policies (Ibrahim, 1988b).

The colonial government also resorted to using prison and conscript labour and, when these sources proved insufficient, it imported labour from beyond the boundaries of the Sudan. Eritreans were encouraged to come and settle in Kassala from as early as 1907, and from that date onwards a pattern of seasonal labour migration developed whereby Eritrean peasants would come to the Sudan after harvesting their own crops (McLoughlin, 1965). Other workers came from Egypt and Yemen and, following the collapse of the Ottoman Empire, the Sudan witnessed an influx of skilled and semi-skilled workers from European countries which had been under Ottoman rule.

The most serious attempt by the colonial government to solve the labour shortage was, however, implemented through a policy to encourage West African 'Fellata' (Hausa, Bornu, and so forth) to come and settle in the Sudan not only as wage labourers, but also as domestic producers of primary exports (Hassoun, 1952; Balamoan, 1976; Duffield,

1980, 1981, 1983). At present, descendants of West African immigrants are estimated to be around ten per cent of the population of northern Sudan.

Subsequent to the establishment of the Gezira Scheme (a large agricultural scheme in the central region of the country) in the 1920s, the demand for cheap seasonal agricultural labour became substantial and imported labour could not meet all the requirements. The involvement of local labour, particularly during the cotton picking season, became imperative. In keeping with its stabilization policies, the colonial administration sought to induce a pattern of seasonal wage labour migration rather than to set into motion processes of wholesale dislocation of domestic producers. The measures undertaken to that effect were initially confined to increasing the demand for cash. Noting variations in the responses of domestic producers to the need for more cash (some started to migrate while others intensified cash cropping), the colonial government started to provide 'incentives' to encourage seasonal migration. These incentives included a free (one-way) ticket to the Gezira during the cotton picking season; shifting of time for tax collection to coincide with the picking season; the provision, at subsidized prices, of commodities in short supply to those who came to the scheme; and the encouragement of tenants of the scheme to grow fodder in order to attract pastoralists.

Over time the small producers' need for cash continued to increase. Simultaneously, labour migration and market-oriented production (cash cropping and the sale of animals) became integral components of production processes in the so-called 'traditional sector'. The participation of small producers in systems of labour migration was thus continually growing in both scope and intensity. The post-colonial introduction and expansion of large-scale mechanized rain-fed farming provided a new and steadily growing demand for labour.

Notwithstanding the colonial government's attempts to stimulate systems of seasonal wage labour migration, relatively few Sudanese peasants and pastoralists were attracted to the wage labour market during the colonial era. The labour shortage during this era (particularly during the cotton picking season in Gezira) was never definitively solved. On occasions of extreme shortage, the colonial administration conscripted school children in order to obtain the labour force they required (Ali, 1974:30ff). Indeed, it was not until the achievement of 'flag' independence that seasonal labour migration by Sudanese peasants and pastoralists started to accelerate.

Proletarianization in post-colonial Sudan

In considering the main post-colonial developments within the domestic form of agricultural production, it should be emphasized that the emergence of a 'national' administration has not undermined the processes of the colonial-type trade economy. Expansion in primary export production is still viewed as 'development'. But, whereas during the colonial period an integral aspect of the imposition of primary export production was the conservation of the domestic form of production in the so-called 'traditional sector', during the first two decades of the post-colonial period stabilization policies were almost totally abandoned. As a result of this, the continuity of domestic production has become dependent almost exclusively on the willingness and/or ability of domestic production units to maintain their 'autonomy'. This continuity has for large sectors of domestic producers proved very difficult to achieve without regularly resorting to seasonal labour migrations.

The processes that resulted in the acceleration of semi-proletarianization in post-colonial Sudan are several and complex and can only be outlined here. Though some of these processes are 'nation-wide' and apply to all domestic producers in the country, others are specific either to particular regions and/or groups, or to particular forms of production. A central 'nation-wide' process was, and to a large extent continues to be, the relaxation of the constraints which the colonial administration imposed upon the interaction between traders and domestic producers. The consequences of this relaxation of constraints include the widespread incidence of *sheil* [1] and other forms of debt relations which involve exorbitant interest rates (sometimes exceeding 200 per cent), and the emergence of parallel markets, particularly in rural areas, whereby goods normally in short supply in cities can easily be obtained, albeit at double the 'official prices', in villages. These situations are well documented in micro-studies from all parts of the country (Awad, 1966; Apaya, 1971; Barnett, 1977; Omer, 1979; Abdel Ghaffar M. Ahmed, 1980; Ahmed & Abdel Rahman, 1979; O'Brien, 1980; Ibrahim, 1980; El-Mustafa, 1983; Ahmed, 1986).

The unfettered monopoly status enjoyed by traders has led to, on the one hand, a sharp decline in the proceeds from cash crops accruing to the domestic producers and, on the other, a steady increase in prices of goods furnished by merchants. Public corporations monopolizing exports of oil-seed and gum-arabic also contributed substantially to depressing the proceeds to farmers by offering very low prices compared with what the commodities were sold for on the international market. A study of marketing of gum-arabic recently showed that the producer price amounted to no more than 45 per cent of the Port Sudan price – the difference being government taxes and profit margins for traders.

Pastoralists have been particularly affected in recent decades by accelerated proletarianization processes. The expansion of large-scale agriculture mostly took place in what had been the richest grazing areas for the herds of pastoralists. It cut out grazing areas, disrupted nomadic routes (*maraheel*) and blocked access to watering points. Pastoralists have consequently been forced to concentrate in relatively marginal lands where the carrying capacity is insufficient to meet the demand. Over-stocking and over-grazing are the unavoidable consequences of this marginalization.

In this context an intensification of the commercialization of pastoralism was set in motion. Not only were the products of pastoral production increasingly brought to the market, but even the two essential inputs, water and fodder, became commodities to be bought, particularly during the hot dry season. While these developments opened a world of opportunities for the relatively resourceful pastoralists and those who penetrated the livestock sector (mainly merchants and owners of rain-fed agricultural schemes), they simultaneously implied a thorough impoverishment of poorer pastoralists. In the hands of the former categories, pastoralism is being transformed into a full-fledged capitalist enterprise based on waged herders and commercialized inputs. In the meantime, the vulnerability of small pastoralists has been further exacerbated, and increasing numbers are being forced to become sedentary farmers on marginal land (and as such are becoming subject to the processes experienced by small farmers), or to become migrants looking for wage employment, and are thereby ending up as displaced persons.

In the eastern and Darfur regions, the problems facing pastoralists have been further complicated by the armed conflicts across the border in Ethiopia and Chad. The border districts in the Sudan and Ethiopia (and the Sudan and Chad) historically constituted a single grazing zone and pastoral border groups used to practise forms of transhumance whereby they moved, according to the season, from one side of the border to the other. But the armed conflict in Eritrea made access to the rich grazing area across the border a costly, if not high-risk, venture. Access entailed making payments to the military of both countries as well as to the liberation fronts, and also held the prospect of an encounter with bandits. Bandit activity is even more widespread in Darfur than it is in eastern Sudan. By disrupting the traditional patterns of transhumance, armed conflicts across the border have contributed further to the forced concentration of herds in relatively poor pasture.

Proletarianization processes are by no means unique or confined to the so-called 'traditional sector'; the communities of tenants in the 'modern' irrigated schemes are also sources of generations of migrants. In view of the fact that large-scale irrigated schemes for a long period constituted a major source of employment for unskilled labour in the Sudan, it might appear paradoxical to observe proletarianization processes among tenant communities. But tenants are not only a highly differentiated group, they also experience a severe problem of social reproduction (O'Brien, 1984a). Unlike on the rainlands where, depending on the availability of water, the new generations may be stabilized in domestic agricultural production, in the irrigated schemes the tenancies not only are limited in number, but also cannot be divided (in inheritance) below a certain limit (half tenancy). Possibilities for 'fragmentation' among the poorer sections of the tenantry were virtually exhausted in the late 1940s. In such a context, the deployment of the labour of all family members by a tenant with two or more sons would maintain the household for only a brief period in the early stages of its developmental cycle. As the sons grow up they find it imperative either to stay in their respective units and receive labourers' wages (which means a decline in their standard of living) or to seek alternative employment.

The crisis of social reproduction in tenant communities was also recognized during the colonial period. The colonial administration sought to overcome the problem through promoting educational services in the Gezira whereby the descendants of tenants were to become 'more competitive' in their search for alternative careers. In spite of a dramatic post-colonial expansion of educational services in the Sudan in general and the Gezira in particular, there is still severe competition for places in higher education. Only a small percentage of the descendants of tenants are able to lead careers in professional and administrative positions. The majority end up as 'drop-outs', and are consequently driven into the wage labour market as semi-skilled and unskilled workers. In the meantime, with the exorbitant increases in the costs of production and the dramatic decline in productivity since 1973–4 (El-Mustafa, 1979), and the differentiation process taking place within the Gezira tenantry, many needy tenants have become thoroughly proletarianized (O'Brien, 1984a; Barnett, 1983).

The intensification of the processes of semi-proletarianization in the decades since independence coincided with a rapid expansion of large-scale (irrigated and rain-fed) agricultural schemes which generated substantial opportunities for seasonal agro-labour (Galal El-Din, 1978; O'Brien, 1980, 1983a, 1983b; Taisier Mohamed A. Ali, 1982, 1983; Shepherd, 1983). It was because of this expansion that during the first two decades of independence the government was more concerned with the shortage of agro-labour than with the consequences of the destabilization of the 'traditional' domestic producers.

The operation of agricultural labour markets

Although no reliable data or rough estimates are available for the degree to which post-colonial expansion in large-scale agricultural schemes boosted the demand for agro-labour, it is nevertheless quite safe to assert that well over 80 per cent of the demand for unskilled wage labour in the Sudan originates in rural agriculture. Well before the emergence and acceleration of the mass displacement of the 1980s, O'Brien has noted the difficulties in estimating the numbers of seasonal migrants in the Sudan, and contended that 'between 1.5 and 2 million seasonal labourers, mostly peasants and pastoralists for the rest of year, work in weeding or harvesting operations in state and private plantations annually' (1983a:16). The way agricultural labour markets in the country operated, however, progressively enticed migrants to move towards urban areas.

The terms and conditions of employment, as well as the composition of the labour force, used to vary between irrigated and rain-fed schemes. In rain-fed agricultural schemes the main operations are harvesting and threshing of sorghum and sesame. These operations are very demanding and the labour force involved consists almost exclusively of young able-bodied male migrants. Given the desolate locations of rain-fed schemes, the labour force is also expected to endure hardships in terms of accommodation, maintenance and health care.

In contrast to the situation on rain-fed schemes, on the irrigated schemes the bulk of the demand is for the undertaking of cotton picking. This is a relatively undemanding operation in which children over the age of ten as well as old people can attain the same productivity levels as able-bodied female and male adults. Unlike on the rain-fed schemes, then, the work-force on irrigated agricultural schemes consists of family groups.

Until the mid 1970s relatively significant variations between the rain-fed and irrigated schemes were observed in terms of the wages paid to labourers. Wages on the rain-fed schemes were said to be up to 50 per cent higher than on the irrigated schemes. Nevertheless, because all family members over the age of ten could participate in cotton picking, the net returns for families migrating to the irrigated schemes were usually higher than what accrued to those families which sent only their adult male members to the rain-fed schemes. With the deepening economic crisis during the 1970s, however, able-bodied men from families which used to participate in cotton picking started to migrate to the rain-fed schemes. Women, children and old people continued to migrate to the irrigated schemes (Galal El-Din, 1978). The result of this has been a steady increase in wages for cotton pickers and a general tendency for wage rates to equalize between the two segments of the agricultural wage labour market: a truly national agricultural labour market was emerging (O'Brien, 1983a, 1984b).

The differences in the wage paid on irrigated and rain-fed schemes were not solely a reflection of the differential composition of the work-force. They were also the result of the method by which wage rates are determined in the Gezira Scheme. The method used not only kept wages for cotton pickers at the lowest possible level, but also helped maintain low and stable wage rates for unskilled labour throughout the national economy. Although the Gezira Scheme is commonly known as 'the world's largest plantation under one administration', the Gezira Scheme Board has no direct relation with the seasonal labourers. The labourers are hired by individual tenants, and consequently comprise an atomized work-force. Having received advances from the Board, each tenant seeks, in the negotiation of wage-rates, to keep for herself or himself at least part of the advances. This is particularly true of the majority of tenants who are needy and in debt to village merchants and informal financiers. For these tenants the advances are, at least in part, badly needed to meet current consumption requirements.

The decentralization of wage determination served to maintain exceptionally stable, albeit depressed, wage rates for picking labourers between 1945 and 1975. Accounting for the situation up until the mid 1970s, Nigam concluded that, 'it is understood from the Gezira Board that wage rates have not increased much during the last decade, and over the last 20 years have increased by about 3 per cent a year which does not even cover the rise in prices' (1977:156) .

That seasonal cotton pickers continued to accept such low wages is, of course, underlain by the fact that they were not a thoroughly proletarianized wage labour force. They were semi-proletarianized domestic producers and their consumption requirements were largely satisfied through subsistence agricultural production. With the undermining of the viability of domestic agricultural production, however, previous patterns of seasonal labour migration have become difficult, if not impossible, to continue. The seasonal nature of agricultural employment and the depressed wages have made it necessary to search for alternative income-generating opportunities. Rural activities such as wood-cutting and charcoal-making provide some opportunities, but the most attractive alternative has turned out to be migration to urban areas, and this often leads to emigration to the oil-rich Arab countries.

In the context of mounting economic crisis, emigration to the Arabian Peninsula has become very attractive to Sudanese. Although it was initially an option mainly for the highly-educated (professionals and civil servants), since 1978 it has involved considerable numbers of skilled, semi- and un-skilled workers. At present it is estimated that over 20 per cent of the entire Sudanese labour force is working abroad. Indeed, there is hardly a family in northern Sudan which does not have one or more of its members working abroad. Those abroad are shouldering a considerable burden of supporting families and relatives in the Sudan through the current economic crisis. In addition to remittances, Sudanese working abroad also send home a multitude of consumer goods, ranging from clothes to such basic commodities as sugar, toilet soap and toothpaste. As remittances are mainly sent through informal channels (usually foreign currency is sold on the parallel market), the government has virtually no access to the earnings of those working abroad. The only exception to this is the annual tax which must be paid before passports will be renewed or exit visas will be issued. Over the last five years, however, the oil boom in the Gulf started to subside and the demand for foreign labour started to shrink. As a result of these developments, the pace of emigration has started to slow down and the return of migrant workers is becoming a problem.

The mid 1970s thus witnessed the undermining of the apparent segmentation of the agricultural labour market. However, the tendency of wage rates to increase was soon halted and real wages for agricultural labour (as for all wage earners and salaried workers in the country) started to fall steadily. The escalation of the economic crisis and the consequent inflationary processes in the country were major factors behind the fall in real incomes. In the particular case of agricultural labour, and a few other wage-earning sectors, an added factor was the steady influx of increasing numbers of refugees, particularly from Eritrea. Although the first wave of Eritrean refugees was provided plots of agricultural land to settle as domestic producers, the Sudanese authorities later adopted a strategy of settling refugees in areas abutting agricultural schemes. The refugee populations thus started to become an important source of agro-labour. In the 1980s when food aid was extended to refugees, they apparently started to accept wages below levels acceptable to the Sudanese labour force.

The era of displacement

The economic crisis that started to escalate in 1978 has contributed substantially to the undermining of the viability of domestic agricultural production. In eastern and western Sudan small producers in particular have been subjected to a rapid process of impoverishment. With the failure of rain and a consequent crop failure in two successive seasons, the vulnerability of small producers became evident. An exodus from the rural areas of these two regions ensued, and a major famine relief operation was required to solve the short-term problem. The long-term task of eliminating, or at least of mitigating vulnerability is still to be taken up.

The characterization of mass displacement in western and eastern Sudan as a consequence of drought and/or environmental degradation constitutes a 'forced theoretical abstraction' which amounts to a distraction. Blaming nature is a tendency that converges with another that blames an external enemy (the most unpopular is the IMF, although demonstrations in the Sudan continue to chant slogans against the World Bank!). Both tendencies explain away the socio-economic transformations that took place in recent decades in the Sudan. Not least, they draw attention away from the extent to which the policies and measures adopted by successive governments, from the British colonial administration to the May Regime, effectively contributed to the generation and exacerbation of the vulnerability of small producers.

Corroboration of the *internal* socio-economic basis of vulnerability needs no speculation. Neither drought nor structural adjustment has affected the different social categories in the same way or to the same extent. A minority has indeed benefited from both drought and structural adjustment measures. Such differential impacts raise the question of the nature and dynamic of this differentiation. The main point in the preceding sections was precisely to illuminate both the nature and dynamic of vulnerability.

The exodus of 'drought victims' was compounded by massive war displacement following the renewal of armed conflict in southern Sudan in 1983. The ensuing atmosphere of insecurity set into motion processes of population destabilization of considerable magnitude which, if not reversed by the restoration of peace conditions, promise to thoroughly depopulate the combat zone. Already three million southern Sudanese are said to be displaced.

The issue of displacement is not simply a question of the number of people who involuntarily leave the places of their original or normal domicile (Ibrahim, 1990). It is also, and more significantly, a phenomenon which results from a *socio-economic* process whereby otherwise self-reliant people are reduced to destitution and, as a result, become vulnerable. The war has further accelerated the erosion of the viability of domestic production processes in southern Sudan, processes that were already subject to the 'nation-wide' marginalization discussed earlier. The overwhelming majority of those who have undertaken involuntary *spatial* movement have been subjected to this process of destitution. The two aspects of the concept of displacement should not be conflated, however, as some of those who experienced spatial displacement have not been impoverished.

Social displacement is, in essence, a manifestation of proletarianization, that is to say of divorcing domestic agropastoral producers from the means of production. One major and immediate problem facing the displaced is that of finding alternative employment and a relatively secure source of income. With regard to the search for employment, significant variations are observed among different categories of the displaced. There is some evidence which suggests that those who are displaced within southern Sudan, together with those who end up in rural areas in other regions, do not seem to experience social displacement to the same extent or in the same way as those who end up in the large urban areas. In the countryside agricultural employment provides considerable opportunities, but its seasonality poses severe problems. In that respect urban areas are relatively better as the opportunities they provide are not as seasonal. Some displaced men managed to establish themselves as unskilled construction workers, or to enter into the already inflated tertiary activities of the so-called urban informal sector, but the majority are unemployed. The sheer size of the population in urban centres provides considerable opportunities in the social and personal services sector, but this sector seems to be highly selective in its recruitment of the displaced and provides far more opportunities (such as domestic services, the sale of local beer and alcoholic drinks, and prostitution) for women than for men. This seems to have had a significant impact on the customary gender roles among the displaced as households have increasingly come to depend on their female members.

Future prospects

To a large extent, the distinction between 'voluntary' and 'involuntary' patterns of labour mobility in the Sudan is superfluous. Both are rooted on-going processes which result in the erosion of the viability of domestic agropastoral production in the country. The only difference seems to be that in the case of involuntary mobility (displacement), an alleged external and/or extra-social factor (drought or war) is assumed to be the immediate, if not the primary cause for the mass exodus.

Intra-rural labour migration is commonly viewed as positive as these migrants move towards the agricultural schemes. In contrast, rural–urban migration is generally viewed in negative terms, and the authorities are keenly pursuing measures which refer migrants either to their places of origin or to one of the agricultural schemes where they may be engaged as agro-labour. Such measures, needless to say, fail to consider the conditions and processes which brought migrants to the cities in the first place.

The common conception of displacement does not differ much from that of 'voluntary' labour migration. The transformation experienced by the displaced, however, is sometimes viewed in positive terms which emphasize its social revolutionary potential. This view seems to be based on the assumption that if the civil war or drought had not occurred, the displaced would have continued to live within the traditional sector pursuing activities in virtually the same way as their ancestors did centuries ago. The positive impact of displacement is accordingly identified as the disintegration of the traditional order. On that basis it is argued that similar disintegration processes were part and parcel of the industrial revolution and the emergence of the modern nation-state in Western Europe. What is taking place in present-day Sudan, however, cannot legitimately be construed as a re-enactment or reiteration of that historical process. There are, beyond a doubt, significant differences between contemporary Sudan and eighteenth century England. The colonial experience, the transformation of the country into a supplier of raw materials for international markets, excessive external debts, and the disequilibria in the balance of payments are but a few aspects of underdevelopment which England did not have to face at the dawn of its industrial revolution.

In the context of a growing economic crisis, the proletarianized labour force is finding itself to be largely redundant in a labour market that is both saturated and stagnant. Relief thus has to be perpetually extended to the displaced. As long-term relief is untenable (relief is by definition intended to be temporary and short-term), the revolutionary potential of the proletarianized may be lost to its anti-thesis – a destructive physical force.

It does not seem unwarranted to assume that the authorities have a clear understanding of this destructive potential and consequently seek to evacuate the displaced from the large cities.

Upon the restoration of peace conditions, a major task will be to formulate a comprehensive strategy for population stabilization and redistribution. The components of that strategy obviously will depend on the nature and orientation of the social forces that come to power. What is virtually certain, however, is that for the strategy to be viable it cannot adopt administrative measures to restore pre-war forms and social relations of production. Such an objective would be untenable because of the pace and extent of the decomposition of domestic agropastoral production. A comprehensive population strategy should bear in mind the socio-economic realities of present-day Sudan. Small producers in regions far from the combat zone are consistently being marginalized and displaced, and for this reason it cannot be assumed that by returning the war displaced to their original areas stabilization processes will be operative.

A viable population policy clearly has to be based on the skills, resources and potentials of the small producers, on their consent and participation, and on the objective of benefiting them most. Such an approach will render the development process itself a tool of peace. Other courses of action, particularly those based on past experiences of development planning in the country, may prove irrelevant, unacceptable and counter-productive. They may also exacerbate grievances and perpetuate civil war in the south or in other regions and, in the process, further intensify the mounting crisis in the country.

Note
1 *Sheil* is a system of credit whereby farmers sell their future crops for fixed prices to local merchants.

References

Ahmed, Abdel Ghaffar M. 1973. 'Nomadic competition in the Southern Funj' *Sudan Notes and Records*, 53.

Ahmed, Abdel Ghaffar M. 1980. *Rural-Urban Interaction in the Sudan*, a report presented to UNESCO.

Ahmed, Abdel Ghaffar M. and Mustafa Abdel Rahman. 1979. 'Urbanization and exploitation: the role of small centres' *DSRC Monograph Series*, 11, Khartoum, Khartoum University Press.

Ahmed, Abdel Ghaffar M. and Paul van der Wel. (eds.) 1986. *Perspectives on Development in the Sudan*, The Hague, Institute of Social Studies.

Ahmed, Mustafa Babiker. 1986. 'The development of peasant commodity production in Dar Hamar: Incorporation with immiseration' in Ahmed, Abdel Ghaffar and Paul van der Wel (eds.) *Perspectives on Development in the Sudan*, The Hague, Institute of Social Studies.

Ali, Omer Mohamed. 1974. *Mushkillat al-A'taalla* (The Unemployment Problem), Khartoum, Economic and Social Research Council.

Ali, Taisier Mohamed A. 1982. 'The cultivation of hunger: Towards a political economy of agricultural development in the Sudan, 1956–1964', Ph.D. thesis, Toronto, University of Toronto.

Ali, Taisier Mohamed A. 1983. 'The road to Jouda' *Review of African Political Economy*, 26.

Apaya, W. 1971. *Agricultual Credit in the Gezira*, M.Sc. thesis, Khartoum, Khartoum University.

Awad, Mohamed Hashim. 1966. *Al-Istighlal wa Fassaad al-Hukm fi al-Sudan* (Exploitation and Corruption of Governing in the Sudan), Khartoum.

Balamoan, G.A. 1976. *Migration Policies in the Anglo-Egyptian Sudan, 1884–1956*, Cambridge, Harvard University Center for Population Studies.

Barnett, T. 1977. *The Gezira Scheme: An Illusion of Development* London, Frank Cass.

Barnett, T. 1983. 'The labour market in the irrigated areas of the Sudan' in *Self-Reliance for Refugees in Sudan, A Programme for Action*, Volume II – Technical Papaers and Projects No. 82/AP/SUD/LS/26/ Geneva, ILO.

Barnett, T. and Abbas Abdel Karim. (eds.) 1988. *State, Capital and Transformation in the Sudan*, London, Croom Helm.

Duffield, M. 1980. 'West African settlement and development in the towns of northern Sudan' in Pons, V.G. (ed.) *Urbanization and Urban Life in the Sudan*, Hull.

Duffield, M. 1981. *Maiurno: Capitalism and Rural Life in the Sudan*, London, Ithaca Press.

Duffield, M. 1983. 'Change among West African settlers in northern Sudan' *Review of African Political Economy*, 26.

Elhassan, Ali Mohamed. (ed.) 1977. *Growth, Employment and Equity: Selected Papers Presented to the ILO Employment Mission*, Khartoum, Economic and Social Research Council.

El-Mustafa, Mohammed Yousif A. 1979. 'Al-Wafidoun wa A'Lagat al-Intaj bi Mashrou' al Jazira' (The Immigrants and Production Relations in the Gezira Scheme) in El-Din, Galal and Mohammed Yousif El-Mustafa *al-Hijra al-Wafida ila wa al-Hijra al-Dakhiliya gi al-Sudan* (Immigration and Internal Migration in the Sudan), Khartoum, Economic and Social Research Council.

El-Mustafa, Mohammed Yousif A. 1983. *Capital Accumulation, 'Tribalism' and Politics in a Sudanese Town*

(Hassaheisa): A Case Study in the Political Economy of Urbanization, Ph.D. thesis, Hull, Hull University.

Galal El-Din, Mohamed El-Awad. 1973. *Internal Migration in the Sudan Since World War II, With Special Reference to Greater Khartoum*, Ph.D. thesis, London, London University.

Galal El-Din, Mohamed El-Awad. 1974a. 'The factors influencing migration to the three towns of the Sudan' *Sudan Journal of Economic and Social Studies*, vol. 1, no. 1.

Galal El-Din, Mohamed El-Awad. 1974b. 'Development, income distribution and labour utilization the Sudan', paper presented to the *13th Inter-African Public Administration Seminar on Managing Unemployment in Africa*, Khartoum.

Galal El-Din, Mohamed El-Awad. 1978. 'Ba'dh Qadaiya Al-Sukkaan wa Al-Tanmiya fi al-Sudan wa al-A'llam al-Talit' (Some Issues on Population and Development in the Sudan and the Third World) *DSRC Development Studies Books Series, 1*, Khartoum, Khartoum University Press.

Hassoun, Isam Ahmed. 1952. ' "Western" migration and settlement in the Gezira' *Sudan Notes and Records*, 33.

Ibrahim, Salah El-Din El-Shazali. 1980. 'Beyond underdevelopment: Structural constraints on the development of productive forces among the Jok Gor, the Sudan' *African Savannah Studies, Bergen Occasional Papers in Social Anthropology*, 22. Bergen, University Printer.

Ibrahim, Salah El-Din El-Shazali. 1985. *Peripheral Urbanism and the Sudan: Explorations into the Political Economy of the Wage Labour Market in Greater Khartoum, 1900–1984*, Ph.D. thesis, Hull, University of Hull.

Ibrahim, Salah El-Din El-Shazali. 1986. 'Theory and ideology in Sudan urban studies: Towards a political economy of peripheral capitalist urbanism' in Ahmed, Abdel Ghaffar M. and P. van der Wel (eds.) *Perspectives on Development in the Sudan*, The Hague, Institute of Social Studies.

Ibrahim, Salah El-Din El-Shazali. 1988a. 'The emergence and expansion of the urban wage labour market in colonial Khartoum: Explorations into the political economy of peripheral capitalist urbanism' in Barnett, T. and Abbas Abdel Karim (eds.) *State, Capital and Transformation in the Sudan*, London, Croom Helm.

Ibrahim, Salah El-Din El-Shazali. 1988b. 'The structure and operation of urban wage labour markets and the trade unions in the Sudan' in O'Neill, N. and J.J. O'Brien (eds.) *Economy and Class in Sudan*. Aldershot, Avebury.

Ibrahim, Salah El-Din El-Shazali. 1988c. 'The South Kassala nomadic survey: The conditions of pastoralists in the eastern Sudan refugee reforestation project' *Consultant Report*, submitted to Care-Sudan.

Ibrahim, Salah El-Din El-Shazali. 1990. 'War displacement: The socio-cultural dimension', paper presented to the Conference on *Internal Migration and Displacement Issues in the Sudan*, organized by the Population Studies Centre, the University of Gezira, Medani.

Khalifa, Mona. 1979. 'Fertility differentials in urban Khartoum' *Economic and Social Research Council Bulletin*, 81.

Kursany, Ibrahim. 1983. 'Peasants of the Nuba Mountain Region' *Review of African Political Economy*, 26.

Manger, L.O. (ed.) 1984. 'Trade and traders in the Sudan' *Bergen University Occasional Papers in Social Anthropology*, 32 Bergen, University Press.

Martin, P.F. 1970. *The Sudan in Evolution: A Study of the Economic, Financial and Administrative Conditions of the Anglo-Egyptian Sudan*, New York, Negro Universities.

McLoughlin, T.G. 1965. 'Labour market conditions and wages in the Gash and Tokar Deltas' *Sudan Notes and Records*, 47.

McLoughlin, T.G. 1970. 'Labour market conditions and wages in the three towns, 1900–1950' *Sudan Notes and Records*, 51.

Munslow, B. and H. Finch. (eds.) 1984. *Proletarianization in the Third World*, Beckenham, Croom Helm.

Nigam, S.B.L. 1977. 'The labour requirements and supply situation in agriculture in the Sudan' in Ali Mohamed Elhassan (ed.) *Growth, Employment and Equity*, Khartoum, Economic and Social Research Council.

O'Brien, J.J. 1977. 'How "traditional" is traditional agriculture?' *Economic and Social Research Council Bulletin*, 62.

O'Brien, J.J. 1980. *Agricultural Labour and Development in the Sudan*, Ph.D. thesis, Connecticut, University of Connecticut.

O'Brien, J.J. 1983a. 'The formation of the agricultural labour force in the Sudan' *Review of African Political Economy*, 26.

O'Brien, J.J. 1983b. 'The political economy of capitalist agricultural in the central rainlands of Sudan' *Labour, Capital and Society*, vol. 16, no. 1.

O'Brien, J.J. 1984a. 'The social reproduction of tenant cultivators and class formation in the Gezira Scheme, Sudan' *Research in Economic Anthropology*.

O'Brien, J.J. 1984b. 'The political economy of semi-proletarianization under colonialism: Sudan 1925–50' in, Munslow, B. and H. Finch (eds.) *Proletarianization in the Third World*, Beckenham, Croom Helm.

Omer, El-Haj Bilal. 1979. *Local Traders and Agricultural Development in Dongola Area: A Study in Rural Capitalism in Northern Sudan*, Ph.D. thesis, Hull, Hull University.

O'Neill, N. and J.J. O'Brien. (eds.) 1988. *Economy and Class in Sudan*, Aldershot, Avebury.

Pons, V.G. (ed.) 1980. *Urbanization and Urban Life in the Sudan*, Hull, Department of Sociology (Hull University) and Khartoum, Development Studies and Research Centre (Khartoum University).

Shaa'Eldin, Elfatih. 1981. 'The mechanisms of proletarianization in the Sudan' *DSRC Seminar Series Discussion Paper, 6*, Khartoum, Development Studies and Research Centre.

Shepherd, A. 1983. 'Agricultural capitalism and rural development in the Sudan' *DSRC Seminar Series, Discussion Paper, 32*, Khartoum, Development Studies and Research Centre.

Comment ABBAS ABDELKARIM AHMED

Population mobility is one of the best reflections of the changes occurring in the economic, ecological, political and socio-cultural structures. By establishing the reasons for population mobility – that is, migration – and examining its impact on the region, we learn a great deal about the roots of problems and the development challenges in the region.

As external migration is largely outside the scope of Salah El-Shazali Ibrahim's paper, which focuses on internal migration in the Sudan, a few words should be said on immigration from other countries to point out some priority areas for future research. It must be noted at the outset that none of the countries of the Horn has any reliable data on migration. All estimates made arise merely from observational guesswork. We have, for example, a range of different estimates that suggest the number of Sudanese migrants lies between a few hundred thousand and five to six million. The number of immigrants from neighbouring countries is normally estimated, or rather inflated, in the Sudan in accordance with our governments' efforts to attract foreign aid.

Four types of reasons for migration can be identified: economic, political (which includes refugees of wars, and those segments of the population that are forced by authorities to leave for alleged security reasons or due to other allegations), ecological, and socio-cultural. All four types are evident in the external migrations of all Horn countries; however, different types acquire different levels of importance at different periods.

In the Sudan, for example, political reasons were more important in the 1950s and 1960s, and again from the mid 1980s onwards due to the war, while economic reasons predominated in the 1970s and early 1980s. From the late 1980s onwards we can safely estimate that the number of Sudanese migrating from the south to other African countries exceeds the number settling in the Arab oil-producing countries. However, this political type of external migration is often ignored by officials and academics; they only take into account migration that brings back money. Politically motivated external migration acquired special importance in Ethiopia from the mid 1970s; in Eritrea it has been evident since the early 1960s. Ecological factors started exerting increasing influence in all the countries concerned from the late 1970s.

In terms of absolute numbers, emigrants from Ethiopia, Eritrea and the Sudan exceed those from Somalia; however, in relative terms (comparing the number of migrants to the total population or total labour force), Somalia more or less stands on an equal footing with Ethiopia and the Sudan. External migrations from the different countries of the Horn bear some resemblance in terms of the reasons which lead to the phenomenon itself and the countries and regions to which migrants move. Significant numbers of emigrants turn to other countries within the region itself, and a relatively large number move to the Arab oil-producing countries. In contrast to Sudanese migrants, Somali, Ethiopian and Eritrean migrants have also settled in large numbers in Europe and the United States. During the period of reconstruction and development, migrants could have a significant role to play in their home countries. Planning this involvement must rest on solid data which is now lacking. The data needed extends to a variety of economic and social indicators and also to the aspirations of the migrants and their views on the nature of their possible participation in the development of their home countries. Careful analytical studies based on that data should precede all future development planning.

Migration and the formation of a Sudanese wage labour class are inseparable social phenomena. During the early period of British colonial rule (1898–1956) three categories of people who were sources of wage labour and who became labourers in places other than their places of origin can be identified:

1. people freed temporarily or permanently from their lands during Mahadiya rule (1881–98) as a result of the continuous warfare;

2. people who had been freed from slavery; and
3. migrant labourers coming mainly from Nigeria and what was then French Equatoria. This source of wage labour became particularly important after the establishment of the large agricultural Gezira Scheme in the central region of the country in 1926.

After this initial period, migrant labour from western Sudan increasingly became the major source of agricultural wage labour in the Sudan. Over two thirds of the settled wage labour in Gezira camps, which comprised 170,000 labourers in 1980, came from western Sudan. Seasonal wage labourers in the scheme, who normally are greater in number than the settled wage labourers, also come from western Sudan, as well as from the pastoral groups of the White and Blue Nile regions in central Sudan. Data from another agricultural region, Gedaref, which is at present the largest in the country, also suggest that 89 per cent of the labourers in 1983 were migrants from the western and southern regions, Ethiopia and Eritrea.

Migrant labour has also been fuelling the wage labour army in towns. A survey conducted in 1983 revealed that 73 per cent of industrial workers were not born in the area in which they were working. These points exhibit the relationship between rural migration and the creation of a wage labour class in the Sudan.

The second point which should be touched upon is the claim made in the paper that a truly national agricultural labour market was emerging. This statement is based on J. O'Brien's research which was carried out in 1980. However, surveys undertaken in 1982 and 1983 tend to show that the Sudanese agricultural labour market is segmented and not yet national. This finding is based on three facts:

1. wage differentials for the same type of job exist not only among different agricultural regions, but also within each region;
2. the data available does not suggest the free movement of wage labour from one agricultural region to another; and
3. non-market mechanisms of recruitment of wage labour still exist in some areas, such as in Gezira.

One last point that should be brought up in the presence of Sudanese political activists and legal workers is that, while agricultural workers constitute the larger segment of the Sudanese wage labour class, there are no labour laws to protect their interests in the same way that service and industrial workers are protected. Those workers who have joined the rural labour market in the Sudan know very well the unfair contractual relationship between agricultural employers and workers. It might be true that it is not easy to formulate labour laws for a casual labourer who works for a number of employers. However, what is lacking is not the legal capability, but the political will.

Reference

O'Brien, J.J. 1980. *Agricultural Labour and Development in the Sudan*, Ph.D. thesis, Connecticut, University of Connecticut.

Appendix 1 THE REGIONAL SIGNIFICANCE OF SEA PORTS IN THE HORN OF AFRICA

JOHN MARKAKIS

Some of the sea ports in the Horn of Africa have regional, economic and strategic significance which makes them a political factor that underlies some of the major conflicts in the region. Unless this factor is addressed, lasting peace in the Horn is not likely to be achieved. The paragraphs that follow, drawn from a panel discussion on the ports held during the workshop, focus attention on some aspects of this factor which should receive more attention and investigation in future research.

1. Ethiopia is threatened with the loss of both Massawa and Asab due to the irresistible rise of Eritrean nationalism. Reversion to being landlocked, as it was before it annexed Eritrea, is a condition Ethiopia cannot easily accept. If this condition is forced upon it, this will be a source of renewed conflict in the future. Consequently, the issue of the ports will figure prominently in the negotiations to resolve the Ethiopia–Eritrea conflict. The two ports are not of equal significance to Ethiopia. Asab is located relatively nearer to the centre of the country and to the regions where modern economic activity has developed. Throughout the 1980s, Asab handled about 85 per cent of the total tonnage handled by Ethiopian ports. Massawa's relative insignificance during this period is due not only to its remoteness from central Ethiopia, but also to the insecurity created by the armed conflict in Eritrea. Consequently, Asab is likely to be the main focus in the negotiations. There are examples in other parts of the world where such issues have been settled to the satisfaction of both parties through a 'free port' arrangement; as in the case of Trieste, for example, between Italy and Yugoslavia after World War Two. They could serve as models for the resolution of similar disputes in the Horn of Africa. Needless to say, accommodation will serve Eritrea's interests since transit trade to Ethiopia is the main source of revenue for both ports. Massawa is of primary importance to Tigray, the northern region that has been fighting for autonomy within Ethiopia and seems to be on the verge of achieving this objective. Access to that port will have to be negotiated between Eritrea and Tigray.
2. Other ports in the Horn also serve regional needs, albeit unofficially, following a practice that pre-dates colonialism and the appearance of the present states. Trade from northern Eritrea historically was channelled through Suakin in eastern Sudan, but for the past 30 years the Eritrean nationalist movement has relied on Port Sudan to serve its logistical needs. That port could usefully continue to serve both regions in the future if proper agreements were reached. Likewise, trade from Ogaden in Ethiopia has always gone through Berbera and, to a lesser extent, Zeyla in northern Somalia. Despite the many obstacles and risks involved, this pattern has not been interrupted simply because it is essential for the pastoralist economy of the Ogaden. Therefore, any solution to the conflict in that region must provide access for the pastoralists to these ports. Djibouti also serves a regional function as the entrepôt of most illegal trade that takes place across its own borders and those of Ethiopia and Somalia. It should be noted that virtually the only cross-border trade that takes place in that region is smuggled trade.
3. Still other ports could play a regional role for the benefit of all concerned. For instance, if the railway connection between Eritrea and the Sudan was completed, Massawa could serve parts of eastern and central Sudan – where commercial agriculture has flourished – more economically than Port Sudan which is further away. For some years now, trade and aid into southern Sudan has come through Kenya and Uganda. While this has been the result of the ongoing conflict, it also follows the logic of the

market. Indeed, the Kenyan port of Mombasa on the Indian Ocean is best situated to serve southern Sudan, and a future autonomous regime in that region is certain to consider this possibility.

The point here is that these ports serve regional functions that are essential and adhere to a pattern that is both historical and economically logical. All the measures taken against this practice by both the colonial and the independent states have not stopped this activity. In recent years, the breakdown of central government control in all the states of the region, save Djibouti, has allowed such activity to flourish, albeit illegally. Indeed, regional trade in the Horn is conducted largely through such illegal channels. It would be best to take account of this reality in the process of resolving the manifold conflict, and seek to reach agreement on a bilateral or regional level to facilitate it.

PART

III

RECOVERY AND LONG-TERM
DEVELOPMENT
**Rural Production Systems:
Crisis and Sustainability**

**Rural Production Systems in the Sudan:
A General Perspective**

ABDEL GHAFFAR MOHAMED AHMED

Introduction

The Horn of Africa's strategic location on the one hand, and its need for humanitarian assistance on the other has kept it on the agenda of administrations of the developed world. With the cold war behind us, the silent struggle for securing the maximum possible share of the raw materials of the third world shall become the new arena for confrontation among developed countries. Under such circumstances the need for securing the passage of these raw materials will force itself to the top of the world powers' agendas. The stability of the countries of the Horn, which overlook one of the most important passages for these materials, the Red Sea, has to be closely monitored by the concerned powers. This is perhaps what makes a keen observer recognize that settling the conflicts in the Horn and halting the environmental degradation in the area are the next items on the international agenda now that the Gulf crisis has been somewhat resolved.

It is not surprising that thoughts about the vast problems that shall face the peoples and governments of the Horn after the existing conflicts have been resolved come to the fore and occupy the minds of those concerned with the well-being of the region. The urgency for thinking ahead arises from the fact that the problems to be dealt with are complex, interrelated and cut across national boundaries. Their complexity is due to the fact that the problems are multi-dimensional because of the physical nature and social characteristics of the countries of the Horn themselves. These countries are characterized by religious, ethnic and ecological diversity and harsh conditions in which the average life expectancy is around 45 years.

The predominant economic activities in the region, agricultural and pastoral production, have been facing continuous challenges over the past two decades. The region is unable to produce enough to feed its population and hence famine dominates the scene. The reason for this food shortage is the inability of these countries to deal with deforestation, desertification, drought, population growth, civil conflicts, and the consequent reduced potential to produce food. Human intervention in the form of over-intensive farming and overstocking of animals without close consideration of the carrying capacity of the land remains a major contributor to the desertification of the region.

The combination of over-intensive land use and forced human and animal mobility has created a situation which is almost impossible for the existing institutions to comprehend or resolve. The state, which is supposed to be a source of security and provide problem solving mechanisms through its established formal and informal institutions, has failed to do so. Instead the state is advancing policies that foster individual and group insecurity in the face of an increasing ecological imbalance and an economic recession.

With its failure to address the immediate problems of underdevelopment and assist those incapacitated by drought and famine, or to offer peaceful solutions for civil conflicts, the state in the countries of the Horn only has coercion at its disposal to impose its legitimacy and assure its survival (Mohamed-Salih, 1990).

The rural production systems in the Sudan have to be seen within the context outlined above. As the Sudan is by all measures a microcosm of the countries of the Horn and the African continent, depicting the mechanisms operating in its rural areas shall offer a good basis for reflecting on the complex issues that need to be faced. Suggestions for the rehabilitation of these production systems attempt to incorporate a food security strategy for the Horn which considers the existing and potential resources and conditions in the Sudan.

Rural production systems in the Sudan

The context

In the mid 1970s the Sudan was described as a potential 'bread-basket of the Arab world and Africa'. During this period hopes for the development of the country's economy were high and the investment of Arab oil-generated revenues in the Sudan's agricultural sector seemed to hold immense promise. Vast areas of hitherto unused arable land could be brought under cultivation. The resultant produce was expected to transform the Arab world and most of Africa as a region of food deficits was to become a region of food surpluses and these surpluses would lay the basis for the development of extensive processing industries in the country. However, against all hopes, economic crisis, reflected primarily in the decline in production and productivity in all sectors, dominated the scene. This crisis began in the late 1970s following a short boom which accompanied a vast expansion of commercially financed investments. These investments, which were hastily made, have failed to raise outputs and, consequently, have failed to increase exports or decrease imports. This failure in terms of returns is one of the main reasons for the crisis which has steadily worsened, and for the resultant problem of foreign debts.

The early months of 1985 witnessed the end of these high hopes. Agricultural and industrial production had been declining in per capita terms over the years, and external debt had risen to above nine billion US dollars. Even the interest on the external debt could only be paid by negotiating new loans. Imports were three times the level of exports, and massive food aid was needed to save large parts of the population from starvation as the 1984 grain harvest of 1.47 million tons fell 1.9 million tons short of the country's needs. Some of the major projects which were expected to transform the economy had been terminated and many industries had ceased production. The value of the Sudanese pound against the US dollar had fallen to less than 10 per cent of its 1978 value. The disintegration of the economy was exacerbated by the renewal of the civil war in southern Sudan, ethnic conflicts in the south and other regions, the impact of the Chadian war on western Sudan, and the continuous flow of refugees from civil wars in neighbouring countries. The post-Nimeiri period (after April 1985), with all the political promises it carried, did not result in a marked improvement in the economic performance of the country. On the contrary, the situation seemed to worsen as both sides in the civil war expressed their firm commitment to achieving military supremacy rather than a peacefully negotiated settlement.

Economic performance: An overview

The democratic government that took office in 1986 after the downfall of Nimeiri's regime attempted to curtail economic deterioration in certain spheres. The economy was pulled up from a negative rate of growth of 6 per cent in 1984–5 to a positive rate of growth of 7 per cent in 1986–7. This impressive turn around was mainly due to the recovery of agricultural production after years of drought. By mid 1987 the country was self-sufficient in some basic food products and possessed a strategic reserve of sorghum. Good weather and the timely provision of imported agricultural inputs contributed to the creation of such a situation.

While economic growth fluctuated during the last decade, it averaged only about 1 per cent per year. With the population growing by about 2.9 per cent per year, per capita income has declined at an average annual rate of 1.9 per cent. The general weakness of the country's economy is reflected by the inflation rates which increased to almost 70 per cent; by the decline in the levels of exports and imports as a proportion of the gross domestic product (GDP); by the budget deficit which rose to about 14 per cent of the GDP; by stagnant consumption which absorbed virtually all of the GDP; and by the declining rate of investment.

Sudan's economy depends predominantly on agriculture, which accounts for about 33 per cent of the GDP. The agricultural sector employs about 80 per cent of the population which, as already mentioned, amounted to 21.6 million in 1983. According to the Sudanese Ministry of Planning and the IMF, per capita income is estimated to be in continuous decline (World Bank, 1990). Given its dominant role, the agricultural sector's performance reflects the performance of the Sudanese economy. In the drought years of 1982–3, 1983–4 and 1984–5 the real domestic product declined by 5 per cent, 1 per cent and 7 per cent respectively. This is a total reversal of what was experienced during the 1970s. Between 1972–3 and 1977–8 the GDP increased 8 per cent per annum and per capita income increased about 5.2 per cent per annum. The rapid expansion during this period was achieved at the expense of a widening external resource gap and mounting foreign debt. This led to the intervention of a series of IMF stabilization programmes between 1978 and 1984 which included the devaluation of the Sudanese currency from US$:LS 2.8 to US$:LS 0.40, the creation of a free foreign exchange market, control over government deficit and bank credit, tax increases, the reduction of subsidies, and the replacement of the joint account system in the irrigated agricultural subsector by a unitary account system. These programmes, however, did not manage to reverse the situation. Exports continued to decline, imports increased, the trade gap widened, inflation soared, and foreign debt accumulated. Income distribution became increasingly unequal, especially in rural areas in general, and in southern and western Sudan in particular, and the emergence of a powerful parallel market economy also became evident.

Unexpected and unplanned population increases in certain border areas and internal mobility from marginal areas due to the civil war and drought have also contributed to the poor performance of the economy. The influx of refugees from neighbouring countries is estimated to have added an extra 5 per cent or more to the population of the country, thereby overburdening strained food and water supplies, education facilities, health services and other public provisions. One of the major problems the country is facing is how to provide food security and self-sufficiency in food production for refugees. The influx of refugees was accompanied by a drastic decline in the country's food production due to a persistent drought in four consecutive seasons. The drought affected an estimated eight to ten million people. The worst hit areas were Darfur, Kordofan and the Red Sea regions, and this led to the displacement of 1.8 million people from these areas. The situation in the south is difficult to assess in relation to the drought, but as a result of the civil war and possibly the drought, over three million people have been displaced so far. The result is an absolute decline in the region's population and the creation of unpopulated areas where the agricultural potential is very high.

The high level of food (in)security in the Sudan is a good indicator of the lack of efficiency and the malfunctioning of the economic system. Table 1, which shows the regional net cereal production and food demand for 1986–7, illustrates this point. Domestic food flows are indicated by the regional food balances shown in the table. The transport and marketing of surpluses emerges clearly as an enormous task. Approximately two million tons of surpluses have to be moved out of the surplus areas. The Agricultural Bank of the Sudan handles approximately 700,000 tons. The private sector also handles a substantial amount of this surplus although no reliable estimates exist. These surpluses have not been able to reach the areas where they are most needed, namely Darfur and southern Sudan, due to the lack of an efficient transport system. This makes the price differential very high and reinforces the inequality among the population in the country at large.

Table 1   Net Cereal Production and Food Demand 1986–7 (in thousands)

	1987 Population	1986–7 Production	1987 Food demand	Balance
Northern region				
North & Nile	535.3	64.8	178.0	–113.2
Eastern region				
Kassala	1,901.0	1,243.0	278.0	+965.0
Red Sea Hills	883.0	10.8	129.0	–118.2
Central region				
Gezira	2,385.0	289.8	348.0	–58.2
White Nile	1,179.0	315.9	172.0	+143.9
Blue Nile	1,206.0	1,055.7	176.0	+879.7
Kordofan region				
North Kordofan	2,104.0	196.2	307.0	–110.8
South Kordofan	1,502.0	252.9	219.0	–33.9
Darfur region				
Northern Darfur	1,594.0	72.9	233.0	–160.1
Southern Darfur	2,118.0	246.6	309.0	–62.4
Khartoum	2,101.0	307.0	–	–307.0
Southern region	6,138.0	188.1	560.0	–372.0
TOTAL	24,337.0	3,937.5	3,217.0	+720.5

Source: FAO, 1986.

With such abundant resources in the country, there is no logical reason for there being so many poor people and so much food insecurity in the Sudan. A country which was once described as the bread-basket for the Arab world and Africa should have no difficulty feeding itself either from domestic or foreign sources. However, some explanations for the present situation in the country can be offered. Growth in the GDP has averaged little above 1 per cent a year over the last decade and this has been accompanied by a decline in per capita income. Food policies in the country have been inadequate for coping with the substantial fluctuations in domestic production. The government has generally been unable to reduce fluctuations in grain prices through imports, interregional trade or stock policies. Furthermore, the government's provision of financial support for the development of semi-mechanized agriculture has tipped the balance toward the growth of large-scale farming. This has resulted in a substantial increase in employment in this sector and has attracted labour from the traditional subsector where most of the rural population earn their income.

Fluctuating production and employment in semi-mechanized agriculture has led to fluctuating incomes for wage earners and hence to transitory food insecurity for those dependent on wages. The rapid growth of the population and labour force in urban areas, without any significant growth in the industrial sector, has made it difficult to find well-paying jobs in the cities. The result of this situation is that urban wages have been forced down and access to food is being reduced.

The civil war in the south has caused extensive destruction of productive resources, and has led to extreme poverty, dislocation of families and starvation. Villagers can no longer depend on their traditional agricultural sector for food production due to lack of security in rural areas of the south where over 90 per cent of the population used to live. The semi-mechanized agricultural projects on the borders of the Blue Nile, Kordofan and Darfur regions have either ceased to produce or their production areas have been greatly reduced for the same reason. This affects the food situation in the southern region and in the country as a whole. Refugees from the civil wars in neighbouring countries have also put pressure on available jobs, social services, and food supplies. Drought has added to the deteriorating situation and led to the escalation of the magnitude of the suffering of rural and urban populations through adding to the number of displaced people.

Pastoralism and small-scale cultivation under stress

National and regional planners in the Sudan seem to have a bias against pastoralists and small cultivators. Planners either neglect and marginalize them, or offer them opportunities under unfavourable conditions. Since the 1940s this sector has been subjected to state intervention. They have been evicted from their home areas and denied the use of their animal routes, grazing lands and water points in order to allow for the expansion of large-scale semi-mechanized schemes. The contribution of the pastoralists' livestock to the GDP, which at times has exceeded 10 per cent, is not thought of as an activity that deserves promotion. The small cultivators, although willing to join the market economy under harsh, competitive circumstances, are not given the same treatment as the large-scale semi-mechanized farmers who mostly are members of the elite and are able to influence decision-making at regional and national levels.

The interests of pastoralists and small cultivators conflict with those of the state which, with the emergence of group interests and inequality in Sudanese society, came to represent the interests of the middle and upper strata and the urban population. Planners and decision makers have adopted the attitudes of these emerging power groups and have hindered any policies that may serve the rural poor. Fertile lands that used to be traditionally utilized by small cultivators and pastoralists continue to be appropriated by the state and given to rich farmers for the purpose of establishing 'modern' farms. The location of these farms in the intermediate land between the semi-arid zone and the rich savannah has become a source of conflict between the traditional users and the newly established owners (Ahmed, 1973, 1987, 1989; Mohamed-Salih, 1979, 1990).

With these policies being implemented and with the degradation that is taking place in the different ecological zones which used to be utilized by pastoralists and small cultivators, the marginalization of rural people has reached an unprecedented magnitude. The famine between 1983 and 1985 further deteriorated the situation of pastoralists and small farmers. The rural production system could not continue to operate under the ecological stress to which it was subjected and rural people could no longer provide the essential food supplies they needed, nor could their animals survive. This situation led to the migration of approximately four million people to towns (90 per cent of them came from the semi-arid zone). The traditional migration of pastoralists, which can easily be mapped up until the early 1970s, was disturbed and lacked direction due to the unplanned expansion of the semi-mechanized schemes, an expansion which is well known to the state yet no effort has been made to halt it.

While doing its best to provide agricultural inputs and financial support for the irrigated agricultural sector and for semi-mechanized rain-fed schemes, the state has paid very little or no attention to the demise of the pastoralists and small farmers. It either fails or refuses to provide credit to small cultivators and even when banks and international organizations venture into this area there seems to be no genuine interest and support from the regional and central governments. Small-scale rural development projects initiated by some regional ministries, with financial and technical support from international organizations and the willing participation of the local rural communities, seem to die out due to the lack of enthusiastic support from the state (Fadlalla, Ahmed and El Sammani, 1982).

Industries related to agricultural or livestock products are no longer found in rural areas as the entire countryside has become an area of population mobility toward small and large urban centres. Given the failure of the rains in 1990, it can be expected that

1991 will witness the movement of even more people who hope to live on national or international charity in towns and relief centres. It is clear from personal observations made during a trip to the Red Sea Hills in December 1990, that the situation of famine in 1991 was made more difficult than that of 1985 by the state's delayed recognition of its grievous dimensions.

Production systems in the civil war zone

In addition to the argument provided above regarding state policies, it has to be emphasized that the civil war in the southern part of Sudan contributes substantially to declining production. The annual rate of growth has generally remained negative since the renewal of the civil war in 1983. This negative growth rate in all sectors of production can be attributed to the disruption of productive activities due to displacement, lack of security and lack of inputs. Almost all the large-scale production schemes in the war zone, whether under the government's or the Sudan People's Liberation Army's (SPLA) control, have ceased to function. This situation has led to the total collapse of the economy in the war zone and has made the area entirely dependent on commodities imported from other parts of the country or from abroad through relief organizations.

Traditional forms of production, essentially agriculture and raising livestock, have virtually ceased to operate due to the fact that the land on which these activities used to be practised is no longer accessible. In many areas land mines planted by the fighting forces prevent people from attempting to move out of their villages or the garrison towns to which they have been displaced. The use of mines has also totally paralysed the transport system and, consequently, no agricultural inputs can be delivered to those who need them in the war zone. Some villagers claim to have stopped their production activities because they fear their crops will be taken by the rebels roaming the area.

Grazing of animals has also become problematic since there is the risk of coming across land mines. In areas where nomads from other regions – such as Blue Nile, Kordofan and Darfur – used to move for part of the year and establish symbiotic arrangements with the local population, these practices have disappeared. If these nomads want to move in southern areas they have to do so without these symbiotic relations. They also have to depend on the protection of their own militia and the government army, or strike an agreement with the SPLA troops whereby they provide these troops with food in exchange for the freedom to graze their livestock in the area under control. Although none of the warring parties would admit that such agreements exist, the nomads themselves acknowledge their existence and explain that this is the only way they can sustain their animal wealth.

As a result of the civil war, most of the resources in rural areas have been subject to neglect and destruction. The rural environment can no longer support any population pressure and has gradually been marginalized. The traditional sector that characterizes rural areas used to produce beyond the subsistence level and support the small and large urban centres in the region. Now that no small-scale cultivation can be steadily practised and cattle herding generally cannot be maintained due to the lack of security, what used to be agriculturally productive or high potential grazing areas in the southern region have become empty lands only frequented by SPLA members, government soldiers or armed militia. The local people have been forced to move toward the centres held by the SPLA or the government, or have fled the region altogether.

Indirectly related to the civil war in the south is the rural insecurity which is increasing in parts of western Sudan (Kordofan and Darfur) where rural life is being undermined by banditry and inter-ethnic conflicts. In certain parts of this region cattle rustling has become so wide spread that rural people are selling their animals and moving out of the livestock sector. Cattle rustling seems to be going on in the SPLA held areas in Equatoria, Bahr el Ghazal and Upper Nile, as well as where relations between ethnic groups continue to be extremely tense.

In view of the lack of reliable information on the war zone, the impact of the war on production can only be established by looking at the position of some economic projects which operated in the southern region prior to the renewal of the civil war in 1983.

These projects are located in the primary sector, secondary sector and service sector, and are executed by public institutions and private or donor organizations. The performance of such projects during peace time may not have matched the objectives that led to their initiation, but they at least started the process of development. When these projects are prevented from operating, development in the region is retarded and the margin of inequality between the southern region and the rest of the country is increased.

The magnitude of the destruction of economic resources is indicated by the number of projects that had to stop functioning in the primary sector. According to the final report of the National Dialogue Conference on Peace held in Khartoum in September and October 1989 (to some extent an up to date document on the issue), a large number of projects in the agricultural sector had to be suspended with substantial sums of money or materials lost at the expense of both the region and the country as a whole. Reference is made particularly to the large-scale projects run by the regional government and donor organizations. Among these, for example, is the Aweil Rice project whose target was to have 7,000 feddans annually under cultivation. The project is financed by the EEC and the Sudan Government at a total cost of LS 40.4 million, 34 million of which was contributed in foreign exchange. Only 700 feddans were cultivated when the security situation in the area started to worsen and the size of the labour force started to fall. At present only 200 employees are taking part and the agricultural activities have been limited to the area adjacent to the town.

Another project produces coffee and used to cover 12,000 feddans. Its production reached 2,100 tons annually during the 1978–83 period. This project is no longer operational due to the lack of security and the fact that most of its area is no longer under government control. A milk production scheme in Bahr el Ghazal had a similar fate when the foreign experts had to leave and 200 senior and junior staff members were dismissed. Still about 600 workers are kept on the project's pay role without any tasks to perform. A tea plantation, sawmill, and other agricultural projects in Eastern Equatoria have had to stop functioning and some of them, such as the forestry project which was funded by the European Development Fund and cost up to 47 million US dollars, have been destroyed. All the semi-mechanized rain-fed and irrigated schemes in the region have ceased functioning since 1983. Other rural development schemes which were to be financed by the UNDP or the World Bank had to be abandoned together with the accompanying agricultural training institutes. A Norwegian Rural Development Project in Eastern Equatoria has also been closed and work on the Juba–Nairobi road has had to stop.

Sudan's contribution to future development in the Horn: A proposition

Any contribution to the future development of the Horn which comes from the Sudan has to be based on the realization of the full human potential of the region and the full land potential of the country. However, it should be recognized that although these two essential assets are physically available on sight in the Sudan, their utilization is somewhat problematic. The human potential available, in addition to that in local communities, mainly consists of Eritrean and Ethiopian refugees who have been coming to the Sudan for almost 20 years to date. According to the Commissioner's Office for Refugees, the number in the eastern region is over 734,000 (El Bashir, 1990). The majority of these refugees come from the regions of Eritrea and Tigray. Since some of them are staying in established settlements or camps, they have had a conspicuous impact on the rural production systems. These production systems, as indicated above, have had to contend with the war and drought in addition to the influx of these refugees. When considering these factors, combined with the present weakness of the economy in general and the increasing commercialization of agriculture in particular, and an unstable and inequitable food system, it can be said that these refugees have entered a country on the verge of collapse.

Within such a context, and with special reference to the rural production systems in the eastern region, the refugees have had both positive and negative impacts. Their positive impact can be seen in their contribution to the rural commercial sector. They have been instrumental in the great expansion of horticulture and have contributed to the development of mechanized agriculture. In the subsistence agricultural sector, however, their enormous numbers have added to the other processes already driving the region toward environmental deterioration (Kuhlman, 1990).

The positive and negative impacts of the refugees may be balanced if the other required asset, land, can be made available on easy terms. Given the large area of arable land in the region, it would seem that this should not be a problem. However, given the land tenure systems in the region and the customary rights of the traditional users, land is not as easily available as might be thought. Unused land always has people claiming traditional rights over it. An attempt to effectively combine the human potential of the refugees with the land, in order to start working toward self-sufficiency in food production in the region and toward generating a surplus for the rest of the Sudan and the Horn of Africa, will require that the state intervene to solve conflicts that may arise over the use of land. Perhaps ethnicity and kinship, which link the population across the national borders, may act as moderators and reduce any serious impacts of harsh state intervention.

It is important when considering such an issue as land use to start identifying priority areas. It has to be emphasized that no effective action can take place without there being an improvement in the productive basis of the economy in the region as a whole. Given the present situation in the Sudan, such an effort would require inputs which go beyond the resources of the state, and hence requires the participation of the international community. Such participation has already started as can be seen by the initiatives undertaken by the Sudanese authorities and the United Nations High Commission for Refugees (UNHCR) which are designed to help both refugees and their local hosts. The World Bank has also expressed its willingness to join such a venture.

Efforts to support the traditional systems of production of small cultivators – to help them produce their necessary food commodities, and perhaps also engage in income generating activities – can eventually lead to the start of a process of sustainable development. Ideas about the possible rehabilitation of grazing lands and the provision of water through water harvesting systems have already been floated and pastoralists may have something to look forward to. However, there is a need for more information on the socio-cultural conditions relevant to such suggestions so that the effective participation of the local communities can be secured. Further studies which provide baseline data need to be undertaken by national and international academic institutions working in close collaboration with regional and local government institutions. A current example of this is the Red Sea Hills research programme which is run jointly by the Universities of Bergen (Norway) and Khartoum.

Once such information is available the targets for sustainable development in the region can be clearly identified. For instance, one key target should be the integration of the defused and fragmented production systems into systematized and well integrated rural development programmes. Such programmes have to be built on models which allow for the real participation of target communities in all stages of the project. Furthermore, such projects in the eastern region have to be premised on the assumption that the refugees will be integrated into the local communities. Plans for such a project should be guided by the possibility of creating a uniform production and administrative unit which may perhaps lead to the emergence of unified communities across the borders and, consequently, to the creation of a joint entity run by the two neighbouring countries. The socio-cultural characteristics of the local communities suggest that such a proposition is credible. The model of integration proposed for the eastern region in relation to the regions of Eritrea and Tigray can also apply to the south-eastern part of the Sudan in relation to Ethiopia, where there are currently approximately 375,000 Sudanese refugees.

A concrete proposal for the Horn region

Establish a political, economic and social council whose major objectives are:
  1. to facilitate the optimal utilization of existing resources through encouraging specialization in production and working toward complementarity;

2. to settle conflicts, rehabilitate the displaced population, restructure the infrastructure and create joint administrative regions in areas where the population (ethnically) and the natural resources can easily merge.

Many projects can be jointly run under these administrative arrangements. The water harvesting projects, for instance, and other projects of similar magnitude can benefit pastoralists and small cultivators on the Sudan–Ethiopian/Eritrean borders. The area also has the potential to integrate ethnically related populations on both sides of the borders in already existing schemes. Before these schemes can offer further employment to a larger number of people, however, contributions of some basic inputs are needed from concerned national and international organizations. Some of these schemes already have refugees working alongside local people; what may be needed is an expansion of the area and the means that make this integration possible.

It could be said that such a proposal as outlined above could easily be undertaken by the Inter-Governmental Authority on Drought and Development (IGADD) since one of the major development objectives of IGADD is to work for the establishment of food security in the region. However, it must be noted that this proposal goes beyond IGADD's mandate when it suggests the creation of joint administrative regions which would have far-reaching implications for political development in the Horn.

Concluding remarks

The difficulties facing the Horn of Africa are many. An attempt to solve any or most of these difficulties has to start by providing security for the people of the region through settling the existing civil conflicts. This in itself is a major task and demands some drastic structural changes in the governing systems of the states of the Horn. Basic to these changes will be the upholding of freedom of expression and of equal participation of all people in determining the future both of these countries and of their relations with the international community. Once having achieved this, the countries of the Horn will be in a position to reconsider their production capabilities and to start utilizing their immense resources. Plans for the optimal utilization of these resources should consider the idea of complementarity within the context of the region. Since there are already ethnic and cultural similarities as well as similarities in the systems of production and of securing a livelihood in general between the border peoples of the Horn countries, complementarity and integration in these areas can be targeted as test cases for a wider scheme. The need for such integration can be supported by the argument that it is not possible, in the near future, to think of the Horn countries as self-sufficient. The wealth of resources in the region is not equally distributed and the countries need to combine their assets if sustainable development is to be achieved in the region. To take just one example, if the abundant arable land in the Sudan was combined with the abundant labour power of Eritrea and Ethiopia, the whole food security situation in the area would definitely change.

There are, of course, political decisions to be made and national and ethnic feelings to be controlled before the model of joint administrative regions suggested here can be realized. However, if there is to be any future for peace, recovery and development in the Horn, what is needed is leadership that has the will and courage to make such dreams come true.

References

Ahmed, Abdel Ghaffar M. 1973. 'Nomadic competition in the Fung area' *Sudan Notes and Records*, 54.

Ahmed, Abdel Ghaffar M. 1976. *Some Aspect of Pastoral Nomadism*, Khartoum.

Ahmed, Abdel Ghaffar M. 1987. 'National ambivalence and external hegemony: The negligence of pastoral nomads in the Sudan' in Mohamed-Salih, M.A. (ed.) *Agrarian Change in the Central Rainlands: Sudan*, Uppsala, Scandinavian Institute of African Studies.

Ahmed, Abdel Ghaffar M. 1989. 'Ecological degradation in the Sahel: The political dimension' in Hjort af Ornas and M.A. Mohamed-Salih (eds.) *Ecology and Politics*, Uppsala.

Bailey, J., Marget Buchanan-Smith and Simon Maxwell. 1990, December. 'Famine in Sudan: the proceedings of a one day symposium' *Institute of Development Studies, Discussion Paper No. 283*, Sussex, IDS.

El Bashir, Z.S. 1990, December. 'The social and economic impact of refugees in the Sudan', a paper presented to the conference on *Problems of Internal Migration and Displacement in the Sudan*, Sudan, Gezira University.

Fadlalla, B.O., Abdel Ghaffar M. Ahmed and M.O. El Sammani. 1982. *A Rural Credit Institution for Kordofan Region*, Kordofan, Sudan, Regional Ministry of Economy and Finance.

FAO. 1986. *Global Information and Early Warning System on Food Agriculture*, mimeo, Rome, FAO.

IGADD. 1987 (unpublished). 'The birth of IGADD' *First Donors Conference*, Djibouti.

Kuhlman, T. 1990. *Burden or Boon: A Study of Eritrean Refugees in the Sudan*, Amsterdam, VU University Press.

Mohamed-Salih, M.A. 1979. *The Socio-Economic Basis of Inter-Tribal Conflict in South Kordofan*, M.A. thesis, Khartoum, University of Khartoum.

Mohamed-Salih, M.A. 1990. 'Ecological stress and political coercion in the Sudan' *Disaster*, vol. 14, no. 2.

Mohamed-Salih, M.A., Abdel Ghaffar M. Ahmed, El-Shazali and El Nagar. 1990. *The Impact of War on the Sudan*, a report submitted to UNICEF, Nairobi.

Sudan Government. 1983. *Sudan Population Census*, Khartoum, Department of Statistics.

Sudan Government. 1989. *Final Report of the National Dialogue Conference on Peace*, Khartoum, Sudan Government.

William, T. 1990. 'Sudan: Twenty years on' *Refugees*, no. 72.

World Bank. 1990. *Toward an Action Plan for Food Security in the Sudan*, Washington DC, World Bank.

15 Attempts in the Transformation of Ethiopia's Agriculture: Problems and Prospects

MULUGETTA BEZZABEH

Reflection on some issues of transition

Introduction

The most tragic event of the 1980s has undoubtedly been the mass hunger in Ethiopia. Despite the litany of explanations and protestations, the debate on why this hunger happened in a country often described as a water tower of Africa has not subsided. Some argue that Ethiopia is caught in a Malthusian population trap. Others downgrade the tragedy as a momentary pain which will be overcome by the ending of the war. There are still others who see the crisis in terms of malfunctioning policies and institutions: some suggest that Ethiopia lost touch with the original objectives of the revolution, the implementation of the democratic phase of the socialist revolution; for other critics, whose vision of society is rooted in classical liberal capitalism, it was the very policies of the Mengistu regime that were the anathema.

A completely open and comprehensive analysis of the situation cannot be undertaken now, given the state of the Ethiopian polity. Moreover, a serious analysis of Ethiopia's food systems can only be undertaken through a wider interdisciplinary review which considers the interaction of culture, ecology, the heritage of Ethiopian nationalism and independence, the political/ideological position of the regime in power *vis-à-vis* the transition to socialist economy, bureaucratization and politics and the international dimensions of Ethiopia's national and agrarian development. These essential parts of the analysis cannot be fully undertaken in detail in a short paper of this kind. Neither can we avoid them altogether. However, the time frame allotted for this paper's preparation and its objective precluded attention to the international dimensions.

Theoretical considerations: Agrarian transformation in a backward economy

A review of Ethiopia's smallholder agriculture should first be seen against the background of recent agrarian policy. The policy articulated by the Dergue (the Military Committee which overthrew the regime of Imperial Ethiopia and declared the country a Marxist-Leninist State) had as its central objective the transformation of Ethiopia from a country with essentially feudal forms of production relations to one containing the basic features of a transition to a socialist mode of production.[1] The implanting of new institutional arrangements included the creation of rural mass organizations and new production structures, and the introduction of political and cultural programmes, especially literacy. The changes in production relations centrally involved the physical transfer of land.

By any criteria of evaluation, Ethiopia's agrarian transformation effort was massive. One central question, however, is whether there was the same kind of serious debate on the nature of the transition, including the means and ends which the transition entailed, as happened in countries that embarked on a similar course of action such as China, Cuba, Vietnam and Nicaragua. In the early period of the Ethiopian revolution, limited national debate did take place, largely through the use of the national media, on the question of the transition to socialism. However, this debate was monopolized by Marxist movements and parties and was largely confined to general issues of ideology and political power. The agrarian question was hardly touched upon, much less the specificity of Ethiopia's agrarian systems. What followed, therefore, were national policy declarations and instruments, largely derived from the general theories of the political economy of Marxism-Leninism, which were applied uncritically to the conditions in Ethiopia.

The difficulties which have now emerged and the consequent reversals of political/ ideological positions in recent times can partly be attributed to the absence, during the formative years, of critical analysis of the specific relevances of Marxist political thought to the agrarian conditions of Ethiopia. There were, and still are, no ideologues with an empirical orientation to undertake the historic task of constructing a body of knowledge and policies applicable to transforming Ethiopia from a backward feudal type economy to the society envisaged in a Marxist-Leninist model: egalitarian but at the same time containing the structure, institutions and know-how for continuous accumulation.

A more fundamental problem, however, is rooted in Marxist theory of transformation. Marxism has not produced a political/economic theory for pre-capitalist societies like the one provided for capitalist economies. Neither have those states that brought Marxism to power in backward pre-capitalist societies been able to evolve a systematic body of theory and practice relevant and applicable to the day-to-day organization and management of an economy in transition to socialism. This dilemma was faced by Ethiopian policy makers. There was hardly time for well thought out actions as policy makers operated in an environment of continuous crisis management and could only hope that some of their decisions would be fruitful. Agrarian policy went through a series of acrobatic somersaults which culminated in a set of programmes – some in contradiction with each other (such as investment priorities between state and peasant farms; villagization versus investment for increasing production and productivity). Some policies were inherently counterproductive: pricing and marketing policy was ostensibly adopted as a weapon for breaking the 'exploitative exchange relations in production', but was terminated ten or more years later because it was unworkable.

This somersaulting of agrarian policy will only settle on firm ground when the existing model of development reflects the objective conditions of the agrarian question and when policy actions are interpreted accordingly. It is precisely for these ends that it becomes essential to undertake a brief review of the extent to which Marxist and neo-Marxist thought on the transition to socialism has been relevant to the contemporary reality of agrarian Ethiopia.

In addressing the problem of applying Marxist thought, Bettelheim and other neo-Marxists see 'every reality as a structured whole which has to be analyzed as such' (Bettelheim, 1978:148); each transition is materially different, therefore conceptually different. Furthermore, the transition to socialism requires 'the passing of state power to the working class, or a coalition of formerly exploited classes within which the working class plays a dominant role' (Bettelheim, 1978:21).

This perspective prompts a number of fundamental questions. That a revolution took place in Ethiopia is not in question. The Ethiopian revolution was a popular mass insurrection led by students, workers, peasants, and all other democratic forces. This insurrection culminated in the major towns after many years of overt and covert agitations. Although the military did not join the insurrection until a much later date, it played a crucial role in tipping the balance of the insurrection and in the subsequent shift to policies of 'socialist' orientation. Prior to and following the overthrow of the *ancien régime,* there was a popular appeal for change especially for land reform. The impulse which was generated after the revolution was directed mainly toward a general democratization of life, as evidenced by numerous mass demonstrations for civil liberties. On the other hand, the socialist project, as it subsequently unfolded, was only supported and spearheaded by a tiny minority of students and intellectuals. There was no working class movement or political party advocating socialism. The political decision to follow a socialist programme was made in the absence of a free discourse on alternative directions. State power passed to the military on the grounds that the 'military is part and parcel of the exploited classes of the peasantry',[2] a justification similar to that advanced by early Bolshevik leaders ('state power by substitution') for their playing a dominant role in the maintenance of state power instead of the working class which was unorganized and decimated by the civil war. Even if the military had not been in the picture, it is difficult to imagine how Ethiopia's working class, essentially of peasant origin and with little or no history of struggle, could have maintained state power, either by itself or in collusion with other marginalized classes.

Basic premises

Transformation measures which took place in Ethiopia have their basis in the writings of Marx and Engels. Among the agrarian measures that they proposed should follow the seizure of state power were the abolition of property in land, the integration of agriculture with industry, the gradual eradication of the distinctions between town and country through a *more equitable* distribution of the population, the expropriation of large landowners' land and, of great relevance, the persuasion of peasants with small holdings to join co-operatives and enjoy the advantages of large-scale farming:

> When we are in possession of state power we shall not even think of forcibly expropriating the small peasants. . . . Our task relative to the small peasant consists . . . in effecting a transition of his private enterprise and private possessions to co-operative ones, of social assistance for the purpose. (Marx and Engels, 1972:644-5)

Lenin further emphasized the importance of gradual co-operativization of the peasantry; his essay, 'On Co-operation', indicated that the transformation of the peasantry would take many years, at least two decades, given the need to implement a comprehensive literary programme. After Lenin's death, voluntary co-operativization was abandoned and replaced by collectivization and state controlled co-operatives.

The decisive issue in the transformation process which preoccupies policy makers in developing countries attempting a transition to socialism, is the need for an all-round increase in the level of production. Unless this is done, countries embarking on a trans-formation to socialism can only aspire, as Mandel says, to a 'socialism of poverty' (1968:610). To achieve socialist accumulation a large part of the national income needs to be invested in productive development activities. This objective has been achieved in the two major socialist countries, China and the Soviet Union, using different approaches: the Soviet Union used the 'squeezing agricultural surplus' model while the model used by China involved providing incentives for agricultural development so that it could be the basis for industrialization. Within both strategies a number of economic and financial issues assume importance during the transition. It is now recognized that the Soviet model of concentrating on capital goods at the expense of consumer goods undermines the two sectors as workers do not have the incentive to work hard in the capital goods sector, thus making accumulation difficult.

The experience of all socialist countries indicates that the most sensitive and politically volatile economic issue in the transition has been pricing and marketing policy. The Soviet model involved the mobilization and exaction effort, to siphon surplus from agriculture for investment in industry. This meant very low prices for agricultural produce, hence very low standards of living for those in agricultural occupations. In contrast, the Chinese model has been more innovative, recognizing that the agricultural sector must be provided with continuous price incentives to produce for itself, for the urban areas and for industry (see Mao Tse-Tung, 1956). This approach, together with institutional arrangements at the grass-roots level, explains the relatively good performance of Chinese agriculture.

Agrarian transformation in Ethiopia favoured the Soviet approach, with some variations and exceptions. However, unlike in the Soviet Union, there was no forced collectivization. The material conditions in the country did not permit venturing on such a course. Co-operativization was and is still based on voluntary membership. However, neither the co-operative sector nor the peasant non-cooperativized sector have made a substantial contribution to accumulation. The pricing and marketing policy which has been in force for the past decade – which depended largely on lower producer prices and the use of a quota system for the collection of farm produce – has not contributed to higher production, the extraction of surplus, or accumulation.

The fundamental premise informing Ethiopia's national and rural development effort since 1975 has largely been derived from Lenin's thought that in order to develop a productive base it is important to depend initially upon a combination of capitalist relations in production and strong centralized state control of the economy to achieve 'complete material preparation for socialism' (Lenin, 1976:445). This assumption directly implied the need for dictatorship and coercion during the transition period, thus precluding the 'peaceful' transition advocated by social democratic parties throughout western Europe. Undoubtedly Lenin's approach not only influenced policy directions in Ethiopia, but became the cornerstone for the organization and management of national development and politics.

The direct implication of this policy direction was the establishment of mass organizations in the rural and urban areas, linked vertically to central power and planning structures of the state. Such a system helped facilitate and implement the decisions of the centre without delay, and would have contributed enormously to accumulation, at least in the short run. But the political situation in the country, especially in the northern part, was not amenable to central control. Subsequent policies of the state failed to find remedies to this crucial issue. As a result, more than 65 per cent of the national budget was devoted to defence, depriving the rural areas of essential investment resources without which it is not possible to talk about sustained growth of the agriculture sector. Here lies Ethiopia's dilemma.

Resources for development

Human resources

Ethiopia is the third most populous country in Africa. By the year 2010 it is estimated that the population will reach 100 million. It is also estimated that more than 60 per cent of the population live in the northern highlands. By present standards of technology and institutional arrangements, food security will be a preoccupying factor in national policies for many decades to come, at least until the country is in a position to control population growth and its effects on fixed resources, food availability, and social and infrastructural services.

As part of the reform measures, Ethiopia embarked on a comprehensive literacy programme. It is estimated that close to 70 per cent of the rural population has been provided with the basic skills of reading and writing. Due to a lack of data, it is not possible to verify the extent to which literacy has had an impact on increased output and productivity, particularly in agriculture.

Ethiopian farmers have practised agriculture since primordial times with technology sufficient to sustain food supplies for low population levels. Here lies the present dilemma: the technology/human resource balance has been upset over time. The conjunction of high population growth and limited technology has created a serious dichotomy with enormous policy implications. On the one hand there are the northern highlands which have been substantially degraded as a result of inappropriate land use practices over the centuries. Furthermore, 50 per cent of the area is unsuitable for agricultural production using the present level of technology and know-how. On the other hand, in the southern areas the person–land ratio is low and the potential for developing a sustainable agricultural production system is generally high. This emerging dichotomy between north and south, containing within it acute social, ethnic, linguistic and cultural differences, increasingly acts as a deterrent to the evolution of a stable national development policy or a stable production and distribution system.

Degradation and stagnation

The mountainous topography of the country in which traditional agriculture has been practised for centuries, the ox-plough technology of Ethiopian agriculture, as well as the population pressure have turned the highlands into areas displaying the worst features of soil degradation. Soil fertility has been greatly diminished through deforestation, overgrazing, overcropping and resultant erosion. The degradation extends also to the other highlands of the country (see FAO, 1986 and IFAD, 1989). It is important to understand the dynamic causes behind degradation, fragmentation and the general deterioration of the environment. Failure to see the cause and effect relationships will lead to neglect, and this will lead to more degradation and disasters.

The highlands as a whole constitute 53.6 million hectares or roughly 44 per cent of the total area of the country. Of the 53.6 million hectares of land, 6 millon are highly degraded, 8.5 million are degraded, and 13 million are only moderately degraded. This means that more than 50 per cent of the highlands area is unsuitable for agriculture production using the present technology and know-how. The gravity of the problem of degradation is underscored by a case study of Wollo where within one zone 1.5 million people are living in a hostile environment for agriculture and need to move out of the area (Bezzabeh, 1980:5–6). The situation in terms of degradation in Tigray, northern Shoa, eastern Harrarge, eastern Gondar and a large part of highland Eritrea is believed to be worse than Wollo. In the northern highlands particularly millions of people have lost their capacity for subsistence and survival. The policy options are extremely limited; only an orderly resettlement programme can avert future disasters and save the lives of millions of people as well as protect the environment.

A problem closely related to degradation is the extreme fragmentation of cultivable land. Fragmentation of holdings, which has its historic basis in the evolution of the land tenure and production systems of the country, has increased tremendously since land reform, following land redistribution and land allocation to new adult members of rural households. In one decade the fragmentation of cultivable land has increased by at least 25 per cent. This resulted in a situation where, by 1989, 51.3 per cent of the farming population had less than one hectare to work. At present the national average landholding per farming household is 1.2 hectares, down from 1.5 only a decade ago. With increased fragmentation, given the present level of technology, there is little doubt that output and productivity will also have declined.

Feudalism started in the northern part of the country and has contributed to the degradation. The north was a region where many internal wars were fought and where foreign expansionist wars met resistance. These wars had devastating effects on the environment as forests had to be cut to maintain the energy needs of contending armies and the land had to be cultivated intensively to meet the food requirements of a growing population, including the growing appetite of landowners. Every actor living in the north – the nobility, the armies, the peasantry – contributed to the present crisis. The nobility, with their extravagant pattern of consumption, including the maintenance of their armies, wasted considerable resources; the poor destroyed the land and other resources to which they had access and which they desperately needed for survival. Thus inequality, dependence and environmental degradation are closely linked aspects of a development crisis. The solution to the problem lies in mobilizing the same actors who contributed to degradation to contribute to regeneration by using, at the local level, a development strategy which is based on the concept of self-reliance. What makes the situation alarming is the urgency of the need for such a strategy.

Resources for stable policy

The situation outlined above may give the impression that the country has no hope for recovery and adjustment. However, Ethiopia has extensive natural resources, mainly agricultural, located in the south. Presently only 9.5 million hectares of land are under crop production, or roughly 8 per cent of the land area. By conservative estimates the area under cultivation could easily be doubled since reliable estimates indicate that 19 million hectares can be classified as suitable for crop production. This potential offers scope for revitalizing the agricultural system. Ethiopia has 77 million head of livestock with a large grazing area (64 million hectares or 51 per cent of the total area) to sustain it. This sector remains largely undeveloped. Here, again, a national development policy could take advantage of such rich potential.

Recent events have given the country the image of being dry and barren. However, the major rivers and tributaries in the country potentially could generate about 60 billion kilowatt hours of electrical energy. The total electrical energy produced at present is estimated at only 1.2 billion kilowatt hours. With such water-flows the potential for irrigation, especially in the lowlands, is also considered to be very high.

The present scenario

With a GNP per capita of 130 US dollars in 1987 and a growth rate of 0.1 per cent from 1965–87, Ethiopia is one of the poorest countries in the world in light of the average 290 US dollars and growth rate of 3.1 per cent for low income countries. Using similar indicators, we find that the GDP grew by 2.7 per cent from 1965–80 and only by 0.9 per cent from 1980–7 as compared to 5.4 and 6.18 per cent for the low income countries. The sectoral indicators are even more alarming. Agriculture grew by 1.2 per cent between 1965–80 while it declined by 2.1 per cent per annum between 1980–7. These negative growth rates were taking place alongside a high population growth rate of over 2.5 per cent. It can therefore be said that for approximately 10 years stagnation and deterioration have prevailed in Ethiopia. This deterioration was aggravated further in recent times as the country was entangled in an economy of war and scarcity.

In terms of direct revenue through taxation, agriculture's contribution is insignificant, contributing less than one-fifth of the total annual government revenue. Because standards of living are low and output above subsistence insignificant, it is difficult to increase savings by compressing the level of consumption. Increasing the level of savings will require a fundamental rethinking of development policies and strategies, including the opening up of high potential areas and the distribution to co-operative and private investors of agricultural areas controlled and managed by the state. A series of fiscal and monetary measures will need to be introduced to accelerate the monetization of the economy, as will other measures which will increase local initiatives in planning and implementing development programmes at the grass-roots level.

Transforming agriculture: The process

Basic structural changes

The peasant mode of production

The Ethiopian revolution introduced far-reaching structural changes, including the abolition of ownership of land in both the rural and urban areas. Like most of the reform efforts, this was undertaken swiftly without a prior decision by a political party or parties and, consequently, without a truly national debate and consensus on the means and ends. Through a series of military style mobilizations, a highly entrenched feudal type of agrarian production system had to be dismantled in accordance with some of the best Leninist traditions of centralism. These measures helped shape the course of Ethiopian life and politics, and Ethiopia was destined not to be the same again. Massive rural and urban institutional structures involving millions of people evolved in no time. Initially these structures involved no less than six million rural households, or roughly 80 per cent (1980) of the population. Later, with the consolidation of some of the smaller peasant associations into larger ones, and after the gradual erosion of the system in northern Ethiopia, the country came to have 16,000 peasant associations which involved well over four million households or roughly 60 per cent of the population.

Although some critics see these associations as Stalinist prototypes organized by a few elites to control the lives of the Ethiopian people, these associations, with all their institutional weaknesses, demonstrate the capacity and perseverance of the underprivileged to take control of their own destinies, struggling against bureaucratization and politics. Peasant associations remain mass organizations having the freedom and flexibility to perform important tasks such as land redistribution. Although data on income redistribution are not available, the improvement in the standard of living of the rural people, especially in the southern areas, is considerable due to the fact that the redistribution programme entailed gaining access to the income of the former landowners which accounted for about 30 per cent of the rural sector's net output. It is possible to speculate, however, that real incomes per capita may not have increased in the northern areas as there was very little or no change in the net transfer of land resources from landowners to tenants or the landless. Incomes in these areas may actually have stagnated, not because of land reform, but because of the recurring droughts, the effects of which were exacerbated by the war.

The delivery network in the rural areas which supports the local peasant associations merits some attention. Ethiopia has 3,518 service co-operatives (1989–90) whose essential task has been the delivery of consumer goods and input supplies, marketing of produce and, in a limited way, the delivery of credit and associated services to more than 15,000 peasant associations which service four million households or roughly 83 per cent of the total membership of the associations. Ethiopian agriculture operates with very low levels of inputs per capita. Fertilizer consumption is less than half the level used per hectare in Kenya; less than 2 per cent of Ethiopia's farmers use improved seeds and the volume of institutional credit remains at 12 US dollars per household. Surprisingly, the pattern of credit delivered is highly skewed such that three out of the 15 administrative regions absorbed more than 85 per cent (1988) of the total credit to small farmers. In effect, Ethiopia's poor smallholder farmers operate with virtually no modern inputs or technology. Neither has the nation been able to develop the capacity to produce alternative inputs such as organic fertilizers which could save foreign exchange.

Producer co-operatives
Next to smallholder peasant agriculture, the small sector of producer co-operatives is the second important mode of production in the rural areas. In theory producer co-operatives are supposed to be implemented in two stages. The first stage involves the cultivation of land collectively with implements and draught animals hired by the co-operative from members. The members retain some of their land for individual cultivation and share co-operatively generated income on the basis of labour contributions. Payments are also made to those who have provided oxen and implements. The second stage involves the pooling of greater portions of the land, and implements are pooled for collective use. The income is distributed according to a work point system.

Up until March 1990 over 250,000 households were members of producer co-operatives, or roughly 5.5 per cent of the total number of households in the peasant associations. The new policy declaration of 7 March 1990, which called for a 'mixed economy' in Ethiopia, introduced tremors into the already shaky situation of producer co-operatives. Peasants voluntarily disbanded their co-operatives so that only 170 of the 3,500 continued to exist. Thus producer co-operatives have almost ceased to exist as a distinct mode of production. The fact that the peasants rejected producer co-operatives does not, however, invalidate their usefulness. It only shows that the peasantry did not have a say in how these co-operatives should be organized and managed. In the past, members of producer co-operatives were drawn from the poorest strata of the peasantry. In a country where a significant number of households have no implements and no draught animals,[3] and where the average area of cultivable land per household is diminishing every year, it is difficult to minimize the importance of producer co-operatives. Greater benefits could be obtained by using a participatory methodology wherein the co-operatives would be geared primarily toward collective accumulation rather than collective cultivation. Co-operatives could be regarded more as instruments for promoting investments by organizing labour for capital construction and by amassing special funds for accumulation, involving local grass-roots activities.

Settlement farms

The other transient mode of production which recently gained international attention is the settlement farm. Although the tradition of spontaneous resettlement has a long history in Ethiopia – involving people voluntarily moving from drought prone areas of the northern highlands and resettling in southern areas – it almost ceased to exist. Spontaneous resettlement lost its importance for several reasons: hiring wage labour was prohibited by the land reform proclamation and this discouraged potential migrant settlers, security reasons were also a deterrent factor; the periodic land redistribution system became a disincentive for migration as potential migrants were afraid of loosing the piece of land they 'owned' in their peasant associations; the social and economic environment which was conducive to migration and resettlement was breaking down and the potential benefits from migration were no longer attractive.

With the decline in spontaneous resettlement came the officially sanctioned and organized massive resettlement programme which reached an unheard-of magnitude following the 1984 drought in northern Ethiopia. Since 1984 about 200,000 families or 600,000 people were moved from the north, especially from northern Shoa, Wollo and Tigray, and resettled in southern and south-western areas. The international controversy which arose as a result of this programme, and the programme's exorbitant costs, led to its de-escalation. According to reliable estimates, the official resettlement programme cost 5,000 US dollars per family, absorbing more than 50 per cent of the total capital budget for the years 1985–6. The programme's military approach raised controversy and contributed to a lot of unjustified results. Such an approach, quite apart from its involuntary nature, could not be sustained and therefore had to be discontinued.

It is important to consider Ethiopia's long-term recovery and rehabilitation of the northern highlands in terms of relieving the population pressure in these areas and of land use conservation measures. Present resettlement costs are indeed exorbitant. However, these costs were incurred during a period when the planning and management systems were in a panic situation. A more orderly programme could be developed at significantly reduced costs.

A programme similar in its planning approach, the villagization programme, met the same fate as the resettlement programme. In one of the most remarkable mobilization efforts ever undertaken by a developing country, more than 21,000 villages were created in a span of less than five years. More than 12 million people (1988), or roughly 38 per cent of the rural population, moved into new villages. This programme had to end mainly for reasons of viability and sustainability.

The state farm mode of production, which involves the cultivation of about 240,000 hectares of land, is undoubtedly the sector that destabilizes Ethiopia's agrarian policy most significantly. This sector absorbs the largest share of official credit (40 per cent) with most of these funds remaining in arrears. To date state farms have been the government's insurance against food shortages, with almost all of the produce channelled to the urban areas through the Agricultural Marketing Corporation. This insurance is no longer viable. The high operating costs of the state farms will likely lead to a sharp de-escalation of their importance in the next few years.

Policy in crisis or the crisis of policy? Some conclusions

From the analysis undertaken so far, it is obvious that we cannot answer definitively whether we are facing policy in crisis or the crisis of policy. There is, first and foremost, a crisis in agriculture. How else, except in terms of 'crisis', can one explain the sense of fear and hopelessness which has prevailed among people who once believed that Ethiopia was chosen by God to be green and to feed the inhabitants of the desert kingdoms surrounding it? Yet the grim reality has been that within a matter of two decades this country, which was a net exporter of food, has turned into a country acutely dependent on food aid.

The effects of agricultural policy usually take a decade to show signs of regeneration or degeneration, and perhaps two or more decades to become stable, productive and sustaining. This is assuming these policies make a dispassionate assessment of the past and an open and critical assessment of the present as both influence the future. However, varying and conflicting attitudes, motivations, interests, values, institutions and structures all make reconstruction difficult even though, one way or another, reconstruction is inevitable.

Ethiopia has undergone a lot of changes, although the gains made are not numerically measurable. The country's agrarian policy developed in sequences at an amazing pace. That peasants became usufructuary owners of the land they cultivate affirmed their legitimate rights; that the peasantry was freed, through hard struggles, from the bondage of feudalism confirmed the long-view of history; that the peasantry had, for the first time, its own voice articulated through its own associations and production structures added new dimensions to power relations at the local level, through which new rights and privileges could be translated into higher incomes on a sustained basis. The long overdue resettlement schemes which were executed in a style which indicated a poor planning process only proved human fallibility. However, the process brought the issue of resettlement to the forefront of the national agenda.

The movement of millions of peasants living in scattered households into organized villages in only a matter of few years may raise serious conceptual problems of human rights prioritization in a planning process. Yet, the programme proved that the impossible could be done through the 'boundless creative power of the people' (Mao Tse-Tung, 1956); after a short period of time millions of people can read and write because of the high level of commitment and motivation expressed by so many people. Many more examples of the positive effects on rural areas could be cited, but emerging problems also need to be recognized – with *honesty and accountability*. It is precisely the failure to admit the existence of serious policy flaws that led to fluctuations and contradictions in policy prescriptions over the past decade and resulted in lost opportunities for future accumulation and reconstruction.

High on the list of missed opportunities is the fact that in the formative years of agrarian policy, no critical assessment was made of what is required and what could be achieved. If this had been done, Ethiopia would not have embarked on a policy of diverting huge amounts of its very scarce resources to support a programme of state farming, leaving millions of its rural farmers desperately in need of inputs and services. This is only one example. Perhaps this is intellectually pardonable. After all, part of the 1.5 billion birr credit in arrears due to state farms has gone into infrastructural investments.

One unpardonable plan of action was the pricing and marketing policy which Ethiopia adopted for over a decade. This policy was adopted, undoubtedly, with the aim of curtailing the exploitation in production relations and achieving the objectives of equity and accumulation, conflicting as they are. That such a policy should not have been adopted during the 'democratic phase' of the transition to socialist accumulation is not even a point for debate. But on the economic side of the issue, simple microeconomics indicates that in a situation of inelastic supply, control measures (state interventions) only result in creating internal parallel markets, external illicit trade, higher price margins for consumers and loss of revenue for the state. In this situation agricultural producers are at a disadvantage since the investment capacity of the state is hampered. No one benefits from the programme; the damage to the economy is incalculable, to say the least. This, indeed, is a clear case of a crisis in policy itself.

There continue to be a number of outstanding constraints to consider. The newly established agrarian structures are facing serious organizational constraints. These top-down structures were tolerated by the peasantry only on account of the politics in command. New grass-roots structures have to replace them. The bottom line is that Ethiopia has only experimented with institution-building processes which model the Soviet approach, which is still struggling to find a viable and sustainable way to achieve the objective of growth with equity. Finally, the regeneration of Ethiopia's high export potential, which has been negatively and drastically affected during the past decade, is one outstanding constraint that awaits a workable and effective policy framework.

The current main agricultural policy of the country involves a concentration of effort and resources on high potential areas. This policy, which was officially discarded in 1971 (but discretely applied even after), is yet another of the many agrarian policies that require critical scrutiny. The policy is cushioned in the growth model. Econometric work conducted by the Office of the National Committee for Central Planning (ONCCP) revealed that 83 per cent of the difference in agricultural production is explained by variation in rainfall (ONCCP, 1988:9). Indeed water is a critical element and concentration should have been on a selective organization of irrigation works. The so-called high potential areas, given a conducive climate in price policy, for instance, could achieve the objectives of growth even without a concentrated deployment of scarce resources. The policy concentrating in high potential areas will definitely aggravate personal and regional incomes, a situation which cannot be corrected through the 'trickling down' effects of the growth model. In the long-run the stability of the nation falls into question.

What is to be done?

In our analysis we have purposely avoided covering two fundamental issues which have drastically affected agrarian transformation in Ethiopia – the war and the bureaucracy. These two issues are awaiting the interest of researchers. Matters related to policy formulation also require a much broader public debate. Whatever the nature of this discourse, all indicators point to one central issue: Ethiopia needs to find remedies to the critical resource constraints outlined in this review. These constraints can, however, be overcome only if the people concerned – the peasantry – are motivated to organize and manage institutions of their own. The policy option open for Ethiopian agriculture is to adopt a participatory methodology for planning and implementing development programmes at the grass-roots level.

The Ethiopian path to development, with contradictions and shortcomings, was meant to lead to the empowerment and economic advancement of the rural poor. Institutions for group activities have been established. The task ahead is to make these institutions truly participative. It would, therefore, be most counterproductive to the cause of the rural poor if international economic trends toward privatization were to sweep away the achievements made in terms of equity and the potential for group action and development. This would leave the rural poor vulnerable to the vagaries of the market and the exploitation of economic entrepreneurs.

Notes

1   Despite a recent policy declaration in favour of a 'mixed' economy, there was not explicit renunciation of the policy objectives of creating a socialist society as contained in several official documents of the state, including the constitution.

2   This was the political line repeatedly argued in the media to justify the military leadership of the Ethiopian revolution. Using a purely class approach to the question of leadership, the military, as a group, had more legitimacy as a member of the oppressed classes than the intellectual elites who come from a well to do urban class. In the old days joining the military, except for those who were forced to join the Military Academy at Harar, was an occupation for the poor who had no other alternative except being a soldier.

3   It is worth noting that 38 per cent of rural households have no oxen at all, 32 per cent have one ox; 24.5 per cent have two oxen; 3.7 per cent have three oxen; and only 2.1 per cent have four oxen or more.

References

Bettelheim, C. 1978. *The Transition to Socialist Economy*, Brighton, Harvester.

Bezzabeh, M. 1980. *Revolution and Land Reform: A Study of the Impacts of Agrarian Changes in Wollo Region*, Rome, FAO, ESH.

Engels, F. 1974. *The Peasant Question in France and Germany*, Moscow, Progress Publishers.

FAO. 1986. *Ethiopian Highlands Reclamation Study*, Rome, FAO.

IFAD. 1989. *Special Programming Mission To Ethiopia*, Rome, International Fund for Agricultural Development.

Lenin, V. 1976. *Selected Works*, Volume I, New York, International Publishers.

Mandel, E. 1968. *Marxist Economic Theory*, Volume II, New York, Monthly Review Press.

Mao Tse-Tung. 1956. *The Ten Relationships*, Peking, Beijing Review.

Marx, K. and F. Engels. 1972. *Selected Works*, New York, International Publishers.

ONCCP. 1988. *Growth Scenarios of the Ethiopian Economy. 1987/88/1989–93*, Addis Ababa, Office of the National Committee for Central Planning.

16 Somalia: Rural Production Organizations and Prospects for Reconstruction

HUSSEIN M. ADAM

The underlying historical reason for the failure of Somali rural production systems to meet food security and employment requirements, has been the integration of an export-oriented Somali state into the global capitalist economy. Abdi Samatar has argued this point extensively:

> The transformation of northern Somali rural life since the turn of the century entailed more than just agrarian change. It encompassed the entirety of the Somali political economy, material, cultural, and social. The development of peripheral-capitalist 'tribal' politics and the mercantilist nature of accumulation spawned a politico-economic development strategy dependent on foreign sources, and led to the exploitation of rural producers in the sphere of circulation for its maintenance and to the demise of rural production. (1989:161)

This externally oriented mode of production has, following a long period of gestation and maturation, precipitated 'the current Somali development crisis – a crisis of social reproduction' (Samatar, 1989:161). Several factors contributed to this failure and acute crisis, including neglect of domestic food production in favour of crop and pastoral export production, pricing policies and bureaucratic measures against peasant/pastoral producers, droughts and floods, the Ethiopian–Somali war, and the decentralized civil wars waged to overthrow the Siyad military regime.

The following excerpts from Peter Conze and Thomas Labahn (1986) illustrate the dimensions of this crisis:

> The sharply rising government budget deficit and the extremely low allocations to production services assumed alarming proportions.
>
> Agricultural performance in Somalia from 1970 to 1984 was extremely poor ....sectoral output (54% of total GDP) grew by only 0.4% per year, slightly more rapidly in the livestock sector (35% of GDP) and considerably slower in the crop sector (11% of GDP). Per capita food production declined during these years by nearly 3% per year, and the country's dependence on imported grain and cereal aid rose from 40,000 to 350,000 tons. With nearly $600 million invested in the sector during these years, agriculture's poor performance contributed directly to Somalia's present external debt of $1,500 million, about equal to total GDP. This debt has resulted in an extreme balance of payments/foreign exchange shortage during 1980–1985. (18)
>
> For almost one decade the backbone of the Somali farming society – the small- and medium-scale private farmer – has been neglected. Instead, development of crop production was expected to mainly emerge from large-scale farming of the state farm type. With the implementation of this strategy, the government has established some centrally organized services which have increasingly failed to function, and in some cases have even prevented development. (53)

From developmental dictatorship to tyranny

The Siyad regime came to power in 1969 following a military coup. During its early years it constituted a top-down, socialist-oriented developmental dictatorship. The major national campaigns mounted by the government during that early period included combating the movement of sand dunes, control of land degradation and planting trees; writing the Somali language and spreading literacy in urban and rural areas; expanding health and education services to meet the needs of most parts of the country; eliminating rural armed conflicts; improving livestock health and management; resettling the nomadic populations made destitute by the 1973–4 'long-tailed' (*Dabadheer*) drought; and implementing a large number of infrastructure projects through self-help initiatives.

This was a period of a relatively creative personal rule system in Somalia. Even though most of the campaigns were conducted on an *ad hoc*, unsustainable basis, Somalia attracted favourable world-wide attention. President Nyerere, while attending the 1974 OAU Summit in Mogadishu, remarked: 'The Somalis are practicing what we in Tanzania preach' (in Farer, 1976:95). Most of the current opposition leadership can share deserved credit for such programmes because they were involved in their initiation and implementation. They are, therefore, in the best position to promote a learning process based on previous experimentations.

By 1975–6, Siyad began to consolidate his personal rule and transform it into an autocratic regime. Governance became 'more a matter of seamanship and less of navigation – that is, staying afloat rather than going somewhere' (Jackson & Rosberg, 1982:18). Siyad emerged as the typical 'autocrat [who] commands and manages; the country is his estate; the ruling apparatus is ultimately his to deploy and direct, and the party and governmental officials his servants and agents' (Jackson & Rosberg, 1982:78). Inclined toward action for action's sake, Siyad began to dictate policy programmes in areas where knowledge was virtually non-existent and the appropriate policy tools unavailable. He pursued separate and often conflicting policy goals simultaneously. The greatest difficulties came when he advocated unrealizable policies. He declared, without much serious consultation, that Somalia should attain food self-sufficiency by 1980. As for policy tools, Siyad avoided providing incentives and inputs for the benefit of pastoral and peasant producers; instead he poured large rent-oriented resources into the state farms – the Agriculture Crash Programmes – modelled after Soviet state farms. Material and coercive instruments were used to siphon urban unemployed elements into these semi-militarized state farms. By 1978, it had become embarrassing to even mention the national slogan advocating food self-sufficiency by 1980.

Following the 1977–8 war with Ethiopia, the regime lost its stable source of expensive arms – the USSR – as well as its developmental pretensions. For a while, however, it seemed that the regime might undergo a gradual process of democratization as a result of the combined effort of Western/Arab donor and international organizations (the EEC, UN, World Bank and the IMF). In 1979, the FAO helped the Somali government prepare its first '1981–1990 Rural Development Strategy Paper'. The paper introduced the concept of basic needs while at the same time relying on the narrow project approach to rural development. In a 1985 review and revision of the strategy paper, it became evident that where such projects had been established semi-autonomously, they had drained talent and commitment from line ministries. When situated directly under ministries, their management and finances were subsumed under other ministerial priorities. It was necessary for the government to be less ambitious and to accept the fact that progress would be painful at best. The Deputy Director of UNICEF tried to offer a simplified quantitative tool to measure rural developments: 'Progress in rural development can ... be measured by falling death rates for infants and children' (in Adam & Ford, 1986:31).

The Somali Unit for Research on Emergencies and Rural Development (SURERD), a voluntary development organization, organized a national review conference in 1985 on behalf of the government and international and national voluntary development organizations (VDOs). The key role of voluntary organizations at the 1985 National Conference on Somalia's Rural Development Strategy (1981–1990) reflected a certain respect for the needs and activities of Somalia's neglected rural producers. International private or non-governmental organizations (PVO/NGOs) came to Somalia in 1980–1 to help care for the over one million Somali and Oromo refugees from Ethiopia. By 1983–4, a number of these organizations sought official permission to work in non-refugee rural development settings.

Somalia has had a number of local and regional indigenous voluntary organizations and many rural development initiatives have been in their hands. However, in 1981 SURERD became the first national intermediary VDO. SURERD's interest in influencing official policies on behalf of other VDOs and the rural poor obliged it to opt for a semi-NGO status, that is, it functioned as a financially autonomous unit working next to the ministry charged with co-ordinating rural development – the Ministry of Interior. In 1984, Haqabtir became the first Somali national private voluntary development organization. At the time of the 1985 National Conference, SURERD facilitated the establishment of another national intermediary organization, the Horn of Africa Relief and Development Foundation (HARDF). By the time of the subregional NGO/VDO Conference held in Khartoum in January 1988, there were 18 Somali national VDOs.

A preliminary analysis of such organizations, particularly of the vision of their founding leaders and their development activities, permits us to divide them into two main groupings (Adam, 1990a:40).[1] The first group can be labelled 'return to the source' because their founders are urban elites who have decided to de-link themselves from official policies and, instead of going into exile, have decided to stay in and work in rural parts of the country as long as they can. This represents a form of Amilcar Cabral's 'return to the source' (Cabral, 1973). Influenced by dependency theory in their development orientation, they stress the need for national and international structural transformations. Accordingly, they are oriented toward policy issues. The second category consists of 'transmission belt' VDOs which serve as extensions or conduits for aid flows from industrialized to the third world countries. VDOs of this group manifest a technocratic development orientation. The technocratic VDOs want to implement discrete projects; the transformation VDOs want to go beyond projects to become involved in the overall process of development. The transmission belt VDOs represent those VDOs which lack their own clear-cut identity/vision and self-determined role in national development.[2] Should they be allowed to dominate the scene, they would pose a serious threat to the task of establishing an effective, authentic non-profit sector that would contribute to Somalia's auto-centred development.

Voluntary rural development organizations

During the early 1980s, as Director of SURERD I criss-crossed rural Somalia and became fully aware of the spontaneous activities of rural people which constituted authentic rural development initiatives. This entrepreneurship has two sides – a private/profit and survival side, as well as a public spirited collectivist side. Abdi Samatar gives an example of a peasant survival strategy: 'Small producers who are immobilized in this system may adopt crops and/or methods of production that may not serve the "general public interest" but may temporarily alleviate the crisis of peasant and pastoral production' (1989:150). In this case, the crop grown is *kat* (a drug).

The public spirited response is provided by local co-operatives and other forms of community level organization. During SURERD's regional and district surveys, a myriad of artisan grass-roots organizations were encountered: co-operatives, traditional water management committees, development activities undertaken under elders' councils, village councils, grazing associations, Islamic Sufi orders, traditional Islamic settlements (*jamaha*), and production oriented Islamic co-operatives. SURERD worked with the *alindi* cloth weavers in Gelib and encouraged OXFAM (UK) to assist those in Merca. Both towns are situated about three hours south of Mogadishu. These and other co-operatives have escaped government attempts to regulate Somali co-operatives along Soviet lines, and have retained control over their property and their spirit of voluntarism.

SURERD's 1982 survey of the Nugal region came across the Timoweyne (Salihiya Sufi order) Co-operatives whose members combine livestock production and limited farming with Koranic instruction. Among the numerous rural Islamic organizations, SURERD had the opportunity to work with the two leading and most impressive co-operatives: the Eil Bardaleh community in the north-west and the Sheikh Banaaney Solidarity Co-operative in the south. Both represent modernized forms of the traditional *jamaha* in which the economic productivity aspect is given much more attention than in an ordinary *jamaha*. These communities are not against modernity as such, they simply reject an undiscriminating acceptance of Westernization as modernization. Their selective approach to modernization has allowed them to adopt appropriate technologies without sacrificing their religious, cultural and local political autonomy.

The Eil Bardaleh community was established in the early 1950s. The spiritual leader, Sheikh Mohamed Raghe, guided the community in religious matters leaving technical and administrative matters in the hands of his able co-operative secretary general, Mohamud Jama. The latter, who had received agriculture training in England, briefly served as Minister of Agriculture in the 1960s. The community is located in a mountainous zone near the town of Gebileh, west of Hargeisa in the northwest region. Eil Bardaleh has resettled drought victims voluntarily and had attained self-sufficiency in food when SURERD visited in 1982 and 1983. The community grows a limited amount of *kat* to earn cash for developmental needs. However, they feel very uneasy about this and *kat* chewing is forbidden among community members. A variety of crops, including coffee, have been grown experimentally to try to replace *kat* as a profitable cash crop. Former community members serve as its representatives and agents in Berbera, Djibouti and Mogadishu.

The Banaaney Solidarity Co-operative was established in 1959. The founding Sheikh later visited Eil Bardaleh in the north to learn from Eil Bardaleh's agricultural, marketing, organizational and spiritual experience. As of June 1987, the religious co-operative had cultivated 22,525 hectares in three religious economic centres situated in two regions south of Mogadishu, and owned about 10,000 head of livestock. Beginning with the simple tools of an average Somali farmer, the co-operative, through self-reliant efforts, has come to possess four small tractors, one bulldozer, four diesel water pumps, one oil pressing machine and a large truck. The truck plays a major role in marketing and in shifting labour around its three main settlements which are located between three and five hours drive of each other. In 1984, OXFAM America, acting on SURERD project proposals, donated three solar pumps to the community. The community has taken several loans from the Somali Development Bank and, unlike most of the top-down government sponsored co-operatives, has been able to pay its debts regularly and punctually.

The co-operative's crop production activities include experimenting with several specimens, and growing a variety of vegetables and crops such as sorghum, maize, sesame, groundnuts, beans, sunflowers and bananas. Each co-operative family devotes part of its labour time to collective activities, the rest is spent on private plots. Within its multi-sector development strategy, the co-operative devotes about 25 per cent of its resources to livestock production and in 1985 was able to sell 489 camels, 976 oxen and 3,520 sheep and goats. The co-operative operates at a profit, experiences no labour shortages and is able to withstand periods of drought such as the one which afflicted the region in 1986. It is even able to open its doors to new members who wish to join from among the drought victims. The co-operative meets the basic food, shelter, clothing and other necessities of its members. It operates an eight-year formal school which meets national curriculum standards but is taught exclusively by teacher-members of the religious community. In 1987, the total membership consisted of 10,300 people (4,300 in Bay and 6,000 in Lower Shabelle region involved in large-scale irrigated agriculture which is labour intensive). The co-operative does not use chemical fertilizers, and insecticides. Instead members use animal manure and compost from dead leaves, branches, husks and stems. This frees them from relying on imported fertilizers the supplies of which are unpredictable due to the serious shortage of foreign currency. Members' environmental awareness has led them to discourage the activities of private charcoal burners in and around their areas (Farah, 1989).[3]

Sheikh Banaaney Solidarity Co-operative is run by a general assembly which meets at least once a year to elect an executive council of five. It was chaired, until 1987, by the Sheikh himself. The assembly also elects four committees: public and external relations, administration and production, public works, and inspection and auditing. These committees function for two–year periods. Women have their own somewhat similar structures giving them levels of participation in keeping with the complementary tasks they perform.

Sheikh Banaaney's charisma was not simply based on profound religious knowledge. He was also well equipped with skills pertaining to indigenous technology. He was reputed to be highly skilled in discovering underground sources of water – a precious commodity in Somalia's arid climate. His followers say this was part of his *baraka* (blessing) as a saintly figure; however, in 1984 he modestly claimed he acquired such techniques during extensive travels within Somalia and in Ethiopia and Kenya. His institution building abilities were suddenly brought to an end by his tragic vehicle accident in March 1987. The Qadiriya community continues to function under the new leadership of his colleague Sheikh Hussein Ali, who was elected by the general assembly established by the founder.

To complete the VDO categorization, the Eil Bardaleh and Sheikh Banaaney regional VDOs may be considered to constitute the most authentic type of voluntary development organization in Somalia. Their originality lies in their insistence that the courage to look forward to one's posterity must be combined with the humility to look backward to one's history, culture and religion. Accordingly, this group can be labelled the 'seize the past' VDOs. Their approach of development through empowerment is focused on grass–roots conscientization activities. Collaboration between 'seize the past' and 'return to the source' VDOs could ensure the hegemony of their self–reliance orientation within the non–profit sector of civil society, and thereby contribute to Somalia's auto–centred development.

In 1985, SURERD's strategy was to create a national NGO/VDO umbrella organization as a first step toward developing and strengthening a Somali non–profit sector within civil society to balance the excessive reliance on the public and private sectors. The 1985 National Conference on Somalia's Rural Development Strategy (1981–1990) recommended that 'indigenous NGOs, both those rooted in time–tested community processes and those that are local affiliates of national organizations, should be encouraged and trained to develop the capacity to assume leadership of NGO activities' (Adam & Ford, 1986:124). The government accepted this and all other recommendations contained in the document revising the 1981 rural development strategy. However, it did not take SURERD long to find out that the government was reversing its earlier policy which waged rhetorical wars against hunger, disease and ignorance. The new version saw the government actually waging savage wars against its own people, and culminated in the destruction of most of Somalia's modest cities.

The effects of war

From the preliminary information received, the Eil Bardaleh string of village co–operatives in the north–west were drastically affected by the civil wars. Sheikh Mohamed Raghe and Mohamud Jama were both said to have fled to the Harta–Sheikh refugee camp in Ethiopia. Recent accounts state that both they and their followers are getting ready to get on with the daunting task of rural rehabilitation and reconstruction. Perhaps the Banaaney co–operatives have been less affected by the wars. In any case, these and other similarly organized rural producers would be in the best position, once peace and stability are restored, to embark on short– and medium–term relief and rehabilitation, as well as long–term sustainable development.

Large–scale agriculture projects became attractive, easy targets during the civil war. Kenneth Menkhaus, researching rural transformation in the Lower Juba Valley, wrote:

The Mogambo Irrigation Project was abandoned in 1989 by Australian managers after government military forces fought Ogaden rebels on the project and then occupied project housing; the state farm now is said to be idle, after investments of $40 million by German (KFW) and Kuwaiti (KFAED) development banks. The Juba Sugar Project, a $200 million investment, continued to function through 1989 but now has been raided for vehicles, cash, and other supplies and operates at only a fraction of its capacity. (1990:10)

Traditionally, Islam played a constructive role in Somali society promoting mediation, peace, learning and inter-clan co-operation. The civil wars unleashed a vicious culture of violence demonstrated in the wars for Burao, Hargeisa and finally Mogadishu. It will take many years to heal the physical and psychological consequences of these wars. The relatively moderate resurgence of Islam among the Somalis could serve a positive role in this regard. Beginning in the 1950s, Islamic co-operatives have begun to play a leading role as models of indigenous rural production units.

A further more general impact of the decades of militarization has been the introduction of land grabbing practices encouraged by the Siyad military state, about which Menkhaus observed:

> Where settled communities have a vested interest in protecting access to and development of their land, territorially-based local government is imperative. Some form of federal governance, at least for the interriverine region, is the only configuration of power which promises the possibility of protecting an ethnic minority group from still further state-sponsored expropriation of their land. (1990:38)

The emerging policy context

The fate of rural development policies – or any policies for that matter – obviously cannot be separated from the general course of politics. What follows are general speculative reflections on the post-Siyad policy context.

The Siyad military regime was overthrown as a result of the combined efforts of fragmented armed regional opposition groups. The most organized of these, the Somali National Movement (SNM) has waged successful guerrilla wars to free the northern regions since June 1988. By late 1990 the SNM held most of the countryside in the north, and on 13 May 1991 it opted for full independence. The second most successful armed opposition was that of the United Somali Congress (USC) which waged operations in the central parts of Somalia, including the regions around Mogadishu. By the end of December 1990, the USC felt confident enough to attack Siyad's main base in Mogadishu and before the end of January 1991, the Siyad military regime fell from power. A group of soldiers from western Somalia (Ogaden), sent by the government to fight the SNM and subdue the northern revolt, defected in 1989 and reconstituted themselves as the Somali Patriotic Movement (SPM) in the south of the country. The first regionally based armed resistance, the Somali Salvation Front (organized in Ethiopia by 1981) suffered major defections and was never able to wage a successful campaign. It drew most of its support from the central north-eastern parts of the country.

The weakening of the Siyad regime by regional armed opposition forces facilitated the rise of internal non-violent opposition groups. The first of these consists of prominent leaders of the Somali parliamentary regime. It is named the Manifesto group as a result of the pro-democracy Manifesto they issued on 15 May 1990 (15 May 1943 marked the birth of the Somali Youth League (SYL), the main Somali nationalist organization). The other main internal opposition group, the Islamic Movement, issued a formal declaration, the Islamic Call, on 7 October 1990. It is expected that these groups, as well as other movements, will collaborate in the process of forming national unity coalitions and in drafting a new post-Siyad constitution.

Unlike the period following the Siyad coup of 1969, when the new Somali government appeared highly united and centralized, the emerging policy context is one of disarray and fragmentation. Pessimists fear that Somalia may even be facing a period of prolonged civil wars. Whatever policies emerge from such a context, truly Aristotelian skills will be required to create functional coalitions out of the myriad of regionally organized special interest groups, most of which are making narrow appeals.

The overthrow of Siyad has occurred during the post-Cold War period when Somalia is no longer viewed as a strategic state in the Horn of Africa. Obviously the Gulf war has played an important role in drawing world media attention away from the bloody Somali civil war. Nevertheless, structural changes due to the eclipse of the Cold War point to an emerging phase of international benign neglect of Somalia. For those who have advocated a policy of national and subregional self-reliance for Somalia, the post-Cold War context offers both challenges and opportunities. The Somali state, suspended above civil society due to extraordinary amounts of foreign aid received since independence, will now have to learn to tango with its rural producers if it is to extract adequate fiscal resources (Samatar, 1989:149).

The civil war practically destroyed the Somali Army – once considered one of the largest, best organized and well equipped in sub-Saharan Africa. The new state is, therefore, not in a position to extract rural surplus by force. The new authorities will need to devise fiscal and other related policies that contain few elements of coercion; policy tools that encourage voluntary compliance in keeping with the traditional 'pastoral democracy' ethos will be needed. In waging the anti-Siyad wars, the opposition groups relied on rural militias. Pastoralists are a traditionally armed people. The civil war has caused many of them to be armed to the teeth, and it would be counterproductive to try to coerce an armed people. The main rationale for the Somali pro-Western, parliamentary regime establishing such a large national army with Soviet aid, was the question of western Somalia (the Ogaden under Ethiopian rule). To wage armed struggles against Siyad's army, the opposition groups thus sought Ethiopia's help. As one of the leaders of the armed opposition movement explained:

> The flight of these human waves of persecuted Somalis into Ethiopia, and the experience of the Somali National Movement in its formative stages in Ethiopia . . . is the reflection of a deep and dynamic change in the attitudes which has highly positive implications for future Somali-Ethiopian relations. We believe that new initiatives for peace could be built on this change between the peoples of the two sisterly nations in a post-Siyad Barre era. (Hurreh, 1990:19)

It is easy, in the abstract, to recommend that the Somali state redirect public expenditure from the large military establishment to rural productive forces and socio-economic development. What is more crucial is to analyse the feasibility of such a recommendation. The current situation – the destruction of the Somali army and the potential of a policy of peaceful coexistence with Ethiopia – has removed the need for a large national army.

Another emerging element is the policy that can be labelled 'unitary-federalism'. According to SNM documents (information about the other movements, especially the USC, shows that they share major points in common),

> the political program of the SNM . . . [has as] its main thrust: decentralization of power.... The system of government the SNM proposes is a unitary one with strong decentralization features .... The central government will be lean and efficient. It would consist primarily of national defense, foreign and national economic and financial policies and monetary guidelines. (Hurreh, 1990:20–1, 22)

Somalia would be divided into agreed upon regions with elected governors and regional assemblies. Each region would have its own development plan, administrative system and judicial apparatus (in uniformity with the other regions). The regional governments will take charge of key areas that affect the lives of the Somali people, such as social services including health, education up to university level, electricity, roads, public transport and related services (Hurreh, 1990:21). In addition to regional offices, other key district level offices, such as town mayors, will be elective posts.

Even though 'there is nothing to prevent a citizen of Somalia from working, having business or residence in any part of the country of his [or her] own free choice', the SNM programme stresses that 'to restore a public spirit in public servants...it is essential that each region, district, city, town, village and rural settlement be served by its indigenous people. They would know the areas they are serving very well, have a stake in its economic advancement, its social service systems, and above all, have pride in its advancement' (Hurreh, 1990:21).

The Siyad regime, particularly during its declining years, became notorious for its corrupt rent-seeking officials. Central appointments for public jobs in Hargeisa, Burao, Berbera and other parts of the north were highly prized by the get-rich-quick deputies of the regime. The region was leading in the lucrative livestock trade and in receiving remittances from Somali workers in Saudi Arabia and the Gulf. This policy of local staff autonomy is offered as an antidote. The sense of belonging and living in a particular community is utilized to enhance public service accountability.

This trenchant regional/local approach reflects deeply felt Somali political values such as fairness and equity. For years the Siyad regime centralized everything such that the people in the north, for example, could not travel to nearby Djibouti or Saudi Arabia without first spending considerable sums of money going to Mogadishu to get passports. Those working in the Gulf could not come home by air directly without first landing in Mogadishu. When it reached the point of too little, too late, Siyad opened a passport office in Hargeisa and allowed Somali airlines to land in Berbera on its way to and from the Gulf. Cut-throat rent-seeking and related corrupt practices continued to irritate the people of the region. In this and other matters, the people of the regions have come to value decentralization as fair and equitable. It remains to be seen, however, whether these common goals of democratic decentralization are realizable, especially after the disagreements which led to the north declaring a separate independence.

Article Fifteen of the SNM programme talks about the need to replace the Siyad regime with 'a system of *pluralistic democracy*'; it also states that 'both regional and central authorities will be constitutionally under obligation to actively encourage the teaching and practice of Islam' (Hurreh, 1990:20, 23). Obviously it is too early to tell what the future Somali political system will really look like. An electoral multi-party system requires the evolution and maturation of a relatively stable party system which is able to harmonize fragmented interests and regional interest groups for the national objectives: 'maximizing democracy and economic development' (Hurreh, 1990:23). It will be important to adopt an electoral system that minimizes societal fragmentation. It would be wise to heed I. M. Lewis' remarks concerning Somali competitive party elections (1960–1969):

> The democratic parliamentary system which had seemed to combine so well with traditional Somali institutions, and had begun with such verve and promise, had turned distinctly sour. The National Assembly was no longer the symbol of free speech and fair play for all citizens. On the contrary, it had been turned into a sordid marketplace where deputies traded their votes for personal rewards with scant regard for the interests of their constituents. (1972:397)

Experience from Nigeria and elsewhere has shown that 'the swollen state has turned politics into a zero-sum game in which everything of value is at stake in an election, and hence candidates, communities and parties feel compelled to win at any cost' (Diamond, 1988:69). Partly to offset this tendency for the central state to control all external and internal resources, the opposition programme cited above states: 'The finances of the central government will come from tax levies on the region's sources of revenues, and will be a fraction of the revenues of the regions to be stipulated in the future' (Hurreh, 1990:22). Should this policy be pursued successfully, it could discourage people from caring too much (as they did in the past) about national electoral outcomes. The post-Cold War dwindling of foreign donor funds and the channelling of existing funds through international and national VDOs, rather than through inflated central government bureaucracies, may contribute to this process. Unitary federal, pluralistic democracy might reduce emotional and tangible stakes in national electoral outcomes, and allow candidates and their supporters to contemplate defeat within a new spirit of civic culture. Democratic stability requires moderation and restraint.

Partly as a reaction to the bitter trap of expecting overachievement, which was encouraged by the Siyad Afro-Marxist military regime, Somali political actors are trying to assign a modest, reduced role to the emerging state. The current adage states, 'expect nothing, avoid disappointment'. Somalis, as a result of their history, have joined the global movement wherein citizens appear to be turning away from the government as a source of solutions to problems. During the transitional period, policy making is bound to be highly disjointed and not easily amenable to rational models. As the new regimes learn from past failures and seek corrective actions, the 'irrational' process involved may disguise trends that are historically quite 'rational'. History never moves in a straight line, and the zig-zags may, in the long run, gradually delink Somalia from internationally exploitative and distorting relationships.

Policies also have symbolic values related to the need for self-esteem, dignity, and personal rectitude. This partially applies to the need to enhance the role of Islam in the new Somalia. All the opposition movements have vocal Islamic blocs within them. The SNM Islamic wing, for example, has advocated basing the new constitution on the Islamic Sharia, while 'Somali traditional law will apply except when contrary to the Islamic Sharia' (Compagnon, 1990:43). Assuming that Somalia evolves into a multiparty state, the Islamic movement will face various options. It may decide to unite all the various organized Islamic groups in the urban and rural areas and reconstitute itself into a political party. Will the new regime allow it to call itself the Islamic Party? In Tunisia, for example, the government has argued that since almost everyone in the society is a Muslim, the party could not monopolize 'Islam' in its name. The movement could avoid becoming a political party and pursue hegemony by penetrating and influencing all political parties, cultural and educational institutions, the media and voluntary associations. Whatever option it takes, the Islamic movement is here to stay. It is no longer valid to wonder whether political Islam has a future in Somalia; the relevant question is what form will it take and with what outcomes? If Islamic ideology can functionally unite the highly fragmented Somali elite and allow them to 'work according to the twin priorities of maximizing democracy and economic development,' then it would have played a historically successful role.

The Siyad military regime fabricated webs of regulatory requirements which generated huge quantities of red tape, imposed crushing burdens on society, and created fertile grounds for corrupt officials. The opposition movements have given every indication that they will abolish most of these regulations. They believe that in the past top-down government programmes created the problems that in turn demanded governmental solutions, and that needless regulations have contributed to Somalia's runaway inflation. They intend to use economic incentives as a substitute for regulations. Given the context and the reaction against Siyad's bureaucracy, price incentives for public intervention may be more efficient. Providing deep water wells through water charging systems, for example, would not reduce the potential for fraud and abuse if such a system was controlled by the national Ministry of Water and Mineral Resources.

The stress on putting such services under local community control is intended to eliminate or minimize fraud and abuse, while enhancing a community's ability to control by reducing administrative complexity. Pure market controls, however, pose the danger of creating inequalities and social conflicts. Besides, experience has shown that the realistic choice is often between an imperfect market and an imperfect regulatory system. The reaction against Siyad's exploitative bureaucracy has, dialectically as it were, promoted a veritable privatization fever in Somalia. However, the new leaders will have to check such knee-jerk reactions and provide a new basis for indicative planning and related regulations. 'If rural development', observed Dan Aronson in 1985, 'is to be an activity in which planning plays a part and which has broad social benefits, and not just the sum of individual entrepreneurial actions with large net costs to Somali society, then this contradiction [between public policy and practice] must somehow be resolved' (in Adam & Ford, 1986:41).

Voluntary development organizations provide another bridge between the interests of the private and public sectors. For example, VDOs tend to be small and flexible and able to target grants to communities where such resources would be most effective. A government bureaucracy would tend to broadly distribute such resources in a slow, cumbersome manner, unaffected by concrete and diverse local needs and initiatives.

Similarly, organic VDOs tend to eschew individual entrepreneurial actions in support of collective community needs and organizations. While there is reason to believe that voluntary organizations will be encouraged in the newly emerging order, the opposition movements have not, at least to my knowledge, issued clear policy statements on the role of voluntary organizations in a new Somalia. The Islamic movement, in their *Islamic Call* of 7 October 1990, expressed reservations about certain 'so-called' Christian evangelical organizations posing as relief and development agencies.[4] Some of the armed opposition movements have welcomed the efforts of relief and rehabilitation agencies working with them.[5]

As part of the 'return to the source' response described above, a number of professional Somalis from the north decided to return home and serve their people during the 1980s. A few of these were doctors who worked with a German NGO, the German Emergency Doctors, to try to improve working conditions and facilities at Hargeisa Hospital. Others worked with a regional VDO, SAMAFAL, established by local elders. The Siyad regime, weakened by the 1977–8 war, and under Western pressure to recognize NGO/VDOs decided to temporarily tolerate the Mogadishu-based ones. Its policy of regional divide-and-rule would not permit it to accept the Hargeisa and Burao based organizations. These VDO and private sector leaders were all arrested by the end of 1981 and were only released in 1989 as a result of internal and external pressures co-ordinated by Amnesty International.

Since their move into the NGO/VDO sector answered deeply felt needs, most of those released went back to what they had been doing before their arbitrary arrest. Some went to the refugee camps for northerners who had fled SNM and government clashes in Burao and Hargeisa; others went abroad where they established the Somali Relief and Rehabilitation Association (SORRA, registered in the USA) and supported the formation of the Somali Relief Association (SOMRA) established in London.

It is critical that potential aid givers understand how to extend aid so that it supports the efforts of people to achieve social and economic development in Somalia (and the Horn generally). There are several case histories which illustrate the ease with which dependency patterns can be established among disaster victims, despite the subjective intentions of international relief agency staff (Anderson & Woodrow, 1989). Perhaps one of the best ways to ensure that relief and development are directly related is to work patiently with the Somali institutions, neither by-passing them nor overwhelming them.

Successful policies must be based upon adequate research about the causes of problems and the outcomes that will occur if particular policy strategies are pursued. Without a good grasp of such relationships, the selection of any policy is simply a gamble. The new leaders may well see the connection between relevant research and viable policy as most are highly educated and a number have been members of Siyad's various cabinets. However, it is too early to say whether they will be able to use policy oriented research.

Somalia remains one of the least researched and documented countries in Africa. Documentation on Somalia has, however, increased considerably since the 1960s. There is, for example, a great deal of descriptive project reporting. A number of documents have been produced which review rural development strategies and programmes mostly from the modernization school of development studies. Recently, however, a growing number of publications of the radical dependency approach have appeared (see Swift, 1977, 1978; Aronson, 1980; Hoben et al., 1983; Ahmed Samatar, 1988; and Abdi Samatar, 1989). The radical approach has shed much needed light on the relationship between the post-colonial state, emerging classes and the global economy. It has criticized the gap between policy and practice and indicated the impossibility of governmental actions aimed at ameliorating the lives of the majority of all Somalis who are still dependent upon livestock and peasant farming. However, neither approach has been able to adequately answer the question, what is to be done? It may be more practical to carefully examine concrete peasant/pastoral coping and development activities. The spontaneous activities by rural people themselves offer necessary clues for creating an implementable rural development strategy. The process involves learning from both Somali and non-Somali successes and failures, and seeking corrective actions. It also involves encouraging voluntary development associations to spearhead rural development policy innovations that strengthen self-reliance and democratization.

Viable development for Somalia in the long run can be achieved within the context of local, national and subregional self-reliance. A strategy of collective subregional self-reliance could free Somali rural producers from disease, hunger and poverty, create schools and hospitals, and provide clean drinking water and electricity. It would allow the pastoralists to move freely according to their time-tested, ecologically sensitive movements. The current crisis goes a long way toward proving that the case for subregional economic co-operation is a compelling one. Nevertheless, it will have to rest on adequate national development strategies based on economic realities and potentials. A short-term focus on austerity and limitations on imports must be balanced by a vision of broader transformations based on productive rural producer oriented investments. The Inter-Governmental Authority on Drought and Development (IGADD) offers the eastern African states of Djibouti, Ethiopia, Kenya, Somalia, the Sudan and Uganda the prospects of evolving a collective common market to promote sustainable development. However, this is a potentiality to be realized when circumstances change.

At the international level, it is necessary for PVO/NGO/VDOs in collaboration with democratic, humanistic reformers everywhere (scholars, students, development practitioners) to put the necessary pressures on donors to ameliorate the debt burden and to devise aid programmes that favour the majority of the poverty stricken rural producers. The peasant-centred development approach requires strategic interventions at the local, national, subregional and international levels. Above all, it is important to realize global South–South and North–South PVO/NGO/VDO exchanges and collaborations.

Notes

1   This typology is derived from my research with Sahelian VDOs and my experiential knowledge of Somali VDOs.
2   Purely for illustrative purposes, we may group SURERD and GARGAR, for example, as 'return to the source' VDOs, while Haqabtir, HARDF and DARYEEL represent 'transmission belt' type VDOs.
3   Most of the data on the Banaaney Co-operative cited in this paper comes from the case history prepared by Mohamed H. Farah (1989) based on a 1987 field study.
4   See 'The Islamic Call', Appendix I in Hussein M. Adam (1990b).
5   A striking example is SORA which works with the SNM in northern Somalia and among refugees from the north in Ethiopia.

References

Adam, Hussein M. 1990a (unpublished). *Building Capacity in Rural Areas: The Role of Sahelian Voluntary Development Organizations*.

Adam, Hussein M. 1990b. *Islam and Politics in Somalia*, mimeograph.

Adam, Hussein M. and Richard Ford (eds.) 1986. *Somalia: Towards A Revised Rural Development Strategy*, Worcester, SURERD/CLARK Publications.

Anderson, Mary B. and Peter J. Woodrow. 1989. *Rising From the Ashes*, Boulder, Westview Press.

Aronson, D. 1980. 'Kinsmen and comrades: Towards a class analysis of the Somali pastoral sector' *Nomadic Peoples*, no. 7.

Barker, Kelly E. 1984. *Towards the Establishment of Somali NGOs: Needs Assessments*, Mogadishu, USAID.

Cabral, Amilcar. 1973. *Return to the Source: Selected Speeches*, New York, Monthly Review Press.

Compagnon, D. 1990. 'The Somali opposition fronts: Some comments and questions' *Horn of Africa*, vol. XIII, nos 1 and 2.

Conze, P. and T. Labahn (eds.) 1986. *Somalia: Agriculture in the Winds of Change*, Saarbrucken-Schafbruche, epi Verlag.

Diamond, Larry. 1988. 'Nigeria: Pluralism, statism, and the struggle for democracy,' in Diamond, L., J. Linz and S. M. Lipset (eds.) *Democracy In Developing Countries: Africa*, Boulder, Lynne Rienner Publishers.

Farah, Mohamed H. 1989. *Sheikh Banaaney Solidarity Co-operative*, a mimeographed case history prepared for the International Relief Development Project, Harvard University.

Farer, Tom J. 1976. *War Clouds on the Horn of Africa: A Crisis for Detente*, New York, Carnegie Endowment for International Peace.

Hoben, et al. 1983. *Somalia: A Social and Institutional Profile*, Boston, Boston University African Studies Center.

Hurreh, Ismail. 1990. 'Peace for the Horn of Africa in the political program of the SNM', proceedings of the *Fourth International Conference on the Horn of Africa*, 27–28 May 1989, New York, Center for the Study of the Horn of Africa.

Jackson, Robert H. and Carl G. Rosberg. 1982. *Personal Rule in Black Africa*, Berkeley, University of California Press.

Lewis, I. M. 1972. 'The politics of the 1969 Somali coup' *Journal of Modern African Studies*, vol. 10, no. 3.

Menkhaus, K. 1990. 'Alternative futures for Somalia: Legacies of the Barre regime and prospects for a post-Barre government', paper presented to the *African Studies Association Annual Conference*, 1–4 November 1990, Baltimore, Maryland.

Samatar, Abdi I. 1989. *The State and Rural Transformation in Northern Somalia, 1884–1986*, Madison, Wisconsin University Press.

Samatar, Ahmed. 1988. *Socialist Somalia: Rhetoric and Reality*, London, Zed Books.

Swift, J. 1977. 'Pastoral development in Somalia: Herding co-operatives as a strategy against desertification and famine' in Plantz, M.H. (ed.) *Desertification*, Boulder, Westview Press.

Swift, J. 1978. 'The development of livestock trading in a pastoral economy: The Somali case' in *Pastoral Production and Society*, Cambridge, Cambridge University Press.

17

The Role of Small-Scale Rural Industries in the Recovery and Development of Southern Sudan

BENAIAH YONGO-BURE

Small-scale industry, as well as agriculture, has a contribution to make to the reconstruction and development of rural production systems. In the case of southern Sudan its importance is understood by the fact that this is the only significant subsector outside primary production. Formal industrial development had hardly started in southern Sudan before the outbreak of civil war in the 1960s brought it to a halt. A spinning and weaving mill, an oil processing and a fruit canning factory were about all that had been established, apart from a few sawmills. Traditional handicraft remained the major form of manufacturing.

Industry in southern Sudan

After the 1972 peace, a few private industries started operations in the south. They manufactured ready-made clothes, processed and manufactured tobacco, built boats, and produced soft drinks, mineral water and ice. A number of small-scale production units for tailoring, carpentry, blacksmithing, motor and bicycle repairs, miscellaneous mechanical and electrical repair and so forth, were also established. Most of these activities were concentrated in the major towns, especially the largest three, namely Juba, Wau and Malakal.

To boost industrial development, the southern regional government in Juba initiated a number of industrial development projects, including the Kapoeta cement factory (but only to the feasibility study stage), a foundry, a fruit processing plant, a plastic and steel pipes factory, and a bicycle and motorcycle assembly plant, plus handicraft industries (RMFEP, 1977). In addition, the central government included in its development plans the completion, rehabilitation or reactivation of a number of on-going or dormant projects in the south which were at various stages of implementation in 1972. These included the Nzana Agricultural Production Corporation, the Wau fruit canning factory, the Tonj Kenaf project, the White Nile brewery at Wau, the Melut and Mongalla sugar projects, and the Mongalla textile (weaving) project (RMFEP, 1977).

At the time of the outbreak of the second civil war in 1983, neither the regional government's nor the central government's projects had materialized. Those that had been operational and needed rehabilitation or overhauling, such as the Nzana complex, deteriorated further. Although these projects continued to be included in the government's development budget, in practical terms work on them had stopped by the end of the 1970s. The only central government projects that continued to be vigorously implemented or pursued in the south were the controversial Jonglei canal and the Bentiu oil.[1]

166

The regional government issued private sector licences for the establishment of a few basic consumer goods factories, but only about 11 in total – all urban based. Even the government handicraft industry was planned for location in Juba, Malakal and Wau. While assistance to handicraft activities in the urban centres is not to be dismissed, greater efforts should be directed in the recovery period to encouraging these activities in the rural areas where the employment, output and income effects would be greater. Growth and development of rural cottage and handicraft activities would also contribute to minimizing rural–urban migration and the uneven distribution of development opportunities between urban and rural areas. Furthermore, it would meet urgently felt needs.

The skills for the revival of this subsector exist and, given the less demanding complementary facilities and inputs this sector requires, it could respond much more quickly to the recovery of the south than the encouragement of large-scale industry. Moreover, this subsector is of immediate direct benefit to the rural population through agricultural production, employment and income and, together with peasant-based agriculture, it provides a sound basis for further development. Rural industry also contributes to food security as it supplies and repairs the farm tools and implements. It increases the market for agricultural output and thereby encourages increased food production. Part-time rural industrial activity reduces underemployment, and therefore increases the income of the rural population and enhances their ability to purchase food and have a diversified food basket. In case of crop failure, rural industrial employment can provide earnings for food purchases from other areas.

Developing small-scale rural industries

Agricultural tools and implements

The immediate basic objective, when peace is realized, will be to attain a reasonably adequate food supply with the goal of food self-sufficiency in the medium run and the realization of surpluses for export in the long run. To achieve this objective, the availability of farm tools (such as hoes, axes, pangas, matchets, slashers) and implements at affordable prices is one of the key policy measures. Facilities for the repair and maintenance of these tools and implements are a must. While a lot of these tools and implements probably will be supplied along with the relief needs, their maintenance and repair will be a local responsibility. Given the scattered nature of the population in the vast area of southern Sudan, it will not be possible to establish maintenance and repair centres for most farmers. Hence, the traditional village blacksmith will be crucial in providing the bulk of these services.

Virtually all of the south's peasant farmers rely on simple hand tools and implements. There is a considerable need for farm equipment innovation to lift peasant farmers from subsistence production to higher objectives which include increased employment, larger acreage under cultivation, higher farm incomes and better living conditions generally. However, domestic farm technology innovation is likely to be a medium- and long-term objective. In the short-term period of reconstruction and rehabilitation, improved farm tools and implements will be met by imports although, as in the 1970s, imported farm tools and implements will not meet most of the peasants' needs. Thus, the local blacksmith will be vital.

Animal-powered and other inexpensive but appropriate and well designed farm equipment/implements can make an important contribution to increasing agricultural productivity, labour use, and the growth of output and employment among rural-based manufacturing firms. At least the making of parts such as handles and frames, as well as the repair work, should be encouraged. Experience in the 1970s showed areas of success in ox-ploughed cultivation.

To boost food production, the former Southern Ministry of Agriculture, in collaboration with the Lutheran World Federation (LWF), the Norwegian Church Aid (NCA), and the Sudan Council of Churches (SCC), introduced oxen implements in 1974–5 for cultivation in the cattle areas. The NCA ox-ploughing programme was the most success-ful. It established six training units adjacent to its Rural Development Centres in Torit and Kapoeta districts. The most successful units were those in the Acholi and Madi areas. These ethnic groups are sedentary. In addition, during their migration and refuge in Uganda, they became familiar with the use of oxen for farming.

Seasonal labour constraints at the time of cultivation and weeding serve to limit the area cultivated by a family and, hence, in the absence of yield-increasing technological inputs (including improved farm equipment), the amount of food produced. There is evidence from Gogrial district that the seasonal labour constraint is a primary limiting factor on agricultural production (ILO/JASPA, 1983:188). There occurs a brief period of intensive activity when both cultivation and the first weeding coincide. At the peak it is estimated that the actual labour input exceeds by 38 per cent the arbitrarily defined sustainable level (six hours per day for six days per week). Time lost cultivating at this time reduces the area planted, while time lost weeding reduces the yield per unit area; consequently, the opportunity cost of labour is high.

This labour constraint may in principle be relieved by increasing either the power applied or the efficiency of the equipment and implements in use. The available power in the traditional sector is limited to human power, the majority of farmers use hand tools and implements. The prevailing labour constraint can be considerably eased not only by improving the efficiency of existing tools and implements but, above all, through a step by step introduction of innovations, first represented by animal cultivation.

Crop marketing

The availability of bicycles and lorries is a must if crops are to be bought from surplus areas and sold or distributed in deficit areas. The bicycle is a basic capital good for the peasant in the marketing of his or her crop. Initially, bicycles will be imported but later an assembly plant must be established locally. For the lorries, and hence the marketing system, to function efficiently and be effective, it will be necessary to establish garages and fuel stations in many places, close to the farmers. The maintenance and repair of the bicycles will need even more dispersed bicycle repair units down to the village level.

The availability of grinding mills and water boreholes at the village level will also contribute to increased agricultural production. The availability of these facilities will ease the work of women, and thereby enhance their productivity as more of their time and effort will be released for other activities. Hence, the training of many borehole and grinding mill mechanics to maintain these facilities in the various villages is a necessity, as is the availability of spare parts and tools.

Crop processing

Being a basically agricultural area, the south will have to establish processing plants for its major crops. Mefit's study of the 1970s identified processing projects for groundnuts, pineapples, cocoa, tea, tobacco and sorghum (1979). Coffee and sugar processing plants will also be necessary. However, for most of these crops, this will be a medium- and long-term undertaking to be pursued after crop production has been substantially increased. Given the diversity in ecological zones, it is expected that these processing activities will be dispersed all over southern Sudan.

A short- to medium-term crop processing activity is tobacco. Tobacco has been processed in the south since the 1950s, and its manufacture could be revived within a year or two of the end of the war. By 1965, when flue-cured tobacco production came to a standstill, the crop had been adopted by smallholder producers in Kerepi and Magwi in Torit district in the east bank, and in Maridi and Yei districts in the west bank of the White Nile in southern Equatoria.

In the 1970s, the crop was reintroduced by the National Tobacco Company (NTC) in the same districts except for Maridi. Unlike previous requirements whereby small-holders had to produce the green leaf, the company required individual farmers or groups of farmers to construct curing barns. This greatly restricted the number of smallholders willing to adopt the crop because of its labour intensive nature. From 1974 to 1979, the output of the flue-cured leaf in the south increased eight-fold compared with a decline of half in the north. The number of smallholder households involved in production in 1981 was about 1,200. This is a small number and could be increased considerably if the companies provided central curing barns for smallholders who are unable to run their own barns because of labour bottlenecks. With the provision of small, dispersed central curing barns for smallholders, employment output and income could be considerably increased in rural southern Sudan.

Animal products processing

About two-thirds of the southern Sudanese are pastoralists. The livestock population in the south was put at 6.912 million cattle, 3.141 million sheep and 2.211 million goats in 1979–80 (Yongo-Bure, 1988). There are also large populations of wild animals and trapping is widespread. Crocodile and other reptile skins are also produced in southern Sudan. Production of hides and skins in the south was estimated at 148,835 pieces annually in the mid 1970s. However, the quality of these hides and skins needs to be improved. Past experience shows that both hides and skins lose a great deal of their quality and hence value due to poor treatment during drying and storage.

A hides and skins improvement project was initiated in the mid 1970s. This project was intended mainly to provide experimental and demonstration units, as well as extension services to the private sector for improving the quality of hides and skins produced in the south. This was to be realized by introducing the techniques of shade and frame drying and by building better slaughter houses and stores. Employment, output and income could be increased considerably from both domestic and wild animal sources if an efficient hides and skins marketing system was established.

Fish processing

The inland waters of southern Sudan cover an area of more than two million hectares. The fisheries resources of this vast area have, to a large extent, remained underexploited. Production has been estimated at between 12,000 and 18,000 tons per annum, while the estimated potential ranges from 140,000 to 150,000 tons per year (Bassa, 1986).

Traditional fishing gear comprises harpoons, spears, cone-shaped fishing baskets, barrage traps, plant poisons and dug-out canoes. In addition to purchasing ready-made nylon fishing nets, the traditional fishers have also learned how to make modern gear which consists of gill-nets, beach seine-nets and cast-nets. These had become common before the war and were already displacing the traditional fishing gear. Further improvements and the spread of more efficient fishing technology to the remote areas could increase the catch of the small-scale fisher.

The transportation of fresh and processed fish is extremely poor. Landing facilities for fresh fish are non-existent even in the towns. The fishing camps are usually situated in areas which are remote from steamer calling points; in the areas where steamers do operate, there are no facilities for storage. Transport by road is possible for only a few months of the dry season, especially in Jonglei, Lakes and Sobat areas as most roads in this zone are impassable during the rainy season. To boost the participation and catch of the small-scale fisher, improvement in local fish processing is essential as the problem of transportation in the main fishing area – the swamps of the south – will continue to constrain fast access to the market in the short and medium run.

Conclusion and policy implications

The task of reconstruction and development of the southern Sudan is great. A special difficulty arises from the fact that the essential infrastructure and skills are very thin indeed as they did not exist before the war. These prerequisites are not easily and quickly produced. Hence, the immediate major activities to be undertaken should largely consist of those which do not demand elaborate infrastructure or sophisticated technology which requires advanced skills and organizational frameworks. The promotion of peasant farming will definitely have to figure prominently among the directly productive activities.

In the industrial sector, the encouragement of small–scale activities of the kind exemplified above could give more certain and faster results than emphasis on large-scale industry. Small-scale operations are probably the most efficient way to deliver a wide range of products and services as well as impart skills in a poor and sparsely populated territory.

Note
1   See Peter Nyot Kok, 'Adding Fuel to the Conflict: Oil, War and Peace in the Sudan' in this volume.

References
Bassa, Gabriel K. 1986. 'Fishery resources of southern Sudan' in Zahlan, A.B. and W.Y. Magar (eds.) *The Agricultural Sector of Sudan: Policy and Systems Studies,* London, Ithaca Press.
Binyason, S.A. Koi and S.J. Dima. 1986. 'Background and economy of the southern Sudan' in Zahlan, A.B. and W.Y. Magar (eds.) *The Agricultural Sector of Sudan: Policy and Systems Studies,* London, Ithaca Press.
ILO/JASPA. 1983. *Appropriate Farm Equipment Technology for the Small-Scale Traditional Sector: Synthesis Report,* Geneva/Addis Ababa.
Mefit, S.P.A. 1979. *Regional Development Plan: Key Projects,* vol. 1, Part Two, Third Phase, Rome.
RMFEP. 1977. *The Six-Year Plan of Economic and Social Development, 1977/78–1982/83,* Juba, Regional Ministry of Finance and Economic Planning.
Yongo–Bure, B. 1988. 'The first decade of development in the southern Sudan' in Arou, Mom K.N. and B. Yongo–Bure (eds.) *North-South Relations in the Sudan Since the Addis Ababa Agreement,* Khartoum, Institute of African and Asian Studies/Khartoum University Press.

18 Rural Development in Post-Conflict Eritrea: Problems and Policy Options

BERHANE WOLDEMICHAEL

Introduction

Thirty years of ravaging war and the severe drought of recent years have critically undermined the production systems of rural Eritrea. The destructive nature of the war which resulted from Ethiopia's colonial occupation extends far beyond the high material and human losses sustained; the very survival of the social fabric of the people has been under threat. Nearly a third of Eritrea's population is estimated to be living as refugees outside their country and thousands more left their homesteads to settle in relatively safer areas within Eritrea. A considerable proportion of the population is thus at the very edge of existence and depending on the trickle of food aid provided by humanitarian organizations.

The Eritrean People's Liberation Front (EPLF) is well aware of the enormous task Eritrea faces with the cessation of the conflict. While engaged in the military struggle for self-determination, the EPLF developed a quasi-governmental system which has been laying the foundation for the long-term objective of achieving a self-reliant economy. Both have been undertaken while the EPLF has been occupied with crisis management with regard to the current famine situation.

The aim of this paper is two fold. In the first place, an attempt is made to draw a picture of the existing agrarian production systems. The second part consists of an analysis of the policy options available for rural development in post-conflict Eritrea. The EPLF has broad policy objectives already in place and the aim here is to elaborate on the hard choices that will need to be made and the means available to the EPLF for doing so.

However, these options should be considered against the background of the larger issues pertaining to development in the less developed countries (LDCs). A common denominator to the state of affairs in these countries has been that they all have an ongoing conflict of one kind or another. The problems in sub-Saharan Africa are, by and large, of a political nature, but a distinction should be made between national and international politics which are equally responsible for Africa's ongoing problems. National politics refers to African decision makers at the central level – the state leadership. Most African leaders, even those who came to power through popular support, have not lived up to expectation.

The crude politics of many countries in the industrialized world also have a direct bearing on development problems in Africa. The conditionalities imposed by the IMF and the World Bank – two powerful instruments of the industrialized countries – on poor nations are well known and it suffices to point out that for every dollar Africa gets in aid it transfers four to the industrialized world in debt servicing. The irony is that in Africa it is the poorest peasant who pays the heaviest sacrifice as a direct result of the inadequacy of the central leadership and of the greedy policies of the industrialized countries.

One thing Africa can learn from history is that no country in the world has achieved progress without having a nationalist and highly interventionist government. Development cannot take place without having a government that can play a determined role in fostering, guiding and protecting development investment. The priority in sub-Saharan Africa today is, of course, not rapid industrialization but rapid action to alleviate mass poverty. This requires determined leadership and good government. Should that not come about, the hope for real improvement in sub-Saharan Africa will predictably remain gloomy.

Background

The present rural population of Eritrea is estimated to be 2.4 million.[1] This estimate does not include the many – more than a million according to some estimates – who fled the rural areas to take refuge outside their country. The population of Asmara, the capital city of Eritrea, is estimated to have soared to about half a million over the last few years because of the war situation. The other towns in Eritrea combined would probably account for about a quarter of a million people, which brings the total population of Eritrea to just over three million. If the Eritreans in diaspora were to be included, this total figure would be in the region of four million.

According to one author writing about Eritrea, 'in no other part of Africa of equal area has nature brought together such contrasts of physiographical conditions' with which people have such a 'close relationship' (Abul-Haggag, 1961:4, 6). In a broad sense, however, Eritrea may be divided into three main geographical areas, following the EPLF's classification: the highlands are above 2,000 metres in elevation; the midlands lie between 1,000–2,000 metres; and the lowlands are below 1,000 metres. Again following the EPLF's classification, the rural population may also conveniently be aggregated into three occupational activities.[2]

1. *Agriculturalists* are sedentary farmers whose livelihood depends primarily on the cultivation of crops. Livestock are mainly reared for the purpose of farming; for instance, oxen are used for ploughing and pack animals for various farm transport needs. Other domestic animals such as sheep, goats and chickens may also be reared, but their importance is minimal in terms of the overall livelihood requirements.
2. *Agropastoralists* depend on both crop and livestock husbandry. They live in permanent homesteads but seasonal movement (mostly involving only some members of a household) in search of pasture is common.
3. *Pastoralists* do not live in permanent homesteads. Livestock are the primary means of livelihood.

According to the EPLF's 1987 survey, agriculturalists constitute 62 per cent of the Eritrean rural population, agropastoralists 33 per cent, and pastoralists 5 per cent. The geographical distribution of these three occupational groups follows a distinct pattern. The highland and midland areas are exclusively inhabited by agriculturalists, whilst the lowlands are largely occupied by agropastoralists and pastoralists.

Land ownership systems

Traditionally, the main social and political unit of the peasantry in most of the highland and midland areas of Eritrea has been the village. The village is not only the focus of all social interactions, but is also an autonomous and self-contained political unit. It has well defined boundaries and administers its territory by a mechanism of communal control. A chief (*Chikka*), supported by elders, presides over all matters and disputes which involve decision making.

The land ownership system within a village varies from area to area. In some areas villages practice family land ownership, and in others communal ownership. However, the distinction between the two systems is not very significant. The family land ownership system may have started with the division of the village land among family members, possibly brothers, and with time each forming a unit of its own. The village has become, in effect, an amalgamation of small villages. The mechanisms for land control and distribution in both the communal and family systems are more or less similar. The land within a village's territory is allocated to various uses such as to cultivation, grazing, forest, water points, community activities and so on. The village manages this vital resource – land – through a complex set of rules and regulations that every village member must abide by.

Cultivation plots are graded into three types on the basis of the fertility of the soil. In the communal land ownership system, farm plot redistribution takes place usually every five or seven years, at which point every adult member of the village community gets a share. There is a mechanism whereby individuals who reach adulthood in the intervening period also receive their share of plots. Following the land gradation system, the farm plots of an individual family could be some distance apart. Land cannot be inherited in the communal system since upon the death of an individual the village community resumes its right of ownership. In the family land ownership system, however, land is inherited by the next of kin and remains with that person until the next round of redistribution, the timing of which is decided by family elders.

In some parts of the midland and lowland areas of Eritrea land is relatively more plentiful and does not act as a constraint on agricultural production systems. In the lowland area of Barka, for example, it is a lack of animals and a shortage of labour which are the main constraints on production. Ownership of livestock and the balance of producers to consumers, not land, are what differentiates poor and rich farmers (Silkin, 1989:17–18).

However, the impact of the prolonged drought and war on the production systems of the pastoralist and agropastoralist populations has been such that many have been forced to diversify their economic activities. Gamaledin and Fre (1988), for example, explain the major changes that occurred in the occupational structure of the Afar population in Danakil region – from pastoralism and agropastoralism to fishery.

There is a misguided belief which regards pastoralists as aimless wanderers, based on the assumption that pastoralists do not own land (see Gamaledin's paper in this volume). In the pastoralist and agropastoralist populations of Eritrea land is owned communally; private land ownership is not known among these communities. All pastoralist communities follow specific patterns of movement, passionately protecting the water points and pasture lands within their own territory.

Traditional village life in Eritrea has been shaken to its foundations by the armies of the Ethiopian colonial regimes, particularly the military regime of Mengistu Haile Mariam. The socially closely-knit villages became convenient targets for exploitation and control. Under Ethiopia's rule the village chief was not chosen by the village communities, but implanted by the government and entitled to command obedience through indiscriminate terror. Forceful conscription of village youths to the Ethiopian army and summary execution for refusal was common. In many cases entire villages were destroyed and their inhabitants massacred.

As mentioned above, the pastoral population has dwindled to a mere 5 per cent of the total rural population. This is far less than might have been expected as in 1944 the British Military Administration in Eritrea estimated the pastoralist population at 26 per cent of the total population. It is likely that war and drought are the main reasons for this decline. The Ethiopian army plundered the pastoral community by taking their animals for food. Some pastoralists managed to escape to the liberated areas but the drought of recent years cruelly depleted what remained of their livestock.

The effects of war and drought on rural production systems

The EPLF survey of 1987 attempted to establish the factors limiting the production of cereal crops in 1986 and 1987. From the findings of the survey, the ten factors listed in Table 1, ranked according to their impact in terms of limiting production, provide a clear picture of the problems in rural Eritrea today.

Table 1   Ranking of Factors Limiting Production of Cereal Crops in Rural Eritrea

	% of total limiting factor	
	1986	1987
Oxen	27	23
Rain	14	27
Labour	13	8
Ethiopian Army atrocities	13	11
Seeds	10	5
Pests, excluding locusts	9	4
Ploughing implements	8	9
Low price for products	3	4
Land	2	1
Locusts	1	8
Total	100	100

Source: EPLF, food and agriculture production assessment study in Eritrea (see also preliminary report submitted to the emergency relief desk by a consultancy team in 1987:22).

The lack of labour and Ethiopian army atrocities could both be categorized as war factors and thus combined would become the second most important limiting factor after the lack of oxen in 1986, and third behind the lack of rain and oxen in 1987. It is important to recognize that in 1986 and 1987 the Ethiopian army was pinned to its garrisons after suffering successive military defeats by the Eritrean People's Liberation Army (EPLA). Had a survey been conducted in earlier years the war factor could well have led the ranking by a large margin. The fact that a shortage of oxen and rain scored highly in 1986 and 1987 is not surprising as it is a reflection of the severe drought that affected the country in 1984 and 1985. The considerable lack of seed in 1986 is worrying as the crop types genetically adapted to Eritrean conditions may become extinct should the drought situation persist.

The cumulative effect of all these factors on the Eritrean rural economy has been disastrous. The 1987 survey established that 62 per cent of the Eritrean population live below the poverty level. Rich and poor are defined in the Eritrean context; the rich peasant has just enough grain to last until the next harvest. Within this context, it is not difficult to imagine what poverty means in Eritrea. The struggle to bring Eritrea to a point of being able to stand on its own feet socially and economically is by no means going to be easy. So, how should Eritrea tackle its problems?

Post-conflict rural land policy options

Communal or village land

At a conference organized by the Eritreans for Peace and Democracy in the USA in November 1990, an Eritrean academic, Dr Ghirmai Abraham, argued in favour of privatizing the communal land system in independent Eritrea. The central points of his argument against the communal land system were that, (a) the individual has no incentive to take care of his (or her) land and that he (or she) has worked the land to exhaustion by the time the next rotation comes, and (b) the farm plots are far from one another and hence waste time. For these reasons, Abraham's conclusion was that the communal system is not conducive to progress. The same arguments were also raised by some British officers who found the communal land system quite unusual during the British Administration period in the 1940s.

An anthropologist who served in the 'native affairs' section of the Secretariat of the British Military Administration in Eritrea, S.F. Nadel, was exceptional for his outlook.

Nadel had a clear understanding of the communal land system:

> The argument [against the communal land ownership system] ignores an important fact – the spirit of communal responsibility in these communities.... The rules of fallow-lying and the building and upkeep of terraces, which outlive individual tenure, prove this community spirit convincingly...'resti' (private) ownership involves absenteeism and various forms of tenancy, which can hardly be called a spur to improvement and interest. (1946:15)

Nadel was critical of those who favoured privatization on the grounds of progress and improvement, and of their 'thinking in terms of modern methods of agriculture – irrigation by means of wells and pumps, artificial manuring, market gardening – methods which are far above the average native group; methods, in other words, which follow the principles of individualistic and capitalistic enterprise' (1946:15). Nadel made the point that since no attempt had been made to improve agriculture on a communal basis or to explore the potentialities of the 'communal spirit', the economics of free competition and individualistic enterprise should not have even been discussed.

In the context of Eritrea's current reality, there are additional pressing arguments which testify against privatization of the communal land system. How would the now communal grazing land, water points and all the other communal facilities of a village be shared? How is fairness to be exercised in the redistribution of land given the differences in soil fertility from area to area? Privatization would result in the dispersal of the population over a wide area and thereby create problems in terms of the provision of social services. Perhaps the most crucial question is, what is to be done with the excess farmers which privatization will inevitably create? And what will happen to the poor farmer without oxen whose needs are currently being met by the village system?

The EPLF has been treating the management of land with the caution that it deserves. Its strategy has always been not to dictate from above but to be a facilitator and an implementor of decisions reached through democratic mechanisms (Cliffe, 1989). For example, in the early 1970s, when a large part of highland Eritrea was under the complete control of the EPLF, some village communities under the *tsilmi* land ownership system wished to turn it into the *dessa* system, that is, from family ownership to village ownership. On the basis of the popular wish of the village communities, the EPLF then took action by introducing land reform in those areas.

A credible policy in Eritrea would be one which dwells upon what already exists. A radical change for its own sake should never be contemplated in post-conflict Eritrea. The Eritrean village is the envy of many, the past rulers of Ethiopia in particular. Whilst trying to destroy it they engaged in emulating it in their country.

Private land

In areas of Eritrea where there is private land ownership there may well be a need to equitably distribute it. However, no policy should attempt to impose the village communal land system on these areas as this is something that people will do by themselves if they so wish. The Eritrean village took centuries to evolve into its present form and it cannot be simply inserted into a different social system. This would seriously disrupt those involved and would waste resources which Eritrea can not afford to lose.

The goal which should determine future agricultural policy in Eritrea is the eradication of hunger. Private land ownership using 'modern' farming methods could play a role in this provided effective control mechanisms are in place to ensure that the overall policy will not be compromised. This approach may be more effective than developing big state farms which are cumbersome to manage and usually end up being a burden on the national economy rather than contributing to it.

Pastoral land

Based on the assumption that pastoralists are aimless wanderers, many countries have tried to settle them. Nowhere has this been successful. What must be understood is that pastoralists are not rejecting progress by opposing government-imposed settlements, but that the settlements do not provide a better life for them. Governments' settlement policies for pastoralists are usually engaged for sinister motives, that is for control and for the appropriation of tax.

For the reasons mentioned above, Eritrea should not follow a policy which favours the settlement of pastoralists. For a start, it is not a viable policy option. Eritrea, coming out of a long drawn-out war, is not in a position to provide the experts required to develop such a policy, or the financial assistance needed to encourage pastoralists to change their way of life. Independent Eritrea can best assist pastoralist societies through upholding their rights to land and providing veterinary, health and education services at strategic locations. In general, the aim must be to provide services which are compatible with the available resources, both human and financial.

The management of aid

Eritrea's own resources alone are not sufficient to cover the costs of post-conflict recovery and reconstruction. Out of sheer necessity it has to look for assistance. However, even in this desperate situation Eritrea must take note of the evils of certain kinds of aid. There are numerous examples where the burden of aid has become a barrier to development. Eritrea must, therefore, avoid the trap of joining the club of debtor countries.

Aid from non-governmental organizations, usually associated with small rural projects, could play an important role in Eritrea's recovery and reconstruction. But, even humanitarian aid of this nature can be a burden rather than a help to a country if not properly managed. There may well be a need to establish a department which is solely responsible for the management of aid in post-conflict Eritrea. Ideally this department would be attached to the body responsible for planning. In whatever way the management of aid is organized, the aim must be not to exercise petty controls, but to guide project proposals so that they fall within the overall development objective. Aid assisted projects should be based upon certain guiding principles:

1. they must operate under and as part of the appropriate local institution;
2. they must aim to provide compatible and sustainable levels of services;
3. they must aim to develop self-reliance by emphasizing the building of institutional capacities to plan and implement programmes and projects.

Concluding remarks

In conclusion, the function of state leadership in development needs to be stressed. Any government's mandate is only to manage the duties of the state on behalf of the people. The role of a responsible government must always be to create a climate conducive to development. It is responsible for the maintenance of law and order, for upholding and respecting the democratic rights of the people, for the provision of adequate levels of social services, for the improvement of transportation, communication and marketing networks, for making credit and other essentials like fertilizer and seed available to the people, and so forth. Development cannot take place without these essential ingredients. By and large, the role of governments should be, therefore, to protect, control, advise and provide services to the people. Whether in agriculture or other industries, governments must guide and encourage private enterprise as this forms the engine for progress. The exercise of control is important, but the actions of governments must not stifle individual or group initiatives and be an obstacle to development.

Notes
1   This is the EPLF's estimate based on its 1987 survey. No census had ever been conducted in Eritrea before, and the EPLF estimate is the most reliable to date.
2   Artisans such as blacksmiths, although part of the rural economy, are numerically too insignificant to merit their aggregation by occupation.

References

Abraham, G. 1990. 'The privatisation of the diesa in independent Eritrea: Towards an agricultural research and policy agenda', paper presented at international conference organized by the Eritreans for Peace and Democracy.

Abul-Haggag, A. 1961. *A Contribution to the Physiography of Northern Ethiopia*, London, University of London, the Athlone Press.

Cliffe, L. 1989. 'The impact of war and the response to it in different agrarian systems in Eritrea' *Development and Change*, vol. 20, pp. 373–400.

EPLF. 1987. *National Democratic Programme*, Eritrea, EPLF.

Gamaledin, M. and Z. Fre. 1988. 'Pastoral development challenges in Eritrea: Preliminary notes on policy options', paper presented to the *First Conference on Research and Development*, Winna, Eritrea.

Nadel, S.F. 1946. 'Land tenure on the Eritrean plateau' *Journal of the International African Institute*.

Norwegian Church Relief, The Emergency Relief Desk. 1987. *An Independent Evaluation of the Food Situation in Eritrea*, Agriculture and Rural Development Unit, Centre for Development Studies, University of Leeds.

Silkin, T. 1989. *Nara of Mogarib and the Beni Amer of Forto (Lower Barka): Implications for the Mogarib-Forto Community Development Project*, a consultancy report for CAFOD.

19 Pastoralism: Existing Limitations, Possibilities for the Future

MAKNUN GAMALEDIN

This paper addresses some specific problems facing pastoralism, particularly focusing on existing limitations and possibilities for the future. A central point is that the nature and role of the nation-state which was born out of the colonial state needs to be reconsidered because its ethos and philosophy are not compatible with the aspirations of pastoralists. The proof is self-evident in the Horn of Africa, where the conflict between the state and the nationalities, with the exception of Tigray, started in pastoralist areas. A number of viable options for future co-operation between the Horn countries are presented.

Present limitations for pastoralism

The emergence of the colonial state and later the post-colonial state disrupted the political, social and economic lives of pastoralists. The emergence of colonial ports and the development of a modern transport system not only disrupted the ancient trade network on which pastoralists partly depended, but in addition all traditional markets in the coastal areas disappeared, thus bringing to an end a way of life. The consolidation of the state and the creation of artificial borders limited the size of territories available to pastoral groups, thereby disrupting their finely balanced use of varied ecological zones. This was in the interest of controlling movement and imposing taxes. The accumulated effects of the state policy have resulted in devastation, which has been accentuated by recurrent droughts.

The example of the Awash Valley is used to illustrate issues relating to land rights and pastoralists' experience with a centrally organized development agency. But, before proceeding to show how the Ethiopian state under Haile Selassie and Mengistu Haile Mariam subordinated the interests and the aspirations of the Afars to that of the centre through land policy, it is useful to highlight some of the current limitations to the development of pastoralist societies in the Horn of Africa. Some of these limitations are summarized below.

1. The creation of artificial borders has limited the traditional patterns of movement of nomadic groups.
2. The state's refusal to recognize the land rights of nomadic groups has meant that they are denied access to water and pasture. The state's need for cash and commodities for its growing bureaucracy has resulted in it limiting land rights in nomadic areas using legal instruments. These controls were enshrined in the 1926 State Domain Declaration in Eritrea, and in Ethiopia in the revised constitution of 1955, as well as in the Rural Land Proclamation of 1975.
3. Ministries of Agriculture normally focus their activities on livestock development,

as part of agricultural development, and on the introduction of exotic breeding, neglecting the breeding of indigenous livestock. Ethno-veterinary is not incorporated in training programmes.

4. State policies encourage sedentariness and, therefore, are not geared to the needs and aspirations of pastoralists.
5. State policies and armed conflicts disrupt trade and markets. In the Awash Valley, the post-war redrawing of the boundaries of districts for movement control and tax purposes led to markets being relocated to the hinterland. The wars in Ogaden and Eritrea also disrupted traditional trade and markets. The Beni Amer now have to travel to Kassala in the Sudan for markets.
6. Wars and drought have led to an environmental crisis and this, in turn, has resulted in inter-clan and intra-ethnic conflicts. The continuous fighting between the Issa and the Afar in the Awash Valley is one example. In other areas of the Horn, insecurity has also contributed to increasing the number of cattle raiding incidents, thereby leading to the militarization of pastoralist societies. In western Eritrea cattle raiding has prevented pastoralists from moving out of the wet season areas for years.
7. There is a general lack of research on land tenure, health and indigenous knowledge.

Case study: The Awash Valley

The discussion below attempts to shed some light on development in the Awash Valley, under both Haile Selassie and the Dergue. The legal basis on which claims to land ownership were based by the two contending parties (the Afar and the government) will be explicated, and the dangers associated with centrally organized development agencies without any local accountability will be underlined. This review is intended to help future development avoid the mistakes of the past.

In 1962 the government established the Awash Valley Authority (AVA) to supervise development in the valley. Land ownership was vested in the AVA, ignoring the traditional claims of the nomadic people. Under the management of the AVA, development in the valley took the form of large-scale mechanized commercial enterprises, most of which were managed by foreign agro-businesses in joint ventures with the state. The government's main concern at this stage was to acquire cash and commodities for its expanding military and civilian bureaucracy. Irrigation development in the Awash Valley certainly increased the country's production of cotton and sugar, and large numbers of migrant labourers were absorbed. However, irrigation, the construction of dams, the government's drive for centralization, and drought had a deplorable effect on the nomads of the Awsah.

In order to establish how development was pursued in the valley, and the AVA's role in this process, a Feasibility Study of the Lower Plains (FSLAV) was carried out in late 1973, assessing the physical and human resources of the Lower Awash. It also included a section on the political structure of Awsa and an appraisal of the development projects undertaken by the leadership of the Sultanate of Awsa. The most devastating part of the FSLAV report as far as the role of the AVA was concerned was the sociological study written by Cossins who was known to be sympathetic to the Afar, and was an outspoken critic of the development in the valley. Cossins' original report blamed both the AVA and the Tendaho Plantation Company for having deprived the herdspeople of their prime grazing area. Whilst the study praised the organizational skill of the Afar farmers in the Lower Awash, the Awsean landed aristocracy did not escape Cossins' criticism, although the Sultanate fared better than the AVA and the Tendaho Plantation Company.

Unlike earlier reports of feasibility studies, the contents of which normally appeared in the FAO's periodical report to the Imperial Government of Ethiopia, neither the Interim Report of 1974 nor the subsequent Interim Report carried the recommendations of the FSLAV. This departure from procedure indicates the AVA's dissatisfaction with the FSLAV, which in fact recommended that AVA limit its activities in the Lower Awash Valley to the role of water management only. The feasibility study called for the establishment of a new development organization in which the Afar farmers and the Awsa Sultanate were to participate along with the local government and the AVA.

The first survey showed a lack of political awareness on the part of the government with regard to the valley's people, and this was to cost the Authority dearly. The report also suggested the improvement of grazing land together with irrigated agriculture, the digging of wells, the distribution of watering points and the spreading of flood water from intermittent watering points. But, at the same time it called for priority to be given to large-scale commercial development in the middle valley, and the promotion of family sized farms in the lower valley. The latter was to meet the demands of the lower plains Afar.

AVA and the allocation of land resources

The Ethiopian government had not devised any definition of what it referred to as government land. Nevertheless, according to the government, all lands utilized by semi-nomadic pastoralists were by definition 'state domain', a claim based on Menelik's conquest which may or may not have included the Afar country. The revised constitution of 1955 nationalized all pastoral lands in the Empire. There was some confusion over the definition of government land, but this did not prevent the government or Haile Selassie from actively disposing of such lands by imperial grant or for what was defined as the 'public interest' which was the case in the Awash Valley. In addition, although no Ministry or Public Authority in fact ever turned over land titles to the AVA, the Authority derived that it was the manager of all grazing land within the Awash Valley, given its interpretation of the state's right to all such land. It was on this basis that the AVA formulated its land policies.

According to the revised constitution, the AVA was not responsible for devising ways to settle the Afar on irrigated land. Such attempts were more a response to the alienation of grazing land to concessionaires and the perceived need to compensate the Afar by settling some of them on irrigated plots. Compensation in principle was unacceptable to both the nomadic and settled Afar. The Authority's policy of granting concessions to private enterprises which excluded the Afar did not assist the AVA's attempts to win some Afar to its side. The exclusion of the Afar was exacerbated by the hostile attitude towards the nomads held by the newly established farmers, many of whom constructed elaborate networks of fences, some electric, around their plantations. However, it was the economic tensions arising from the land issue which shaped Afar opinions of the Authority. The crude economic incentive offered to limited numbers of Afar settlers on the Amibara settlement scheme was not enough.

However, it is incorrect to assume that there was a unified reaction of all Afar towards the Authority: attitudes ranged from outright hostility and rejection of the AVA and its activities in the lower plains, to a policy of accommodation in the middle valley. In the latter region the Authority attempted to engage the elders, albeit nominally, in the affairs of the scheme, but the Authority's refusal to provide them with credit facilities and large concessions of the kind available to non-Afar, increased hostility towards the AVA. The middle valley Afar were willing to accommodate the Authority if the latter were to give them equal treatment with other interests in the valley. These elders understood very well the political pressures and the strength of the state, and their economic deterioration caused by the continued drought. They were thus prepared to support the settlement schemes, but remained hostile to the AVA's land policy.

The Afar view was expressed quite clearly by Sultan Alimirah of Awsa to a panel of consultants who evaluated AVA settlement schemes in 1974:

> We are loyal to our government, and we have paid Gibir (*taxation*) for generations. We fought for the land as we fought for the country because the land is ours, just as the country is ours. No man with a piece of paper from Addis Ababa is going to take the right away from us. We live along the frontier of the French occupied territory. Our people on the other side of the border look towards us for advice and leadership. (Asmeron, 1974:37)

This statement is an indication of the political awareness of the Afar leadership, something that the AVA's management seemed to overlook.

Afar claims to land are based on permanent access to watering rights along the river banks or to pasture; some clans have been in their present areas of habitation for more than seven generations. The introduction of mechanized agriculture meant the demarcation of particular plots of land. This was an entirely different approach to the system of utilization of resources employed by the traditional users who had not been restricted either in their movements or in their choice of locations. The Afar were unable to comprehend the AVA's rejection of the traditional rights conferred upon clan leaders as spokespeople in matters related to resources. The AVA's refusal to discuss the matter was incomprehensible in a society where only negotiations and prolonged discussion can lead to agreement. This, combined with the threat of losing resources or livestock, triggered Afar militancy. In addition, the Afar recognized the relationship between drought and the loss of grazing lands and watering points to the concessionaires, and this increased their sense of bitterness.

The Afar leaders of the middle valley challenged the AVA directly. With political and financial backing from the Sultan of Awsa, and a loan of 17 tractors and two bulldozers, they set up their own commercial farms, and allocated concessions to others. This was fiercely opposed by the AVA in the courts, but the Afar were able to exploit the loopholes in Ethiopian law, particularly those related to government land. In 1973 an Afar elder won a legal case against the AVA, and the court upheld his right, as spokesperson of his clan, to dispose of land.

The Dergue and the semi-nomadic Afar

The change of government in Addis Ababa in 1974 further exacerbated the already precarious relationship between the state and the Afar pastoralists. The new regime's programme of nationalization of rural land was rejected by the Afar Sultan of Awsa. This soon led to the formation of the Afar Liberation Front (ALF) in June 1975.

There appeared to be some change from the previous government's position because nomadic people were given 'possessory rights over the land they customarily use for grazing' (Provisional Government, 1975). However, the statement was very vague, and the government's vigorously pursued policy of establishing more state farms in the valley, alienating people and land, was evidence of the state's continued policy of control over nomadic land. This evidence was reinforced by the government's continued reluctance to allow the establishment of local agencies which would be accountable for the development of the valley.

The post-conflict situation

The assumption here is that 'post-conflict' relates to a condition in which the peoples of the Horn of Africa have exercised their full right to self-determination through supervised referendums leading either to a reconstitution of old political entities on a federal basis, or to the emergence of new political entities. It is realistic to assume that in such a situation the new or the reconstituted entities would be extremely busy reconstructing their particular societies which were ravaged by years of war, rather than directing their energies and limited resources to regional co-operation.

However, it will be a tragedy if the leaders of these entities, who have made great sacrifices to achieve the liberation of their people, do not make some provisions to relinquish some of the sovereign rights of the nation-state, particularly in terms of concessions to nomadic people. The concessions might take the form of dual citizenship or the joint management of resources. Such development can only be achieved through a gradual process, and this should be preceded by institutional developments at the regional level and at the local level. At the regional level a political will has already been expressed in the formation of the Inter-Governmental Authority on Drought and Development (IGADD). This regional body should be expanded to include a pastoral development strategy which is people centred as well as action- and needs-oriented. Despite the predominance of pastoralism as a major occupation and part of the economy in the region, no such strategy yet exists. IGADD should explore various possibilities for the joint management of resources in relation to livestock, water authorities and marketing systems. If the undertaking of such tasks requires widening its terms of reference, then an agreement should be reached by a reconstituted IGADD.

At the national level, the focus should be on building local institutions which are accountable to local governments, not to the national government, and which have the power to negotiate directly with organizations with similar objectives across the border. Such institutions could develop ways to co-operate and conduct joint research relevant to their particular area. The recognition of the specificity of each pastoral group and the need for autonomy is expressed by many observers, among them Hassan and Doornbos (1977:137):

> The strategy suggested for the semi-arid zone should be regional, focusing on local problems and providing for their solution. This represents a shift from national sector development efforts which are usually based on aggregated abstractions, and lack spatial considerations or regional comprehensiveness.

Experience in the Awash valley and elsewhere has shown that externally imposed development is geared towards the fulfilment of national goals at the expense of local needs and aspirations. To avoid this, future developments should include the following:
1. the guaranteeing of land rights to nomadic groups;
2. the establishment of local institutions for the development of pastoralism which are accountable to local people;
3. support for the establishment of independent herders' associations and groups campaigning on land rights;
4. extensive use of indigenous knowledge of pastoralism and wider participation by pastoralists in pastoral development;
5. the lifting of the Poll Tax, which has had a very negative effect on production, the structure of markets, and the supply and demand network; and
6. studies of indigenous livestock breeding and their productive characteristics. Investment in the pastoralist sector was previously directed toward the introduction of veterinary services and to livestock breeding. The former has some limited acceptability among the pastoralists who know its benefits, but the latter was rejected as it did not fit their priorities. Hence, in terms of breed improvement, more resources should be put toward helping pastoralists expand the natural selection processes with which they are familiar. Any breed improvement programme should be combined with production system improvements which may include range management and better health provisions. The pastoralists' considerable knowledge of animal production management and plant use could form a basis for technical intervention.

Investment and research priorities should be directed toward land tenure, indigenous knowledge, range management, and animal health. These priorities are the pastoralists' own, and should be the focal point of policy.

References

Asmerom, L., et al. 1974. *Evaluation of the Awash Valley Authority Settlement Programme*, prepared by a panel of consultants for the IEG, Addis Ababa, Ministry of Agriculture.

AVA. 1974. *Master Plan for the Regional Development of the Awash River Basin*, Main Volume, Addis Ababa, Government of Ethiopia.

Dolal, M.B. 1990. 'Pastoral resources, human displacement and state policy: The Ogaden case' *PENHA Informal Talks*, series no. 1, London, PENHA.

Emmanuel, H.W. 1975. *Land Tenure, Land Use and Development in the Awash Valley, Ethiopia*, LTC No. 105, Madison, Wisconsin.

Gamaledin, M. 1986. *The Political Economy of the Afar Region of Ethiopia: A Study in Peripheral Dynamism*, Ph.D. thesis, Cambridge, Cambridge University.

Gamaledin, M. 1987. 'State policy and famine in the Awash Valley of Ethiopia: The lessons for conservation in Africa' *Conservation in Africa*.

Gamaledin, M. and Z. Fre. 1988. 'Pastoral development challenges in Eritrea: Preliminary notes on policy options', paper presented to the *First Conference on Research and Development,* Winna, Eritrea.

Goudie, A.G. 1972. 'Irrigated land settlement' *Informal Technical Report No. 7,* Addis Ababa, AVA.

Hassan, Y.F., and P. Doornbos. 1977. *The Central Bilad-El-Sudan: Tradition and Adaptation,* El Tamaddon P. Press Ltd.

I.E.C. Ministry of Pen. 1962, January 23. *Negarit Gazeta, No. 7,* General Notice No. 229, Addis Ababa.

Provisional Government of Ethiopia. 1975, March 4. *Proclamation for the Nationalization of Rural Lands,* Addis Ababa, Government of Ethiopia.

Voelkner, H.E. 1974. 'The social feasibility study of settling semi-nomadic Afar on irrigated agriculture in the Awash Valley, Ethiopia' *Informal Technical Report No. 23,* Addis Ababa, AVA.

Comment   AHMED HUSSEIN

The problems that the Afar pastoralists confront and the reasons for these problems are clearly detailed by the author of the paper. But, assuming that there was enough time for a more comprehensive study, one would have liked to have seen a broader picture of the entire region and its less known areas. A particular point worth mentioning is the author's suggestion that in the post-conflict period leaders should 'make some provisions to relinquish some of the sovereign rights of the nation-state, particularly in terms of concessions to nomadic people. The concessions might take the form of *dual citizenship* or the joint management of resources' (emphasis added). Although concessions are clearly desirable, pastoralists like other groups in society would prefer to preserve their own identity (national, cultural, and so forth). It would, therefore, be safer to opt for the joint management of resources, the strengthening of IGADD, and the introduction of similar regional- and local-level bodies.

There are some important concerns which are limiting the development of pastoral society at least in some parts of the Horn of Africa. Perhaps the most crucial limitation is the adverse political atmosphere prevailing in the Horn which often seems to victimize pastoralists more than the rest of the population. For instance, as a result of political hostility between the warring groups there is a large number of refugees criss-crossing the Horn region. The bulk of them are pastoralists who have been in exile for over two decades. Over a million Ogadeni refugees in Somalia, for example, were effectively made an unproductive population by the Ethiopian government and became entirely dependent on international community hand-outs.

Biased conceptions of pastoralism and the pursuance of wrong policies were particularly evident under the previous Ethiopian regimes which very often viewed pastoralism as a backward mode of production. Unfortunately pastoralists have not been represented on the circles of policy and decision makers and, as a result, have generally been marginalized by the previously existing state structures. Unlike Somalia, where there is no such stereotyping and pastoralism is well integrated into the national economy as one of the hard currency earning sectors, Ethiopia not only neglected the pastoral sector but was hostile to pastoralists in general, and camel herders in particular. The past governments equated camel herders with guerrillas. Although the camel is one of the pillars in the Ogadeni pastoral economy, there has been widespread ignorance and anti-camel sentiment among the ruling elite in Ethiopia.

Pastoralists in Ethiopia also have to pay the notorious poll tax. This is not a major limiting factor to the development of pastoralism in the country, but remains a main source of conflict and has created a hostile atmosphere and distrust between the Ethiopian state and the pastoral society. This is particularly true in the case of the Ogaden where no services are provided and yet pastoralists are expected to pay the grossly unfair tax. In addition, its collection is impractical; quite often families have to pay on behalf of deceased relatives and people who left the country decades ago. In Somalia pastoralists are provided with the necessary services as are the other sectors and the poll tax is not known. All sectors, including pastoralists, are expected to pay income tax when they sell their products. Consequently pastoralists in Somalia feel neither marginalized nor unnecessarily discriminated against.

20

Pastoral Resources, Human Displacement and State Policy: The Ogadenian Case

MOHAMED DOLAL

The pastoral production of the herding communities in the Horn of Africa is an under-researched practice that deserves further study. The Ogadenian pastoralists are a good example of a neglected society whose problem-solving processes and patterns of dependence on livestock production in this famine and drought frequented unstable region are little understood. The extent to which Ethiopian state policy discourages this indigenous industry also needs to be recognized.

Ogadenian pastoralists practise agricultural techniques in rain-fed dryland areas or on irrigated or flood plains in order to augment the basic household livelihood derived from livestock. The dependence of animals and people on their natural environment for energy and sustenance has, in turn, to be related to the economy and culture of the inhabitants and their territory (Ingold, 1980). The basic pattern is for each person or community to travel over a certain area annually in search of a living; they shift their stocks and homesteads/hamlets across and within the grazing land they possess. In normal periods each pastoral lineage or household may travel around an area of about 200 km² annually. Movement is most marked during the dry seasons (*Jiilaal iyo Hagaa*) of July to September and January to March (Shears, 1976).

Society, ecology and livestock production

More than 70 per cent of the Ogadenian population is engaged in livestock production, trading, and management in a territory at least the size of Somalia and Djibouti put together. They breed camels, cattle, sheep, goats, donkeys, horses and chickens. Hunting and gathering is also practised by certain sections of the community. With the exception of camels (one-humped dromedary) and cattle (zebu type), livestock is used as petty cash to purchase either farm products or large stock. In this connection, stock maximization is the basis of social security for the lineage and the life insurance of the individual proprietor (Swift, 1977). Such practices lead the Ogadenians to boast of having the largest camel population in the Horn of Africa. To some livestock is prestige, to others it is wealth.

The variations in altitude and ecological formations of the territory generally determine the quantity, quality and breed of the stock in each geographical region. The mountain ranges of 1,800–2,500 metres in elevation receive 800–820 mm annual rainfall and have a livestock density of 50 head per km². Those of 1,600–1,800 metres in elevation support 80–100 head per km². Animal density increases on the lower slopes and the basins of Shabelle and Ganaane (Juba) rivers which rise to 1,000 metres above sea level. Here the mean annual rainfall is less than 450 mm (Le Houerou, 1977), but the average monthly

185

temperature remains between 20–28 degrees centigrade in Qalaafo, which is situated in the most eastern region of the Shabelle river depression. The alternative is the relatively mild climate of Harar plateau in the west where the temperature fluctuates between 10 and 20 degrees centigrade in the summer and winter respectively.

Given these climatological conditions, cultural values see the camel as the most suitable or favoured animal. It is said to represent the 'capital goods' that make another obtainable, that being livestock. This capital asset of the lineage, community and individuals is supplemented by agriculture or small livestock for security and life insurance. Camels are the medium or measurement for calculating compensation or redress for physical or moral damages. A hundred camels for a man and half of that for a woman is paid to compensate manslaughter (Lewis, 1955). Camel meat and milk are served at all important events.

Subsidiary activities

Sorghum and maize are widely grown wherever there is adequate water. Normally these two crops ripen within 90 days in the lower plains, but double that period is needed on the plateaus (Dolal, 1988). Highland and agropastoral communities grow coffee, vegetables, beans, peanuts, fruit – such as bananas, avocados and oranges – and chat. These products are locally exchanged and exported to some extent to Somalia, Djibouti and Europe. However, pastoral products have a higher value than plants in the local exchange system. This economic understanding has nothing to do with the labour expended on the commodity or the principle of supply and demand equilibrium mechanisms. Rather, the cultural conception of values of commodities determines the value of the product. Pastoralists actively promote their products, and this has enabled them to convert their products into hard currency. In other words, pastoralists and their products have entered society at large. Anyone forcefully challenging their system, intruding into their culture, or longing to possess the land they occupy confronts an animosity well remembered in the tradition.

State policy

The advent of the Ethiopian occupation, which began in 1897 and totally engulfed the territory in 1954, actually spawned a camel holocaust and 'concentration camps', so the central authority could impose its rule over the colony and misappropriation of livestock by the government's occupying forces became eminent and negative policies on pastoralism were experienced. The incompatibility of the occupying culture precipitated and contributed to the droughts, wars, pastoral displacements and famines in the territory.

The Ethiopian government discouraged livestock production by pastoralists, introducing sedentarization and villagization programmes, and levying 30 Ethiopian birr as a pastoral 'head tax' (*zelaan gibir*) from 1960 to 1970. It was this policy which was largely responsible for the famine in 1962. In 1987 the same tax was levied, this time 100 Ethiopian birr, on the Ogadenian pastoralists. Instead of rehabilitating the victims of the 1984 famine, the state imposed its grip on the pastoral subsistence economy. In both cases the tax was payable by all ages of pastoralists in polygamous communities (OAG, 1989). The off takes of livestock became unbearable at both the household and community levels. The International Livestock Centre of Africa (ILCA) guards against this trend. Almost 75 per cent of the land area in the Ogaden (90 per cent of which was pasture) is now used for crops (ILCA, 1977).

The Ethiopian authorities misappropriated 112, 647 cows, 3,582 camels, 77,895 sheep and goats, and 216 donkeys. While defending their property, 892 unarmed herders were slaughtered (Wais, 1978) between 1964 and 1971 in Diri-dhabe region alone. Similarly, since September 1988 the Ethiopian government has seized 2,390 camels, 544 cows, 15,890 goats and sheep, and 70 donkeys from the region of Godeey. Seventeen herd owners have been murdered in the process.

These factors and others contributed to the destructive contradictions which caused incalculable human suffering and ecological damage. The Ogadenian famine of 1984 and the present one are arguably both the end result of misguided state policy. The 100

Ethiopian birr 'head tax' and, due to the lack of currency, the substitution of two adult camel/cattle for the annual tax of two persons were devastating. Livestock can only be replaced gradually using earnings from the Gulf states. In the meantime, the Ogaden is facing another famine. If this policy were to be continued and the Ogadenians' right to self-determination still denied, misery and political pressure would only increase.

Currently more than a million Ogadenian refugees are located in Somalia, Djibouti, Kenya and beyond Africa as a result of occupationist policies of past Ethiopian regimes and, to some degree, the irredentist policy of Somalia. In sum, these wars and the human displacement they entailed, patronizing policies, and the persistently denied rights of nations and the individual, led the pastoral mode of production to collapse. The end result has been famine both for the victims and the victors. Furthermore, the effects of the state's negative attitude towards pastoralism have been exacerbated by ecological depletion caused by the burning of forests for charcoal, by commercial farming, and by the clearing of bushlands for security reasons by the Ethiopian government during and after the 1980s.

The Ogadenian response to state policy

State policies were met with varying levels of resistance. Some resistance was politically organized by liberation fronts; some arose simply in reaction to suppressive state policies. In 1963–5 the Ogaden Liberation Front (OLF), otherwise known as *Al-Nasrullaah*, mounted an armed struggle against Ethiopian colonial rule in Ogadenia. That struggle was responsible for the influx of thousands of thousands of 'invisible' refugees from Ogadenia to the neighbouring countries. Decades later, the Marxist-Leninist inspired Dergue practically implemented the old policy of the *Naftenya* (land conquerors) which valued 'the land, not the people'. Hence, adherence to rapidly adopted policies, the Dergue's adamant rejection of the principle of self-determination of nations, its undemocratic government, and the nationalization policy which included the communal pasture lands, were arguably the catalysing factors which activated the nationalistic fervour that engulfed the empire state of Ethiopia in the early 1970s. Perhaps the intensification of the dissatisfaction was enhanced by the unswerving non-dialogue stand of the Dergue.

The whole pastoralist mode of production has been upset by the struggle, leaving the pastoralists in a most vulnerable position. In response to incompatible state policy, the Western Somali Liberation Front engaged in armed struggle against the Ethiopian state from 1976 to 1979. The confrontation resulted in there being about 1.5 million Ogadenian refugees in Somalia alone, and about 400,000 in other neighbouring states. The refugee influx was followed in 1984 by famine and another wave of human migration. With there being no solution to the problem which caused the confrontation, famine is again prevalent in Ogadenia.

Concluding remarks

To avert the perpetuation of famine in Ogadenia it would be advisable, firstly, to lift the pastoral head tax which reduces livestock production and marketing. Secondly, constraints on livestock production should be removed. Adequate drinking water and the maintenance of animal security and health should be ensured. Thirdly, it is essential that the people's right to self-determination is recognized.

Organizing mobile or semi-mobile livestock extension projects with self-equipped public health clinics and veterinary drugs would help maintain the health of livestock. To enhance marketing, feeder roads, regularly inspected wells, and range lands are essential. The nature of these options could be developed by pastoralists and agro-pastoralists themselves, but the development and enhancement of any project for the most needy people depends on the stability of the territory, and that cannot be maintained without a recognition of the people's rights.

References

Dolal, M.S. 1986 (unpublished). *Oiimaha Dhaqanka Koonfur Soomaaliya-Gobalka Bay* (The Cultural Values of Somalia-Bay Region), Mogadishu, Somali Academy of Sciences and Arts.

Dolal, M.S. 1988. *Socio-Economic Relations of Social Groups in Southern Somalia-Bay Region*, M.Sc. thesis, London, University of London.

Evans-Pritchard, E.E. 1940. *The Nuer, A Description of the Modes of Livelihood and Political Institutions of Nelotic People*, Oxford, Oxford University Press.

Geshekter, C.L. 1972. *British Imperialism in the Horn of Africa and the Somali Response 1884–99*, Ph.D. dissertation, Los Angeles, University of California.

ILCA. 1977. *Report and Assessment of Jigjiga Development Project*, Addis Ababa, ILCA.

Ingold, T. 1980. *Hunters, Pastoralists and Ranchers*, Cambridge, Cambridge University Press.

Le Houerou, H.N. 1977. *Jigjiga Range Lands Development: Survey of Present Land Use and Preliminary Assessment*, ILCA/AC/4/ADD1, Addis Ababa, ILCA.

Lewis, I.M. 1955. *People of the Horn of Africa: Somali, Afar and Saho*, London, International African Institute.

Malinowski, B. 1922. *Argonauts of the Western Pacific*, London, Routledge and Kegan Paul.

Marx, K. 1964. *Precapitalist Economic Formations*, Hobsbawn, E.J. (ed.), London, Lawrence and Wishart.

OAG. 1989. *Newsletter Report*, London, OAG.

Rigby, P. 1985. *Persistent Pastoralists, Nomadic Societies in Transition*, London, Zed Books.

Sahlins, M. 1960. 'Political power and economy of primitive society' in Dole, G.E. and R.L. Carneiro (eds.) *Essays of the Science of Culture*, New York, Crowell.

Shears, P. 1976. 'Drought in south-eastern Ethiopia' in Hassan, Abdul Majid (ed.) *Drought and Famine in Ethiopia*, London, International African Institute.

Shirokogoroff. 1922. *The Tungus in Siberia*, Moscow.

Swift, J. 1977. 'Pastoral development in Somalia: Herding co-operatives as a strategy against desertification and famine' in Glantz, M.H. (ed.) *Desertification and Environmental Degradation in and Around Arid Lands*, Colorado, Westview.

Wais, I. 1978. 'An account of the colonial experience of western Somalis (Ogadenians)' *The Horn of Africa*, vol. 4, no. 4.

Watson, R.M. 1973. *Aerial Livestock and Land Use Surveys of Jigjiga Area, 1971–73*. Nairobi, Ethiopia Resource Management and Research, Survey Division.

21 Agrarian Crises and Strategies for Recovery in the Horn: A Comparative, Regional Perspective

LIONEL CLIFFE

These comments, on a series of papers that were, inevitably, country based, attempt to bring out some of the common features of the agricultural predicament faced by the countries of the Horn, and some of the regional dimensions of that predicament – features that any development strategies ignore at their peril. Their main concern is to see how far a comparative and regional perspective illuminates some of the key strategy issues raised in the papers.

It is not possible to say anything meaningful about what policies to follow for rural reconstruction and development without coming to some conclusions about the current agrarian crises. Without these conclusions strategies will be misdirected. If, for instance, it is decided that the chief debilitating factor is war itself, then the restoration of peace and some reconstruction should automatically bring about recovery. If the basic cause of the crisis is mistaken policies with regard to prices and which crops to encourage, then the recovery task will involve charting new policy directions. If the basic problem is one of environmental decline, then recovery will not be automatic and wholesale changes in the ways in which the environment is used will have to be contemplated. Should the decline be irreversible, population movement might be advocated. Some argue that the underlying problem is the increasing marginalization of the most vulnerable. If this is the case, emphasis should be given to redirecting support services and productive investment to different social groups, and possibly to redistributing productive assets through, for instance, land reform.

Agrarian crises: common features

The harrowing evidence of famine – in Eritrea, Tigray, Ogaden, Wollo and western and southern Sudan – underlines the extent to which not only people but whole agricultural systems are in jeopardy. But apart from this immediate shared crisis, there are, with some variations, several common characteristics of the agrarian systems.

Regional food imbalances

Many areas of each of the Horn countries regularly experience a food deficit and rely on imports from a few surplus areas such as Kassala and the Nile provinces of the Sudan, and Gojam in Ethiopia. These surplus zones also feed areas in neighbouring countries. All the countries of the Horn are now food deficit countries at the national level. Somalia and Eritrea have fitted into this category for many years, but the Sudan has just developed a national deficit having continued to export grain to Saudi Arabia up until 1989, despite internal food shortages. The workshop papers suggest that Somalia and Eritrea both import about 40 per cent of their grain needs, while the latest figures for the Sudan put grain imports at 700,000 tonnes (although almost 200,000 tonnes were exported).

Thus one crucial issue of strategy, food security, immediately raises the question of the level at which food self-sufficiency should be sought. To seek it at the national level would be inappropriate: in the Sudan national self-sufficiency did not prevent acute food shortages in certain areas, while in Somalia, Djibouti and Eritrea the ecology may make it a too distant goal. Food security for the Horn as a whole might thus be the most appropriate and realistic level to aim for, but would require trade networks and the funding of cross-border transfers to work. A regional strategy and programme of work would have to be established – an urgent task for IGADD. At the same time, the problem of hunger may well arise because individual households and communities may have been reduced to below the level of producing enough food and of having the means to purchase – a failure of entitlements which may require the reconstruction of production systems as part of a policy of pursuing food security for all households. Thus national agricultural policies will have to be couched in ways that guarantee food security at the household and community levels, and will have to take into account the features of the present situation outlined below.

The prevalence of pastoralist and agropastoralist populations

All of the countries of the Horn have large populations which depend more on livestock husbandry than crop husbandry, although the proportion of those who are exclusively 'pastoral' rather than agropastoral is often exaggerated. In southern Sudan, 66 per cent of the rural population are classified as pastoral or agropastoral; in Eritrea these two categories constitute 40 per cent of the rural population; in Somalia the proportion is perhaps nearer 70 per cent; the Sudan paper refers to 11 per cent of the whole population being 'nomads'. (In fact, this widely used term is often inappropriate, for even among pastoralists, who must move animals to new pastures periodically, such movement may be around a single point, or between two established, seasonal poles (transhumance), and even where this follows a genuinely nomadic pattern, it may only be the herders who move, not whole families).

It also has to be recognized that pastoralism may be the *most sustainable* pattern of livelihood and of land use in very dry and fragile environments. This fact is often ignored by the anti-pastoral *bias* of much public policy. This is the case even in Somalia, according to Hussein Adam's paper, despite the fact that the majority of the people in that country are pastoralists (or agropastoralists). It must further be recognized that pastoral and agropastoral modes of livelihood cannot, by definition, be based on *subsistence production*. As these people consume mainly grain, their economy has always been based on the *exchange* of livestock for grain. Drought, war and other disasters endanger their livelihood not just by directly destroying their animals, but by drastically worsening their 'terms of trade'. Hunger and the fear of losing animals force pastoralists to sell and, consequently, to face a buyer's market for livestock and a seller's market for grain. Other long-term shifts in their relative political and economic status can also threaten their terms of trade with the outside world and thus the survival in this means of livelihood, and indeed the physical existence, of the poorest pastoralists. One possible strategy for sustaining as many people as possible in this potentially productive livelihood would be to stabilize their situation by, for instance, fixing the relative exchange price of animals for food grain. Recovery also dictates a need for the replenishment of some minimum herd for the poor through subsidies and credit. The alternative is their continued reliance on welfare or a further flood into town.

Increased commoditization and its effects

Various papers point to certain long-term trends which are all related to the increase in the production of commodities for the market, and the resulting tendency for basic social entities and relationships to take on a monetary form.

1. The commercial production of grain and export crops has grown and, in the Sudan in particular, has become the preponderant basis of supplying the national and external markets, rather than peasant commodity production.

2. Increasing numbers of rural as well as urban dwellers rely on purchasing a proportion of their food requirements (pastoralists have always done this); peasants who are land poor or resource poor cannot sustain production at a subsistence level; 'improved' seed has to be purchased each year. This increased tendency to *buy food* or the wherewithal to produce it makes food security more precarious and increases vulnerability.

3. Most peasant/pastoral households have to find ways of earning money from their labour to purchase food and other necessities. Due to declining land, livestock or other productive assets, declining terms of trade for their produce, and periodic disasters, it is necessary to engage in local casual or seasonal work, annual or longer migrations, petty trading and so forth.

The extent of this reliance on off-farm earnings is very great. Salah Ibrahim's paper on 'Patterns of Internal Wage Labour Migration in Sudan', indicates that 20 per cent of the labour force works abroad and the number of internal seasonal migrant labourers is between 1.5 and 2 million. Evidence from Eritrea suggests that earnings from labour in towns and commercial farms in eastern Sudan helps sustain a majority of poor peasant households in the north and west.

These trends, particularly labour migration which is largely undertaken by males, have had an uneven gender impact. The division of labour in peasant agriculture is changing, generally increasing women's burden. A large proportion of households are in fact made up of female adult members and children – groups that are among the most vulnerable. However, male absences may also have some liberating impact as women gain greater access to their own sources of income. More study is needed to document the extent and specific forms of women's situation in different agricultural systems, and to indicate what forms of support (agricultural inputs, provision of resources, alternative income sources, or welfare provision to reduce the domestic labour load) would be most appropriate for women.

Effects of war

Abdel Ghaffar Ahmed's paper is one of the few attempts to document some of the specific impacts of war on agricultural production and on the economies involved: the ending of work on the Jonglei canal and the curbing of seasonal pastoral movement in the Sudan are two such impacts. A similar catalogue has been attempted for Eritrea (Cliffe, 1989) which stresses that it is the indirect disruption of normal trading and grazing patterns of pastoralists and agropastoralists in particular that has a greater long-term impact than the confiscation, the destruction of fields and animals, and so forth. The resulting changed patterns of livelihood need to be understood if recovery is to be accomplished. With peace and 'normality', economies can hopefully be less fragmented. However, this reorientation will not necessarily occur automatically and will need to be structured.

Agrarian crises: Identifying causes to get prescriptions right

The papers rightly avoid any single factor explanation of the crisis in any one country. Hussein Adam points to official policies in Somalia which encourage export crops rather than food production, and set prices that do not encourage the production of surpluses. The general squandering of resources by bureaucracies that simply content themselves with extracting a 'rent' from rural producers is another contributing factor, the impact of which is worsened by drought and war. Abdel Ghaffar Ahmed offers a further contribution to what is a rich ongoing debate about the causes of the Sudan's crisis in the 1980s – one that is given added impact by the fact that the country survived relatively unscathed the similar drought conditions in 1973–4 which reduced the Sahel and the rest of the Horn to famine. Hence natural causes alone cannot explain the hunger of the 1980s. He argues that war and the overall debt crisis have made the Sudan more vulnerable to drought, but that these calamities have impacted on a worsening general situation facing many peasants and pastoralists who have been marginalized by inappropriate prioritizing of partially-mechanized commercial farming and non-productive state investments.

Other writers on the Sudan (such as O'Brien, 1986) have given explanatory weight to the policy emphasis in pricing of export crops, paralleling Adam's argument on Somalia and Mulugetta's analysis of causes of the Ethiopian famine. Clearly an important element in recovery strategies if food security is to be emphasized is appropriate pricing policies, but whether even the right prices and a reorientation of public support to smallholders and small herders would be enough to turn the tide must be doubted. The lack of price incentives and the government preference for large-scale production, also the case for Ethiopia as indicated by Mulugetta, do not explain why farmers who are regarded as 'subsistence' producers do not have enough food; that condition can only develop if their situation has changed so that their access to productive resources has been curtailed, perhaps as a result of the trends listed under the second and third headings of the previous section, and they are less able to grow their own food and are more vulnerable. Insofar as this is the case in particular areas – and a lot of area case studies are needed to reveal how different localities now stand – efforts to improve the production system of the more marginal populations will be needed.

Wasteful use of public resources and other inappropriate government initiatives point to the other factor that contributors mention as responsible for worsening the position of peasants and pastoralists: the extraction by state bureaucracies of 'rent', often enforced by such institutions as the central marketing body in Ethiopia. The famine in that country in 1973–4 was, of course, attributed to that kind of exploitation – landowners might take as much as half the produce of peasants. The 1975 land reform should have rid peasants in the areas concerned of that burden, and in theory allowed them a bigger share of their produce. That this was not enough to stave off famine points to other factors, such as the bureaucracy's extraction of rent, worsening production conditions or lack of incentives, more than offsetting any gains from land reform. However, this experience questions the potential contribution of land reform.

A further factor to which blame is often attributed is environmental decline. Some analysts put this down to 'natural' causes; 'desertification' is often mentioned, as are the long-run adverse trends in rainfall. All that can be said here is that although these trends are discussed in a way that takes them for granted, the actual evidence for both is still insufficiently conclusive to be a firm basis for policy formulation and planning. Moreover, even if one concedes that such trends do affect some areas, it is not clear what can or ought to be done about such areas and the people who live in them. One common response has been to suggest that whole areas have declined to the point where they cannot sustain their present populations, and the only solution is large-scale population removal. That was the logic behind Ethiopia's massive resettlement programme; similar proposals have been made in relation to parts of western Sudan and other areas. Others attribute environmental decline to the way land is used – either farming methods are not sustainable, communities and their traditional ways of running their affairs cannot manage the 'commons', or simply there is over-population. These views are essentially opinions, often based on prejudice and assumptions that peasants and herders are by definition backward. The prescriptions that follow these views are not self-evident; they are arguments which can be used to justify the privatization of land and the commons, the modernization of farming practices, or resettlement.

Resettlement is only logical if evaluations confirm that whatever damage to the environment has occurred, whether 'natural' or 'human-made', it is in fact irreversible. But such a concept, so often bandied about, is in fact very difficult to define, let alone measure. Moreover, such a conclusion is often based on a simplistic approach to environmental issues which compares the carrying capacity with the human and/or livestock population without reference to the production system being used, or to the fact that production systems are not static and can be improved to become more sustainable.

Strategy issues for reconstruction

Apart from the issues of prices for produce, government investment priorities, and the extraction of rent on a·scale beyond the 'surplus' of peasants where it eats into the production necessary for their survival, the experiences of the countries of the Horn offer examples for evaluating the potential for major policy initiatives, especially in the areas discussed below.

Resettlement or land rejuvenation?

Ethiopia has been the site of one of the most dramatic and ambitious programmes to combat famine in Africa. In the ten years following the 1973–4 famine, approximately 46,000 families were resettled, most of whom were from the drought-affected northern provinces of Wollo and Tigray. A programme which would move 1.5 million people the government classified as 'environmental refugees' was announced at the time of the famine in 1984; almost 600,000 people were resettled during the next two years. Resettlement was resented because it was partly enforced; it involved working as labourers on state-run collectives for an indeterminate share of the eventual produce; the new land in the resettlement areas was itself quickly degraded by hurried clearance; the areas people left were often not rejuvenated as those who remained were hesitant to undertake the hard work of conservation for fear of being resettled; and because those who were exempt from resettlement were usually those who owned the most livestock – a prime cause of degradation (Dejene, 1990). Although resettlement has been abandoned, opinion about it is divided: was it a failure of a well-intentioned plan simply as a result of enforcement, undue haste and too ambitious a target, or is the rationale to reduce population densities to some ideal (and pseudo-scientific) carrying capacity fundamentally unrealistic because it is always resisted and uneconomical?. An evaluation of the Ethiopian experience and more modest proposals in Kordofan and Darfur in the Sudan is needed to settle this issue. What is at issue is whether environmental change is irreversible – a matter that cannot easily be resolved, despite the multitude of *ex cathedra* pronouncements to this effect made by politicians, journalists and researchers.

Efforts have, of course, been made in several of the Horn countries to introduce conservation practices and measures, such as afforestation, designed to reverse this decline. These have not always been successful, and some have even been counter-productive largely because specific rules or measures have been applied in isolation and grafted onto the existing farming practices regardless of the indirect effects. For instance, overgrazed areas have been placed out of bounds and this has pushed bigger herders to encroach more on arable land; efforts have been made to control grazing in highland areas and even reduce animals where there is also a shortage of oxen for ploughing. There are simultaneously too many animals for the available grazing lands and too few oxen to do the ploughing, which means that a sustainable agricultural system requires some ingenuity, not simplistic solutions. What is certain is that some modification, but not wholesale desecration, is needed in the production systems, viewed in their entirety, in order to rejuvenate the worst affected areas, provide food security and income generation, and render practices which are environmentally sound.

Villagization

Another negative lesson which hopefully can be learned from Ethiopian experience is that forcing rural people to live in regimented rows of houses in large clusters is very costly, resented, environmentally unsound as it leads to extreme concentrations of livestock and people, and is unnecessary for the provision of services at central points. The latter can be provided at a central place and people can walk to school, clinics, or shops rather than walk long distances to their fields or to graze their animals as they are required to by villagization. Again there is ambiguity in the discussion: some people still believe the Ethiopian mistake was in the mode of implementation and still argue for villagization and the 'settling' of 'nomads', despite the overwhelmingly negative evidence from Tanzania, Mozambique and other countries that have pursued villagization, an approach to regulating rural dwellers which had its origins in apartheid South Africa.

Agrarian reform?

Ethiopia also has experience of land reform, under which land that was owned by non-cultivating landowners was distributed on a basis that more or less equalized the land holdings of the tillers. Such reforms certainly ended extractions from some peasant groups, but seem to have left large differences in *livestock* ownership, and also did little to improve the lot of the peasants in the many areas where the system of land tenure was some variant of community allocation of land for use. There is a need in some areas of other countries to curb the tendency of those who claim some traditional access to land cultivated by others or to incomes therefrom to reassert these rights and 'enclose' land, thereby marginalizing the poor even further. However, as the Ethiopian case shows, the much more thorny issue of redistribution and provision of the basic means for production for the poor in production systems based on livestock instead of or as much as crops has to be addressed. So too does the issue of whether land reform is possible and necessary in areas with community allocation of land rights. Here the little known experience initiated in some parts of liberated Eritrea is worthy of further study as the EPLF sought to resurrect a modified version of the old land tenure system whereby land was periodically redistributed, a version which placed the distribution in more democratically representative hands than those of the local elders and notables who no doubt had used it for patronage purposes.

References

Cliffe, L. 1989. 'The impact of war and the response to it in different agrarian systems in Eritrea' *Development and Change*, vol. 29, pp. 373–400.

Dejene, A. 1990. *Environment, Famine and Politics in Ethiopia: A View from the Village*, Boulder, Lynne Rienner Publishers.

O'Brien, J. 1986. 'Sudan's food crisis' in Lawrence, P. (ed.) *World Recession and the Food Crisis in Africa*, London, James Currey.

The Political Economy: 'Structural Adjustment', the State and Civil Society

22 Debt, Adjustment and Donor Interventions in the Post-War Horn of Africa
RICHARD P.C. BROWN, AHMED NUR KULANE HASSAN AND ALEMAYEHU GEDA FOLE

Debt and policy for longer term economic recovery will no doubt be high on the agenda in the 'post-war' Horn. The reality of the international political-economic environment makes these two issues practically inseparable. The disposition of the accumulated debts of the previous regimes, the role to be played by the IMF, World Bank and donor community, and the economic policies and institutional reforms introduced, will all have implications for the sorts and magnitudes of international capital flows the new regimes can expect to be forthcoming. Both the international donor community on which they will depend for external assistance, and the internal socio-economic groupings on whose support they will depend to stay in power, will make many – and inevitably competing – demands on them.

This paper demonstrates that the official debt and macroeconomic data on which existing economic analyses and policy prescriptions are based can give rise to misleading conclusions about the severity of the debt crisis and the magnitudes of the actual foreign exchange and other resource flows. The *actual* burden of the debt might not be as severe for these countries as data and conventional wisdom indicate.[1] Secondly, the *actual incomes* earned, and foreign exchange and savings potentially available to the state, might be substantially greater than indicated by official macroeconomic data as these exclude the growing levels of informal, *unrecorded* economic activities. Before prescribing policy and donor intervention, one needs first to carefully consider both the qualitative and quantitative characteristics of these economies. Orthodox analyses which fail to consider these characteristics account for much of the failure of policies.

This paper is intended as a modest contribution to the debate. Its main purpose is to show that a proper comprehension of the financial legacy of the 'old' regimes requires more than a purely quantitative approach. In focusing on some of the neglected issues in the current debate, this paper attempts to initiate discussion, debate, and – hopefully – research that could lay the basis for a possible alternative programme for economic recovery in the Horn.

The debt crisis and IMF/World Bank conditionality

Like most sub-Saharan African (SSA) economies, the economies of the Horn are comparatively small, very open and lack much diversification of their production and export structures. They are greatly dependent on foreign exchange for imports to meet both production and consumption needs, and highly vulnerable to external shocks, such as the oil-price hikes of the 1970s and declining markets and prices for their main exports.

Since the late 1970s, the debt/GNP ratios of most SSA countries began to deteriorate as their governments increasingly resorted to foreign borrowing to fill their growing balance of payments gaps (see Table 1). Among the countries of the Horn, continuing external shocks, such as the 1984–5 drought, the Saudi ban on cattle exports from Africa and internally induced economic disruptions associated with escalating political struggles and civil wars, contributed to a marked decline of output, particularly in the production of exports. Foreign exchange scarcities have thus been induced on the demand side by increasing foreign exchange requirements for financing the growing debt burden and escalating civil wars, while on the supply side foreign exchange earnings are declining due to a combination of deteriorating external conditions (such as declining markets, deteriorating terms of trade, decreasing financial flows) and stagnating export production.

Table 1 Magnitude and Composition of Debt, 1980–8 (millions of US dollars)

	1980	1982	1984	1986	1988
Total debt (EDT)					
– Ethiopia	804	1,239	1,524	2,215	2,978
– Somalia	664	1,225	1,487	1,802	2,035
– Sudan	5,218	7,249	8,613	9,808	11,853
Composition of EDT by source					
Official creditors (%)					
– Ethiopia	93.9	91.8	86.2	85.9	84.5
– Somalia	95.8	82.8	88.6	94.9	98.3
– Sudan	89.9	84.2	88.5	87.0	87.9
Private creditors (%)					
– Ethiopia	6.1	8.2	13.8	14.1	15.5
– Somalia	4.2	17.2	14.4	5.1	1.7
– Sudan	10.1	15.8	11.5	13.0	12.1
Composition of official debt					
Bilateral lenders (%)					
– Ethiopia	37.0	43.5	49.2	54.9	55.1
– Somalia	64.2	58.5	57.6	57.3	55.0
– Sudan	57.8	57.5	57.1	55.8	50.2
Multilateral lenders (%)					
– Ethiopia	63.0	56.5	50.8	45.1	44.9
– Somalia	35.8	41.5	42.4	42.7	45.0
– Sudan	42.2	42.5	42.9	44.2	49.8
Ratios (%)					
Debt/GNP					
– Ethiopia	19.5	28.0	31.7	44.1	54.0
– Somalia	99.1	151.2	194.4	206.4	214.9
– Sudan	78.0	99.9	122.3	105.0	105.0
Debt/exports					
– Ethiopia	136.0	230.3	243.1	326.2	468.2
– Somalia	253.4	443.8	1,389.7	1,553.4	2,575.9
– Sudan	504.6	702.4	639.4	914.9	1,233.4
Debt service/exports					
– Ethiopia	7.6	13.8	14.0	23.4	38.7
– Somalia	5.0	7.2	6.5	19.0	5.1
– Sudan	25.3	28.6	8.2	38.7	17.0

Source: World Bank, 1989e.

As the economic crisis of SSA worsened in the early 1980s, development economists, politicians, international organizations and the donor community began to express the need for some solution to the debt crisis. International flows of funds from commercial sources to many parts of SSA declined quite dramatically after the initial explosion in bank lending to the third world around the mid 1970s, and for some, such as Somalia and the Sudan, commercial flows dried up altogether by the beginning of the 1980s. These countries thus became increasingly dependent on external financial support from the international donor and creditor community – the 'official' lenders, consisting of bilateral and multilateral agencies and institutions.

External financial support takes the form of both new loans and grants, and relief on the interest and principal obligations due on existing debts. As all the countries of the Horn fall into the lower end of the low income group of third world countries, a relatively high proportion of their external financial flows are on concessional terms including, for instance, grants from bilateral donors, and the more concessional International Development Association (IDA) loans from the World Bank. They have also enjoyed a limited degree of 'debt forgiveness' when individual bilateral lenders have agreed to write off some of the debts that these governments have been unable to service.

Although donors and creditors cannot hold a country's assets as collateral, as in the case of bank lending to individuals or firms for instance, they can insist that the recipient agrees to implement certain economic policies that the creditor considers to be necessary to enhance the borrower's capacity to repay the debt. The two Bretton Woods multilateral institutions – the IMF and World Bank – are in the forefront of both the political and academic debates over policy conditionality. Through the lending activities of these two bodies, the international creditor and donor community has attempted to impose its preferred set of economic policy instruments on indebted governments. Thus the donor community has become increasingly involved in debates with national governments over economic policy and institutional reforms – the so-called 'policy dialogue'.

The importance of this policy debate cannot be underestimated. The IMF and World Bank make financial assistance available on the condition that the borrower implements a number of restrictive 'corrective' economic policy measures, collectively referred to as either a 'stabilization' or an 'adjustment' programme, which are aimed at restoring internal and external equilibria. The desperation of most African governments for foreign exchange has tended towards 'monologue' rather than 'dialogue', enabling donors to exercise substantial leverage in economic policy formation and implementation. Relief on existing debt obligations is also subject to such conditionality. Official creditors come together at what is known as the Paris Club to negotiate a rescheduling agreement collectively with an individual debtor government, which must first have made a conditional agreement with the IMF. In this way IMF conditionality, and to a lesser extent that of the World Bank, mediates the multilateral debt rescheduling procedures and negotiations between indebted governments and their creditors.

With the IMF and World Bank having increasingly taken upon themselves a co-ordinating role among donors and official lenders, and with donor assistance and debt rescheduling having become increasingly conditional upon the successful conclusion of an IMF/World Bank-supported adjustment programme, the international community has linked its debt management initiatives directly to its interventions on both the external financial and domestic economic policy fronts. Such interventions have come to focus increasingly on the macroeconomic policies of the most debt-stricken, foreign exchange-starved African economies.

It needs to be emphasized, therefore, that in relation to the debt crisis, the roles of the IMF and Bank are not simply financial; an IMF loan agreement in fact brings very little direct additional external finance to the country in question. Often the *existence of the agreement* is more important, in that this can unleash additional financial flows from other sources, and enable a round of debt rescheduling negotiations to take place. The IMF and World Bank have been at the centre of a substantial amount of controversy, particularly given their ability to compel indebted governments to impose politically unpopular austerity measures, and the fact that the preferred market-oriented policy options invariably have some rather substantial distributional implications for particular socio-economic groups within the country concerned. If the burden of adjustment falls on those on whose support the government's legitimacy depends, adherence to the policy package could become incompatible with staying in power.

Thus the 'debt crisis' concerns both the extraordinary financial burden and strain that its servicing implies for a country's foreign exchange situation, and the leverage the international community thereby acquired. The role of any international institution or agency in the economic policy dialogue is therefore a highly political issue and should be understood and analysed as such from the outset.

A debt crisis? For whom?

The qualitatively different debt crisis facing many African governments has some important policy implications, particularly as regards our understanding of its manageability, debtor and creditor behaviour, and the role of the IMF and World Bank. Most SSA governments are indebted to official rather than commercial creditors and, with a larger part of this official debt being owed to bilateral lenders, its effective burden is often not as severe as the aggregate data might suggest (see Table 1). In addition, the implications of defaulting on bilateral and on commercial debts have proven to be different. The Sudan, for example, has been defaulting on its debt service to most creditors, including the IMF itself, for some years (Brown, 1990c and forthcoming) with very little apparent impact on the level of actual foreign capital flows. On the other hand, Ethiopia managed to continue servicing most of its debt, and thus remain creditworthy, yet it does not seem to have benefited greatly from this achievement.

How the term debt 'crisis' is conceptualized is therefore important. In the first instance, it needs to be asked *for whom* there is a debt crisis. Compared with the debt crisis facing the big Latin American debtors such as Brazil, Mexico and Argentina, total African debt is very small. Sub-Saharan African debtors account for only about 5 per cent of total third world debt from private sources; Latin America for over 50 per cent. The form of the African debt is also very different. Most African debt is owed to official creditors (over 70 per cent), consisting of multilateral agencies and donor organizations (30 per cent), and bilateral government agencies (40 per cent). Most Latin American debt is owed to banks and other private lenders (over 70 per cent).

For many African debtors, the restoration of commercial creditworthiness is no longer a realistic short- or medium-term objective. Most African governments have long been unable to raise commercial loans. The Sudan and Somalia have received no new commercial loans since 1982 (see Table 2), nor have any interest or principal obligations been paid on any of these debts for almost a decade. While these debts still formally exist, and the growing arrears continues to build up in the recorded data on the country's debt, in practice they have become non-performing loans with no real significance for the country's actual (or cash) balance of payments situation.

What of the bilateral debts? Most proposals for African debt relief – such as the Lawson Plan[2] – are concerned only with bilateral debt and remain silent on the question of private and multilateral debts (Parfitt & Riley, 1989). In purely statistical terms these account for around two-thirds of official sub-Saharan African debt (40 per cent of their total debt), and thus need to be analysed more from the perspective of the burden they place on these countries' own development, than from their implications for the functioning of the international financial system at large. Africa's debt poses very little threat to the functioning of the international financial system in the event of a default by one or more of its debtors. Default on bilateral debt has little effect on the international monetary system. What does seem to matter, however, is that a growing number of African debtors, including Somalia and the Sudan, have begun to default on debts owed to the IMF itself – the 'grandparent' of the international financial system. As these debts are not reschedulable – the IMF's own statutes make no provision for this – these arrears have come to represent a significant threat to the IMF's financial integrity, particularly as regards

Table 2 Magnitude and Composition of Capital Flows, 1980–8 (millions of US dollars)

	1980	1982	1984	1986	1988
Net capital flows ($mn)					
– Ethiopia	265.9	263.8	459.0	808.7	1,101.1
– Somalia	491.1	580.0	357.7	488.7	440.2
– Sudan	1,272.6	1,449.3	737.2	703.6	1,001.8
Composition of flows by type					
Net loans (%)					
– Ethiopia	35.0	39.4	37.7	30.4	29.6
– Somalia	25.2	36.7	39.1	14.9	10.2
– Sudan	61.7	63.3	34.2	(18.5)	35.0
Grants (%)					
– Ethiopia	65.0	60.6	62.3	69.6	70.4
– Somalia	74.8	63.3	60.9	85.1	89.8
– Sudan	38.3	36.7	65.8	118.5	65.0
Composition of flows by source					
Official sources (%)					
– Ethiopia	87.6	93.6	71.5	90.7	87.6
– Somalia	94.5	92.8	99.7	100.0	100.0
– Sudan	88.6	92.2	100.0	100.0	100.0
Private sources (%)					
– Ethiopia	12.4	6.4	28.5	9.3	12.4
– Somalia	5.5	7.2	0.3	0.0	0.0
– Sudan	11.4	7.8	0.0	0.0	0.0
Composition of official flows					
Bilateral lenders (%)					
– Ethiopia	48.0	45.0	56.3	67.3	61.5
– Somalia	61.2	62.9	58.3	65.5	72.1
– Sudan	60.0	77.0	67.1	66.7	63.2
Multilateral lenders (%)					
– Ethiopia	52.0	55.0	43.7	32.7	38.5
– Somalia	38.8	37.1	41.7	34.5	27.9
– Sudan	40.0	23.0	32.9	33.3	36.8

Sources: World Bank, 1989e; OECD, 1989.

the potential 'moral hazard' implied if African default establishes a precedent for the larger Latin American debtors.

The tendency to exaggerate the *actual* magnitude of the debt burden facing many African debtors arises from a number of factors. For instance, one must be careful to distinguish between debt obligations that are nominally *due* on a country's outstanding debt, as opposed to those that are *actually paid*. The Sudan, with its total debt service obligations *due* accounting for anything from 100 to 200 per cent of export earnings in recent years, entered into five Paris Club rescheduling agreements between 1979 and 1984. These agreements kept its *actual* debt service payments down to manageable proportions (Brown, 1990c). As the economic situation deteriorated during the 1980s and the IMF-supported policy programme broke down, official relief through the rescheduling of bilateral debt at the Paris Club became impossible.

Normally one would expect the combined loss of the IMF's seal of approval and the decline in debt relief to have negative repercussions on the inflow of foreign capital. However, without an IMF agreement the government of the Sudan still 'managed' its debt crisis. The government managed to maintain a sizeable net inflow of foreign capital by simply not meeting the bilateral debt obligations that were falling due. In this way actual debt service payments were kept to a minimum – amounting to 20 to 40 per cent of exports – and the all important debt obligations due to the multilateral agencies such as the IMF and World Bank could be maintained, at least for some period of time.

Both the Sudan and Somalia, though they are defaulting on some or all of their debts, are maintaining an inflow of new loans and grants nearly equal to that of Ethiopia, which has been servicing its debt fully. It seems, therefore, that creditworthiness has not been the main determinant of the actual inflow of capital to these countries (see Table 3).[3] Clearly debt relief proposals for the post-war situation should not argue for formal debt relief which becomes somewhat irrelevant when debts are not being serviced in any case. Secondly, as capital flows are not necessarily determined by actual creditworthiness and are motivated perhaps more by non-economic, geopolitical considerations, neither default nor official cancellation can be expected to significantly affect the magnitude of net capital inflow (see Table 2). Ironically, for the relatively few sub-Saharan African countries that have attempted to keep current with their debt service obligations, debt cancellation could have the opposite effect in the longer term, since it makes regaining creditworthiness among commercial lenders more difficult.

Thirdly, because of the 'preferred status' of multilateral creditors such as the IMF and World Bank, it can be argued that debt relief, whether 'granted' by the creditors, or simply 'grabbed' through default by the debtors, constitutes a 'disguised transfer' of funds from industrialized nations' governments to multilateral creditors, such as the IMF and the World Bank, who refuse any form of rescheduling. In other words, the bilateral creditors are bailing out the multilaterals.

Thus, despite its alarming statistical proportions among these countries, debt is not necessarily a major obstacle to their economic development. Countries like the Sudan, Somalia and Ethiopia may not be suffering a debt 'crisis' at all. Debt relief, or a wholesale write-off of debt, should not, therefore, be seen as any sort of panacea for these war-stricken economies. Even if all of their debts were written off overnight, these economies would still be facing severe balance of payments difficulties in view of their declining official foreign exchange *earnings* and export performance.

A crisis of policy?

Given that the foreign exchange crisis facing countries of the Horn is not a 'debt crisis' as such, it would make more sense to analyse it as a crisis of exports, and of agricultural exports in particular. It is often pointed out that SSA debt service ratios rose at significantly faster rates in recent years due mainly to the concurrent *secular* decline of their export earnings since the late 1970s; this decline has given rise to a steep deterioration of these countries' trade balances in particular (see Culpeper, 1987). The experience of the countries of the Horn are no exception. The causes of their chronic foreign exchange crises relate more to this deterioration of debt-servicing *capacity* than to the accumulation of the outstanding debt and debt service obligations as such – a deterioration which is part of the region's generalized secular economic decline experienced over the last decade or so, particularly in agriculture and exports.

The figures we usually use in analysing and measuring the severity of the crisis – for income levels, agricultural production, foreign trade, balance of payments and so forth – are so hopelessly inadequate that they cannot provide a full account of the actual situation and, in some cases give a totally wrong impression (for Somalia, see Jamal, 1988b; for the Sudan, Brown, 1990a). Indeed, if one were to accept these at face value it would be difficult to explain why and how large parts of Africa's population survive. Such statistics are inadequately collected and compiled. Widespread subsistence farming and the growing informal or underground sector are pushing an increasing proportion of economic activities outside the scope of the official economy and therefore of the national accounts (Jamal, 1988a). Meanwhile, the World Bank, preoccupied with the need for developing countries to 'let the market work', perceives an over-extension of the state

Table 3 Net Capital Flows, 1981–8* (millions of US dollars)

	1981	1982	1983	1984	1985	1986	1987	1988
Grants								
–Ethiopia	54	44	104	158	187	n.a.	n.a.	n.a.
–Somalia	127	163	148	194	204	261	n.a.	n.a.
–Sudan	122	174	462	309	288	412	223	499
Loans								
–Ethiopia	327	139	245	252	359	391	447	503
–Somalia	475	223	214	147	149	128	93	47
–Sudan	810	764	363	253	163	177	216	93
Service due								
–Ethiopia	55	77	103	126	149	n.a.	n.a.	n.a.
–Somalia	47	20	25	22	45	100	n.a.	n.a.
–Sudan	859	1,014	870	1,119	1,082	1,408	1,017	1,179
Net accrued flow								
–Ethiopia	326	106	245	284	397	n.a.	n.a.	n.a.
–Somalia	555	366	337	319	308	289	n.a.	n.a.
–Sudan	73	–77	–45	–557	–631	–819	–578	–587
Service paid								
–Ethiopia	55	73	103	125	149	202	211	267
–Somalia	27	20	25	20	34	78	55	5
–Sudan	706	620	554	292	211	314	194	392
Net actual flow								
–Ethiopia	326	110	246	285	397	n.a.	n.a.	n.a.
–Somalia	575	366	337	321	319	311	n.a.	n.a.
–Sudan	226	318	271	270	240	275	245	200

* The data given in this table differ from those in Table 2 due to both the different sources used and capital flows defined here as net of interest payments.

Sources: Derived from IMF, 1990; IMF, various; World Bank, 1989a & 1989c.

in these economies.[4] It believes that state intervention in the market is excessive in SSA, especially in its insistence on administrative price controls and direct involvement in the production of goods and services.

The Bank also argues that technically and administratively incompetent governments and public sectors in SSA lack monetary and fiscal discipline. Excessive public spending and the associated increases in money supply are understood as the primary sources of inflation and excess demand for foreign exchange. Administratively fixing official exchange rates leads to an overvaluation of the domestic currency, meaning that imports become relatively cheap and exports are discouraged. The resulting incentive structure then works against the traditional export sector, agriculture, in favour of cheap imports and the production of non-tradeables for domestic consumption. The excess demand for goods and foreign exchange that cannot be met through the official markets spills over into the uncontrolled parallel market where prices are seen as more accurately reflecting the true scarcities of goods and foreign exchange.

The decline of agricultural production and the associated balance of payments and debt problems are thus understood by the IMF and Bank as being almost exclusively the result of government policy failures that were seen as increasing the need for foreign exchange and at the same time undermining the capacity of the economy to generate it. Governments then avoided introducing the appropriate policy corrections by resorting to increased foreign borrowing. Fund and Bank prescriptions follow logically from this diagnosis. The internal terms of trade have to be turned in favour of agriculture, particularly for export. Currency devaluation, the liberalization of trade and foreign exchange markets, and deregulation of domestic markets are thus seen as central to the process of 'getting prices right'. These, of course, are to be combined with reductions in the government's budgetary deficit and with control of domestic credit, to bring domestic inflation in line with the world level. On the supply side, the IMF and the Bank want more resources channelled into areas with higher growth potential and towards the larger and more successful farmers; less state intervention in the economy; aid to the private sector, including the privatization of services such as health and education; reduced urban real wages, with user charges levied on all services; and a shift in the industrial sector away from import substitution and towards export promotion.

One of the main problems with this view is its failure to understand the dynamics of the *ongoing* structural adjustments that *have been occurring* in these economies. 'Adjustment' tends to be defined by the IMF and Bank in terms of the adoption of their preferred set of policy instruments and institutional reforms by government to compensate, as it were, for its past 'adjustment failures' and thereby get the economy back to an equilibrium path. The 'adjustments' and their economic implications for individuals and governments are either omitted altogether or left rather vague in the analysis. This is particularly pertinent *vis-à-vis* the informal economy and parallel markets that have emerged alongside and within the various branches of the formal economy.

Hidden adjustments and structural transformation

It should not be assumed that economic stagnation during the last decade or so has been characterized by any lack of 'adjustment' or transformation of the economic structures of these economies. In response to steadily declining real incomes and worsening socio-economic conditions, individual economic agents as well as governments have had to search for alternative economic behaviour and patterns of resource mobilization. As previous options become blocked and new opportunities arise from the disequilibria of recurrent crises, not all agents are necessarily losers. Such changes can have profound effects on the structure of the economy, the relationship between its different actors and sectors, and the capacity of the state to act cohesively. Orthodox diagnoses, based exclusively on the examination of the officially-recorded macroeconomic aggregates, have failed to adequately consider the implications of some of the more prevalent individual, non-governmental responses to the crisis. Most existing analyses tend to concentrate on the appropriate *governmental* policy adjustments (or 'adjustment failures') and the responses to these (but, see Van Arkadie, 1988; Ghai & Hewitt de Alàntara, 1990).

The evolving economic structures of these economies are thus largely hidden. The transformation and adjustment processes accompanying the crisis have meant, for instance, that markets have become increasingly fragmented and the various parts of these – public and private, formal and informal – have become increasingly interconnected and interwoven, in places creating rather complex networks of relationships and transactions connecting the public and private sectors, and official and parallel markets. The functioning and behaviour of one cannot easily be analysed or understood in isolation, yet we know very little about the actual functioning of these markets, the channels and mechanisms through which foreign financial flows fuel the ongoing adjustment process. In formulating economic policies, one cannot therefore rely on general postulates about 'the market' or 'the public or private' sectors, nor about the supposed behaviour of the different agents operating within these. Rather, it is necessary to investigate the specific avenues of accumulation (and their limitations) resulting from the *actual* ongoing processes through which these economies are adjusting and being transformed.

The Sudan, Somalia and Ethiopia have flourishing 'underground economies', consisting of an informal trade, finance and production sector in which those with privileged access to foreign exchange, bank credits and import licences can earn enormous 'scarcity rents'. There is also a very sizeable parallel foreign exchange market in which huge volumes of foreign exchange are traded at prices many times above the official exchange rate, predominantly for capital flight and luxury consumption. Much of this foreign exchange is earned by Sudanese, Somalian and Ethiopian workers in the Gulf states and elsewhere. It is currently estimated that over three million of these nationals, out of a total economically active population of around 40 million, are working abroad. For each worker abroad it can be reasonably estimated that between five and ten individuals depend for their livelihood on the remittances such workers send, largely through the informal network, and which are exchanged on the parallel market. For example, very few of the economic transactions fuelled by these remittances are captured by the official data on the Sudan, although they are quantitatively and qualitatively important to the functioning and performance of Sudan's economy (Brown, 1990a, 1990b). Using survey data on migrants' earnings, the Sudan's balance of payments and national income accounts were reconstructed for the period 1978-88. Conservative estimates suggest that the Sudan's actual gross national income (GNI) is approximately 40 per cent higher than the officially recorded data indicate. Data showing the officially recorded and the adjusted macroeconomic aggregates for the Sudan are given in Table 4.

Table 4   Sudan: Recorded and Adjusted Macroeconomic Aggregates, 1983–4 (thousands of LS in current prices; % GNP in brackets)

	Original estimates		Adjusted estimates	
National accounts				
Consumption	10,788	(0.95)	12,771	(0.80)
Investment	1,792	(0.16)	1,792	(0.11)
Exports	1,495	(0.13)	1,495	(0.09)
Imports	2,603	(0.23)	4,586	(0.29)
GDP	11,472	(1.01)	11,472	(0.72)
Factor payments	−743	(−0.07)	−2,726	(−0.17)
Net current transfers	627	(0.06)	7,211	(0.45)
Current account	−1,224	(−0.11)	1,394	(0.09)
GNP	11,356	(1.00)	15,957	(1.00)
National savings	568	(0.05)	3,186	(0.20)
Capital flows		*million LS*		
Net foreign borrowing	1,224		1,224	
Capital export	0		2,618	
Net capital flow	1,224		−1,414	
		million US$		
Capital export	0		1206	
Migrants' foreign investment	0		1203	
Total foreign investment	0		2,410	

Sources: Original estimates from World Bank, 1987a; revised estimates by author.

Foreign exchange shortages in the domestic market contribute not only to a scarcity of imported consumer goods, but also limit availability of imported intermediate inputs, reducing domestic industrial output and creating scarcities of locally produced consumer goods through formal sector channels. This often means that consumers rely increasingly on the unofficial, underground market for the supply of goods and services, and increasing amounts of their economies' available foreign exchange earnings are then channelled into the unofficial free foreign exchange market, as the gap between the parallel and official exchange rates widens. Huge 'scarcity rents' are then earned by those with access to foreign exchange or imported commodities, especially when these can be obtained at the official rate of exchange. Speculative hoarding of goods and/or foreign currencies ('currency substitution') can also become important in the underground economy, exacerbating the supply problem and reinforcing the inflationary spiral and depreciation of the domestic currency in the parallel market. Therefore, this process has implications for both ongoing adjustment and structural changes in the domestic economy, and for the role and effects of international financial flows in these areas.

In most orthodox analyses, the existence of the parallel foreign exchange market and the premium on the price of foreign exchange traded tends to be explained solely in terms of the demand for foreign exchange for purposes of illegal *trade*, which is seen as arising from inappropriate government interventions in the formal economy. Imbalances in the foreign exchange market are thus analysed in terms of an excess demand for foreign exchange exclusively for 'spill-over' *current account* transactions. The primary objective of exchange rate adjustments and the unification of exchange rates, as well as other related adjustment policies, is then to restore balance in the supply and demand for foreign exchange for *current account* transactions. This ignores the unrecorded export of capital, or capital flight. Most literature on capital flight tends to focus on the larger, commercial borrowers of Latin America. Recent evidence suggests, however, that it is also very significant in SSA. In the Sudan, for instance, it is estimated that the accumulated capital flight that occurred between 1978 and 1987 amounted to over 11 billion US dollars, which was about the same as the country's official foreign debt at that time (Brown, 1990a).

Capital flight is important, not only in terms of its implications for the availability of scarce foreign exchange and capital resources for the country in question, but also for understanding the functioning of the economy and the determinants of its internal and external economic imbalances. The unrecorded transfer of capital abroad represents a very substantial component in the demand for these countries' foreign exchange. Contrary to IMF and World Bank analyses, the adjusted data suggest that countries like the Sudan cannot be said to suffer a shortfall, either of savings or of foreign exchange, from a purely 'national' macroeconomic perspective. The adjusted accounts reveal a huge current account and savings surplus. The 'problem' is that the state in such countries has no capacity to harness these surpluses for productive investment in the domestic economy. In the current political-economic climate in the Horn, which is undermined by the continuing civil wars, the private sector has little incentive to invest domestically. Migrants, who need to remit their earnings to support their families, provide the foreign exchange and the transfer mechanisms through which private entrepreneurs can engage in capital flight.

Given this, can a lack of government fiscal and monetary discipline be blamed for the country's economic imbalances, as orthodox IMF and World Bank analysis suggests? Can inflation, public sector deficits, excessive monetary creation and the pressure on the exchange rate be understood simply as government-induced phenomena, working through the formal economy? Indeed, can the functioning of the formal, recorded economy be understood in isolation from the hidden, unrecorded economic transactions and processes associated with the underground economy? The whole centre of gravity of these economies has shifted toward the unofficial, parallel markets. No analysis based exclusively on officially-recorded transactions of the formal, private and public sector activities can capture the main characteristics of the economic processes that underlie the (mal)functioning of these economies and the resulting imbalances. Faulty analysis leads to faulty diagnosis and, consequently, suggests inappropriate 'adjustment' policies.

Identifying and quantifying such unrecorded transactions and financial flows would not only improve our quantitative analysis of a country's macroeconomic (im)balances, but also our understanding of the dynamics of the processes underlying these macro-economic aggregates. While inflation and excess demand for goods and services will exert pressure on the price of foreign exchange in the parallel market, contributing to the widening gap between it and the price in the official markets, the demand for foreign exchange and the gap between official and parallel market prices must also be understood as a function of the *asset demand* associated with speculative 'currency substitution' and capital flight.

The inflationary spiral spreads from the parallel markets of the underground economy into the closely linked formal economy, since severe supply constraints push consumers and investors to the underground economy for goods and services. The continuous price increases in the underground economy drive up formal economy prices and costs through both wages and intermediate goods price increases. These affect public and private investment costs alike, as both are dependent on local suppliers, contractors, and so forth, who will tender on the basis of actual (or expected) parallel market prices rather than the official formal sector prices. Rising costs and shrinking profit margins for formal sector investors further fuel inflation, particularly through the associated increases in public sector expenditure and the loss of tax revenue as more private sector activities shift from the formal to the underground economy. In other words, contrary to the orthodox IMF and World Bank theoretical views that lack of fiscal and monetary restraint on the part of government is the primary source of internal and external imbalance and disequilibrium in the foreign exchange market, it is argued here that increased public sector deficits and private sector spending are linked to inflationary processes associated with the largely hidden and unrecorded informal economy.

Adjustment and the restructuring of the state's economic role

The manner in which governments and the international donor community have responded to the crises has undermined the state's capacity to intervene effectively in the economic sphere. In view of the openness of most African economies and their heavy dependence on imports for consumption, production and investment, the external crisis has meant that the governments have been forced to reduce their activities, especially in areas such as health, education and other parts of the social and economic infrastructure. The lack of domestic revenues and the inability to 'create' liquidity by bank borrowing mean that foreign exchange must be generated domestically or obtained from abroad. Donors are then able to exert further pressure on governments to reduce the scope of their activities in the economy. By insisting on expenditure-reducing policy reforms as preconditions for assistance, involving, for example, deregulation, privatization, reductions in government expenditure, the elimination of government controls over economic activity and involvement in the production and distribution of goods and services, the institutional capacity of the state to intervene directly in the management of the economy is further undermined.

This has resulted in fundamental changes in the public sector. The erosion of real incomes of public servants has implications for the performance and social character of the public service. Van Arkadie (1988) refers to this process as 'creeping privatization', as public servants become increasingly unwilling to provide public services without some form of extra private inducement, either from the employer (in the form of 'incentive payments') or from the recipient of the service (often as an outright bribe). Corruption offers another important source of supplementary income for government employees, many of whom are reported to resort freely to such activities as the selling of government property on the underground market; not only are scarce basic commodities sold, but also trade licences, official seals and letterheads (Umbadda, 1989).

Increased dependency on official external financial assistance applies contradictory forces to the state's capacity to actually manage the allocation and use of scarce foreign exchange resources. On the one hand, the growing importance of official development assistant (ODA) flows as a source of foreign exchange has meant that an increasing proportion of available foreign exchange inflows to these countries has come to be channelled through the various organs of the state apparatus. On the other hand, the explosion of 'informal', 'parallel' and 'unofficial' financial relations and markets *within* the formal public and private sectors of these economies, and the growing proliferation of donors and donor conceived, financed and managed projects have gradually eroded the institutional capacity of the official state apparatus to perform its regular administrative functions. Donors and the flow of aid monies have come to play an important part in informal markets, with significant implications for the way in which the financial resources available to the state are used and accounted for.

'Creeping privatization', conceived as a positive dimension of the crisis, thus needs closer scrutiny. It tends to reinforce twin notions underlying orthodox interpretations of the nature of informal economic activities, including that of the World Bank in its most recent report on sub-Saharan Africa. The Long-Term Perspective Study (LTPS) holds (i) that there is a thriving informal economy that exists *outside* the public sector, and (ii) that civil servants have come to rely principally on such *external,* informal economic activities to supplement their meagre public sector incomes (World Bank, 1989c). As argued in the case of Tanzania, neither notion is strictly valid (see Samoff & Wuyts, 1989). Much so-called 'private' contracting in the informal sector is based on public expenditures and finance, and very often the service is provided by someone with access to public sector facilities and resources. Also, there is a tendency to exaggerate the extent to which it is possible for public sector employees (or any other wage earners, public or private) to earn an additional income outside the public sector itself. It is very often the case that the individual engaged in so-called private contracting is paid out of one or another category of public funds. In other words, although the income being earned through the informal activity may well be a legitimate 'private income' for the recipient, it is only possible for the person to earn it because she or he is a *public* sector employee with access to *public* sector facilities, and because *public* finances – defined in the broader sense to include donor-financed projects – are available for such an activity.

What is sometimes understood as a healthy process of 'spontaneous or creeping privatization' of public services through the expansion of a dynamic informal economy, which governments and donors should encourage and support, could boil down, therefore, to little more than a process of secondary contracting within the public sector itself. This is a process that needs to be understood as a response to the erosion of official salaries associated with the general economic decline and erosion of the formal sector, which in turn exacerbates the institutional decay in the public sector, bringing with it a basic restructuring of financial management and accountability of public expenditures. Such processes can also become associated with the less desirable practices of patronage, bribery and corruption, and can lead to significant shifts in the relative earnings differentials within the civil service.

Donor interventions, whether in the form of ODA financial flows, micro-level projects, or macroeconomic policy conditionality, must be analysed and understood in this context. The donor community often takes on functions that normally are the responsibility of the national state. 'Planning' in many aid-dependent economies today has increasingly become an exercise in co-ordinating the diverse project interventions of the growing community of official donors and NGOs (Morss, 1984). The state sector's capacity to function properly is further undermined by the demands placed on its scarce skilled and professional personnel by the numerous and uncoordinated requirements of the endless technical and/or advisory missions of expatriate project consultants, evaluators and so forth.

Furthermore, in the face of declining public sector real wages, the best employees are often attracted away from public service to work for expatriate-managed aid projects, sometimes fulfilling the same task on such a project, for a much higher salary, than that which he or she would have been performing in the public sector. This can fundamentally restructure the nature and organization of many basic state services, such as health, as well as their financial and managerial accountability. Whether by intent or not, many donor interventions tend to bypass official decision-making structures, and as a result gradually transfer responsibilities for providing basic services from the various organs of the national government to different agents of the international donor community. Thus, public sector finances and the earnings of public sector employees become increasingly tied to or constrained by the conditions and requirements of donor aid agreements.

Within aid projects donors often make incentive payments and pay extra allowances to staff to encourage greater commitment to their projects. As donor funded projects tend to have more resources than other public sector activities, there emerges a sharp discrepancy in the total volume of incentive payments provided in the two types of activities. Actual financial authority for much of the public sector budget is thereby effectively transferred to the donor financed and managed projects, and the accountability of governmental employees sometimes becomes transferred from their direct state employer to the donor managed project which has become the *de facto* employer. The donor agency, rather than the government, becomes the focus of the attention and the loyalty of many civil servants. This increasing reliance by civil servants on other forms and sources of public finances (including aid monies) or access to public resources (with which to earn extra income) erodes the cohesion of public sector action and adversely affects public sector ethics (Samoff & Wuyts, 1989).

Ample evidence suggests that these sorts of processes are very important among the aid-dependent economies of the Horn. Further research into the interrelationships between aid flows and state sector finances in these economies will be needed if policy-relevant conclusions about future capacity-building of the state in the Horn are to be forthcoming. The processes through which different donor agencies – both official bilateral and NGOs – have become increasingly responsible for the organization, provision and financing of public services need to be properly understood.[5] Any study of the economic crisis and the impact of donor interventions in such economies must therefore examine the way in which these different forms of intervention are organized, and how these contribute to the reorganization and allocation of public expenditures. The main argument being advanced here is that donor interventions are likely to lead to the fragmentation of public sector activity by fostering the operation of parallel earning circuits within the public sector and between the donor agencies and the public sector.

The prerequisites for economic recovery in the Horn are clearly not as straightforward as the World Bank's studies of the African economic crisis suggest. It could be argued that in its most recent Long-Term Perspective Study of SSA, the World Bank clearly recognizes this in the sense that increased attention is given to elements such as the role of the informal sector, the need to enhance the state's administrative and managerial capacities, and the whole 'human resource' angle of the development process (World Bank, 1989c). Privatizing public services, promoting the informal sector, legalizing parallel markets, and improving managerial capacity have become key issues in policy dialogue. But, while the Bank might acknowledge the existence of the informal sector and parallel foreign exchange markets in their studies, they tend to ignore their functioning in the context of the actual, ongoing processes of transformation that are occurring in these countries. For instance, in the LTPS the informal economy is seen only as a potential source of dynamism and a breeding ground for entrepreneurs, as a possible source of employment for displaced public sector employees, and as an impetus to the expansion of the private sector. Few attempts have yet been made to explain its functioning and its relation to the rest of the economy, especially its interrelationship with and dependence on the public sector and donor funded projects. There is clearly a need to go beyond simplistic notions of the traditional divide between 'public' and 'private' sectors, of potentially perfect markets being distorted by 'inappropriate' and 'irrational' government interventions and regulations, and of the rational and more efficient private entrepreneur becoming 'crowded out' by excessive state investment. There is a need to understand, and thus explicitly incorporate into the analysis, the role of the informal economy and its connections with the public sector.

Concluding remarks on aid policy

For any policy package – IMF/Bank-supported or otherwise – to be effective, it is imperative that the state has the technical and political capacity to implement it. The World Bank calls this a problem of 'governance', as in the oft-used notions of 'inefficient' governments, 'lacking political will' and so forth. The processes that have given rise to the states' lack of 'governance' are, however, much more complex than often assumed. It is neither a purely technical nor an attitudinal problem, as is sometimes too readily assumed. Firstly, the necessary bureaucratic competence and autonomy is as much a political and economic issue as it is a technical one. Political leaders must be able to entrust the design and execution of their key economic decisions to a well-trained technocratic bureaucracy. This bureaucracy has to be created and recruited from the most technically qualified people in the country who will require, among other things, prioritized access to human resource development.

Secondly, once the technocratic bureaucracy has been created, the government has to ensure that this bureaucracy achieves independence from the political leadership, and that both are able to avoid becoming captives of and corrupted by their main clients. This is a highly complex problem with historical, political, economic and social aspects and a variety of agents. Without a proper understanding of how the state's 'governance capacity' has been undermined, and under what conditions the political autonomy and administrative capacity necessary to foster a more broadly-based development programme could come about, no amount of foreign aid will produce the economic development intended. As with the substantial levels of unrecorded foreign exchange surpluses earned through remittances and smuggled exports, these aid flows could also end up supporting the capital export and luxury consumption of those clients on whose support the political leadership depends most.

Until such autonomy is realized, the guiding objectives and criteria that should shape the formulation of an aid policy for the post-war Horn economies, apart from providing immediate humanitarian relief, would thus need to include interventions that have the following longer term aims: (1) the restoration of the state sector's technocratic capacities, and in particular the creation (or recreation) of a rigorously educated bureaucracy; and (2), direct and indirect project and technical support to the public sector with a view to enhancing its own capacity to intervene in the provision of services, and in the creation and regulation of markets.

Notes
1   It can even be argued that the Sudan's and Somalia's debts pose a bigger problem for the IMF and donor community than for the governments themselves!
2   This plan was proposed by Nigel Lawson while he was Chancellor of the Exchequer in the mid 1980s.
3   The data available on debt service payments due, versus those actually paid, comes from a variety of sources and needs to be treated with extreme caution. For the Sudan we had access to IMF and World Bank calculations, whereas for Ethiopia and Somalia these are derived from officially recorded data on arrears in their balance of payments tables.
4   For the evolution of World Bank thinking on the African crisis over the last decade, see World Bank, 1981, 1983, 1984, 1986, 1989c. For a useful overview of the debate, see Shaw, 1986, and Ravenhill, 1988.
5   An interesting start to this is made in the paper by Duffield, which can be found in this collection.

References

Brown, R.P.C. 1990a. 'Sudan's other economy: Migrants' remittances, capital flight and their policy implications' *ISS Working Paper*, sub-series on Money, Finance and Development, No.31.

Brown, R.P.C. 1990b. 'Some missing elements in Sudan's policy debate: Unrecorded remittances, the parallel economy, and capital exports' in *Beyond Adjustment: Sub-Saharan Africa*, Africa Seminar Papers, The Hague, Ministry of Foreign Affairs Directorate General for International Co-operation.

Brown, R.P.C. 1990c. *Sudan's Debt Crisis: The Interplay Between International and Domestic Responses, 1978–88*, Ph.D. thesis, University of Groningen.

Brown, R.P.C. (forthcoming). *Public Debt and Private Wealth: Debt, Capital Flight and the IMF in Sudan*, London, Macmillan.

Central Bank of Somalia. 1989. *Annual Report and Statement of Accounts, 1988*, Mogadishu, Economic Research and Statistics Department.

Culpeper, R. 1987. *Forced Adjustment: The Export Collapse in Sub-Saharan Africa*, Ottawa, The North-South Institute.

Degefe, B. 1990. *Growth and Foreign Debt: The Ethiopian Experience 1964–86*, final report, Nairobi, African Economic Research Consortium.

ECA. 1988. *Beyond Recovery: ECA Revised Perspectives of Africa's Development, 1988–2008*, E/ECA/CM.14/31, Addis Ababa, UN-ECA.

ECA. 1989. *Africa Alternative to Structural Adjustment Programmes (AA-SAP): A Framework for Transformation and Recovery,* Addis Ababa, UN-ECA.

Ghai, D. and C. Hewitt de Alcàntara. 1990. 'The crisis of the 1980s in sub-Saharan Africa, Latin America and the Caribbean: Economic impact, social change and political implications' *Development and Change,* 21(3), pp. 389–426.

ILO. 1989. *Generating Employment and Incomes in Somalia,* Addis Ababa, ILO/JASPA.

IMF. 1988, June. 'Supplement on sub-Saharan African debt' *IMF Survey,* pp. 177-192.

IMF. 1990. *Sudan: Recent Economic Developments,* unpublished report No. SM/90/133, Washington DC, IMF.

IMF. (various issues). *Balance of Payments Statistics,* Washington DC, IMF.

Jamal, V. 1988a. 'Getting the crisis right: Missing perspectives on African development' in Jamal, V. (ed.) *International Labour Review,* 127(6), pp. 655–78.

Jamal, V. 1988b. 'Somalia: Survival in a "doomed" economy' in Jamal, V. (ed.) *International Labour Review,* 127(6), pp. 783-812.

Jamal, V. (ed.) 1988. *The African Crisis, Food Security and Structural Adjustment,* special issue, *International Labour Review,* 127(6).

Ministry of National Planning. 1990. *Somalia in Figures,* Mogadishu, Ministry of National Planning.

Morss, E.R. 1984. 'Institutional destruction resulting from donor and project proliferation in sub-Saharan African Countries' *World Development,* 12(4), pp. 465–70.

OAU. 1981. *Lagos Plan of Action for the Economic Development of Africa, 1980–2000,* Geneva, International Institute for Labour Studies.

OAU. 1985. *Africa's Priority Programme for Economic Recovery, 1986–90,* Addis Ababa, Organization of African Unity.

OECD. 1989. *Geographical Distribution of Financial Flows to Developing Countries, 1984–1987,* Paris, OECD.

Parfitt, T.W. and S.P. Riley. 1989. *The African Debt Crisis,* London, Routledge.

Ravenhill, J. (ed.) 1986. *Africa in Economic Crisis,* London, Macmillan.

Ravenhill, J. 1988. 'Adjustment with growth: A fragile consensus' *The Journal of Modern African Studies,* 26(2), pp. 179–210.

Samoff, J. and M. Wuyts. 1989. 'Swedish public administration assistance in Tanzania' *Education Division Documents No. 43,* Stockholm, SIDA.

Shaw, T.M. 1986. 'The African crisis: Debates and dialectics over alternative development strategies for the continent' in Ravenhill, J. (ed.) *Africa in Economic Crisis,* London, Macmillan.

Umbadda, S. 1989. 'Economic crisis in the Sudan: Impact and response', paper presented at the UNRISD/ISER conference on *Economic Crisis and Third World Countries: Impact and Response,* Kingston, University of West Indies.

UNDP. 1989. *Somalia: Annual Development Report, 1988,* Mogadishu, UNDP.

Van Arkadie, B. (ed.) 1986. *External Finance and Policy Adjustment in Africa,* special issue, *Development and Change,* 17(3).

Van Arkadie, B. 1988. 'Adjustment policy and adjustment processes' *Institute of Social Studies Development Economics Seminar Paper No. 11,* The Hague.

World Bank. 1981. *Accelerated Development in Sub-Saharan Africa: An Agenda for Action,* Washington DC, The World Bank.

World Bank. 1983. *Sub-Saharan Africa: Progress Report on Development Prospects and Programs,* Washington DC, The World Bank.

World Bank. 1984. *Towards Sustained Development in Sub-Saharan Africa: A Joint Programme of Action,* Washington DC, The World Bank.

World Bank. 1986. *Financing Adjustment with Growth in Sub-Saharan Africa, 1986–90,* Washington DC, The World Bank.

World Bank. 1987. *Sudan: Problems of Economic Adjustment,* Vols. I–III, Washington DC, The World Bank.

World Bank. 1989a. *Beyond Adjustment: a Participatory Program for Sustainable Growth and Equity in Sub-Saharan Africa,* Washington DC, The World Bank.

World Bank. 1989b. *World Debt Tables: 1988–1989 Edition,* Vols. I–III, Washington DC, The World Bank.

World Bank. 1989c. *Sub-Saharan Africa: From Crisis to Sustainable Growth,* Washington DC, The World Bank.

World Bank. 1989d. *World Development Report 1989,* New York, Oxford University Press.

World Bank. 1989e. *World Debt Tables: 1989–1990 Edition,* Vols. I–II, Washington DC, The World Bank.

World Bank and UNDP. 1989. *Africa's Adjustment and Growth in the 1980s,* Washington DC, The World Bank.

Comment   DUNSTAN WAI

It seems that Dr Brown, Mr Kulane and Mr Alemayehu made six points in their paper. The first is the objective of the paper which they say is to identify some important areas for immediate research and some issues that have been neglected in current debate on the Horn. The second is their argument about the existing data on economic analysis and policy prescriptions which they say are deficient in that the data do not include clear information on informal parallel market activities. Thirdly, Dr Brown and his co-authors refer us to the severity of the debt crisis and the magnitude of the foreign exchange influx; they think that this has been overstated and use the case of the Sudan as an illustrative example. Fourthly, they talk about the impact of the reduction of the role of the state in government activities and the hijacking of state activities by NGOs or foreign donors. Fifthly, they warn us against the rapid growth of the informal sector once state involvement in economic activities is reduced. Finally, they conclude by calling for the restoration of the state's economic and technical capacities. However, this paper does not tackle the problems in the Horn comprehensively and succinctly. It is very important to look at the problems in Africa in a holistic manner; trying to generalize from one particular aspect will generate misunderstandings or misconceptions. As expressed by Dr Brown et al., it is extremely important to understand the dynamics of the forces acting upon the societies in Africa and on the Horn as a whole.

If we are to look at the problems of the financial situation in the Horn of Africa, we should understand the nature and the magnitude of the overall problem. In terms of economic growth and progress, economic and political mismanagement combined with adverse external conditions have led to inefficiency, low productivity, meagre returns on investment and extremely low economic growth. We already know that economic growth in Africa was the only barrier to population growth during the entire period of the 1960s, 70s, and 80s. The concern of some is not so much that there is a reduced population growth rate in Africa, but that the population growth rate is far ahead of the economic growth rate.

The third issue which Dr Brown and his co-authors mentioned is critically important and should not be underestimated. Sub-Saharan Africa's debt has risen 25-fold since 1970 and is now about 140 billion dollars. Relative to its GDP, sub-Saharan Africa is the most indebted region in the world. The outcomes that Dr Brown et al. put forward with respect to taxes and so forth are extremely interesting in the sense that they are new in the vocabulary of economics, but I do not believe that they carry any substance or weight with respect to transactions between nations or in economic discourse. By the way, although the Sudan is defaulting on its IMF loans, it cannot afford to default on its World Bank loans as if it were to do so all the donors would stop their disbursements to the Sudan and, in fact, this would have a greater impact than if the IMF stopped its funding. Consequently, the country pays the World Bank promptly.

Another important point is that the continent is not competitive. Africa accounts for less than 2 per cent of world trade. The Horn of Africa is not even competitive with other African countries. A major problem is that there is definitely a lack of consensus amongst the countries within Africa, and between Africa and the donor community on what needs to be done. This problem needs to be taken up in a holistic way.

The final issue that Dr Brown et al. talked about – the administrative and managerial capacities of the state and investment in human resource development – is very important and I will come back to it later. It should be recognized that the international community has had a role, not only in the Horn of Africa, but in Africa as a whole as in other parts of the world. But we cannot find satisfactory solutions by continually blaming our own saviours, by blaming our own problems on the outsider. The time has come for us to reappraise our own shortcomings within the Horn of Africa or in Africa as a whole and to try to see why Africa has not been able to respond to external shocks as adequately as countries in other parts of the world. It is paternalistic for anybody, any African or outsider, to continually think that Africans are incapable of doing certain things which they should have done, and therefore the best thing to do is to blame outsiders. This notion has existed in Africa and has not brought forth anything useful.

Due to the limited space, it will not be possible to go into the various points that have been mentioned before. However, it should be pointed out that the World Bank does believe in investment in people and that people are the means and the end of development. Contrary to misperceptions in some quarters, the Bank does take a comprehensive view of the problem over the long term and does not only confine itself to macroeconomic analysis. We do look at the sectoral issues as well and in fact most of the Bank's lending to sub-Saharan Africa is really sectoral. Structural adjustments account for only 40 per cent of our lending – over four billion dollars a year – and the rest all goes to agriculture, infrastructure, health and so forth. It is very important to make a clear distinction between macroeconomic adjustment and structural adjustment. Macroeconomic adjustment is very important; it is imperative for every country. Structural adjustment refers also to sectoral adjustment. It is very important to look at pricing policies, whether in agriculture or in industry.

There are several important points that Dr Brown and his co-authors make which should also be referred to here. The Bank does have an analysis of the inflows and outflows of foreign exchange in the Sudan, but what is important to note is that, notwithstanding the inflows from Sudanese living abroad, the severity of the debt problem is there. With regard to capital flight, this money is going to individuals, some of whom keep it under the mattress, and so forth. It is only in circulation when people fly out to buy things outside; this money is not in circulation in the Sudan. We have to be clear on this point. The logic that inflows of foreign exchange are followed by capital outflows is not coherent.

The other point made in the paper is that the food crisis is not as grave as sometimes claimed. In the Bank's analysis, however, more than a hundred million Africans are suffering from malnutrition. It is an extremely grave situation. Anybody coming from the Horn of Africa will not say that the food crisis is not there. Malnutrition is extensive, not only because of the war, but also due to drought and so forth.

A third point is that structural adjustment, to return to this topic, is not imposed. Suggestions that policies of economic reform which involve deregulating the economy and making sure that farmers get the right price for their agricultural produce (and that the selling rate is not overvalued but reflects the economic potential of the country) are imposed from outside are not true. Our problem is the shortage of people internally who can do the analysis, and do it right.

The word 'orthodox' occurs many times in this paper. In fact, adjustment is not orthodox. Adjustment means being flexible, being responsive to the situation as it comes. Let us not think that these things are imposed from the outside. Sometimes there is no other option but to adjust some policies. Of course adjustment is a high-risk activity, but the risks can be reduced, and the point is not to confuse the malady with the remedy. The World Bank now has projects that try to look at social development as a whole and not just at the macro policies; they try to look at vulnerable groups in society.

Incidentally, reductions in education and social services are not made because of structural adjustment. The resources for education, health and so on are already reduced. Governments may say they were spending 35 million dollars on education and health but, because of structural adjustment, they have had to reduce this. Even if it was on paper, that money was not going to the social services. It was going to the military. The military expenditures of these countries are very high, as we all know. And what is the military for? For only oppressing their own citizens. This point is not reflected in Dr Brown and his co-authors' paper. The choice that the Horn of Africa has made is that when there is peace there has to be massive restructuring, not only of the institutions, but also of the economies. As somebody rightly pointed out, the attitude of the people also has to change.

A fourth point is the lack of data. As reported by the three authors, there is a serious lack of data on the informal sector. But the economic process means we cannot wait until we get data. We are continually trying to improve the data. And it is not the case that we do not know about the existence of the informal sector or that we do not consider it in our analysis. The UNDP, the Economic Commission for Africa and the World Bank are working together to improve the statistics for Africa. But the fact that there is a problem does not mean we cannot make some rough estimates in making current accounts or deficits calculations to inform us of some prescriptions.

The extent of the informal sector should not be romanticized. We are fully aware that it is there. It is very important to understand how it emerges, how it operates, who benefits from it and so forth. The informal sector is actually the private sector in Africa. The government makes up the so-called formal sector. Why do people leave the formal sector? They leave because of massive distortions in the economy, because of the deregulations, because the state in our countries is a privatized entity, particularly in the Horn. Look at the state in the Sudan. That state has been privatized. Whoever comes to power, it is privatized. The state is not serving the interests or the expectations of the people. In fact, it is better to reduce the role of the state. Those who control the state are the ones who are benefitting from it by using the state machinery to acquire wealth. What channels are being used to facilitate capital flight, and who is using them? They are being used by those who have access to political power, not by the masses.

Before summing up it is worth mentioning the progress on the debt. As part of a special programme of action more than six billion dollars was mobilized in 1988–90, and another eight billion dollars for 1991–3 to give the low-income indebted countries some relief so that they can at least focus some of their meagre resources on development so that growth can take place. The Sudan and Somalia were benefitting from this until they diverted from adhering to structural adjustment. The terms which accompanied structural adjustment were very favourable as they included the outright cancellation of debts, reducing the interest rates or in fact extending the maturities of the debt. African governments have been working very closely to benefit from this special programme.

Finally, the problem in the Horn and in Africa as a whole is not so much the fiscal imbalances. It is not a question of reaching equilibria in demand and supply and so forth. The problem is governance. That is the critical issue now. The role of the state can be reduced to a government which is responsive to the basic needs of the people, which is accountable and transparent, and which makes sure that there is rule of law, and that there is an enabling environment for the people to be engaged in the productive activities in the society. I agree with Dr Brown et al. that the development of capacities is extremely important. If we are going to have good governments then we must have institutions which are autonomous, which can moderate and which can define group political actions. Institutions which can implement policies and produce tangible results are also needed, and for institutions to function effectively we need people with the capacity to identify priorities, identify and analyse problems, and suggest policy options to those who make the final decisions. So we are with you, Dr Brown, Mr Alemayehu and Mr Kwane. Investment in human institutions is imperative.

23

Social Decay and Public Institutions: The Road to Reconstruction in Somalia

ABDI ISMAIL SAMATAR

Recently one of the most disciplined critics of Siyad Barre, a person who had known the ex-dictator too well and who for too long wished for his departure, remarked that the old devil was the lesser evil compared to those who replaced him. Such reactions from the most civic minded of citizens must be sobering, particularly since Somalis have longed to see the next independence day. The demise of the Barre-led regime was supposed to usher in a fresh lease on life in Somalia. Tragically, the converse has quickly become true. Why has the opportunity which ordinary people have longed for for so long turned into a living hell, a hell in which more people have been killed, maimed, raped, robbed and displaced than during the first 20 years of the old regime? And what is the prognosis for the future? This brief commentary summarizes the social history of this unnecessary, painful, but hopefully useful, lesson.

In the multiparty election held in 1969 the competing factions in the governing class shared similar views about the nature of the development process. In the absence of ideas which distinguished one candidate or party from another, old kinship identities were resurrected, caricatured and served as a means of mobilizing the electorate behind a candidate. As a consequence of this, divisive competition among the governing class and the deployment of tribal rather than kinship ideology led to the formation of 69 political parties in a country with an electorate of about a million. Once the election was over, the successful candidates went about the business of carving up the public largesse, exposing the true colours of the elected politicians and their priorities. The collapse of the 'opposition' parties and the shift of the allegiance of their members to the ruling party spelled the death knell of multiparty politics and the rise of a single party state. This is the first time in the history of African politics where a sizeable opposition voluntarily dissolved their parties and opted for a government dominated by a single party.

If competitive multiparty politics was intended to guarantee accountability and good government, it certainly did not work out that way in the Somalia of the 1960s. Among the principal legitimating excuses used by Siyad Barre and his colonels for taking state power was the abuse and misuse of public power and resources by the elected politicians. Such claims received the overwhelming support of the public, although it was apparent to knowledgeable people that the General himself took part of the spoils and helped the previous Prime Minister rig the elections in parts of the northeast which were highly contested. Within four years, the period for consolidation, it became clear that a new form of government which was accountable only to itself had taken command. The new lords of Somalia, military men and their allies, were different from their predecessors in two ways. Firstly, they made it clear that any criticism of the regime was an act of treason. As such its *modus operandi* was highly repressive in ways unknown in Somali history.

Secondly, it banned and to a significant degree controlled the spoils system for the first few years of its tenure. The latter issue blunted the public's misgivings about authoritarian rule. This political arrangement was derailed by the Somali debacle in the war with Ethiopia in the Ogaden (1977). The shift of Soviet military and ideological support to Ethiopia led the Somali government to solicit assistance from the United States and the West. The Ogaden defeat also flamed dormant intra-class competition for state power and the 'tribal-based' rules of politics of the 1960 were reinvented.

In the meantime, Western donor agencies such as the International Monetary Fund and the World Bank insisted on the adoption of structural adjustment as the prerequisite for loans. Desperate for new financial patrons, the regime signed its first SAP agreement in 1981. Subsequently, the new development motto proclaimed the virtues of private accumulation and the evils of state bureaucracy and the public sector. In other words, public servants were expected to facilitate private accumulation without benefitting from it. Moreover, the very institutions and bureaucracies which these financial institutions claimed caused the economic crisis of the country were expected to lead the way to private prosperity. The demoralization of public servants which this process engendered, and the precipitous decline of their income due to hyperinflation, virtually legalized corruption. Consequently, the bureaucratic and the technocratic capacity of the state fell apart as each individual servant paid little attention to the public project.

The decade of the 1980s, under the guidance of a SAP and Siyad Barre, witnessed the looting of the public purse in ways unforeseen in contemporary Somalia. As the conflict increased among the competing groups of the dominant class seeking to control public resources and the foreign loans, repression reached new heights and resistance to the governing clique fractured along opportunistic 'ethnic' lines. In spite of their short-sighted, personalized and opportunistic clannist strategy, the opposition deployed democratic rhetoric to attain the sympathy of the international community.

The consequences of these struggles can be summed up in two words: decay and disintegration. The decay of public institutions meant that the very conditions which SAP reforms were supposed to cure hopelessly degenerated. The demise of public institutions and the associated indebtedness (over three billion dollars) of the country shows that the reform programme was poorly conceived. The decay of the public sector became total as the police and the military bureaucracies lost their capacity to ensure basic law and order. The incapacitation of a legitimate national military machine and police marked the end of the Barre-led regime and the beginning of a factionalized insidious civil war, war-lordism and the break up of the country. The collapse of the state has brought to the fore the destructive forces it spawned for more than a century.

The real tragedy of recent Somali history is not the dictatorship of Siyad Barre but the legacy left behind by the failed leadership of the Somali governing class. The United Somali Congress (USC), which claims to have unseated the much hated regime in January 1991, has among its leaders some of the senior members of the old regime whose only qualifications are that they are from the Mogadishu region. The Congress's policy of arming the population during the final days of the old regime, without proper leadership and a programme for securing peace and order, has catapulted the country and the capital into a reign of mindless terror. This means that there is no central authority in Mogadishu and that different parts of the city are controlled by a particular armed faction of the Hawiye clan (the airport and the harbour). Moreover, the breakdown of central authority and the reactionary nature of USC leadership has led to the dispossession of all Mogadishu residents who were not Hawiye, and the massacre of anyone who was Darod by birth. This has generated and intensified communal strife and hatred, thus creating new unnecessary and formidable obstacles to reconciliation. Such actions demonstrate once again the poverty of the leadership's imagination.

The deeds of USC factions in the capital (the collapse of the army, the disorganization of its militias, the looting of every Somali who is not a member of the Hawiye clan and the prosecution and indiscriminate killing of Darod people) gave the other major anti-Siyad tribalist group, the Somali National Movement (SNM), the excuse and the opportunity to engage in its own reign of terror. Immediately after the collapse of the central government, SNM militias attacked and destroyed other towns which were the domicile of other ethnic groups, thus inheriting, internalizing and perpetuating the legacy of the old regime. As a result many have been killed, maimed and dispossessed. Furthermore, SNM unilaterally declared the 'independence' of the north. Most of the 'new' cabinet ministers were members of the old regimes, particularly the last one.

The road to reconstruction

Where should reconstruction begin and what can be done? The incompetence of those who currently dominate Somalia can be gauged by the fact that less than a month after the departure of the dictator, all public property and buildings were ransacked and destroyed; what is left of the economy is shattered. Siyad is 'gone' and the country lies in ruin. The restoration of peace and order is simply the most urgent business facing Somalia. The current leaders in both the north and the south are fundamentally incapable of accomplishing even the task of organizing a national conference and controlling their militias.[1] This means that there are no internal forces who have the credibility, imagination, and capability to disarm the population and start the peace process and reconstruction. This leaves the United Nations Organization as the appropriate choice for intervention despite it becoming a vehicle for American imperialism.

The next step, once peace is restored, is the tortuous task of building public institutions which are accountable to the people on the one hand, and which are protected from illegitimate private intrusion on the other. This is an onerous but absolutely necessary project. In order for this to have a chance to work, two practices need to be addressed. Firstly, the nature of the political process and questions of accountability must be thoroughly rethought. Somali politics was dominated by highly competitive parties. However, such competition did not lead to accountability and development. Thus current discussion of and infatuation with democracy and its equation with competitive politics in Africa in general, and Somalia in particular, needs to be carefully reconsidered. Is it conceivable that a democratic and accountable polity can be developed without the kind of political parties this country knew in the 1960s? Secondly, in constructing such a political process, it will be necessary to reconsider the nature and the form of economic development. That is, you cannot have standard competition operating in the private world, particularly if the state has to play a significant role in regulating the economy while insulating concerns from illegitimate private interests. The purpose of the private sector should be to afford equal opportunity to all interested entrepreneurs without resorting to corrupt means. This requires a serious re-evaluation of the nature of competition in the business sector as well.

Two conditions need to be satisfied for the creation of an environment that will encourage productive entrepreneurship and systematic accumulation. The first condition is internal. This entails qualitatively different political and economic institutions. The second condition is external. Somali development programmes have been fully funded by external sources. This made the state the largest and the most important actor in the development process. As such it not only dominates the development agenda, but its purse has always been the focus of private competition. Such an arrangement has far reaching implications. Firstly, given the propensity of those who have commanded the state, rural production continued to be neglected without the development of other productive domestic sectors (Samatar, 1988, 1989). Secondly, the absence of a productive private economy has magnified the role of the state and concomitantly enfeebled civil society's energy. Thirdly, the country's debt of over three billion dollars, which was incurred during the last decade, has mostly been squandered, leaving the future with a dual liability: a devastating repayment schedule, and little evidence of there being any improvement in the nation's productive capacity. Such a debt is bound to have detrimental effects on the health of the economy and on the prospects of any reform and reconstruction programme. Those donors who funded most of the now defunct and destroyed projects have as much responsibility for the crisis as the deposed regime since they continued to underwrite what most concerned Somalis saw as white elephants.

Consequently, donors could do three things: a) write off the debt; b) minimize the use of loans in future agreements; and c) continue supporting development projects during the long transition, using the state only when deemed essential.

Finally, the currently fashionable bandwagon of democracy and multi-party politics must be critically re-examined in light of the fact that the social forces which can sustain that polity are lacking in many of these countries. How else can we explain the madness of communal fratricide in which ordinary people have been taking part? The exploitation of kinship bonds (and their transformation into tribalism) by the competing fractions of the bureaucratic and mercantile classes has poisoned communal relations. What is needed is the union, in a creative and bold manner, of those from the intelligentsia and popular classes who have refused to take part in the prevailing madness. Such a group will constitute the core of a new polity which will emphasize consensus rather than competitive politics, production rather than speculation and commerce, equitable access to public and productive resources, and a non-partisan judiciary. A fundamental point of departure for this programme is the complete demilitarization of the Somali society.

Note
1   The national reconciliation conference just concluded in Djibouti; its outcome supports this argument.

References

Samatar, A.I. 1988. *Socialist Somalia: Rhetoric or Reality,* London, Zed Books.
Samatar, A.I. 1989. *The State and Rural Transformation in Somalia, 1884–1986,* Madison, University of Wisconsin Press.

24

Accountability and Civil Society

PETER ANYANG' NYONG'O

This discussion of accountability and civil society draws lessons from Africa and situates the debate in the current struggles for democratization on the continent. In Africa today people want to find ways and means by which they can get rid of bad governments and place in power regimes which are responsible and answerable to the people. To be answerable to somebody is to be *accountable* to him or her. People want to do this without necessarily taking up arms to fight such bad governments or to evict them from power by force. But people cannot remove such a government as individuals; they can only do so in an organized fashion as a group. The state is an organized system of power which monopolizes the use of legitimate force in society. When force is used by the state to compel obedience its rule becomes illegitimate, but challenging and dislodging those in power is usually an uphill task which may involve forms of violence and civil disorder. These challenges may or may not lead to the successful transformation of an illegitimate form of authority to a legitimate one.

The peaceful way to such a change is through the democratic process whereby conflicts are sorted out through competitive elections which determine who shall represent whom in the government, for how long, and on what grounds. Because people in Africa have historically had experience with this kind of change, they are now putting pressure on governments to democratize. As Amilcar Cabral once said, people do not struggle for certain crazy ideas in the heads of some intellectuals. They do, however, respond to the words of visionaries who portray their real plight in society and who, more often than not, seek to provide them with an image of an alternative and better society which is worth struggling for.

Yet, over the last 30 years a pattern has developed in African countries wherein governments do not tolerate 'active group life' in society. People are rarely allowed to organize themselves into associations, welfare groups, trade unions, professional organizations and even burial societies. This, in essence, is as it must be as the private use of state power (the 'privatization of the state' as it were) requires an authoritarian or totalitarian system of government. These are systems of government which dictate against the development of civil society; they are not the systems that inspired the people to struggle for independence. If anything, the struggle for independence was to negate such forms of political power over the people so that civil society could grow. As authoritarianism has mushroomed in Africa the development of civil society has declined, and consequently political decay, economic stagnation and social disintegration are prevalent.

The people who struggled for independence in Africa fought the colonial regimes so that freedom would be won and democracy and justice would prevail. According to the late Tom Joseph Mboya, speaking in 1955 at a political rally organized in Hamburg on the occasion of the Liberation of African Peoples' Day,

The growing nationalism in Africa today cannot be controlled by troops or by any other armed forces. The solution lies in giving the Africans the right to participate fully and democratically in the government of their countries. To those who have always argued that the Africans were not as yet ready to take over the responsibilities of self-government, I refer them to the Gold Coast, Nigeria, and the Sudan which are fine examples of the Africans' ability to operate the complicated machinery of modern government. (Singh, 1980:224–5)

Mboya was then a young trade unionist who was leading the independence struggle in Kenya. What he said about nationalist struggles then applies with equal weight to the democratic struggles of popular forces in Africa today. For, as Nzongola Ntalaja has very aptly pointed out,

The basic issue with respect to the relationship between public policy and societal goals in Africa today is the extent to which governments are able to satisfy their people's expectations of independence, namely, the sincere hope that freedom from colonial rule would usher in a new era of basic rights and freedoms long denied under foreign or settler rule. (Singh, 1980:225)

Everywhere African peoples have been disappointed. In Zaire they speak sarcastically about the day when independence will come to an end so that they can be free again. In the People's Republic of Congo they speak of the struggle for the second independence (Wamba,1987), an independence which will not put into power the party leaders, but rather leaders from among the people. As Mao Tse-Tung once said, these leaders should come 'from within the belly of the people'.

People do not inherently mind having political power or authority over them; the real issue is whether this authority is acceptable, whether it exists to be of service to those under it, and whether those under it can control it and make sure it is not used against their interests. There is a belief in almost all societies that political domination is wrong, that political power is only acceptable when it is based on the consent of the governed and not imposed on them by fiat. No excuses, however high sounding, even in the name of modernization or national unity, can justify the subjugation of the African peoples by small minorities of political warlords who base their power on the army, ethnic loyalty, or race in the post-independence era.

African people who know how independence struggles were waged cannot excuse the governments of today. The policies, the very style of government, and the attitudes of government toward the people leave a great deal to be desired. It is not unusual to hear an African president declaring that the people are not yet ready to run a multiparty system of government. Yet it was for the same multiparty system of government that the people risked their lives to win the political freedom which put such presidents in power. This contradiction never worries such people as the immense power they wield, without being answerable to anybody, renders their words unchallengeable.

The issue is not really about multiparty politics *per se*, but rather about the forcing of political homogeneity from above in situations where the very heterogeneous structure of society demands pluralism in political organization if the state is to give latitude to the diverse views and interests which exist in society. Democracy recognizes such diversities and seeks to organize politics along these lines, to manage conflicts in society competently, and to ensure that in an essentially heterogeneous situation parties in conflict accept certain basic rules and methods of conflict resolution and abide by the results of such resolutions.

Thus the first step in the struggle to establish a democracy is establishing the rules of the game. In situations where the very rules of political competition fail to recognize diversity, or seek to illegitimize the articulation of heterogeneous interests, a democratic political culture is jeopardized from the start. The failure of the Ethiopian regimes, from Haile Selassie to Mengistu, to recognize that different nationalities have the right to insert themselves in politics has been a great denial of the people's democratic rights. The assumption by the now expelled Mengistu regime that the rules of the game must be defined and imposed from above itself becomes a source of political conflict. People owe no allegiance to such a state, nor are they obligated to obey its laws. If anything, they are justified to rebel against this state since its very existence does not take into account their basic rights and interests.

It should also be realized that this insensitivity to the popular demand for democratic change has a sociological explanation. Once political power is used for illegitimate ends, it becomes increasingly difficult for those who hold this power to submit to a system of governance which will demand accountability. The tendency, therefore, is for those in power to resist democratic change, or to give in to such change only when the pressure is overwhelming and repression becomes impossible to pursue.

Legitimacy and accountability in the Horn of Africa

It is with the above in mind that we need to analyse the internal conflicts in the Horn of Africa. Among other things, these conflicts have to do with the illegitimacy of political authority, the non-accountability of government, the strangulation of the development of civil society by the state, and hence the popular resistance to the imposed order and struggles for an alternative society.

It would be very difficult to find a sound analysis of the conflicts in the Horn which did not take issue with the illegitimate use of state power in the area, the wanton destruction of human and natural resources, and the unimaginative ways in which incumbent governments have tried to resolve these internal conflicts. Wasted opportunities, like the revolution in Ethiopia in 1974, simply breed frustration and at times a sense of hopelessness. According to Lenin, once a society is ripe for a revolution, if the agents who can carry out this revolution successfully are not there, or if they miss the opportunity to do so, such a society can enter into a process of social decay (Lenin, 1987). That, perhaps, summarizes the condition of Ethiopia, the Sudan and Somalia: societies in various stages of social decay.

The tragedy in Africa is not that there are internal conflicts in many countries, with many lives being wasted, but that these conflicts rarely lead to the triumph of the popular forces, or of any force which is pursuing social progress. Perhaps Nigeria is the only exception; perhaps it is not. Compare, for example, the outcome of the American Civil War with that of the Nigerian Civil War. Can Nigeria boast of a stable civil order since the end of the Biafran War? Has a hegemonic social class – or coalition of progressive and dominant national interests – emerged to give order to society in its own image, but an image acceptable to society nonetheless since the end of that civil war?

In Nigeria, just like in the rest of Africa, there is the problem of what will come first – strong social forces to lead the process of orderly socio-economic development, or socio-economic development which, over time, will lay the ground for much more secular social forces to establish democratic polities. Wars and unending civil disorder, however, do not enhance either route, especially under conditions which are already backward in terms of the development of productive forces.

It is easy to jump to the conclusion that these inconclusive internal conflicts should be brought to an end so that societies can begin the serious task of development. But wars and conflicts do not just come to an end by fiat; the social forces engaged in the conflicts must be ready to bring them to an end and the reasons for which such wars and conflicts are fought must be addressed. It is also important to recognize that such conflicts have continued precisely because the state (and state agents for that matter) benefits from them. Cabinet ministers in Nimeiri's government are said to have made fortunes out of military hardware procurements in a situation where there was no proper legislative procedure to ensure accountability. Stories are also told of National Resistance Army officers in Uganda who are interested in the civil wars in eastern and northern Uganda continuing since these wars give them the opportunity to get material supplies from Kampala destined, as it were, for the 'war zone' but eventually diverted to their own self enrichment.

Situations of internal conflict, therefore, always face a terrible dilemma in Africa. One may feel that the state should see the rationale and logic of stopping such conflicts and yet it does not. The self-interest of the individuals within the state who have vested interests in such conflicts may preclude any 'rational' discussion of conflict resolution. What, then, can be done to create an environment conducive to peaceful conflict resolution under such conditions?

To constrain 'state war mongers' they would have to be made accountable to their people for their deeds. For example, to wage war the Ethiopian state under Mengistu had of necessity to be Stalinist. Yet to break this Stalinist war-mongering machine, the challenge had to come from within – from social forces in civil society. Unlike the leaders of feudal Ethiopia who had a legitimate base in society, the Mengistu regime relied more on the terror of the state to rule rather than on ideological hegemony. Thus popular resentment to state oppression, though not verbalized at the heart of the empire for fear of overt repression, always remained latently strong.

We go back to our norm: no part of society has the right to politically dominate another part, no matter how persuasive the reasons given to justify such domination may sound. Ethiopia *tikdem* ('Ethiopia first') puts the unity of the country above everything else. The fact is, however, that Ethiopia *tikdem* cannot sacrifice people's rights to self-determination for its own survival. After all, governments exist to serve people and not people to serve governments. However, it is difficult for a government to respond to what might normally be regarded as 'popular will' when it has no understanding of what this will is.

The emergence and consolidation of a civil society is diametrically opposed to the interests of a Stalinist in Africa; the power of such a ruler rests in the systematic destruction of civil society as its development entails the growth of forces which will compel the leadership to be accountable for its actions, and of forces which will develop interests diametrically opposed to those in power. It is precisely because of these characteristics of civil society that the struggle for democracy is a *sine qua non* for development in Africa; in this struggle lie the possibilities of getting rid of such dictators. In the process of struggle, people build up their knowledge and understanding of what the alternative system will look like. This knowledge is not really lacking; people know what liberty is, what justice consists of and the importance of 'being ruled and yet controlling those who rule'. But dictators do not allow people access to this education or allow them to practice it; they will not let civil society grow. The growth of civil society must be 'thrust upon them' if need be as the struggle for democracy becomes more intense.

The principle of non-interference

At the very founding of the Organization of African Unity (OAU), the heads of state agreed that the independent African states would have to respect the colonial boundaries as almost sacrosanct. Further, they covenanted that no African state would interfere in the 'internal affairs' of another state as this would violate the principle of sovereignty. Yet, as argued above, to what extent can a state violate the fundamental rights of its citizens and still be regarded as a legitimate state?

There is now a feeling in Africa that there must be certain conditions under which members of the civilized community of states – especially those states which subscribe to the Charter of the UNO – are entitled to interfere in the internal affairs of a member state. Interference would be justified when the actions of a state against its own people become the concern of all civilized humanity. Africa, for that matter, should establish a convention which gives the OAU the right and capability to mobilize its members to interfere in the affairs of other members where, for example, such a member carries out genocide against its own citizens, denies them human rights, or is totally incapable of dealing with some natural or human-made disaster.

The recent case of Liberia is worth looking into as a lesson for the rest of Africa. If the Economic Community of West African States (ECOWAS) could, through their Economic Community Monitoring Group (ECOMOG) intervention force, establish a viable process for creating a democratic government in Liberia, then ECOWAS should also be given the capacity to economically reconstruct Liberia so that the democratic system thus created could be sustained and reproduced. This would, no doubt, require the positive support of the international community.

Democratic struggles in Africa today are much more likely to succeed. The end of the Cold War may give a breathing space to the people as dictators are abandoned by military benefactors from abroad. If the international conjuncture is going to give internal democratic forces a chance to regroup, they must act by challenging difficult objective circumstances with purposeful subjective actions. Politics is about using the subjective will to force changes under objective conditions, which is not necessarily easy. If the ECOWAS succeeds in the Liberian case, then the difficulties should not be exaggerated; a lot is possible where there is a positive will. It is this positive will that is needed in Africa and the international scene if democratic and progressive changes are to come about in the Horn of Africa.

References

Lenin, V.I. 1987. *What Is To Be Done?* Moscow, Foreign Languages Press.

Singh, Markhan. 1980. *1952–56: Crucial Years of Kenyan Trade Unions,* Nairobi, Uzima Press.

Wamba dia Wamba. 1987. 'The struggle for democracy in Africa: The Case of the People's Republic of the Congo' in Anyang' Nyong'o, P. (ed.) *Popular Struggles for Democracy in Africa,* London, Zed Books.

25 Prospects for the Future: Recommendations from the Discussions

Many suggestions for practical action were made during discussions in special working groups and in the plenaries which considered the papers. A list of the many that were mentioned follows. No suggestion was debated and agreed upon by the whole workshop as the format and purpose was to develop ideas for an agenda for action, rather than to settle a detailed blueprint. Thus the following points were not necessarily endorsed by all the participants, indeed many were seen as controversial and generated debate. It is hoped they may provoke thought and further investigation and planning.

Theme 1:
Immediate needs and problems that will be posed by peace itself

A. Repatriation of refugees and displaced people

1. Repatriation will be the main solution for refugees after the conflict. However, it must be *entirely voluntary*. There must be no coercion whatsoever by the host government, receiving authority or aid organization, whether through cutting off essential supplies such as food or through other forms of intimidation. Refugees must be satisfied that the conditions which led to their flight have been sufficiently improved to justify their return. This means the removal of threats to life and livelihood, and of persecution on the grounds of race/ethnicity, political affiliation or religious association. Refugee communities should have the right to nominate their own representatives who would visit the proposed site of repatriation and return to report on conditions. All necessary information on their place of origin should be made available. Refugee agencies should also have access to refugee settlements in order to assist in the assessment of the wishes of refugees concerning repatriation.

2. If, however, refugees choose to remain in the country of asylum, they should be allowed to do so. Their stay should be regularized to enable them to be integrated into the society until such a time when they either repatriate or are naturalized in accordance with that country's legislation.

3. There must be adequate co-ordination between agencies in the countries of departure and destination. The UN system should be flexible to deal with situations in which refugees may wish to be voluntarily repatriated into safe areas controlled by a political organization, and also to provide continuing support for those who have to return across the frontier by force of circumstances, such as the Ogadenian refugees who have shifted back from Somalia.

222

4. Resources for rehabilitation must be provided at the destination in the form of shelter, education, health services, and equipment for income generation, such as tools, seeds and, where appropriate, livestock.

5. Where refugees who remained in the home country are returning to their communities, equal treatment should be accorded to both. Those who did not leave should not be made to feel that the refugees have received preferential treatment.

6. Relief and rehabilitation of returnees at places of origin should be seen as an integral part of future development efforts.

7. Women's roles in production, health maintenance and the shaping of future generations must be respected and assisted. Children's needs with regard to readjustment and the minimizing of trauma must be addressed as of now, since their development cannot be 'frozen' until peace is achieved.

8. Those displaced from their home areas but not classified by the UN as refugees should be provided with similar transport, repatriation and rehabilitation facilities. Special assistance from outside the UN system will be needed for these tasks, and special organizations, perhaps of the displaced themselves and the new authorities and/or existing governments, will be needed to fill this gap.

B. Demobilization of ex-combatants

1. Demobilization in general requires a democratic environment.

2. Economic realities and future prospects for peace dictate that only a small proportion of ex-combatants can be absorbed into national armies (this was so in southern Sudan in 1972). Where possible, elements from former opposing factions should be integrated.

3. The general danger of there being whole generations of people used to violence and children brought up in its midst must be recognized and a counter-culture promoted. The threat of demobilized guerrillas and remnants of defeated armies taking up banditry can be faced by amnesties and by active measures for reintegration.

4. Concrete programmes should be developed to enable former combatants to reintegrate into productive activities. Entrepreneurial opportunities, employment and support for a return to rural production should be made available, and some transitional income support if possible (the latter perhaps from international resources).

5. Special attention and facilities must be provided for the rehabilitation and full reintegration into society of disabled combatants, to reflect their special sacrifices.

6. Women ex-combatants may have special problems reintegrating into society and might not find opportunities to realize the emancipation they may have experienced under armed struggle. Special efforts must be made to enable women to retain any legal/political gains they made, to remain independent and equal, and to retain positions of leadership. Special training and the provision of economic opportunities may be needed.

7. Education and vocational opportunities for young ex-combatants must be emphasized.

8. Where needed, counselling and advice services must be made readily available for ex-combatants experiencing difficulties reintegrating into the socio-economic life of the society at large. These services should be locally based and free of charge.

9. There should be no legal, political or economic discrimination against ex-combatants on the basis of their former politico-military group association. This should be guaranteed through legislation.

10.The special problems of prisoners of war (such as the 20,000 in Eritrea) and their repatriation and reintegration need to be addressed.

C. Special needs of children

1. The post-conflict situation will be marked by large numbers of children who are homeless, disabled, uneducated and have been brought up in a war environment. In the process of repatriation, provisions will have to be made for organizations to arrange the reuniting of families, to provide temporary reception centres and permanent accommodation for those who are homeless, and to offer post-trauma counselling.

2. Special education facilities for older children who have to catch up, for disabled children and for those with special problems, and curricula which can help reintegration into society need to be provided.

3. The emotive and controversial situation of those children subject to what is termed 'household slavery' was addressed. It seems to have become more common during the wars. Some argued that this was merely a survival strategy which should not be termed by the western concept of slavery; others said that approach was used to justify a social phenomena which is immoral. The basic rights of the child under the law is something that should be given attention, as should the more modern phenomena of street children.

D. Position and needs of women

1. Arrangements for repatriation and rehabilitation have to recognize that a majority of the adult refugees and displaced are women, and that many will be heads of households who will have to provide for themselves and their children. Training, resources for self-employment and other facilities particular to their needs will have to be devised and provided, including means for labour saving in domestic and other work.

2. A new conception of the role of women in socio-economic life and decision making should be a priority in the post-conflict situation. It should not be assumed, given experiences in such countries as Algeria and in southern Africa, that the relative emancipation of women which has occurred in some parts of the Horn in the course of ongoing struggles will automatically be transferred and continued in the post-conflict era, unless special legal, political and economic measures are taken.

E. External aid

1. The realities of the present global order and the priorities of the developed countries are such that in planning for rehabilitation and coping with peace no massive international aid programme can be envisaged.

2. A self-reliant strategy should build upon the welfare and relief organizations that many of the movements in conflict have formed. It should also aim to foster effective working arrangements between former foes, and across borders – not only as a worthwhile area for co-operation to build links and heal wounds, but as a necessary part of the agenda during a transition when all agencies will have to be involved in programmes wider than their previous area of responsibility. Such programmes should be the priority for what limited international aid can be expected.

F. Food aid

1. The existing supply of food relief for victims of famine induced by war, drought and long-term crises of production and reproduction must continue in the transition. The

victims will continue to need support for some time, and new needs of returnees will have to be met until they re-establish themselves. Such relief should be planned so as to be integrated with programmes for rehabilitation and development. Even so Ethiopian peasants, for instance, who now find themselves back to normal conditions, will have to wait until October 1992 for their first peace-time crop. Relief food will also have to be distributed along new networks, involving new organization and co-operation between former enemies and across borders. The risk of the disincentive effects of reliance on food aid will become greater when some 'normality' returns; this is a contentious issue and further investigations are badly needed to establish to what extent food aid has been undermining 'self-reliance', and whether in particular situations there continues to be a need for it.

G. The role of NGOs

1. Foreign NGOs have come to play a major role, particularly in the supply and distribution of relief, often supplied by foreign governments or international agencies. Different views were expressed about their role: they can usurp local NGOs or even governments because of their strong presence at the local level and the economic crisis and decapacitation of the state, or be the acceptable face of official donors with their own agendas. Emphasis should be put on using their undoubted experience, their international contacts and their access to resources so as to support programmes of local relief organizations and NGOs and to fit in with national plans for reconstruction as these are formulated in the post-conflict situation. They could also usefully facilitate the exchange of information and experience between previous opponents and between countries. Additionally, they could play a role in providing training for local welfare and development specialists, and for local NGO personnel in organization-related matters and in effective dealing with the external aid world.

Theme 2:

Areas of potential regional collaboration and joint management of resources

A. The prerequisites for regional co-operation

1. *Peace, development and co-operation*
   The process of seeking agreements for specific points of co-operation and building up institutions should not be left entirely to some future time after the attainment of complete peace in the Horn; such initiatives themselves can be a means of reducing conflict and of beginning to realize a 'peace dividend'.

2. *Regional organization*
   It should be frankly recognized that different states and areas have different interests and will not always be able to maximize their advantage in every single arrangement for co-operation; there is a need to recognize that trade-offs will have to be made between different programmes and that the overall benefits of co-operation are worth the compromises. Such conflicts over the assertion of short-term, purely national interests will be lessened if governments relinquish some authority to supra-national bodies such as IGADD, UNEP and PTA. Such reductions in the central power of the existing states may help to play down provincial divisions within states and promote cross-border integration among peoples sharing the same culture. Too much should not be expected, however, of existing regional bodies which only have a limited mandate and also include countries beyond the Horn. Discussions about setting up a common trade, transport and monetary authority for the Horn are not premature. In this task, the region can learn the positive and negative lessons from the Southern African Development Co-ordination Conference, the old East African Community and so forth.

B. Promoting regional trade

1. *The problem of export orientation*

It is not the case that the countries of the Horn produce precisely the same goods, but the complementarity which could generate more trade is still limited as they all concentrate on producing primary commodities for export, albeit different ones, and import manufactures from a long distance. In the circumstances, any country will prefer to export abroad for hard currency rather than meet regional needs, such as for food – hence trade agreements, barter deals, currency union and integrated industrial planning all have to be on the agenda. The degree of complementarity and where the comparative advantage of the region can best be realized are matters requiring more systematic investigation. Certainly at a time of low capacity utilization of existing factories, trade should be encouraged.

2. *Informal trade*

There is, in fact, a great amount of informal, and at present illegal, trade across the borders (perhaps 40 per cent of all trade) – to that extent prerequisites and some complementarity already exists – and it sustains many basic needs of the population. One argument then is simply to recognize these facts and allow it to operate, presumably with some efficiency; certainly it does not seem worth massive state efforts being spent to control it as some informal trade is inevitable and, with the size and remoteness of border regions, not completely unenforceable. On the other hand, states do lose revenue from informal trade, although alternative sources of revenue which do not dampen incentives for production and trade can be sought, and in a post-military era the state's obsession with getting foreign exchange may be lessened. Moreover, trade, whether formal or informal, often needs the right kind of stimulus and support services from the state. One alternative, advocated by a Preferential Trade Area (PTA) study, is to regularize informal trade and provide some indirect support which does not imply complete legalization.

3. *Currency and trade arrangements*

Trade will remain limited without there being some sort of payment system; official currency exchange rates in the Horn are often arbitrary and unreal, encouraging informal transactions and undermining the currencies themselves. These problems could be minimized by also fixing common external tariffs on goods transported into or out of the region.

4. *Transport*

The existing Red Sea ports serve hinterlands which are distant and beyond the borders. Hinterland countries and areas are dependent on those who control the ports, but it is often forgotten that those who run the ports also depend on the earnings from the trade going through the ports. The *complementary* rather than conflicting interests need to be recognized. More detailed studies of the post-conflict potential capacity of the ports in relation to the trade needs of the hinterlands they serve are required. Where necessary, these should form the basis for treaty agreements (see Appendix 1, page 130).

C. Resource management

1. *Nile and other waters*

If potential problems are underestimated, the resulting conflicts may be aggravated. Development plans underway require more water than is available from the Nile the way that water has been apportioned among riverine countries. Downstream states which are most dependent on Nile waters are also more powerful than upstream states. What happens upstream to the Nile is of critical importance to Egypt. Nile planning should be regionally evolved and not determined by donor countries involved in the region.

A new agreement concerning allocation of Nile waters needs to be drawn up by all the riverine countries, rather than just Egypt and the Sudan. Realistic long-term plans for irrigation, hydro-electricity and other uses need to be worked out, and data on all such matters made openly available. Similar if less grandiose agreements are needed for other major rivers which cross borders. IGADD should be encouraged to involve itself with UNEP in generating such long-term water development plans.

2. *Oil*
   Difficult decisions will need to be made, and the detailed technical dimensions explored, about the priority use of oil in southern Sudan and elsewhere (national, regional demand or export?) and its transport (the long route to Port Sudan, or the shorter one to Mombasa with its refining capacity), and appropriate revenue sharing. These contentious issues will affect and in turn be affected by what agreements are made to end the conflict within the Sudan, but could be moderated by a supportive environment of regional co-operation.

D. Migration

1. The vast number of refugees who have moved in several directions, seasonal and longer-term labour migrants between as well as within countries, the movement of pastoralists, and the common culture of peoples either side of many frontiers, (which categories are not in practice easily distinguishable) mean that many inhabitants do not belong, in terms of their livelihoods or identities, exclusively to one country. Measures are needed in order to encourage post-war repatriation where appropriate, or resettlement where not, and to dampen these factors as a source of resentment and conflict within countries (such as refugees being seen as cheap labour and cheapening local labour, being given rights and conditions more than locals or being neglected) and between states, and to reduce the unnecessary and resented interference in people's movement, means of livelihood and socio-cultural interaction.

   Measures that need to be considered include: giving refugees and regular seasonal migrants status as 'immigrants' with some labour rights, and removing the statutory limits on their movement which cheapens wages; and granting dual citizenship to pastoralists, labour migrants, ethnic groups and nationalities divided by present borders, or to others in conflict areas, or perhaps some regional transport document could eventually be issued. A regional policy statement on human rights, perhaps even a 'court', could assist these peoples, and also underwrite democratic, humanitarian processes generally. Studies are required on the extent of migration, on the types of migrants and their patterns of movement, on repatriated earnings and the general economic significance of migrants, and on their future role in reconstruction.

Theme 3:
Recovery and Long-Term Development

A. The long-run problem defined

1. Countries of the Horn have suffered for years from a series of accumulating problems. Chronic conflict, the unbalanced use of resources, fragile environments and a series of natural disasters are only part of what have led to worsening poverty, displacement, starvation and the death of millions of people. The lack of democratic institutions has allowed for political and economic mismanagement of the region's policies and resources. Widespread famines have necessitated food imports, which only aggravated the debt problem. A further result is a very real and disturbing crisis of the state.

2. In the agricultural sphere, common predicaments suffered by the countries of the region include exploitation (the legacy of feudalism, continued by state rents and the world economy); inappropriate agricultural policies (pricing, emphasis on large-scale projects at the expense of the smallholder, and emphasis on cash crops); impoverishment and marginalization (seen in the lack of access to resources such as land and livestock, and the need for, but lack of, off-farm income, and the changed gender division of labour); and finally, the disruption of trade and transport.

B. Objectives and strategies

1. A sustainable and self-reliant development strategy which would fulfil the basic needs of the people irrespective of gender, class or ethnic affiliation is a crucial goal. The promotion of democracy is a necessary but by no means sufficient aim.

Such a strategy for recovery might include:

- the development of human capital, and employment creation (as rural areas are no longer self-sufficient);
- equitable access to land, capital, training and technology for the resource-poor to make a livelihood, especially women;
- broadening participation, particularly in the case of women whose roles and impacts on decision-making, policies, projects and their contribution to the economy (as producers, in the household, in the informal sector, and in the organization of community life) warrant long overdue study and consideration;
- altered family policies and laws so that they contain no bias against women;
- the reconstruction of roads, schools, dispensaries, agricultural services, public health programmes, primary health care and adult education;
- the development of agricultural production and policy. This would require making a choice between several strategy options (listed below), bearing in mind that a fundamental concern is integrated food security for the Horn region.

    (i) The reconstruction of trading and grazing routes destroyed in the wars.
    (ii) Is resettlement the only answer to 'irreversible' environmental damage or is rejuvenation of such areas still possible?
    (iii) Agrarian reform? How extensive is 'landlordism'; does it need to be curbed by land reform? How to reform 'communal' sytems of land tenure to ensure that vulnerable households have the wherewithal to produce? What 'reform' is possible to livestock systems – which are typically very unequal – to safeguard poor herders?
    (iv) Incentives are definitely needed to encourage producers, but can they be provided purely by the market or should structured pricing policies which regulate and fix in advance some basic prices be followed?
    (v) To what extent should the state be the main instrument of interventions in agriculture; should it just set priorities, or be even more passive? To what level should NGOs, local or foreign, be encouraged?

C. Urbanization, industrialization and the orientation of strategy

1. Rapid urbanization, fuelled by environmental decline and conflict, will undoubtedly remain important over the coming decade, but policies in rural development and with regard to income distribution should at least not add to this influx, and could slow it down. Thus privatization or other measures which would fuel landlessness and the further undermining of pastoralists' ability to survive should be avoided. Urbanization will call for employment creation, low-cost housing, and the provision of other services.

2. Industrialization is closely linked to changes in agriculture and public policy. There is a need for industrialization, but as part of an integrated development strategy.

3. A policy which is agriculture-led should be avoided as it may not alter the over-reliance on primary exports, even if extra value is added through in-country processing. On the other hand, an export-led approach geared to achieving competitive advantage within the international market may demand levels of subsidy and infrastructural support that are beyond the countries' means.

D. Research agenda: Where do we go from here?

1. The establishment of an on-going working group to assist in the organization of a forum on policies and strategies of rural development in the Horn of Africa would be one means of focusing attention on this key issue.

2. Other working groups and networks could link individual scholars across borders in the diaspora so as to generate sustained investigation on some of the issues identified at this workshop as critical but on which little hard evidence exists, or on specific countries or regions. Some such follow-ups were initiated in the immediate aftermath of the workshop both in the north of England and in Scandinavia among exiles.

Contributors

Hussein Adam is an Associate Professor of Political Science at the College of the Holy Cross, Massachusetts. He specializes in comparative politics, social and political thought, and international development. He has edited several books and published a number of articles on Somalia.

Abbas Abdelkarim Ahmed worked as lecturer and labour market economist in Sudan and the Gulf. He has published articles on Sudanese rural labour markets, *Primitive Capital Accumulation in Sudan* and *Sudan: The Gezira Scheme and Agricultural Transition* (with Tony Barnett). Presently he is working on a research project on Gulf labour markets as an Institute of Social Studies Research Fellow.

Abdel Ghaffar Mohamed Ahmed is Professor of Social Anthropology, University of Khartoum. He has published a number of books and articles (in English and Arabic) on issues related to rural development with special reference to pastoral communities. He is presently engaged in research on the socio-cultural dimension of development assistance in East Africa as well as the impact of drought on food production and food security in the Sudan Savannah Belt.

Abdel Rahman Ahmed Al-Bashir served in the local government in the Sudan and was later appointed Refugees' Commissioner. He was awarded a D.Phil. from Oxford for his study on voluntary and involuntary migration in the Sudan and has been deeply involved in refugee policies and academic research. He was seconded as a consultant for the Omani government. Currently he is with the UNDP in Somalia as a consultant.

Abel Alier was Minister of Southern Affairs in the Sudan when he led the delegation from Khartoum to the talks in Addis Ababa in 1971 which brought about the end of the 17 year old war in 1972. Until 1981 he served as Vice-President of the Republic. From 1972 to 1977 and 1980 to 1981 he was President of the High Executive Council for the Region of Southern Sudan.

Peter Anyang' Nyong'o has lectured in Political Science at the University of Nairobi, El Colegio de Mexico and Addis Ababa University. He is currently Head of Programmes at the African Academy of Sciences, Nairobi. He is editor and author of *Popular Struggles for Democracy in Africa* (1987).

Hizkias Assefa is Associate Professor of International Affairs at La Roche College,

Graduate Program, Pittsburgh, Pennsylvania. Currently he is on leave and working as Director of the Nairobi Peace Initiative. He is author of *Mediation of Civil Wars, Extremist Groups and Conflict Resolution*, and *Regional Approach to Conflict Resolution in the Horn of Africa* (forthcoming).

Hassan A. Abdel Ati is Assistant Professor, Department of Geography, University of Khartoum and co-ordinator of the Red Sea Area Programme (University of Khartoum and University of Bergen). He has specialized in regional and rural development planning and written papers and reports on the environmental impact of irrigation dams, famine and drought, and on NGOs and rural development problems.

Maruye Ayalew is a senior economist with the Ministry of Foreign Trade, Ethiopia, co-ordinating foreign trade projects and following the implementation of trade agreements such as the PTA.

Abdulrahman Mohamed Babu is currently Secretary of the International Initiative for Peace in Eritrea and Chairperson of the African Centre in London. He has held several Cabinet posts in the Tanzanian government since independence and has led several Tanzanian delegations to international conferences and United Nations General Assembly sessions. He has lectured extensively throughout the world on international relations and African affairs. His publications include *African Socialism or Socialist Africa* (1981) and *The African Manifesto* (1980). He is currently researching one-party dictatorships in Africa.

Mulugetta Bezzabeh is a senior economist for FAO in the ECA/FAO Joint Agriculture Division at Addis Ababa. He specializes in systems study with reference to participatory rural development experiences. He is author of several publications on rural development both on Ethiopia and the African region, and has just completed a special two year study commissioned by UNTFAD (United Nations Trust Fund for African Development) on Africa's field experiences in participatory rural development, to be published in 1992.

Richard P.C. Brown is currently Senior Lecturer in Economics at the University of Queensland, Brisbane, Australia. Previously he taught Development Economics at the Institute of Social Studies and researched extensively on problems of debt and structural adjustment in Africa, especially in the Sudan. He has been published widely in journals.

Mekuria Bulcha teaches in the Department of Sociology, University of Uppsala, Sweden.

Lionel Cliffe is Professor of Politics and ex-Director, Centre for Development Studies, Leeds University. He is a founding editor of *Review of African Political Economy*. He has worked on and in East and Southern Africa for 30 years, including several visits to Eritrea. Most recently he co-edited a volume on the Eritrean struggle with Basil Davidson.

Mohamed Dolal trained as an anthropologist and worked with the Somali Academy of Sciences. He is associated with the Ogaden Action Group and works as a researcher with the Pastoralism and Environment Network for the Horn of Africa, based in London.

Martin Doornbos is Professor of Political Science at the Institute of Social Studies. His research and publications have focused on policies and politics of rural development in Africa as well as India, and on state/civil society relationships. He is managing editor of *Development and Change*.

Paul Doornbos worked in the Sudan between 1975 and 1990 as a researcher, lecturer, project leader and consultant. His research interests include Islamization, Arabization, (border) trade and food security issues. He is currently with the International Department of The Netherlands Red Cross as Project Officer, Disaster Relief.

Mark Duffield is a lecturer at the Centre for Urban and Regional Studies, University of Birmingham. His interests include the privatization of welfare. Between 1985 and 1989 he was OXFAM's Country Representative for the Sudan. His publications include a number of articles on the role of NGOs in famine relief and the provision of social security, and *Maiurno: Capitalism and Rural Life in Sudan* (1981).

Alemayehu Geda Fole is a junior lecturer in Alemaya University of Agriculture (Harar, Ethiopia), Department of Agricultural Economics, in the areas of Macroeconomics and Finance. Currently he is following a graduate programme at the Institute of Social Studies in economic policy and planning.

Maknun Gamaledin's doctoral dissertation at Cambridge University is a study of the Afar pastoralists in eastern Ethiopia. He lived and worked in that region until the 1960s, and has followed developments there closely ever since. For some time he worked for the Commission of Eritrean Refugees. Currently he is working with the Pastoral and Environmental Network for the Horn of Africa in London. Among his publications are *Tolo Hanfade's Song of Accusation: An Afar Text*, with R. Hayward (1981), *State Policy and Famine in the Awash Valley of Ethiopia: The Lessons for Conservation* (1987).

Jordan Gebre-Medhin is Associate Professor, Northeastern University. His recent publications include *Peasants and Nationalism in Eritrea: A Critique of Ethiopian Studies* (1989). Currently he is a Research Fellow at the Institute of Social Studies.

Elias Habte-Selassie is a lawyer and development specialist with interests in human rights and development policy. For the past decade he has conducted extensive field research on population migration in the Horn of Africa. He is active in the EPLF Commission for Eritrean Refugee Affairs, recently spending two years organizing CERA activities in the Sudan. He is currently conducting research on the implications of changing socio-political and environmental conditions in the Horn for refugee repatriation programmes.

Ahmed Nur Kulane Hassan is an assistant lecturer in the Faculty of Technical and Commercial Teachers and a part-time member of the consultant team of the Somali Institute for Development Administration and Management (SIDAM). He is currently working on a M.A. in Development Studies at the Institute of Social Studies.

Ahmed Hussein, a member of the Ogaden Action Group based in London, has specialized in irrigation and water engineering and worked in different rural development schemes. He developed a particular interest in pastoralism issues and has regularly contributed to the OAG bulletin, writing on the problems and opportunities of Ogaden pastoralism and pastoralists.

Salah El-Din El-Shazali Ibrahim is Associate Professor, Development Studies and Research Centre, University of Khartoum. He has authored/co-authored books and papers on small farmers and pastoralists, urban labour markets, migration, displacement and refugees.

Solomon Inquai is a member of the UK Relief Society of Tigray Support Committee, London.

Sidgi Awad Kaballo worked at the Sudanese Ministry of Economic Planning and the Economic and Social Research Council of the Sudan National Council for Research. He taught at the Department of Economics and the Development Studies and Research Centre, University of Khartoum. His publications, both in Arabic and English, are on the political economy of the Sudan.

Peter Nyot Kok is a Senior Research Fellow at the Max-Planck Institute for Private International Law in Hamburg. He is co-founder and ex-Director of the Faculty of Law

Legal Aid Project, University of Khartoum, and past lecturer and Head of the Private Law Department, University of Khartoum. His recent publications include *Islamic Law, Human Rights and National Unity in the Sudan* (forthcoming).

John Luk, former Legal Advisor in the Regional Ministry of Legal Affairs, Juba, Sudan is spokesperson for SPLM/SPLA in London. He has contributed to various conferences, seminars and workshops on the political situation in the Sudan.

Bona Malwal is currently Senior Research Associate of St Antony's College, Oxford University, where he also edits the political monthly newsletter, *The Sudan Democratic Gazette*. He is former Minister of Culture and Information of the Sudan and Editor-in-Chief of the English language newspaper, *The Sudan Times*, whose publication was banned by the present military regime in Khartoum. He is also the author of two books on the Sudan: *People and Power in the Sudan* (1980) and *A Second Challenge to Nationhood* (1985). He is currently completing a political history of the Nimeiri period.

Amina Mama is a former lecturer in the Women and Development programme at the Institute of Social Studies.

John Markakis is Professor of African Studies in the Department of History and Archaeology, University of Crete. The Horn of Africa is his area of special interest; he has followed social and political developments there closely for the past 25 years. He has lived and worked in Ethiopia, and carried out research in the Sudan, Somalia and Kenya. Among his publications are *Ethiopia: Anatomy of a Traditional Polity* (1974), *Class and Revolution in Ethiopia* (1978), *National and Class Conflict in the Horn of Africa* (1987).

Samia El Hadi El Nagar is a researcher at the Economic and Social Research Council, National Council for Research, Khartoum. She has published a number of articles on women and development in rural Sudan, women's status in Arab countries, women, children and disadvantaged groups in the Sudan, and women's participation in the labour force in urban areas in the Sudan.

Ali Ahmed Saleem is a Senior Expert at the Inter-Governmental Authority on Drought and Development in Djibouti.

Abdi Ismail Samatar is an Associate Professor in the Department of Geography and Regional Planning at the University of Iowa. His previous fields of interest include the study of the state and pastoral societies. He recently published *The State and Rural Transformation in Northern Somalia, 1884–1986* (1989). His current research focuses on the impact of structural adjustment programmes on agriculture in eastern Africa, particularly Somalia, with special emphasis on food and agricultural exports.

Wubnesh W. Selassie has worked for the National Union of Eritrean Women for over ten years in Africa, the Middle East and Europe. Presently she is a member of the central council of the Union and works as a project co-ordinator in its regional office in Frankfurt.

L. Jan Slikkerveer is an Associate Professor in Anthropology at the Institute of Cultural and Social Sciences of Leiden University. He has conducted fieldwork in Ethiopia, Kenya and Indonesia, focused on the role of indigenous knowledge systems and development in respect to health care, and agricultural and natural resources management. His major publications regarding the Horn of Africa include *Plural Medical Systems in The Horn of Africa; the Legacy of 'Sheikh' Hippocrates* (1990), *Origins and Development of Indigenous Agricultural Knowledge Systems in Kenya, East Africa* (in collaboration with Richard E. Leakey, 1991) and *Indigenous Knowledge Systems: The Cultural Dimension of Development* (in collaboration with D. Michael Warren and David Brokensha, 1991).

Melakou Tegegn was actively involved in the students' and later in the left-wing movements in Ethiopia for 20 years. He was also a central committee member of the Ethiopian People's Revolutionary Party for some time. He has contributed and presented papers to journals and international conferences concerning Ethiopia. He is editor of an Amharic journal, *Medrek* (Platform), published in the Netherlands. Currently he is engaged in a proposed Ph.D. project on Changes in the Social Composition of the Political Elite in Ethiopia from 1960 to 1992.

Terje Tvedt is a Senior Researcher at the Centre for Development Studies, University of Bergen. His publications include: *Water and Politics. A History of the Jonglei Project in the Southern Sudan* (1984), and several articles on questions of water resources and development.

Dunstan Wai is Adviser to the Vice-President, and is Chief of External Affairs, Africa Region, the World Bank, Washington, DC. His past academic appointments include Research Professor of Political Economy at Georgetown University and Visiting Associate Professor in International Relations at the University of California. He is editor of *The Southern Sudan: The Problems of National Integration*, and has published several books and articles on Southern Sudan.

Berhane Woldemichael is a development planner, his specific area of specialization being the socio-economic field of regional planning. He worked for a number of years with foreign aided development projects in Ethiopia and the Sudan. He was formerly a consultant to UNHCR and UNICEF and currently works as a European co-ordinator of the Research and Information Centre of Eritrea in London.

Benaiah Yongo-Bure is a lecturer in Economics, University of Khartoum. He is currently a visiting scholar at the African Studies Center, Michigan State University. His publications include articles on regional disparities in the Sudan, and *Economic Development in the Southern Sudan: An Overview and A Strategy*. He is also co-editor of *North-South Relations in Sudan since the Addis Ababa Agreement*.

Workshop Participants[*]

Raphael Koba Badal, Department of Political Science, University of Khartoum, Sudan.
Aregawi Berhe, Khartoum, Sudan.
Martine Billanou, Eritrea Inter Agency Consortium, The Hague, The Netherlands.
Laraine Black, Cross Border Coalition, OXFAM Canada, Ottawa, Canada.
P. Brandt, Ministry of Foreign Affairs, The Hague, The Netherlands.
R. Buijtenhuijs, Afrika Studie Centrum, Leiden, The Netherlands.
Jobst Conrad, International Peace Research Institute, Oslo, Norway.
Marc Couwenbergh, NOVIB, The Hague, The Netherlands.
Francis M. Deng, Foreign Policies Programme, The Brookings Institution, Washington DC, USA.
Solomon Desta, Tigray Development Association, Amsterdam, The Netherlands.
Ragnhild Ek, Department of Political Science, University of Lund, Sweden.
Gaetane Gascon, OXFAM Canada, Ottawa, Canada.

[*] In addition to the contributors

Fassil Gebre-Kiros, Addis Ababa University, Ethiopia.

Naigzy Gebre-Medhin, United Nations Environment Programme, Nairobi, Kenya.

Myra Geerling, Werkgroep Eritrea, Amsterdam, The Netherlands.

Teshome Ghebtsawi, Rotterdam, The Netherlands.

F. Gheneti, University of Leiden, The Netherlands.

Djamila Hamid, London, United Kingdom.

F.B.A.M. van Haren, Ministry of Foreign Affairs, The Hague, The Netherlands.

Ulrike Haupt, Church Development Service, Dienste in Ubersee, Leinfelden-Echterdingen, Germany.

Barbara Hendrie, London, United Kingdom.

ICCO Representative, Zeist, The Netherlands.

Ria van Iersel, Mensen in Nood, Caritas Neerlandica, 's-Hertogenbosch, The Netherlands.

I.M. de Jong, Ministry of Foreign Affairs, The Hague, The Netherlands.

Ineke van Kessel, *Onze Wereld* and Afrika Studie Centrum, Leiden, The Netherlands.

W. van der Kevie, Ministry of Foreign Affairs, The Hague, The Netherlands.

Sophy Elizabeth Kibuywa, WUCWO Secretariat, Paris, France.

Anke van der Kwaak, Institute of Cultural and Social Studies, University of Leiden, The Netherlands.

Gerd-Ulrich Lenders, MISEREOR, Aachen, Germany.

Geertje Lycklama à Nijeholt, Institute of Social Studies, The Hague, The Netherlands.

Fisseha-Tsion Menghistu, Department of International Communication, University of Amsterdam, The Netherlands.

Gebru Mersha, Institute of Social Studies, The Hague, The Netherlands.

Desta Mogus, Amsterdam, The Netherlands.

Sture Normark, Horn of Africa Project, Life and Peace Institute, Uppsala, Sweden.

Gerald T. Rice, The World Bank, Washington DC, USA.

Beshir Mohammed Said, Cairo, Egypt.

Vanessa Sayers, Tigray Transport and Agriculture Consortium, The Hague, The Netherlands.

S.J.H. Smits, Ministry of Foreign Affairs, The Netherlands.

Gunnar M. Sørbø, Centre for Development Studies, University of Bergen, Norway.

Bea Stolte, The National Committee for Development Education in the Netherlands (NCO), Amsterdam, The Netherlands.

Jennie Street, Sheffield, United Kingdom.

Yemane Teklemariam, Eritrees Ontwikkelingswerk - Nederland, Amsterdam, The Netherlands.

Teame Tewolde-Berhan, EPLF European Office, London, United Kingdom.

Sarah Vaughan, Tigray Transport and Agriculture Consortium, The Hague, The Netherlands.

Peter Verney, Institute of Development Studies, University of Sussex, Brighton, United Kingdom.

Kitty Warnock, Sahel Programme, PANOS Institute, London, United Kingdom.

R.W. Wiersma, Ministry of Foreign Affairs, The Hague, The Netherlands.

Berhane Woldegabriel, freelance journalist, Sheffield, United Kingdom.

Khalid I. Yagi, Withington Hospital, Manchester, United Kingdom.

Staff and participants of the Institute of Social Studies.

Index

grassroots organizations, 156; independence, 112-13; and Islam, 156, 157, 159, 161, 162, 163; livestock, 157; Manifesto group, 159; markets, 98; pastoralism, 183, 190; ports/shipping, 98-9; privatization, 162; refugees from, 17, 18, 33, 160; refugees in, 183; repatriation from, 25; resistance groups, 159-62; rural production organizations, 154-64; statistics, 101; trade, 96, 97; voluntarist rural developments, 156; war aftermath, 158-9; western liberation front, *see* WSLF; women, 73; *see also* Ogaden

SOMRA (Somali Relief Association), 163

SORRA (Somali Relief and Rehabilitation Association), 163

South Africa, 57, 193

Southern African Development Co-ordination Conference, *see* SADCC

sovereignty, national, 61

Soviet Union, *see* USSR

SPLA (Sudan People's Liberation Army), 33-4, 42-7, 54, 54-6, 60, 138; in Ethiopia, 55; in southern Sudan, 54-6, 61

SPLM (Sudan People's Liberation Movement), 33-4, 42-7, 54-6

SPM (Somali Patriotic Movement), 159

SRRA (Sudan Relief and Rehabilitation Association), 43, 45, 46

SSF (Somali Salvation Front), 159

state, farms, 155; public sector, 205-7; women and the, 74-5; *see also* governments

Sudan, 72, 83, 84, 85, 86; agriculture, 50, 135, 136, 191; Blue Nile, 79, 80; Blue Nile (province), 105; business enterprises, 47; central government, 29, 43, 54, 60; 105-10, 112, 138; cereal production/food demand (1986-7), 136; children, displaced, 15-16; COR, *see* Sudan, refugees; Council of Churches (SCC), 16, 167; crops, 139; debt, international, 198, 199, 200, 210, 212; displacement, 15-16, 124-5, 135; economy, 96-8, 134-9, 203-4; education, 16, 17, 18, 45-6, 122; Egypt agreement (1959), 88; emigration from, 123; Eritrean refugees in, 23-37, 139, 191; Ethiopian refugees in, 139; exports, 99, 189; famine, 43, 189; food security, 44-5, 136; future of, 47, 139-41; Gezira scheme, *see* Gezira; health services, 46; High Executive Council, 108; hydro-meteorological surveys, 89; immigrant labour, 119; imports, 189, 203; infrastructures, 45; irrigation, 79; land tenure, 140; liberation army/movement, *see* SPLA/SPLM; macro-economy, 203; Mahadiya rule, 129; malnutrition, 16, 17, 18; markets, 98; May regime, 105, 106, 124; migration from, 128; migration internal wage labour, 117-29, 190-1; migration to, 129; mortality (1987), 17; National Reconciliation (1977), 105; Nile, 81; Nile tributaries, 82; oil conflict, 104-113; population increase, 135; project abandonment, 139; reconstruction/rehabilitation, 42-8; Refugees, Commissioners' Office for (COR), 23-7, 139; refugees from, 17, 34, 140; refugees in, 16, 17, 19, 23-37, 35, 124, 135, 139, 191; *see also under* Eritrea; relief

targeting, 59; Relief and Rehabilitation Association (SRRA), 45; repatriation of Eritreans from, 25-7; roads, 46; rural production systems in the, 134-40; shipping, 99; social services, 45-6; statistics, 85, 101; trade with Ethiopia, 96-7; trade with Somalia, 96; UN operation (UNOLS), 43, 55; underground economy, 203, 204; wage labour migration within, 117-29, 190-1; war zones, rural production in, 138-9; water demand/supply, 46, 83, 86-8, 93, 227

Sudan, central, 83, 93

Sudan, eastern, 79; displacement, 124; pastoralists, 121; trade with Ethiopia, 96

Sudan, northern, 34, 93; elite, *see* Sudan, central government; famine, 52; Nile tributaries, 82; rainfall, 83

Sudan, southern, 83, 93, 130, 134, 135, 138; children, 16, 17; conflict with central government, 104-13, 124; crops, 168-9; economy, 44-5, 138; education, 45-6; exclusion of, 105-10; famine, 52; food delivery routes, 48; future, 168-9; industrial development, 166-7; livestock vaccination, 46-7; oilfields, 105; pastoralism, 190; private sector, 167; refugees from, 42; relief operation, 20, 61; rural industries, 167-70, 190; seasonal labour, 168; and SPLA, 54-6, 60; swamps/Nile flow, 82; war damage, 43; welfare, 58

Sudan, western, 93, 129, 134, 135, 138; Baggara, 54; displacement, 124; welfare, 60, *see also* Darfur; Kordofan

Sudd-projects, 86

SURERD, 156-7, 158

SURERD (Somali Unit for Research on Emergencies and Rural Development), 155, 156

SYL (Somali Youth League), 159

Syria, 81

Takazze, 83

Tanzania, 30, 84, 85, 88, 89, 115, 193; cereal production, 99; hydraulics, 87; irrigation, 93; Nile, 81, 83

tariffs, 98, 100, 103

taxation, 103

Tekle Haimanot, 87

telecommunications, 99, 100

Tessenei, 27

Tigray, 28, 30, 33, 64, 130, 140, 147, 150, 189, 192; relief operations in, 61; repatriation to, 23; *see also* TPLF

TINET (Trade Information Network), 100

tobacco, 168-9

totalitarianism, 217-8, 220-1; *see also* accountability; Mengistu; Siyad

TPLF (Tigrayan People's Liberation Front), 38, 64

trade, administered, 103; African statistics, 94, 210; African world, 210; commodities, transport of, 97; constraints on, 97-9; cooperation potential, 99-100; foreign, 101; global, 210; illegal/unrecorded, 96-7, 103, 130, 131, 200, 202-5, 226; intra-African, 94, 95, 101, 116; intra-Horn, 95-102, 226; intra-PTA, 94; markets, 98; methods, 103; monopolies, 121; network expansion, 94-

INDEX